Giotto

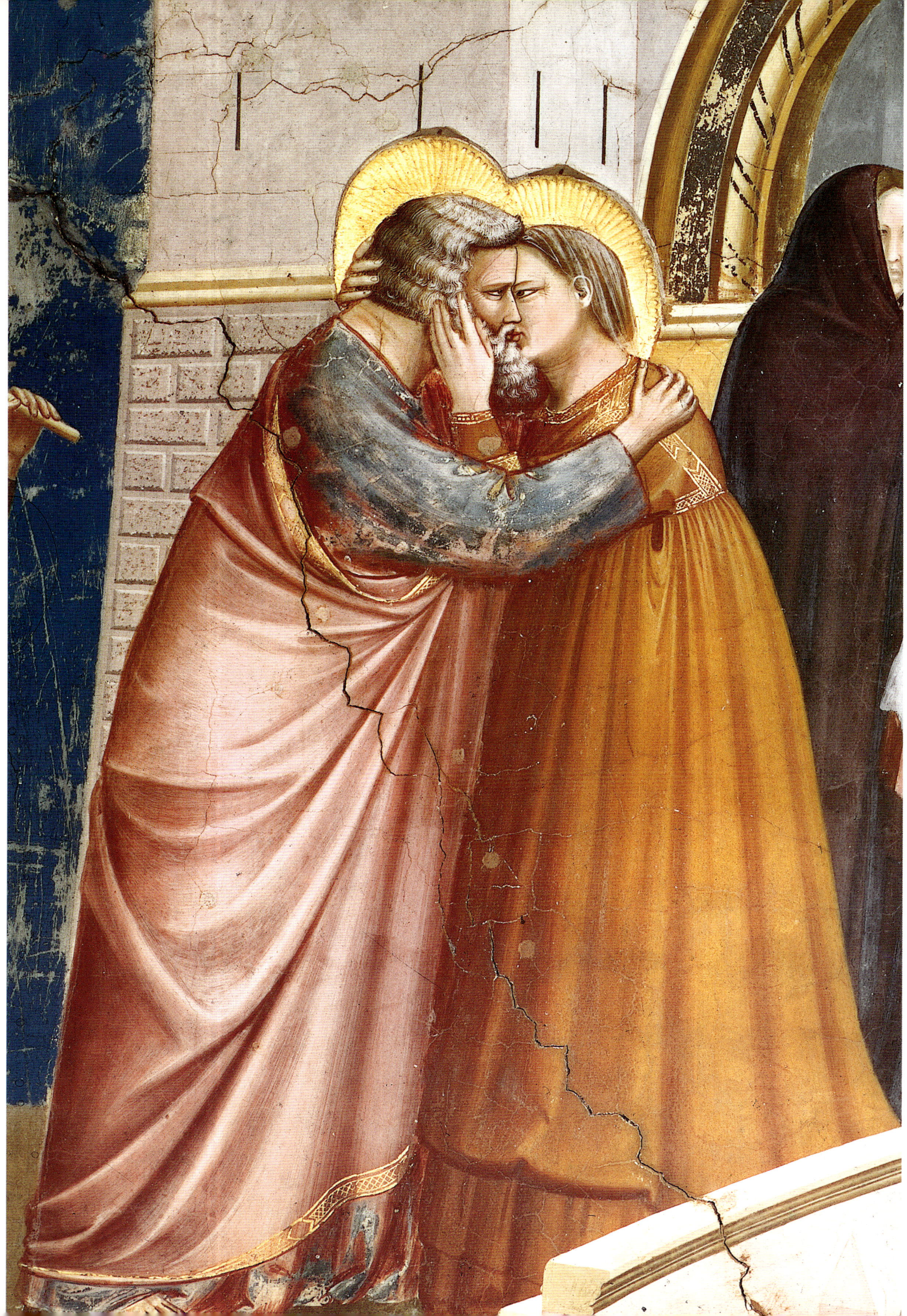

Anne Mueller von der Haegen

Giotto

di Bondone

about 1267–1337

KÖNEMANN

1 (frontispiece)
Meeting at the Golden Gate (detail ill. 69), 1302–1305
Fresco, 200 x 185 cm
Cappella degli Scrovegni, Padua

© 1998 Könemann Verlagsgesellschaft mbH
Bonner Str. 126, D-50968 Köln

Art Director: Peter Feierabend
Project Manager and Editor: Sally Bald
Assistant: Susanne Hergarden
German Editor: Ute E. Hammer
Assistant: Jeannette Fentroß
Translation from the German: Lena Miller
Contributing Editor: Susan James
Production Director: Detlev Schaper
Layout: Sabine Vonderstein
Typesetting: Greiner & Reichel, Cologne
Reproductions: CLG Fotolito, Verona
Printing and Binding: Neue Stalling, Oldenburg
Printed in Germany

ISBN 3-8290-0249-1
10 9 8 7 6 5 4 3 2 1

Contents

"...AND NOW GIOTTO HAS THE CRY..."

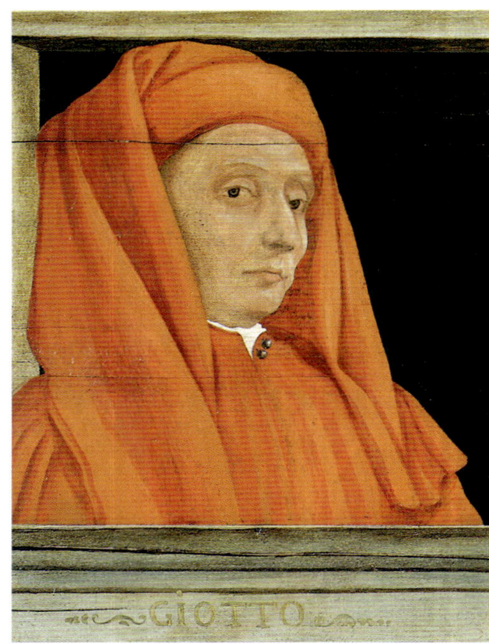

2 Paolo Uccello
Detail of *Five Famous Men (The Fathers of Perspective)*,
ca. 1500–1565
Tempera on wood, overall dimensions: 42 x 210 cm
Musée du Louvre, Paris

The series of five *Fathers of Perspective* by the Florentine
painter of the Quattrocento begins quite naturally with a
representation of Giotto.

Giotto lived in an extremely lively artistic, religious and intellectual environment, and in a period of radical change. Today, his work is regarded as one of the most significant renewals in the history of western art. We see in him the man who invented the self-contained picture and who paved the way for the comprehensive study of nature that was to characterize the art of the Renaissance a century later. The fact that this judgment was already being expressed by Giotto's contemporaries illustrates just how valid it is. From the very beginning, people discerned something completely new in his art.

The first to formulate this assessment was the great Florentine poet Dante Alighieri. In his "Divine Comedy", written between 1310 and 1320, he says in the 11th canto of *Purgatory*: "Oh empty glory of human powers … In painting Cimabue thought to hold the field, and now Giotto has the cry, so that the other's fame is diminished." (*Oh vana gloria delle umane posse … Credette Cimabue nella pittura/ tener lo campo, ed ora ha Giotto il grido,/sì che la fama di colui è oscura.*) Although there was an established tradition in Italy of praising artists, especially in the form of inscriptions on buildings, this passage in the "Divine Comedy" must count as the first literary tribute to an individual artist. Dante mentions Giotto in relation to his teacher Cimabue, and so provides us with what remains, even today, one of the most important points of reference for the art historical assessment of the painter.

Around 1350, Giovanni Boccaccio, another great poet, was the first to emphasize two further aspects which were to determine our picture of Giotto. Just two decades after Giotto's death, Boccaccio writes in his "Decamerone" that Giotto was "of such outstanding genius" that nature, the mother of all things, did not create anything which Giotto "could not depict with his stylus, pen or brush so close to the original that it had the appearance, not of a reproduction, but of the thing itself, often causing people's eyes to be deceived and to mistake the picture for the real thing."

Other important representatives of early humanism in Italy followed suit. The Florentine sculptor Lorenzo Ghiberti finally joined the three aspects – the line of artistic descent from Cimabue, the natural talent and the novel ability to reproduce nature itself in art – together in a striking legend, in around 1452, in his "Commentaries on the Tuscan Artists of the Trecento": On the way to Bologna, Cimabue found the child Giotto at the side of the road tending sheep, and saw how the boy drew a sheep from nature onto a stone slab. Deeply impressed, Cimabue took the boy on as an apprentice. It was to Giotto's particular credit that he later outgrew the *maniera greca*, the style of old Byzantine art, of which Cimabue was considered the most important representative at that time, and created a new art.

This description and evaluation of Giotto's art was to be disseminated widely by the great collection "Lives of the most eminent Painters, Sculptors and Architects", first published in 1550 by Giorgio Vasari, the "father of modern art history". Truth and legend are joined so closely together in it that modern research is still attempting to clarify the issue today.

Reliable accounts of Giotto's life and work are thin on the ground. Giotto was actually born in the Mugello, the mountainous region north of Florence, in which, according to legend, Cimabue is supposed to have discovered the boy shepherd. The house where he was born in the mountain village of Vicchio can still be visited today. When we look at the hills, the houses and the wonderfully lifelike depictions of sheep in the Arena Chapel in Padua, we actually believe that we can recognize the landscape of the Mugello.

The chronicler Riccobaldo of Ferrara reports in around 1312 that Giotto had created magnificent works in the great Franciscan churches of Assisi, Rimini and Padua, as well as in Padua's Arena Chapel.

Others speak of numerous panel paintings, of works in Florence, Rome, Naples and Milan. A great number of works, therefore, can be associated with Giotto. However, there are no signatures to confirm these connections.

We still have no clear idea today of how of an artist's workshop was organized commercially at the beginning of the 14th century. We do know, however, that Giotto was in charge of workshops in various places. Some of his assistants must have accompanied him for many

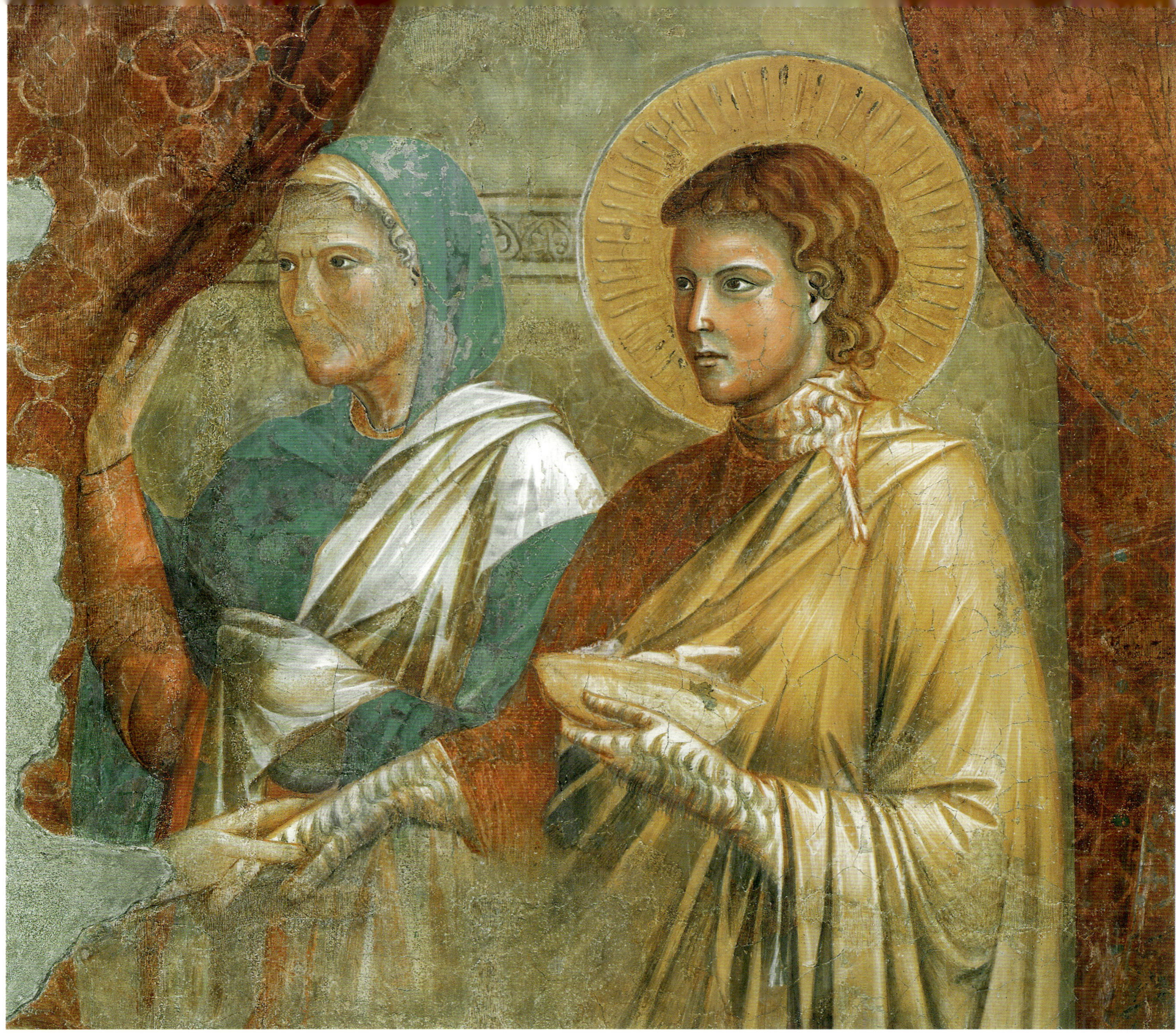

years, others set up their own studios, with works closely adapted from Giotto's style, which sometimes creates difficult problems for researchers as far as attribution is concerned. The widespread emulation of Giotto in all the places where he was active shows that, alongside critics and patrons, it was above all the artists themselves who wished to take part in the renewal of painting which he had begun.

According to Vasari, Giotto was born in 1277. Other sources, however, name 1267 as the year of his birth, which, based on the works attributed to him, is more probable. Giotto would have begun his apprenticeship with Cimabue between the ages of ten and fourteen. A trip to Rome presumably rounded off the young painter's training, after which he followed his master to what was at that time the largest "building site" in Italy, the church of San Francesco in Assisi.

There, Cimabue was in charge of the decoration of the newly erected Upper Church. When he left Assisi to fulfill other obligations, several of his assistants and journeymen, including Giotto, stayed behind. At the same time, Roman painters, led by Jacopo Torriti, arrived in Assisi, so that several studio groups were working alongside one another. A short time later, Giotto became the independent leader of a workshop, and the Franciscan order assigned him the task of continuing with the decoration.

3 *Isaac blessing Jacob* (detail ill. 12), ca. 1290–1295

The second-born son Jacob receives the blessing from the aged patriarch Isaac in place of the first-born Esau. We can clearly make out the skins on his throat and hands, used to feign Esau's greater covering of hair before the blind patriarch. In this depiction, rich in detail and psychologically very accurate, mother and son look towards the father full of suspense. The intensity of their gaze and the precise sequence of the gestures are augmented by the color. The turquoise of the woman's robes stands in strong contrast to the warm golden tones assembled in the figure of Jacob. This coloring supports the dignified expression on his face and emphasizes that, although a human being, he is holy.

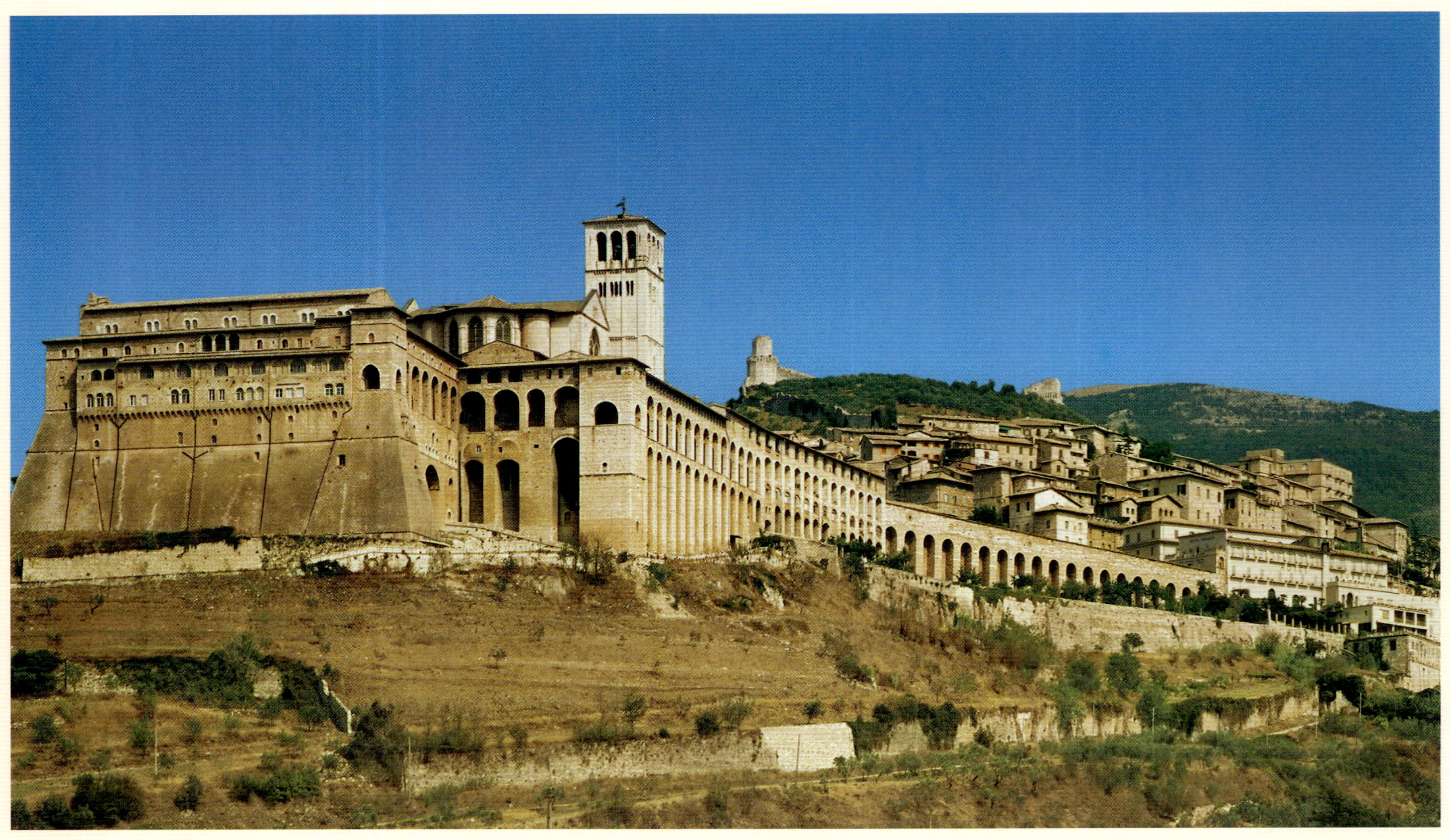

THE BASILICA OF SAN FRANCESCO IN ASSISI

4 San Francesco, Assisi
View from the southwest

Visible from afar, the memorial church of St. Francis juts out from the side of Monte Subiaco over the Umbrian plains. It rises up almost like a fortress on enormous foundations and surrounded by the monastery buildings.

5 (opposite) San Francesco, Upper Church, Assisi
View of the choir towards the west

The Upper Church, with its single nave and tall Gothic windows, has a bright and festive atmosphere. The cross-ribbed vaults, the windows and the nave wall were decorated with frescoes over the period of several decades. The unified program created a kind of pictorial bible.

When Francis Bernardone felt death approaching, he had himself laid down in a small church outside the north Italian town of Assisi, where he died on 3 October 1226. The son of a merchant, he had devoted his life to imitating Christ. This life was thought to be so exemplary by his contemporaries that numerous people gathered around him. Francis drew up a rule for the growing community, which was confirmed by the pope in 1209 and formed the basis of the new order. In it, the founder of the order prescribed the observance of absolute poverty, a life of chastity and obedience to God as the most important virtues.

A simple grave would probably have been more in keeping with the ideas of St. Francis, but the pope and the leaders of the order had quite different intentions: the memorial church of the order's founder was to become at the same time the main and mother church of the whole order. And so the church grounds were donated and an appeal was made by the pope for financial support for the building work as early as 1228 – just two years after the death of the *poverello*. Francis was canonized on 18 July of that same year, and the foundation stone of the new church was laid a day later.

A magnificent construction was erected on the outskirts of the town of Assisi in the form of a double church, i. e.

two churches were built, one on top of the other (ills. 4, 6). Because of its location on the slopes of Monte Subiaco, the choirs of both churches are orientated towards the west, and not towards the rising sun in the east as is usual. The Lower Church was reserved for the remains of the saint: it was here that mass was to be held in his memory. Its sturdy proportions still make it seem like a crypt today (ill. 7). From the outset, the Upper Church was intended as the official place of worship (ill. 5). It opens out towards the town, and also houses the papal throne, for the pope remains a bishop of the church.

As early as 1230, the Lower Church was sufficiently advanced for the remains of St. Francis to be transferred here. This was done in secret, it could almost be said "in the dead of night" for fear that thieves might attempt to steal the relics. The exact location of the saint's tomb remained a mystery until the 19th century. It was not made accessible until 1822, with the construction of a burial chamber. The building of this crypt changed forever the character of the original Lower Church, which had itself once been conceived as a crypt. However, the changes had already begun centuries earlier, when the monastery in Assisi decided, in around 1300, to allow the addition of private commemorative chapels. This meant that the

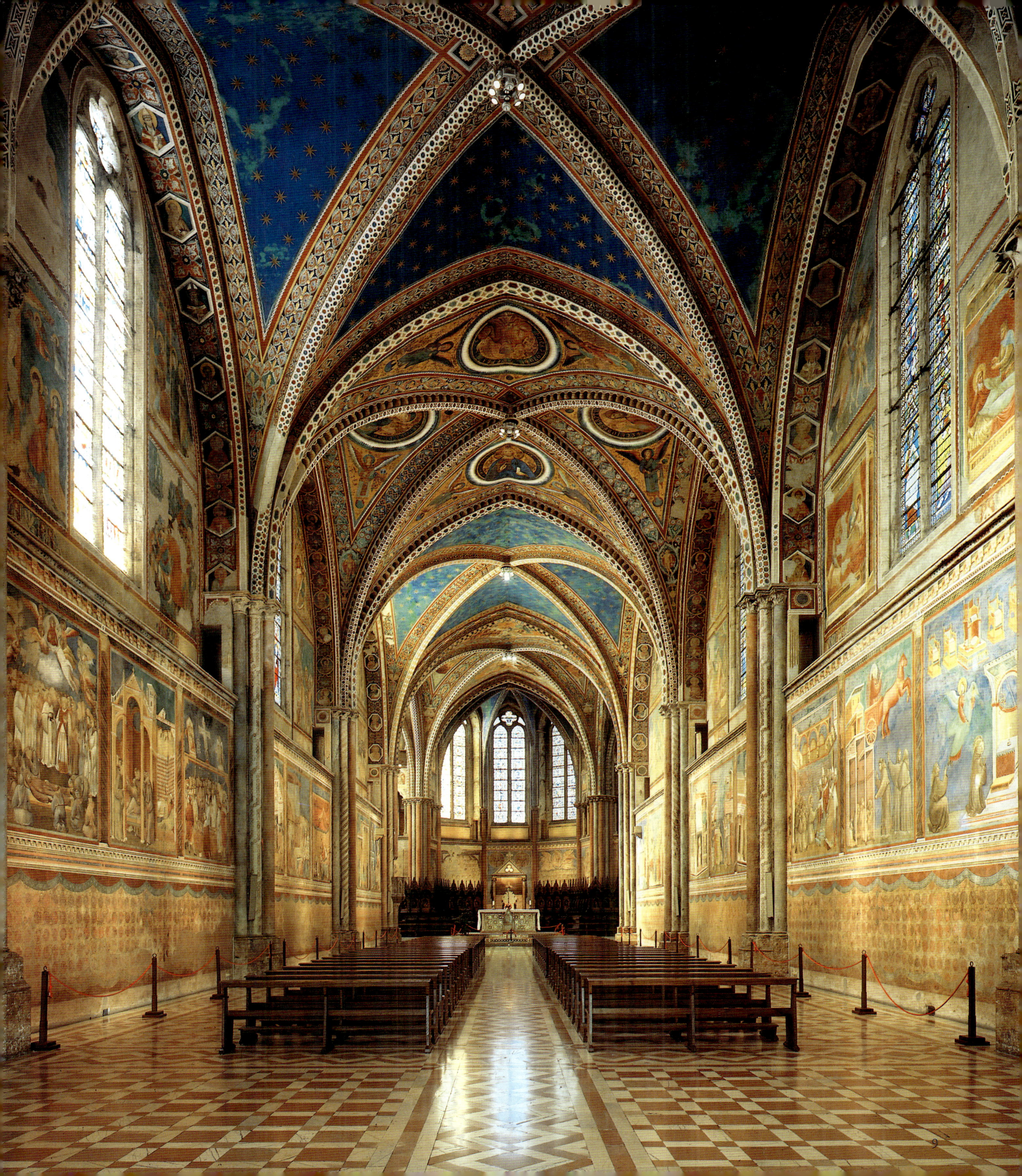

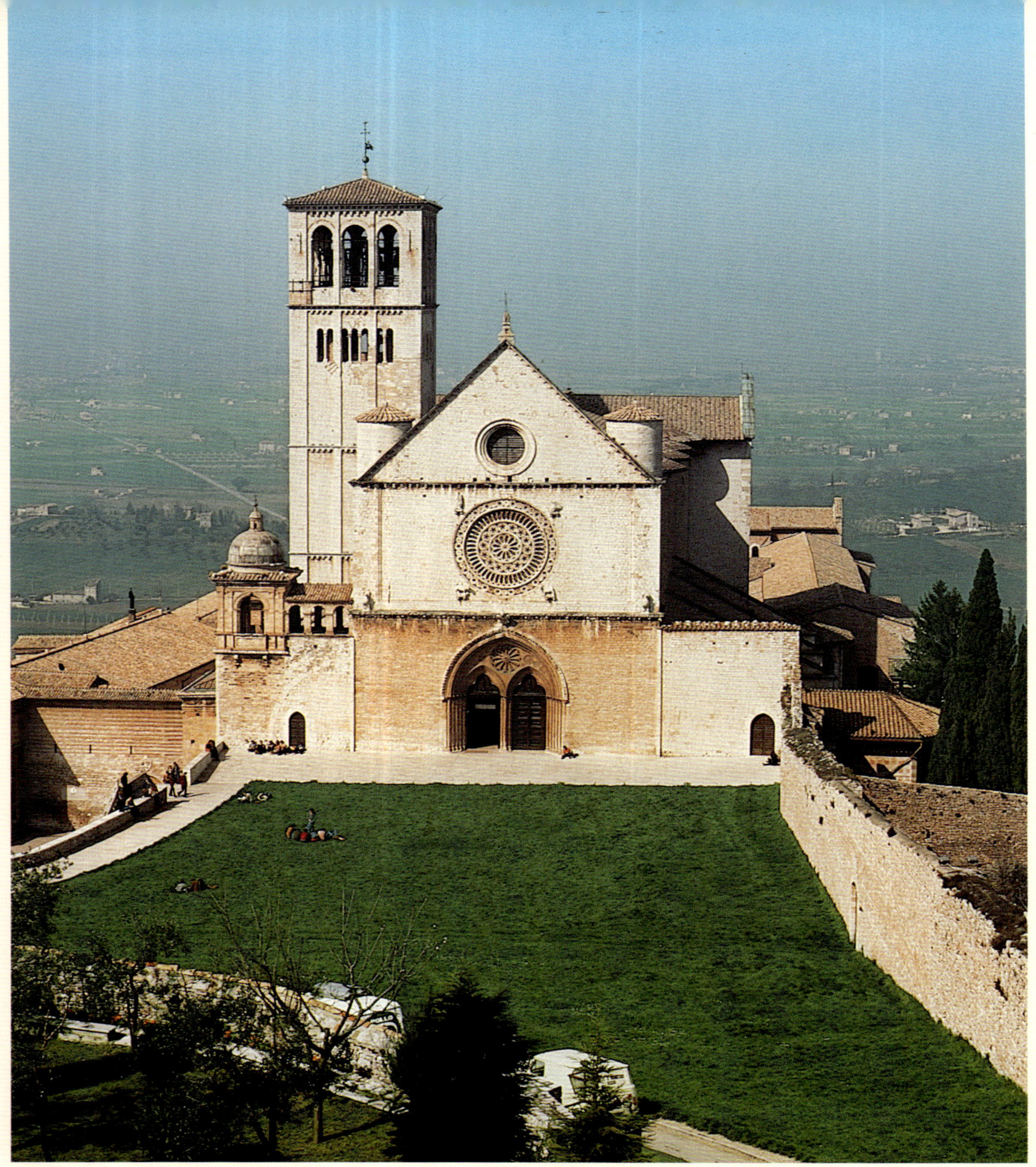

6 San Francesco, Assisi
View from the east

The church where St. Francis is buried opens out towards the city with a ceremonial piazza. Unusually, the solemn façade and the entrance portal lie on the east side of the church.

church interior was now no longer accessible only to Franciscans.

The breaching of the walls to create the new lateral chapels destroyed the paintings on the walls of the nave. These originally showed five scenes each from Christ's Passion and from the life of St. Francis on opposite walls. The order had commissioned this series of pictures as soon as the Lower Church was completed. As the first version in paint to juxtapose the life story of the saint with that of Christ, the cycle became the model for the decoration of all other churches of the order. The great cycle of pictures on the Legend of St. Francis in the Upper Church was completed around 1300. The frescoes in the Lower Church were obviously no longer accorded any great importance after that. From that date, the embellishment of the Lower Church remained in a fragmentary state, although a magnificent program design was to be realized on the occasion of the hundredth anniversary of St. Francis' death. However, only the murals in the crossing and in the transepts were completed. The subject matter of these connects the saint and the allegorical representation of the virtues of the order with both the apocalyptic visions of John the Evangelist and the life of Christ.

The Upper Church consists of a single nave with transept and apse, in which the papal throne stands as a visible symbol of its status as a papal chapel. The proportions of this church are very different to those of the Lower Church, which provided its ground plan (ills. 5, 7). There is no sign here of the dark atmosphere of the Lower Church: soaring, bright and light-filled thanks to its French-Gothic forms, adapted to an Italian style, the church welcomes the streams of pilgrims.

Records tell us that the church was consecrated in 1253, after which work commenced on the decoration of the transepts, presumably by a Roman master and by a northern European one. Cimabue and his workshop begin their involvement in around 1277, painting frescoes, mainly in the apse, the south transept, and the crossing (ill. 16). Scenes from the life of the Virgin Mary, the martyrdoms of the apostles Peter and Paul, representations of the Apocalypse and the Crucifixion occupy this space, which was reserved for members of the order and separated from the nave by a rood-screen.

A different program was designed for the congregation of the faithful, and realized from west to east, i. e. from the choir area to the entrance wall. The surface of the walls was divided into three registers in the process. The two upper tiers of the north wall depict scenes from the Old Testament, and those on the south wall scenes from the New Testament. On the north side the narrative begins in the bay in front of the crossing, in the upper tier, with the *Creation of the World*, and is continued through to *Cain killing Abel*. Beneath this is *Noah building the Ark* and the stories of Isaac and Joseph respectively. On the opposite wall the *Annunciation*, i. e. the beginning of the story of

Christ's infancy, is portrayed above the *Wedding Feast at Cana*. The middle tier is dedicated to *Christ's Miracles* and *Christ's Passion*. These stories from the Old and New Testaments are complemented, and in some cases united, by the saints and fathers of the Church on the vault, and related to the Legend of St. Francis on the lower tier of the walls of the nave (ills. 19–34). Here too, as in the Lower Church, the Christ-like life of St. Francis, the *Imitatio Christi*, forms the basis of the decorative program. However, the parallels in the lives of Christ and of the saint have been expanded through references to the Old Testament. The pictorial program is intended to make the faithful aware of the whole body of theological doctrine underpinning the Franciscan order.

7 San Francesco, Lower Church, Assisi
View of the choir towards the west

The low vault is supported by the massive columns and spans the rather compressed, crypt-like room. To the left and right we see the jambs on either side of the entrance to the lateral chapels, to which the original fresco decorations situated here had to give way.

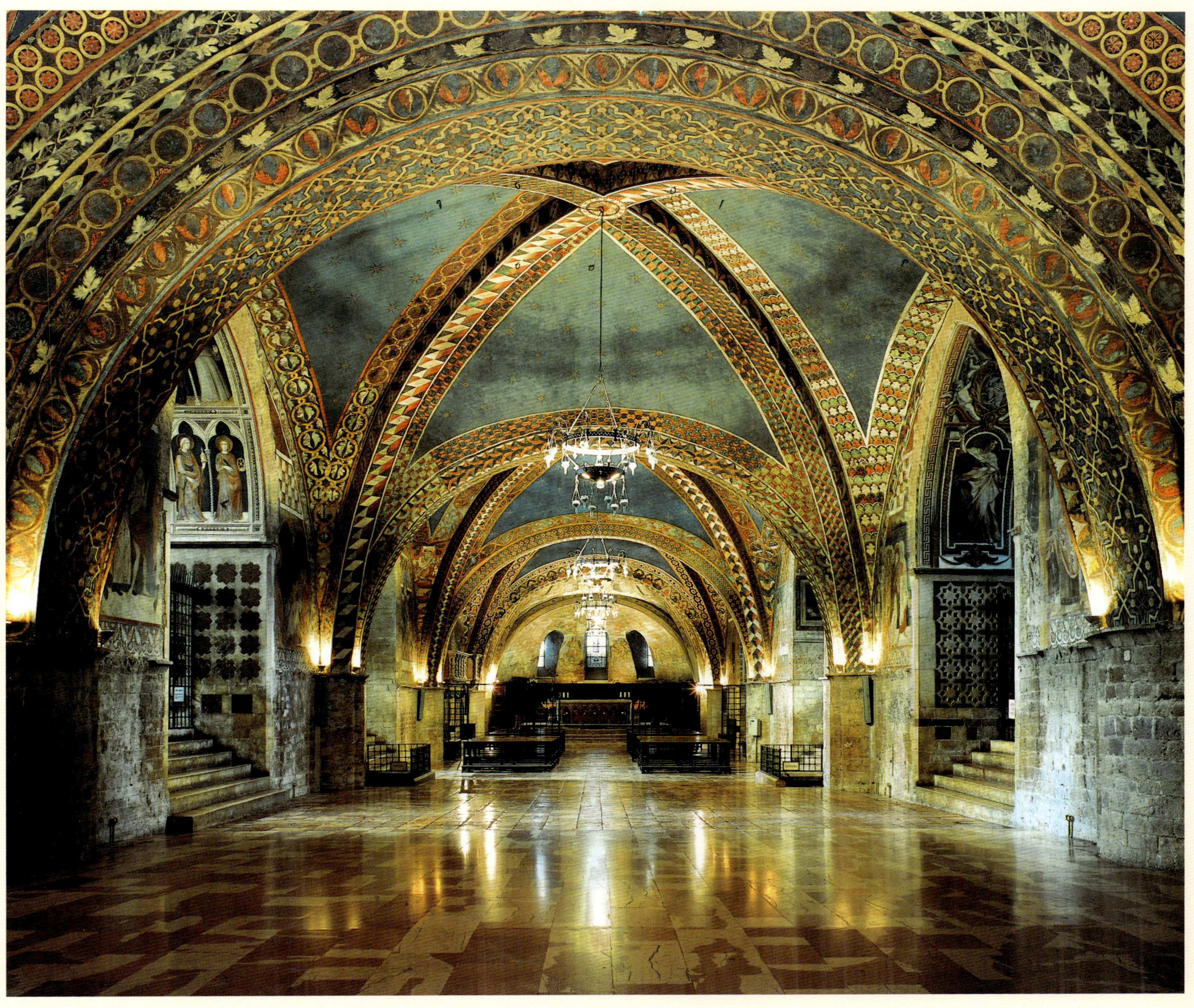

Revolutionary Beginnings in Assisi

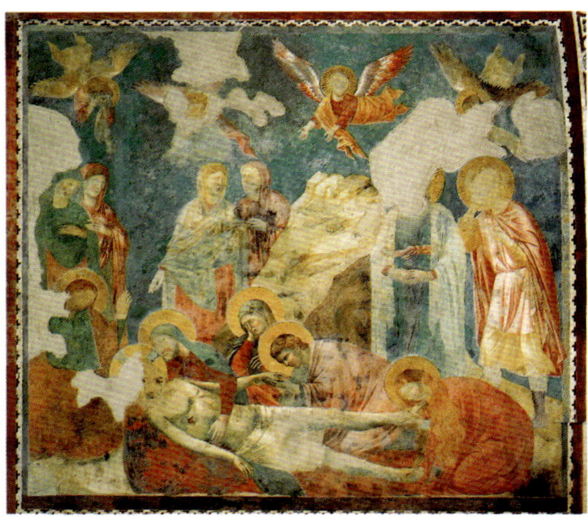

8 *Lamentation of Christ*, ca. 1290–1295
Fresco
Basilica superiore di San Francesco, Assisi

In front of a rocky landscape, Mary holds the body of her dead son in her lap. She looks at him mournfully. John and Mary Magdalene also touch the body of Christ with expressions of great sorrow. The firmness of the composition and the portrayal of human emotions distinguish this fresco by the young Giotto.

9 (opposite) Fourth bay of the north wall (counted from the entrance)
Basilica superiore di San Francesco, Assisi

The walls on either side of the window are again divided horizontally. At the top, the *Creation of the World* can be seen on the left and the *Creation of Adam* (Jacopo Torriti) on the right. Below these are the *Building of the Ark* and the *Boarding of the Ark* (follower of Cimabue). On the walls of the nave we can see the first three stations in the life of St. Francis. The illusionistic framework of the Legend of St. Francis is also visible: the rich console frieze above the coffered ceiling, which is laid out in perspective and supported by twisted columns.

Before Giotto created pictures at Assisi in his own right – when first he becomes visible to us as a painter – other artists had already begun frescoing the walls of the nave of the Upper Church. The pictorial program opens with the five scenes from "Genesis", executed by the school of the Roman painter Jacopo Torriti (ill. 9). As in his earlier works for Santa Maria Maggiore in Rome, Torriti was particularly concerned to achieve a structural firmness in his paintings – using the exact delineation of the horizon and the full circle of the aureole in the fresco the *Creation of the World*, and the clear base line in the *Creation of Eve*. On the other hand, all of the frescoes that form part of the representations from Genesis are characterized by sweeping gestures and dramatic states of ecstasy. The artist from the school of Cimabue, for example, developed the action in the *Building of the Ark* through gestures, which are intertwined in the manner of a garland (ill. 9). The landscape, in particular the rock, serves to separate the scenes, which appear together in the one picture field. Even the *Sacrifice of Isaac* is characterized by the great sweep of Abraham's gesture (ill. 11).

Although the first bay of the south wall has been badly damaged, the surviving fragments allow us to discern that another artist was at work here. Best preserved is the fresco the *Lamentation of Christ* (ill. 8). The landscape is employed here, in contrast to the *Building of the Ark,* to add drama to what is happening in the picture. The gestures of the figures, too, are no longer part of an unchanging series, but are related to the respective figures in a more individual manner.

Grief-stricken, the mourners tend to the body of the dead Christ. His mother cradles her son's body on her knee, John bends over his hand, and Mary Magdalene, who has fallen to her knees, tenderly grasps his foot. Are these not the very feet she dried with her hair? We are however dealing with more than mere symbolism here. This is probably the first time since antiquity that emotion has assumed such a form, that compassion and human grief has been expressed in every gesture. The female figures in the background also demonstrate the artist's familiarity with the art of the ancient world (ill. 10). The way in which their cloaks are draped around their heads and over their shoulders is far removed from the weightless way in which robes painted by Cimabue swing open, or from the ecstatic way their folds are arranged in bundles.

These figures seem to stand out from the landscape or against the background architecture in a particular way – through gravity. And it is precisely this quality that enables the work of the young Giotto to be distinguished from the compositions of the older masters. The brief, brisk movements emphasize the weight and the volume of the bodies, as if the Roman and Florentine schools had been developed in such a way as to achieve a synthesis.

If the surviving fragments of these frescoes make us aware of something new, then this is especially true of two representations in the second bay of the north wall: namely *Isaac blessing Jacob* and *Esau before Isaac* (ills. 12, 13). Such great strides in the history of art are made in both of these depictions that they have been regarded as revolutionary innovations since the late 19th century.

On the one hand, we have the treatment of architecture – only in the art of antiquity was space previously portrayed in such a manner. We are looking into a box-like room, which encloses the robustly voluminous figures, and can see the transition from inside to outside on the right. As in the *Lamentation of Christ*, the figures involved in the action have a firm position. They are clearly standing, and not hovering in space like the figures in the *Building of the Ark*.

On the other hand, we have the portrayal of the protagonists and of their feelings – their faces, their gazes and their posture (ills. 3, 14) express the different emotions of the actors. While the confidence with which the figures act is illustrated in the first fresco by means of their firm stance and their precise, focused gestures, in the second, it is the movement of the bodies and the to-and-fro motion of the gestures which are striking.

This expression of psychological content, the refined handling of color, the delicate modelling of the faces and the superior composition of space, which no longer tilts back and forward between perspectives from above and below: all of these constitute revolutionary steps in the development of art.

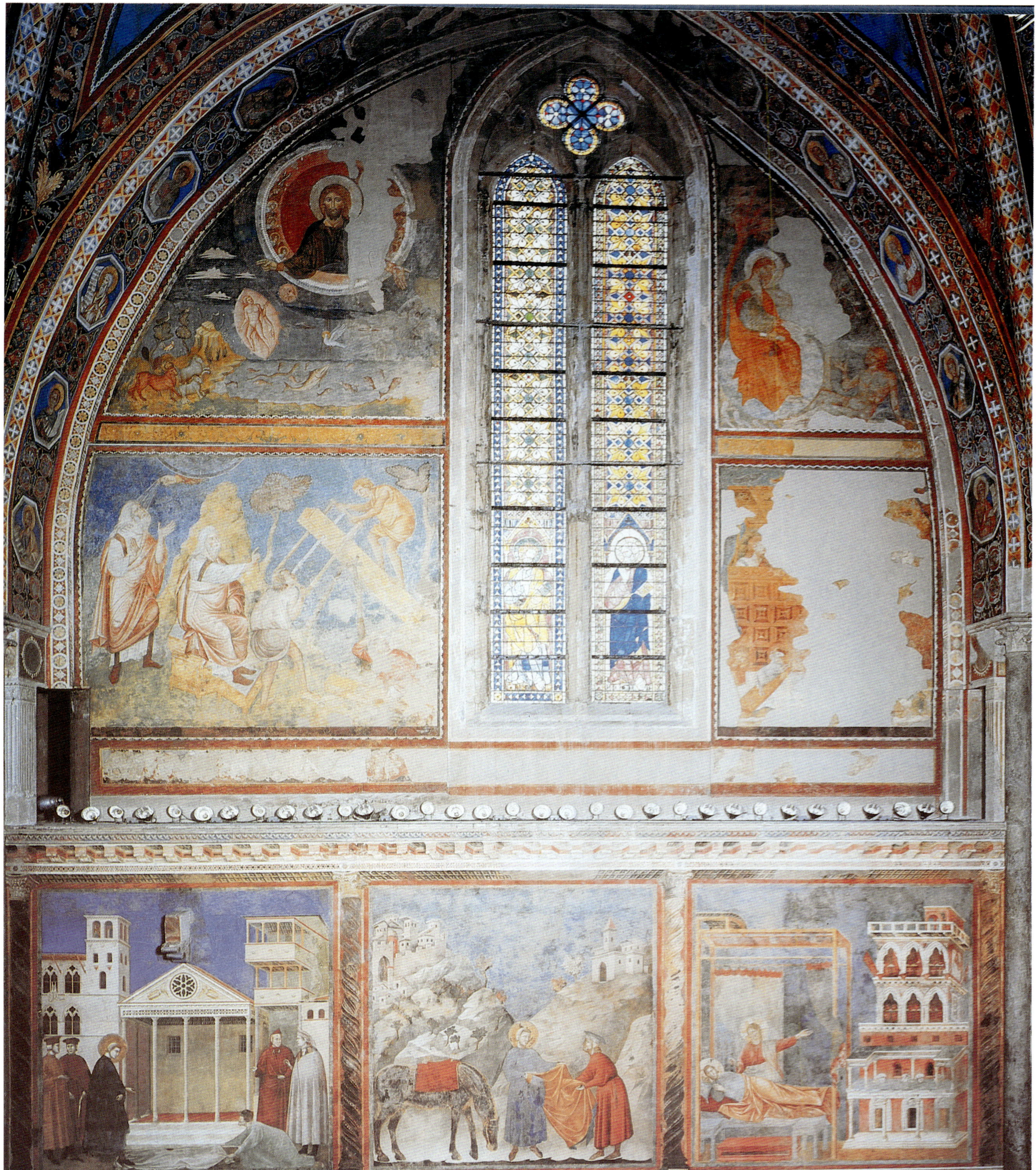

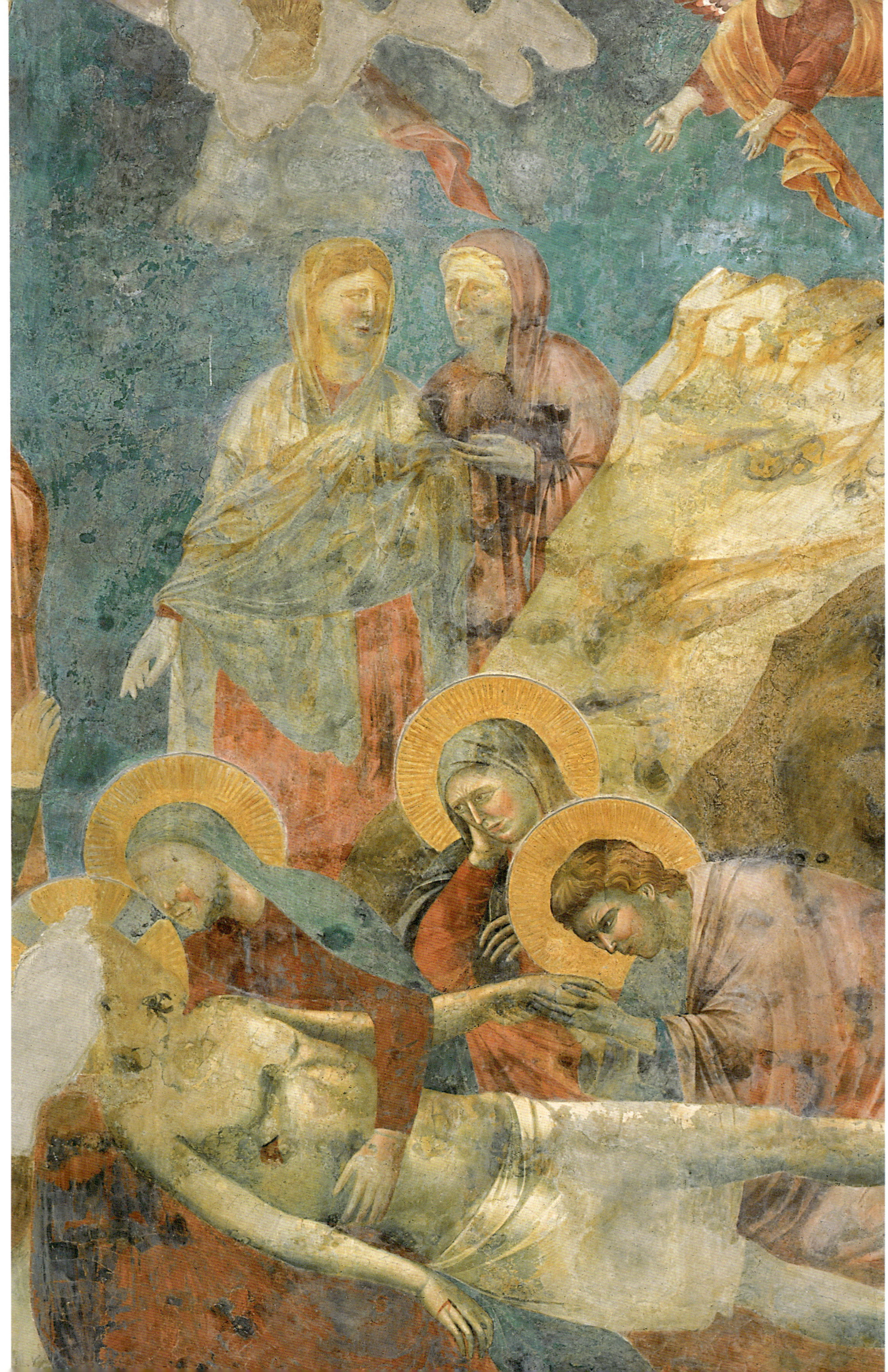

10 (opposite) *Lamentation of Christ* (detail ill. 8), ca. 1290–1295

Two women emerge from behind the rock and approach those who have gathered to mourn around the body of Christ. The women look at one another with understanding, yet shaken. In contrast to the painters of the school of Cimabue, the young Giotto employs figures who add a reflecting comment to the depictions. This difference, which indicates a familiarity with antique art and which will become yet clearer in the *Isaac* frescoes, is also demonstrated both in the relationship between body and garments and in the direct exchange of glances of the figures.

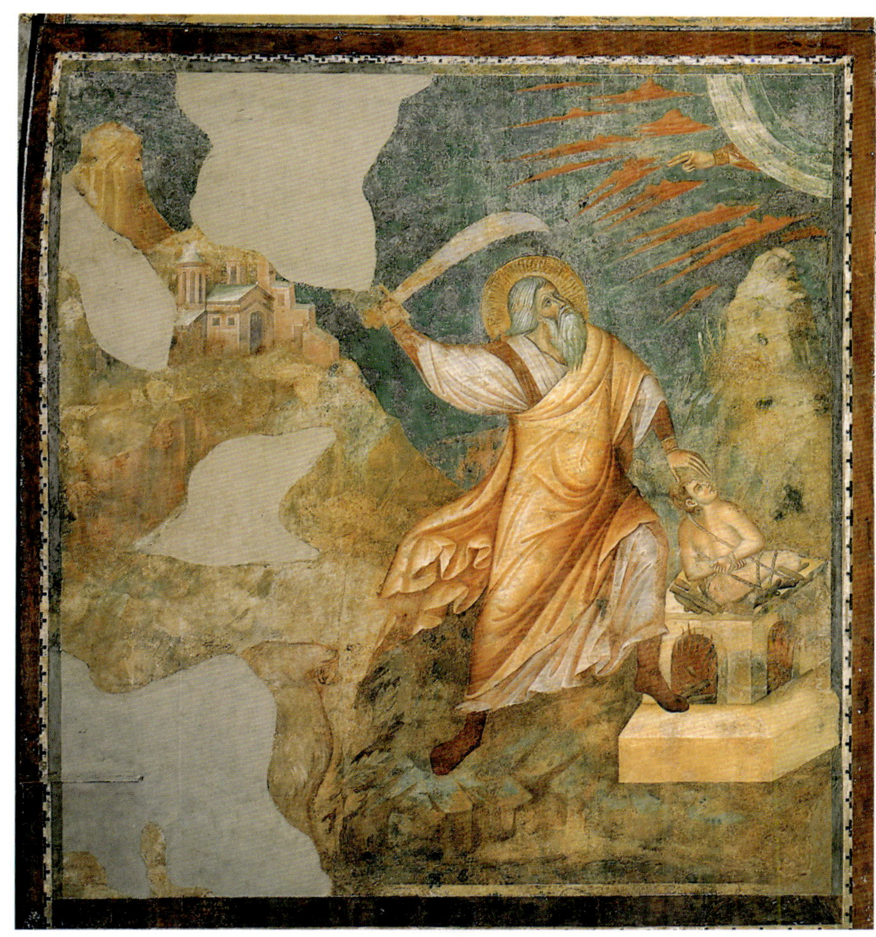

11 Follower of Cimabue
The Sacrifice of Isaac, ca. 1290
Fresco
Basilica superiore di San Francesco, Assisi

The Hand of God arrests the violent gesture with which Abraham intended to kill his son Isaac as a sacrificial offering. This depiction is characterized by the wide sweep of the ecstatic movement. The massive volume of the figure and the plasticity of the altarpiece form a certain contrast to the flatness of the rocky landscape.

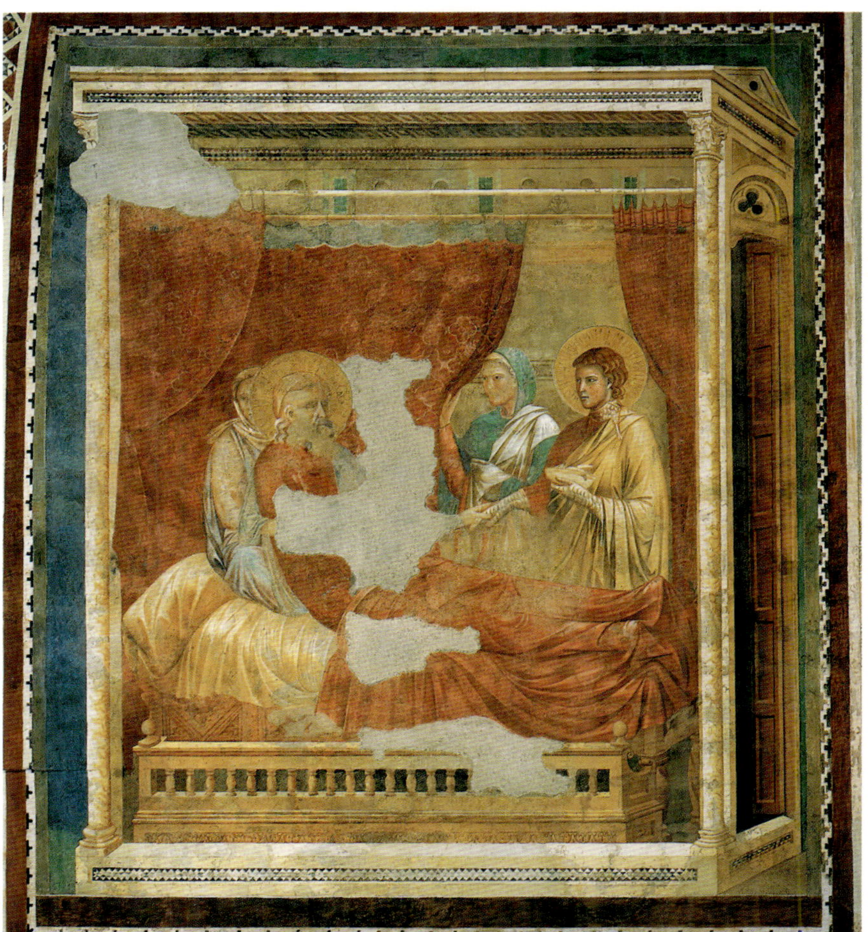

12 *Isaac blessing Jacob*, ca. 1290–1295
Fresco
Basilica superiore di San Francesco, Assisi

Giotto contains the action within a box-like room, the front wall of which is missing. This lends the composition a previously unknown compactness. Jacob, the second-born son of the patriarch Isaac, wearing fur on his hands and around his neck, is ready to deceive his blind father. He approaches the latter timidly and with a hesitant gesture. A woman helps the patriarch into the position from which he gives his blessing.

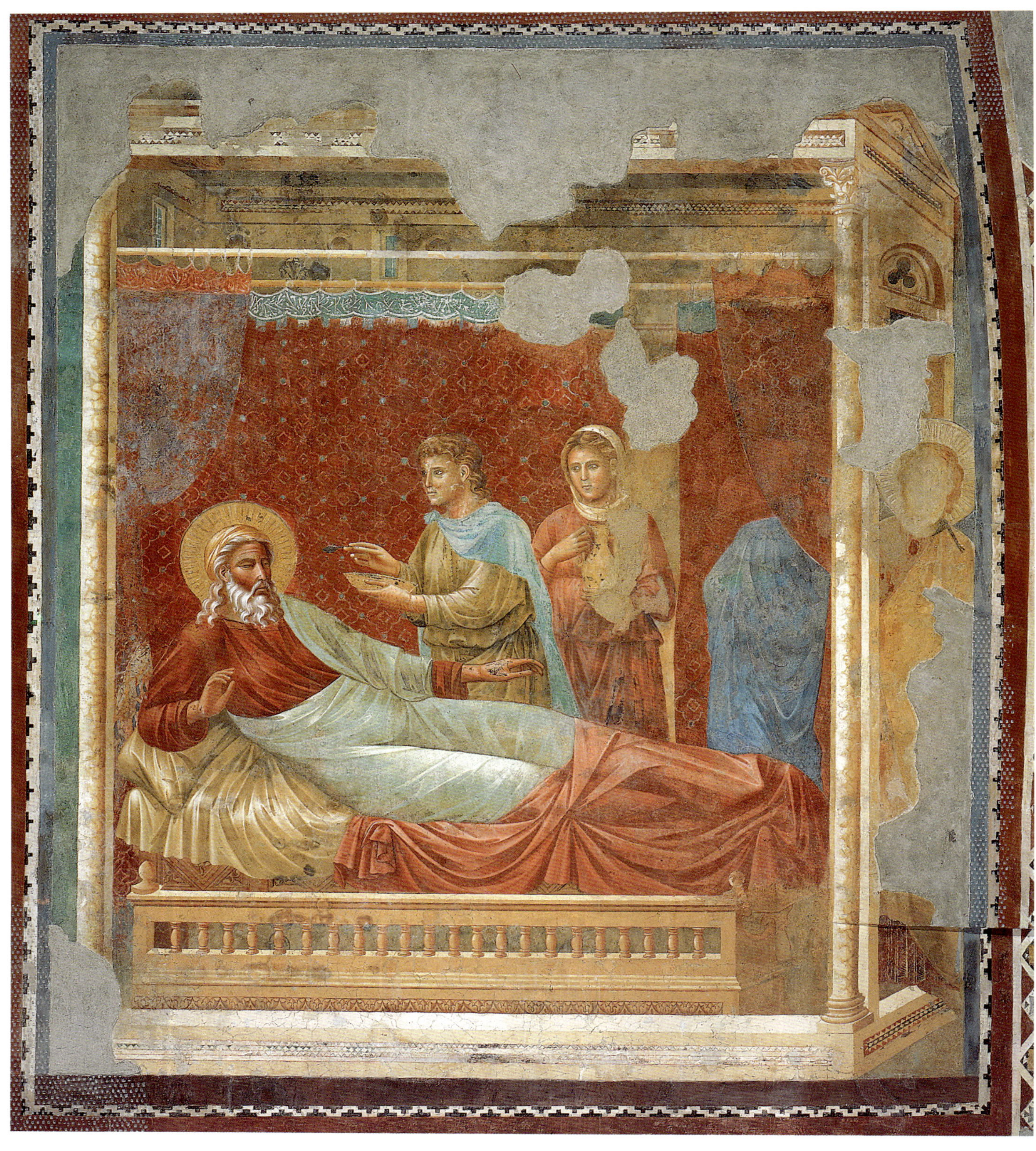

13 (above) *Esau before Isaac*, ca. 1290–1295
Fresco
Basilica superiore di San Francesco, Assisi

The second *Isaac* scene takes place in the same box-like
room as the previous one. On the right, in spite of the
badly preserved state, we can make out Jacob and his
mother Rebecca leaving the room. In this way the
continuity of the two scenes and the explosive nature of
the sequence of events is made very clear.

14 (opposite) *Esau before Isaac* (detail ill. 13),
ca. 1290–1295

The open, questioning gesture of Esau, arrested in his
movement, clashes with the regretful hesitation of the
father. The maid, who just a moment ago had supported
the blind man, observes his reaction attentively and
anxiously. She appears to add extra significance to the
encounter between the first-born Esau and his deceived
father, which is characterized with psychological accuracy.

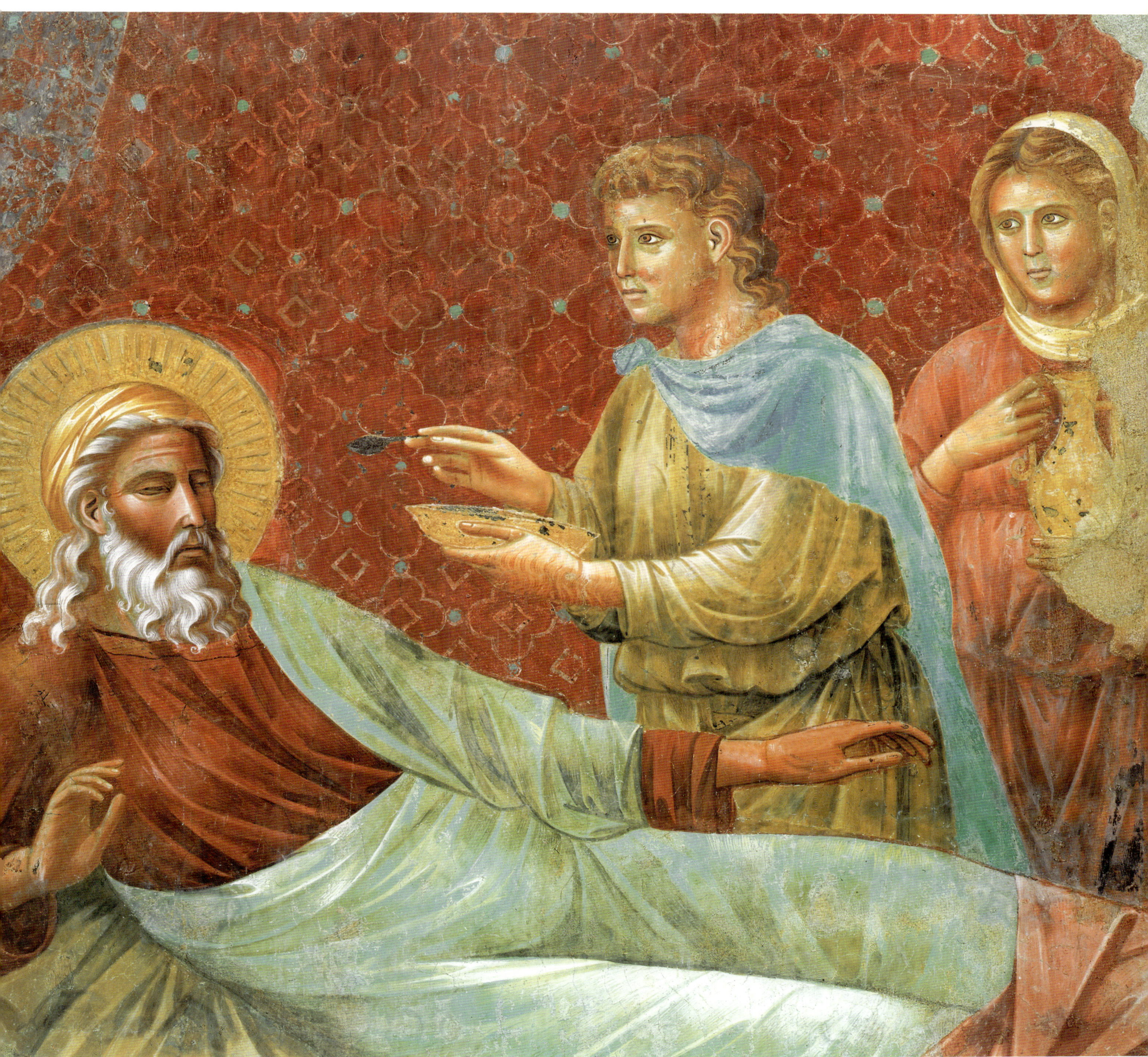

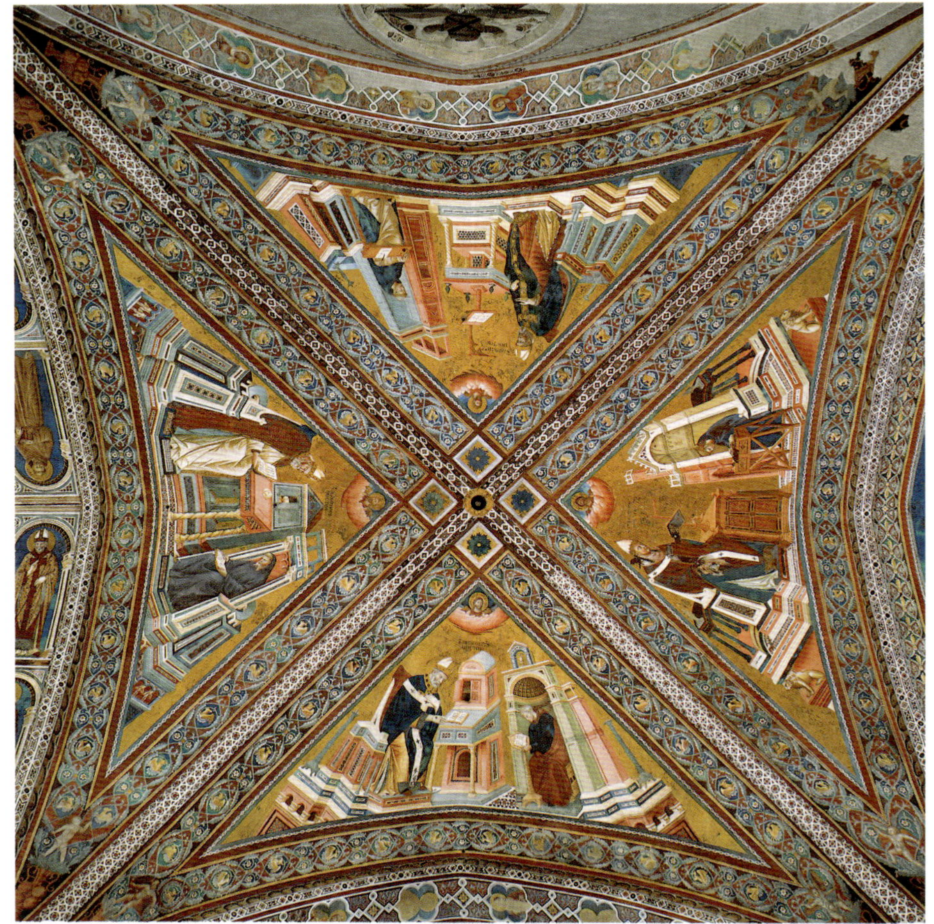

15 Vault of the *Doctors of the Church*, ca. 1290–1295
Fresco
Basilica superiore di San Francesco, Assisi

In the four compartments of the vault in the entrance bay
Giotto portrays the four Doctors of the Church together
with their scribes: in the south (at the top of the
illustration), St. Augustine and, opposite him, St.
Ambrose; in the east (to the left), St. Jerome, and in the
west, St. Gregory. The architectural structures jut up from
below into the gold background. Giotto conveys a definite
idea of the intellectual work of these saints through the
great attention to detail and the perspectival accuracy.

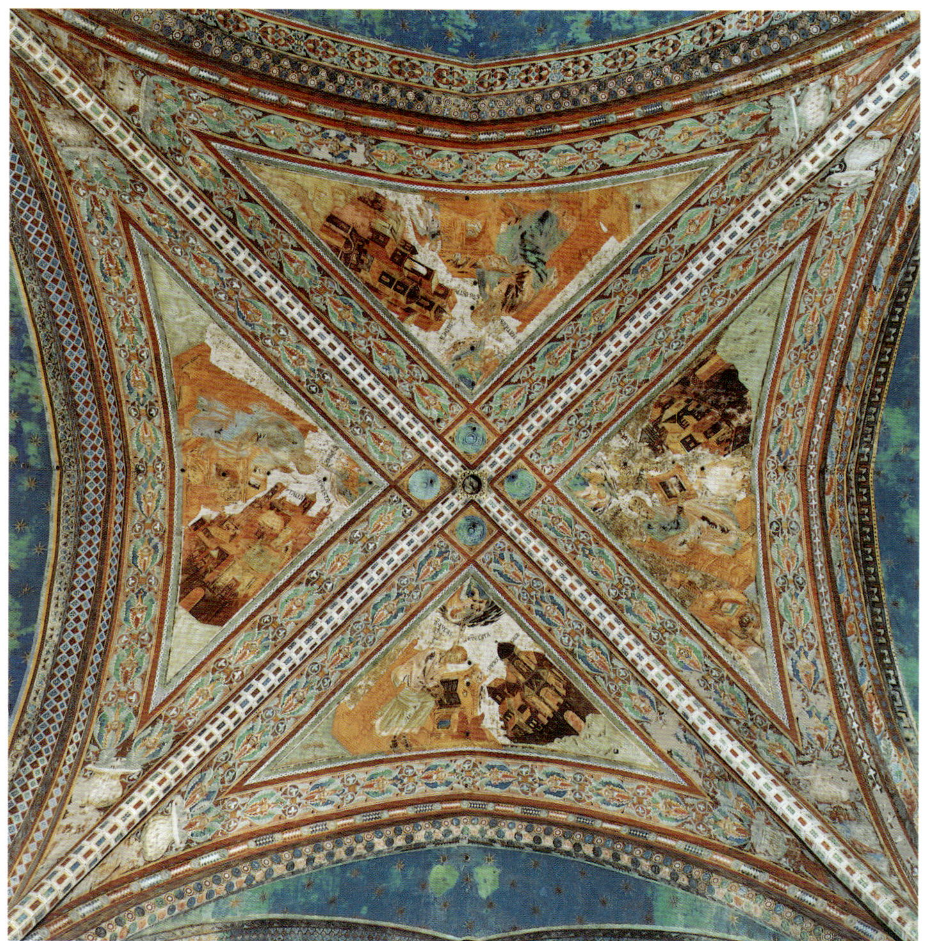

16 Cimabue
Vault of the *Evangelists*, ca. 1280
Fresco
Basilica superiore di San Francesco, Assisi

In the crossing vault, Cimabue portrays the four
evangelists at their writing desks. Matthew, John, Luke
and Mark are each related to the respective cities in which
they worked: Jerusalem, Ephesus, Corinth and Rome.
This vault was badly damaged in the earthquake of
autumn 1997.

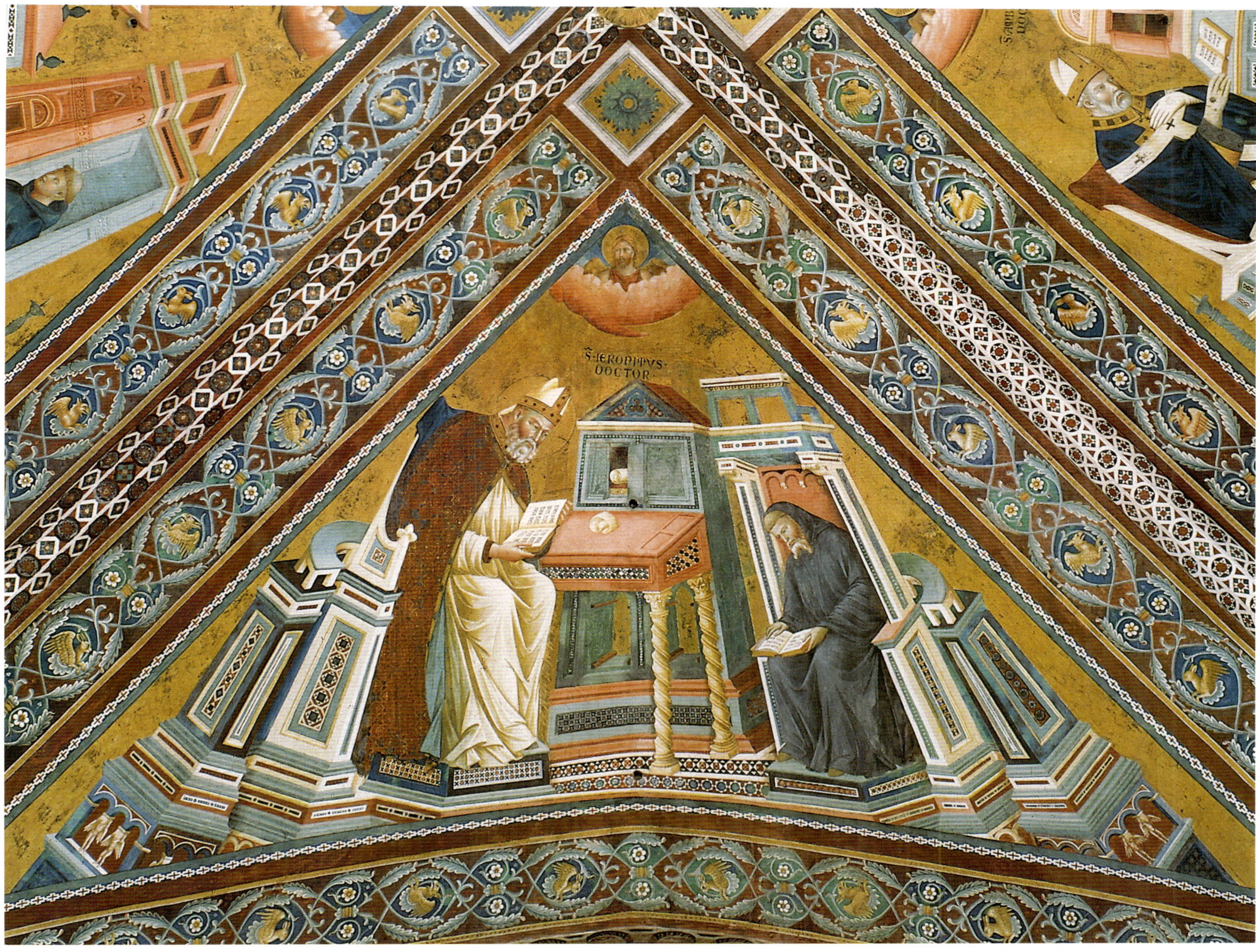

Here, in about 1290, while still a young man, Giotto created a basis from which to develop his future work. Some aspects which still appear clumsy and rough – such as the sharp fashioning of drapery folds, which reminds us of Cimabue, or the relationship of the figures to space – will change and be developed in many different variations.

Just a short time after executing these frescoes, the young master tried out his new discoveries on the ceiling of the Upper Church at Assisi. In the four triangular compartments of the vault depicting the *Doctors of the Church*, his new approach is brought to glorious fruition in the composition of space, in the sculptural effect, in the delight in detail and in the exact characterization (ills. 15, 17).

On very finely constructed thrones, decorated with inlay work, and in marble cabinets, the Doctors of the Church sit opposite their scribes, at lecterns and writing desks respectively. Cimabue himself had filled the awkwardly-shaped triangular surfaces of the vault above the crossing with double items – a single city and a single evangelist are disposed around the vertex of each of the compartments (ill. 16). While in the latter the perspective jumps about, the viewpoint changes, and an otherwise unexplained rock defines the ground, everything is clearer and better structured in the Giotto. The superstructures, all derived from the same basic structure, stand on the same architectural podium, which rises up from below. All the elements, in their entirety, are subordinated to a unified perspective structure. Even the symbolic perspective, which accords the scribes only half the bodily size of the more important Fathers of the Church, is balanced by Giotto by the height of the cabinets in which the servants sit. Just as on the walls of the nave, the artist is here striving towards a unified and "natural" representation.

17 Vault of the *Doctors of the Church*, St. Jerome (detail ill. 15), ca. 1290–1295

St. Jerome sits facing his companion. Both are engrossed in a book. Giotto establishes the connection between the two figures with great understanding for the curvature of the surface. It is striking, too, just how many details – such as those on the writing desk – enliven the scene, although it is at a great distance from the viewer. This fresco was destroyed in the earthquake of autumn 1997 along with the related figures of saints on the wall arch.

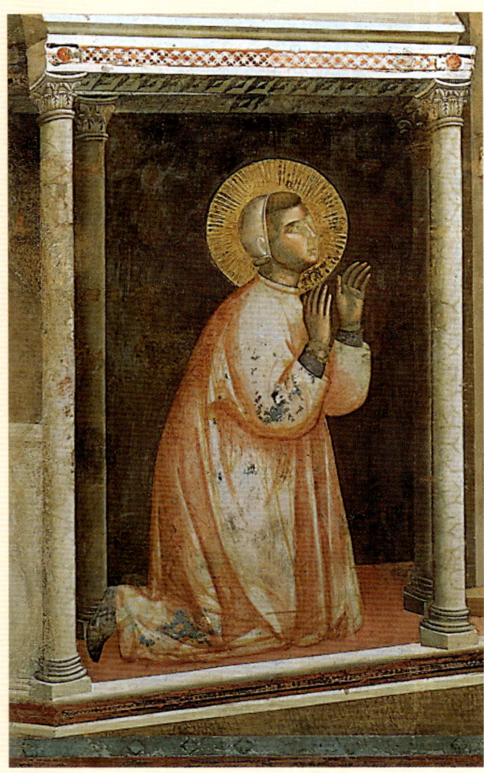

18 *The Crucifix in San Damiano*, Saint Francis (detail ill. 22), before 1300

Giotto depicts Francis with raised, almost shaking hands at prayer in the church of San Damiano. The saint undergoes his first mystical experience in this church, which reinforces the inner break with his previous way of life. Giotto uses gaze and gesture to illustrate the surprise and agitation of the young nobleman.

19 *The Renunciation of Possessions*, 5th picture of the Legend of St. Francis, before 1300
Fresco, 270 x 230 cm
Basilica superiore di San Francesco, Assisi

When Francis' father accuses his son before the episcopal tribune of squandering his fortune, Francis returns to him even the clothes he is wearing, and repudiates him. Giotto illustrates this sensational public separation, which signifies the decisive step towards the saint's future life of poverty, by means of the two groups of people on opposite sides. The buildings further reinforce the gulf between the two worlds.

The admiration and affection shown to St. Francis of Assisi surmount all denominational barriers and indicate just how great is the special aura attached to him, as do the depictions in art – by Giotto and later artists.

Francis is the one who talks to the plants and the animals, who maintains our elemental love of nature. He also remains natural in his dealings with the church, speaking freely and spontaneously to the authorities. He loves the poor and the lepers, and so devotes himself to the oppressed and the minorities. The oldest source for the life of the saint was written at the instigation of Pope Gregory IX by someone who "had heard much straight from the mouth of Francis himself ": Thomas of Celano wrote this so-called "Vita prima" between 1228 and 1230, which was followed roughly twenty years later by a second version with a different slant. About 1260 St. Bonaventure, at the request of the general chapter of the Franciscan order, wrote a depiction of the life of the saint, which was declared the only authorized version.

The so-called "Legend of the Three Companions", which was compiled around the middle of the 13th century by three of Francis' disciples, has a greater popular appeal than the above biographies, which have a specific purpose. It graphically portrays those events in particular that took place in Assisi, and presents us with a picture of the life of the rich young man and of his gradual transformation.

The first son of the rich merchant Pietro Bernadone was born at a time when Assisi was suffering from social unrest and from its enmity with Perugia (1181/82). The father traded in luxury fabrics, which he imported mainly from France. He is supposed to have been away there on a journey even on the day his son was born.

The mother gave the child the name of John, but his father called him Francis – "little Frenchman". Whether he gave him this nickname because of his successful dealings with France, or whether it came about later because the young boy enthusiastically and gaily sang French troubadour songs, must remain an open question. Anecdotes do indicate that the saint was already acquainted with French song from an early age. These songs probably included the spiritual, mystic songs of France's new religious movements, which may have been the inspiration for the path chosen by Francis, as well as for his own poetry.

According to the "Legend of the Three Companions" Francis received an education, which soon allowed him to work successfully in his father's business. In addition, he is said to have wandered merrily and happily through the town with like-minded companions, devoted to gaming and singing. A pleasant nature and a certain liberality are ascribed to him.

Francis was rich, yet he did not belong to the rank of knight, which provided the measure for his clothes, his behavior, and his ambitions. Military action offered him the opportunity of elevation to a higher rank: in 1202 he took part in the battle at Collestrade, on horseback like a knight, but he only returned to Assisi after a year's captivity in Perugia. Shortly after this the opportunity arose for him to lead a campaign to southern Italy. However, he had given his equipment away to a poor nobleman.

Even with new armor Francis did not reach Apulia: he fell ill on the journey and a voice commanded him in a dream to return home and to pursue his true destiny. He returned to his circle of companions a changed man. From that time on his generosity was directed towards others: he gave his cloak to a poor man (ill. 21) and had bread prepared in his father's house – but without his father's knowledge – for the needy. In addition, he undertook a pilgrimage to Rome.

But only when an inner voice made clear to him the complete change in the values he had previously held, and only when he was able to overcome his repugnance of lepers, was Francis able to bid farewell to his former pleasures. He no longer wanted to be a rich merchant, but lived now like a leper, in isolation and solitude. But this "departure from the world" had not yet taken place in the public eye.

The first mystical experience which the legends report showed him the way forward. In the ruined church of San Damiano Christ spoke to him from a painting: he was to rebuild his house (ills. 18, 22). Francis took these instructions literally, sold cloth belonging to his father, and put the money towards the reconstruction of the church. This wastefulness was too much for his father, who was already concerned about the new turn his son's life had taken. He sued Francis for the return of the money. Since the municipal authorities declared themselves not responsible for penitents such as Francis, the trial was heard before the bishop. And so it came about that Francis publicly repudiated his natural father and turned towards the Heavenly Father (ill. 19).

Thus the journey that led to the changes in the young man, who was a popular favorite, culminated in a dramatic event. He met with abhorrence and sympathy in equal measure, and these stimulated the attention that was to be devoted to him and his journey through life from then on.

It is possibly this very attachment to one place and to his middle-class origins which still make us so ready to identify with this saint today. Perhaps it was his spiritual path, which did not develop from religious training, but which was due to his personality, which made him the "modern" founder of the order.

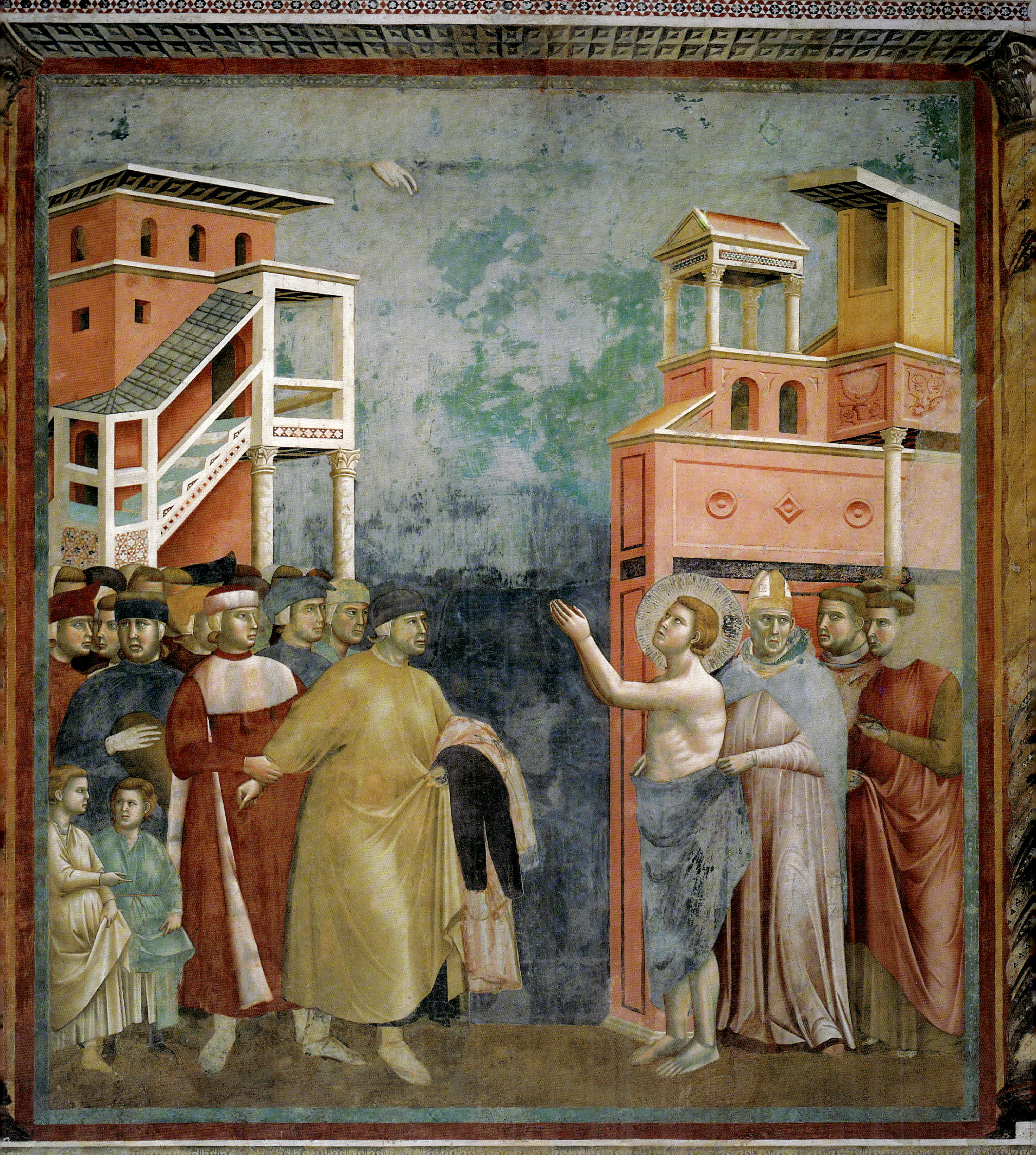

The Legend of St. Francis – First Representation of a Narrative Cycle

Not long after the completion of the upper wall surfaces and of the vault in the Upper Church of San Francesco in Assisi, work would have begun on the lower walls of the nave. At the request of the order, something was to be realized here which had never before been attempted in such a fashion – the history and progress of the great saint and founder of the order, whom the old people of the area might still be able to remember as a living person, were to be brought to the attention of the faithful in the form of a frieze. The intention was to develop a pictorial version of the life story of the saint, which would then act as the model for all further representations.

The patrons recognized Giotto as the artist best suited to this unique undertaking. This cycle of pictures has occupied generations of art historians. The questions of dating – whether they were painted shortly before or shortly after the first Holy Year of 1300 – and of authorship were judged particularly controversial. In the latter case, attributions veer between a Roman artist, Cavallini, and a Florentine artist, Giotto.

However, a simple glance at the framework of the fresco (ills. 9, 20) demonstrates that this must have been the work of an artist with a well-developed sense of architecture, such as we have witnessed in the Isaac series of pictures (ills. 12, 13). The "illusionistic" architectural framework gives the impression that we are looking through an open colonnade with a coffered ceiling, behind which the scenes from the life of the saint take place. Even the painted forms of shadows and the foreshortening take into account the viewpoint of the spectator walking along the nave. Even today we can scarcely overlook the relationship that this creates between the viewer and what is portrayed. How much greater must this effect have been on people in the early 14th century?

The new qualities which, compared to earlier works of art, stood out particularly clearly in the Isaac frescoes, can be found again in so many different aspects and in a more highly-developed form in the Legend of St. Francis that the same artist – Giotto – must be the author of these paintings. Together with his assistants, he executed the whole cycle, from the architectural framework to the individual frescoes.

St. Bonaventure described the life of St. Francis in a great theological work as an example to the faithful. He divided the saint's journey through life into ninety-seven stations, from which twenty-eight scenes were selected for the pictorial narrative, these being further identified by inscriptions (ills. 19–34). The life story begins in the fourth bay of the north wall, that is, directly adjoining the crossing, with the *Homage in the Marketplace at Assisi* to St. Francis (ill. 20), and ends with the *Liberation of the Heretic Peter*, a miracle ascribed to St. Francis after his death.

Following four scenes which describe the journey that will lead the young Francis to make his decision (ills. 20–22), the public announcement of the latter is depicted through the repudiation of his father (ill. 19). Here, the bourgeois world in which he was raised is confronted with the spiritual world in which he will go on to live. Accompanied by the noblemen of the city, Pietro Bernadone, Francis' father, stands furious and helpless before his son. The latter, having handed the former his fine clothes, now turns naked – the Bishop of Assisi covers him with a cloak – towards his newly-chosen divine Father. Two pieces of architecture reinforce the groups of voluminous figures and underline the conflict between them. It is only in the gap between the two that the possibility of dialogue between Francis and the responding Hand of God presents itself. The saint seems to take as little notice of the astonished, somewhat disconcerted representatives of the church as he does of the excited population of the city.

The exactness with which the feelings of the figures and the complete dedication of the saint to his spiritual mission are portrayed distinguishes the art of Giotto. The same precision is applied to describing the location in which these events take place, and to the way the figures appear in the open air, in front of buildings and on the surface of the street.

In this respect, perhaps the most exciting of the representations to take place in an interior is the *Celebration of Christmas at Greccio* (ill. 27). A dominant architectural element marks the scene of the action: the high marble wall, the rood-screen, which separates the choir from the nave behind. We are looking from

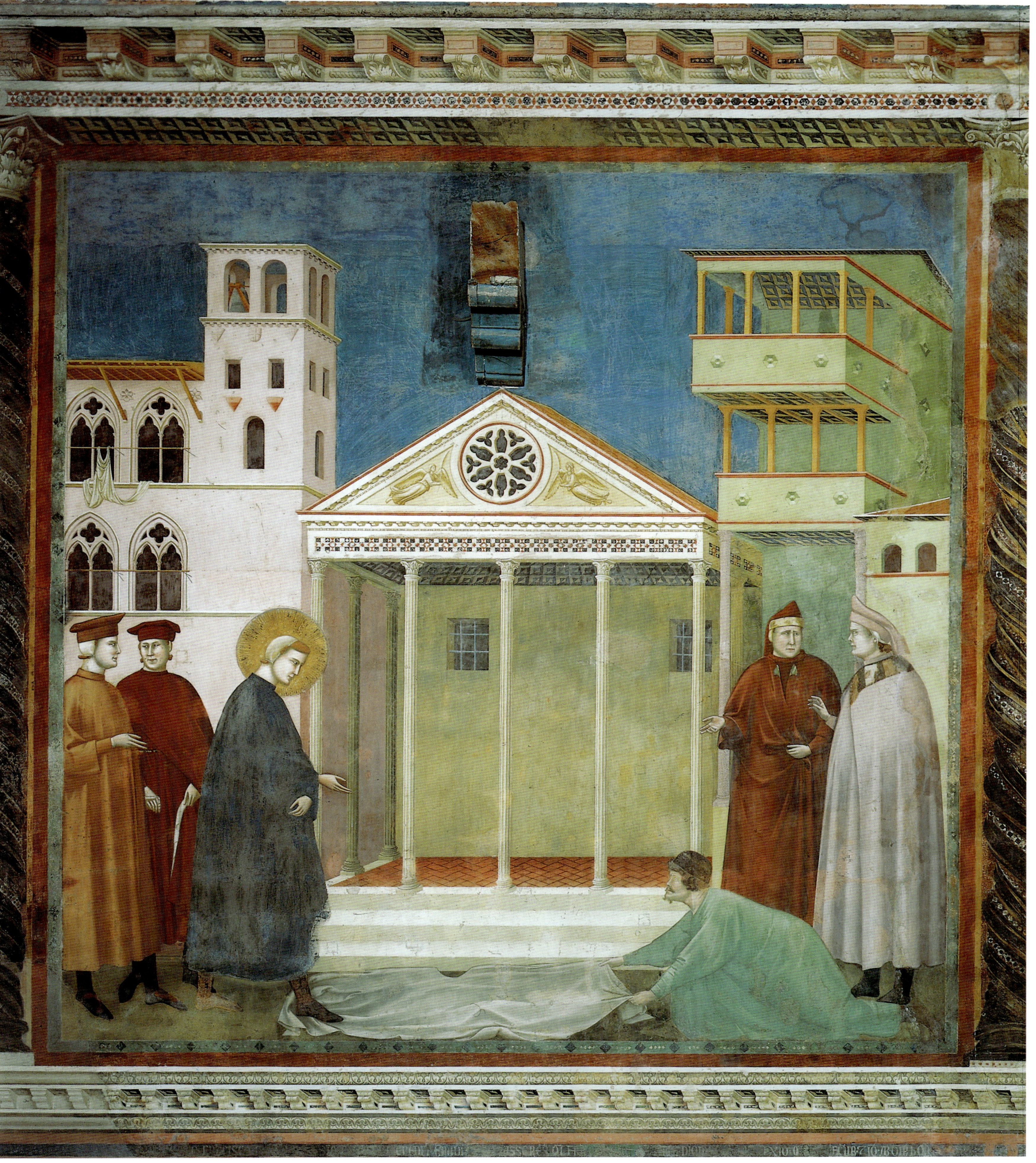

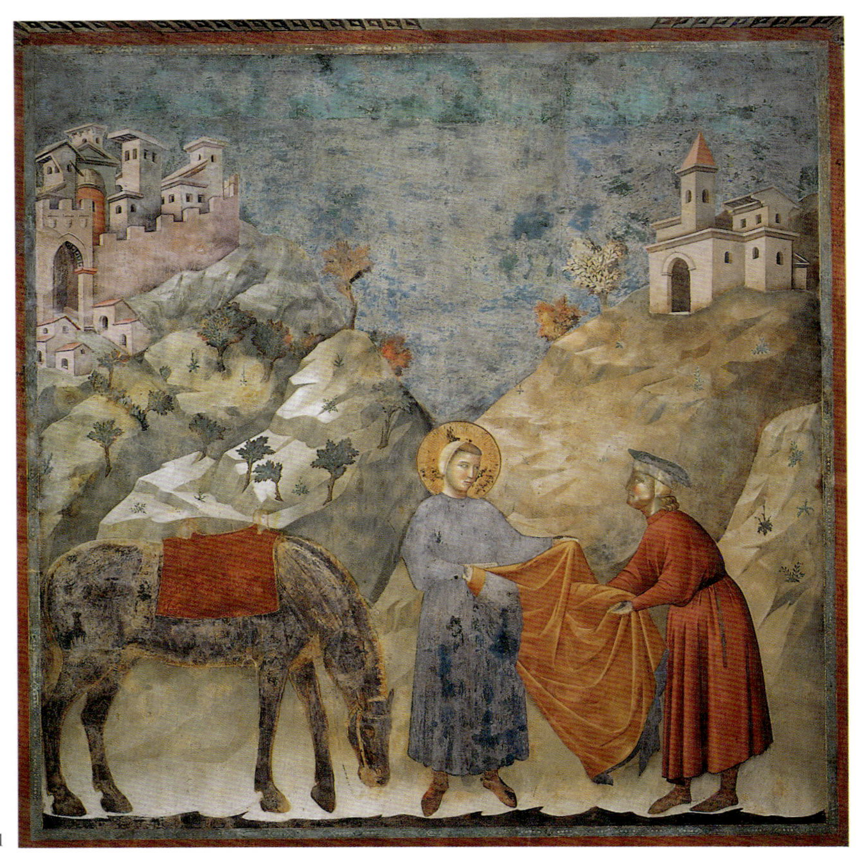

21

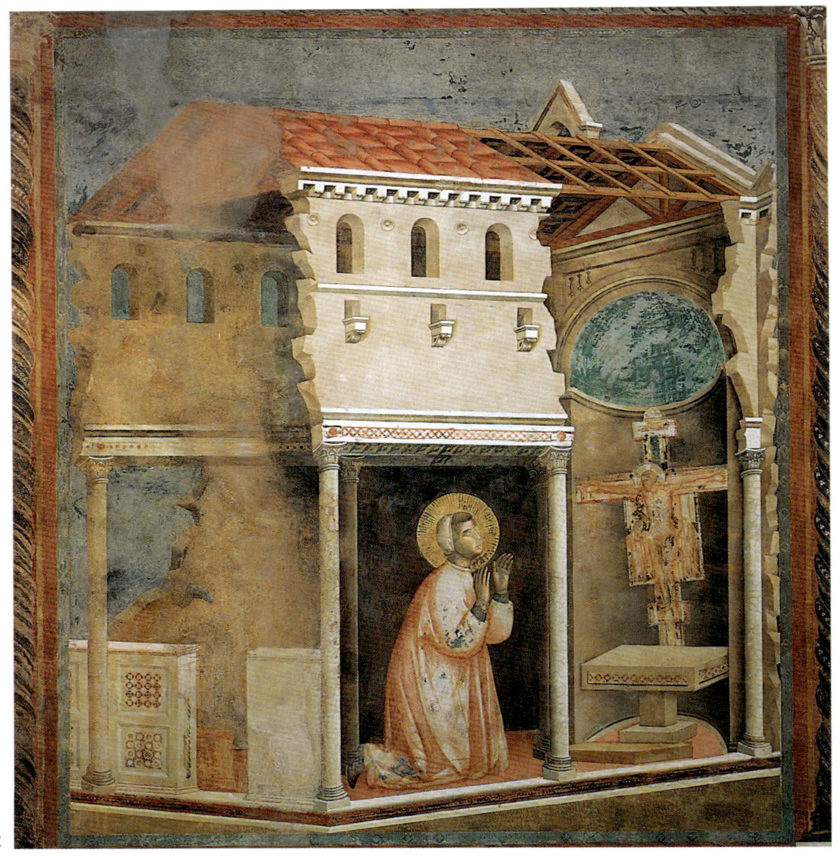

22

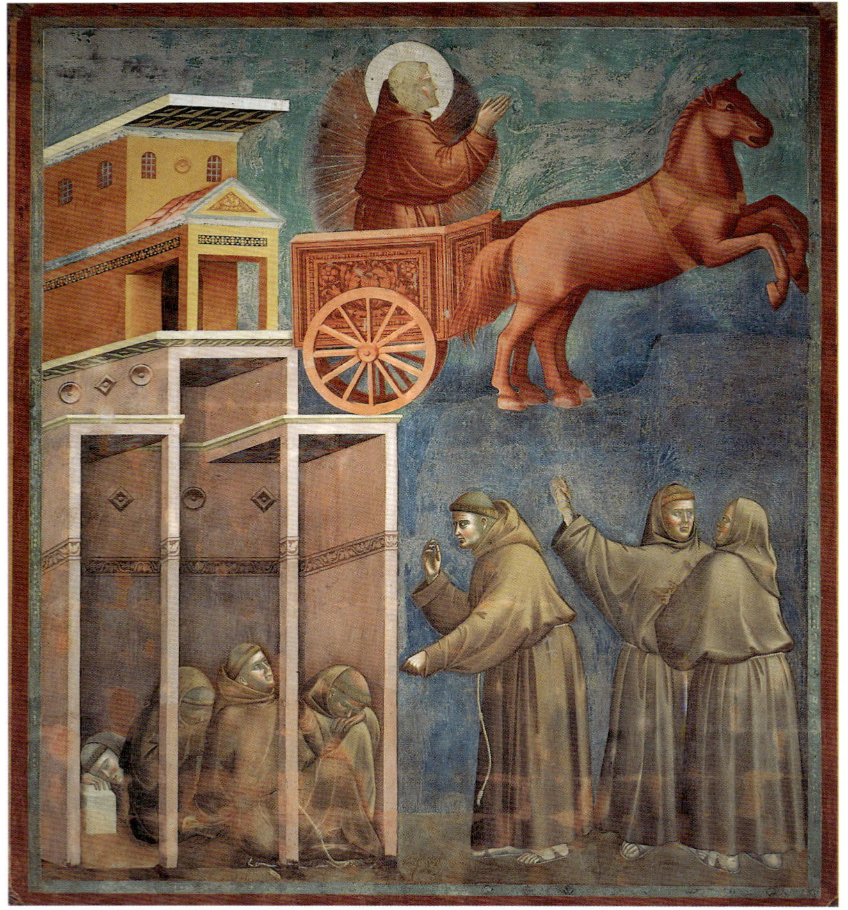

23

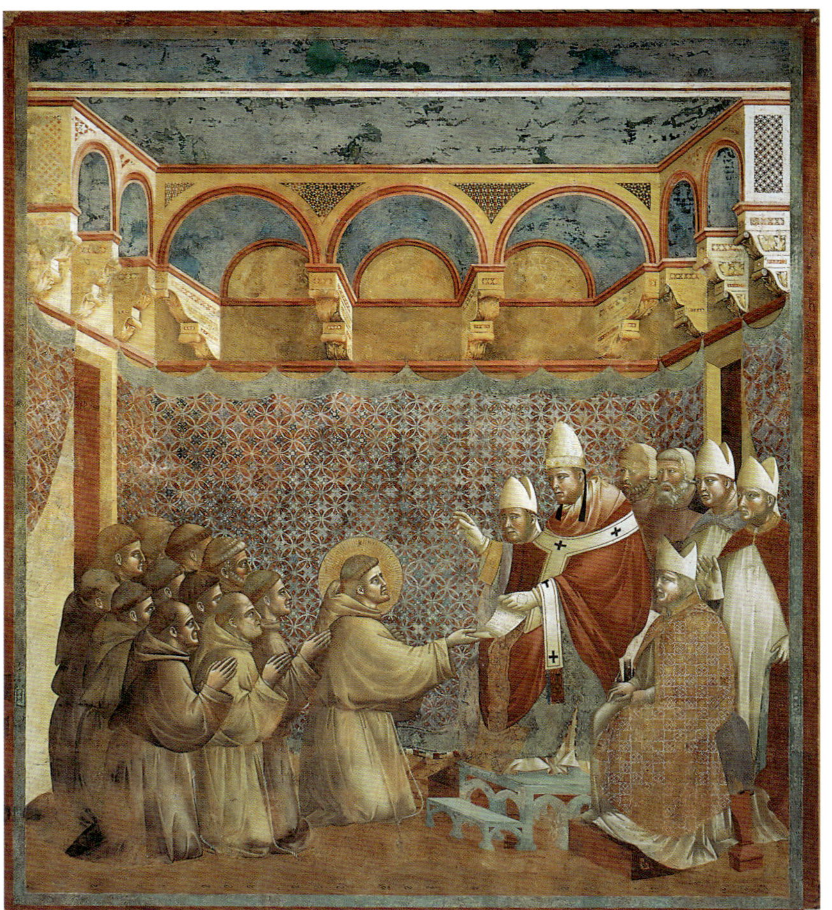

24

21 *St. Francis giving away his Cloak*, 2nd picture of the
Legend of St. Francis, before 1300
Fresco, 270 x 230 cm
Basilica superiore di San Francesco, Assisi

Francis hands his valuable golden cloak to an
impoverished citizen. The scene takes place in front of
two rocky hills, on whose peaks two very different types
of architecture rise up – the world of the city and of the
cloister confront one another here. The descending slopes
meet behind the figure of the saint, emphasizing his
position in the picture, as well as characterizing his
situation in life: this is a first indication that the saint will
decide to lead a secluded life of poverty.

22 *The Crucifix in San Damiano*, 4th picture of the
Legend of St. Francis, before 1300
Fresco, 270 x 230 cm
Basilica superiore di San Francesco, Assisi

According to the legend, the image in the church of San
Damiano spoke to the young nobleman: "Francis, go and
restore my house, which is in danger of collapsing".
Giotto pictures Francis in a half ruined church, where the
saint kneels before the painted crucifix, his arms raised in
fright. This lively reaction and the perspectival structure
make the events in the picture particularly vivid and
intelligible.

23 *Vision of the Brothers at Rivotorto*, 8th picture of the
Legend of St. Francis, before 1300
Fresco, 270 x 230 cm
Basilica superiore di San Francesco, Assisi

Several brothers of the order sleep in a confined
architectural shelter, others stand next to it and
gesticulate excitedly at the curious manifestation in the
heavens: Francis, surrounded by a mandorla of golden
rays, rides in a Roman chariot through the skies. The
saint appears to his companions as the guide and new
leader of Christianity. Giotto distinguishes the spheres of
heaven and earth very clearly through his use of color. In
an impressive manner, he makes evident the visionary
character of the scene.

24 *The Confirmation of the Rule*, 7th picture of the
Legend of St. Francis, before 1300
Fresco, 270 x 230 cm
Basilica superiore di San Francesco, Assisi

Following his vision (ill. 136), Pope Innocent III
confirms the rule of the new Franciscan community. In a
magnificent interior, constructed in perspective, the pope
blesses the founder of the order and his rule. Francis'
companions and the Church dignitaries follow the action
with expressions of concentration. It is not least through
this device that Giotto makes plain the consequences of
what is taking place.

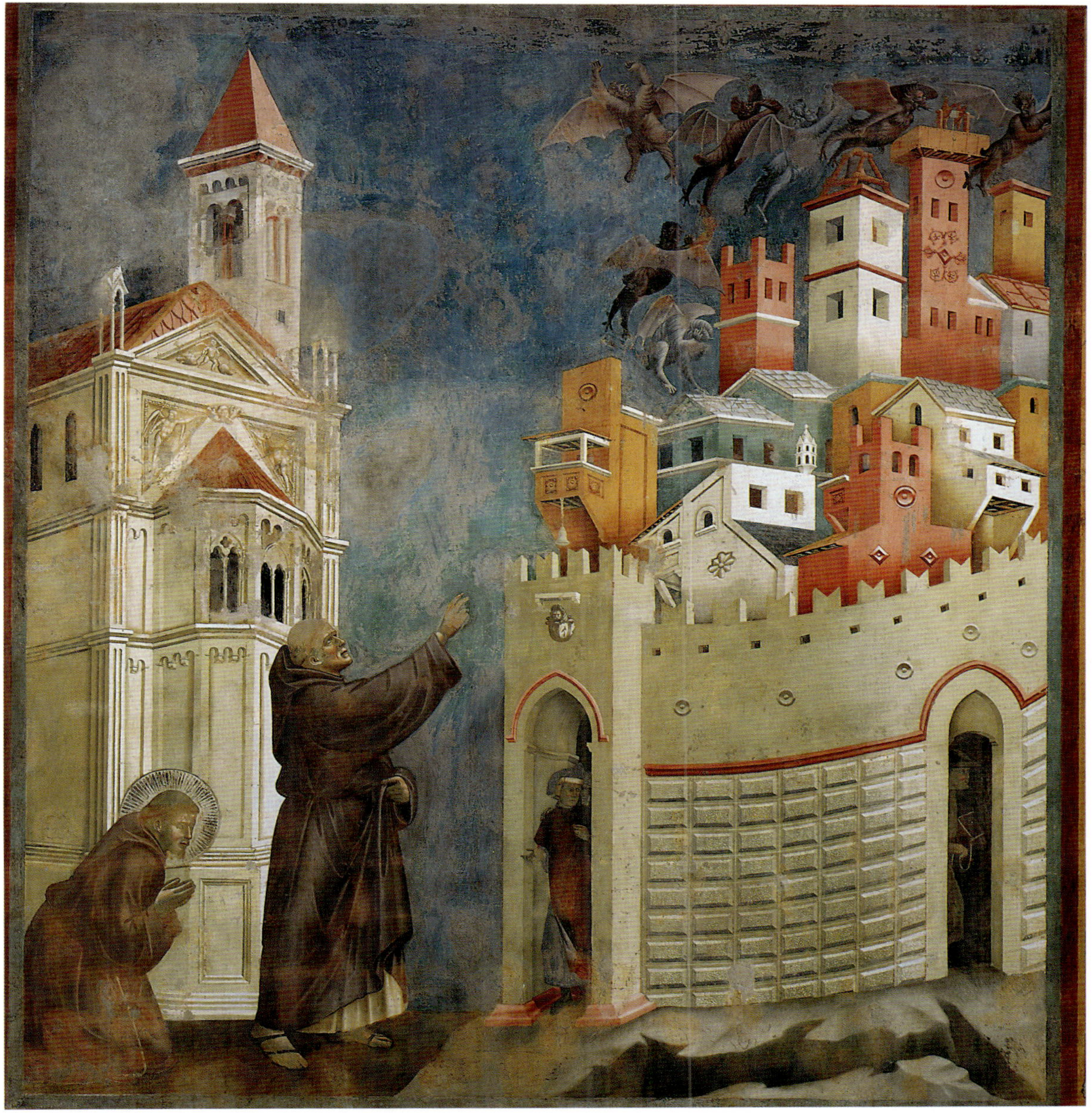

25 *The Expulsion of the Demons from Arezzo*, 10th picture
of the Legend of St. Francis, before 1300
Fresco, 270 x 230 cm
Basilica superiore di San Francesco, Assisi

During the civil war in Arezzo, St. Francis saw demons
over the city. He called upon a brother of his order,
Sylvester, to drive them out. The picture area is
dominated by the architecture of the city, which is
divided from the rest of the world by a crack in the earth,
and by the towering church building. Giotto portrays the
saint deep in prayer in front of the latter. His strength
seems to pass to Brother Sylvester, who raises his hand
commandingly in the direction of the city of towers.
Thereupon the demons flee, and the citizens can return
to their business in peace – they can already be seen at the
city gates.

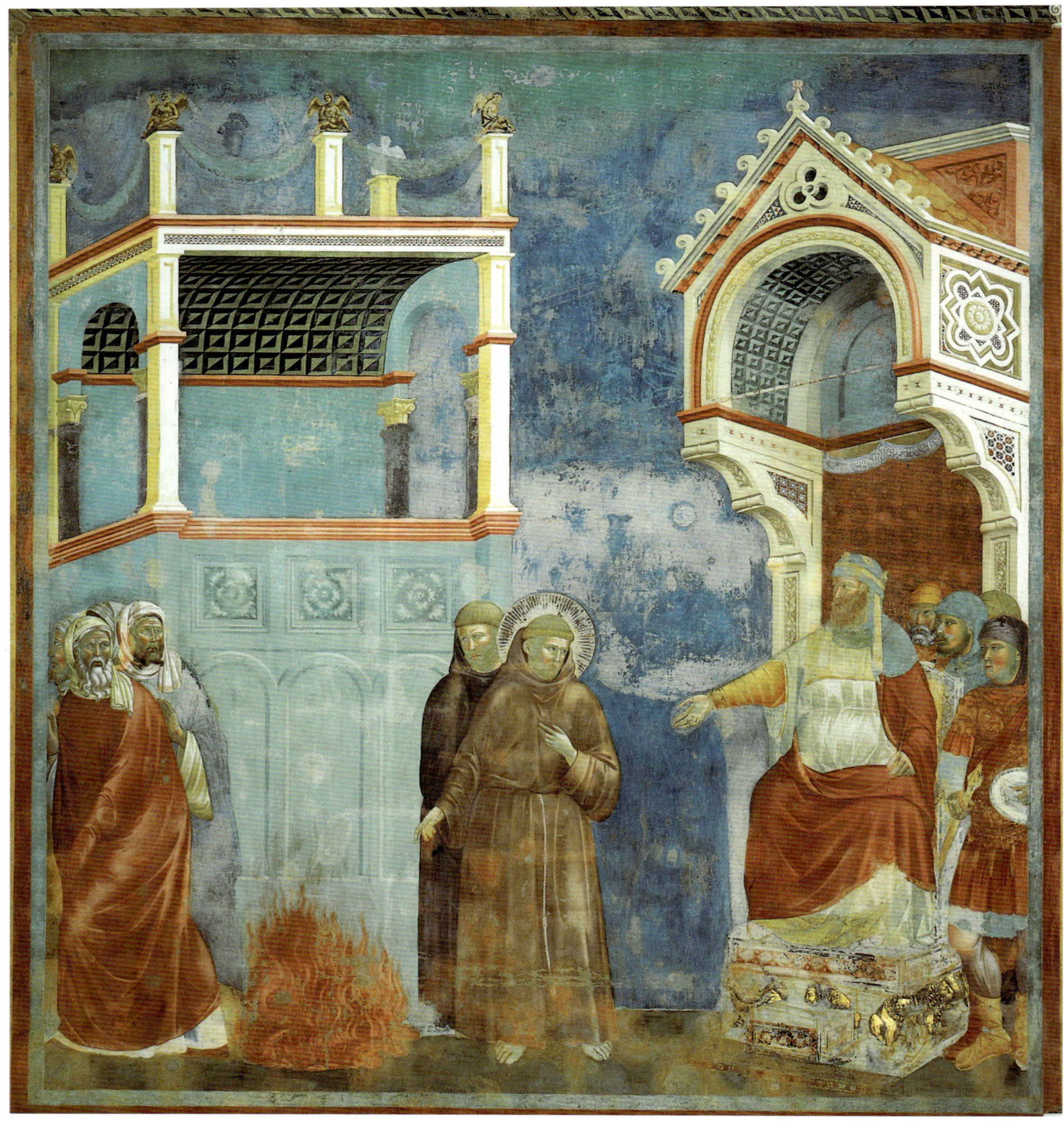

26 *St. Francis before the Sultan*, 11th picture of the
Legend of St. Francis, before 1300
Fresco, 270 x 230 cm
Basilica superiore di San Francesco, Assisi

In order to convert the sultan to the Christian faith,
Francis is prepared to undergo a trial by fire. The saint
stands in the center of the picture, points to the fire and
turns towards the sultan. The latter appears surprised and
annoyed that his own priests are running away. Giotto
pictures the anxious priests and the suddenly powerless
sultan most vividly.

behind towards the pulpit in the choir and at the back
view of a giant wooden cross, installed above the choir
screen, and which juts out at an angle into the nave.
Directly below it, a group of female worshippers are
crowding their way into the choir. Only their faces can
be seen. The narrow cut-out doorway gives the
impression that we are dealing with a great number of
women. Like the men, who enter from the side, the
women also want to take part in the celebration of
Christmas. They do not yet see the miracle that is
taking place: Francis, in a deacon's vestment, lifts the
Christ Child, which has come alive, from the crib.
Some of those present look astonished, others
incredulous, while others again are still wrapped up in
themselves. Several monks fervently sing Christmas
hymns. These human reactions lend a touch of surprise
and reality to what is happening.

Each of those listening to Francis *Preaching before
Pope Honorius III* also reacts in a very different way (ill.
30). The variations in how they listen – from quiet
contemplation to rapt attention by way of sceptical

deferment – are depicted extremely vividly and with a
great knowledge of human nature. Francis preaches in
a Gothic room with delicate columns and fine cross-
ribbed vaulting. Even if we are not dealing here with the
exactly calculated central perspective of the Early
Renaissance, and if the spatial proportions between
floor and ceiling are not quite right, the space has
nevertheless been developed in a very clear and
plausible fashion as far as perspective is concerned. The
strong architectural elements and the blue of the sky
through the windows turn this Gothic hall into a
discernible interior.

Space in which to act and to react and the exact
ordering of figures are not only be found in interiors or
in the city – in Giotto's works the "landscape" can also
become the setting for events, as in the fresco *The
Miracle of the Spring* (ill. 28). Here, the rocky landscape
is used to define space and to articulate the action. In
contrast to the follower of Cimabue in the *Sacrifice of
Isaac* (ill. 11), Giotto fills the space with his rocky
plateau, giving his figures a wider platform. At the same

27 (opposite) *The Celebration of Christmas at Greccio*,
13th picture of the Legend of St. Francis, before 1300
Fresco, 270 x 230 cm
Basilica superiore di San Francesco, Assisi

Francis had a crib built for the Christmas celebrations.
At High Mass, in which he was participating as deacon,
it was observed that he took a sleeping child from the crib
and roused it. The representation of space is particularly
impressive in this fresco. Giotto depicts the choir area
behind the screen, to which the wooden cross, its back to
the viewer, is attached.

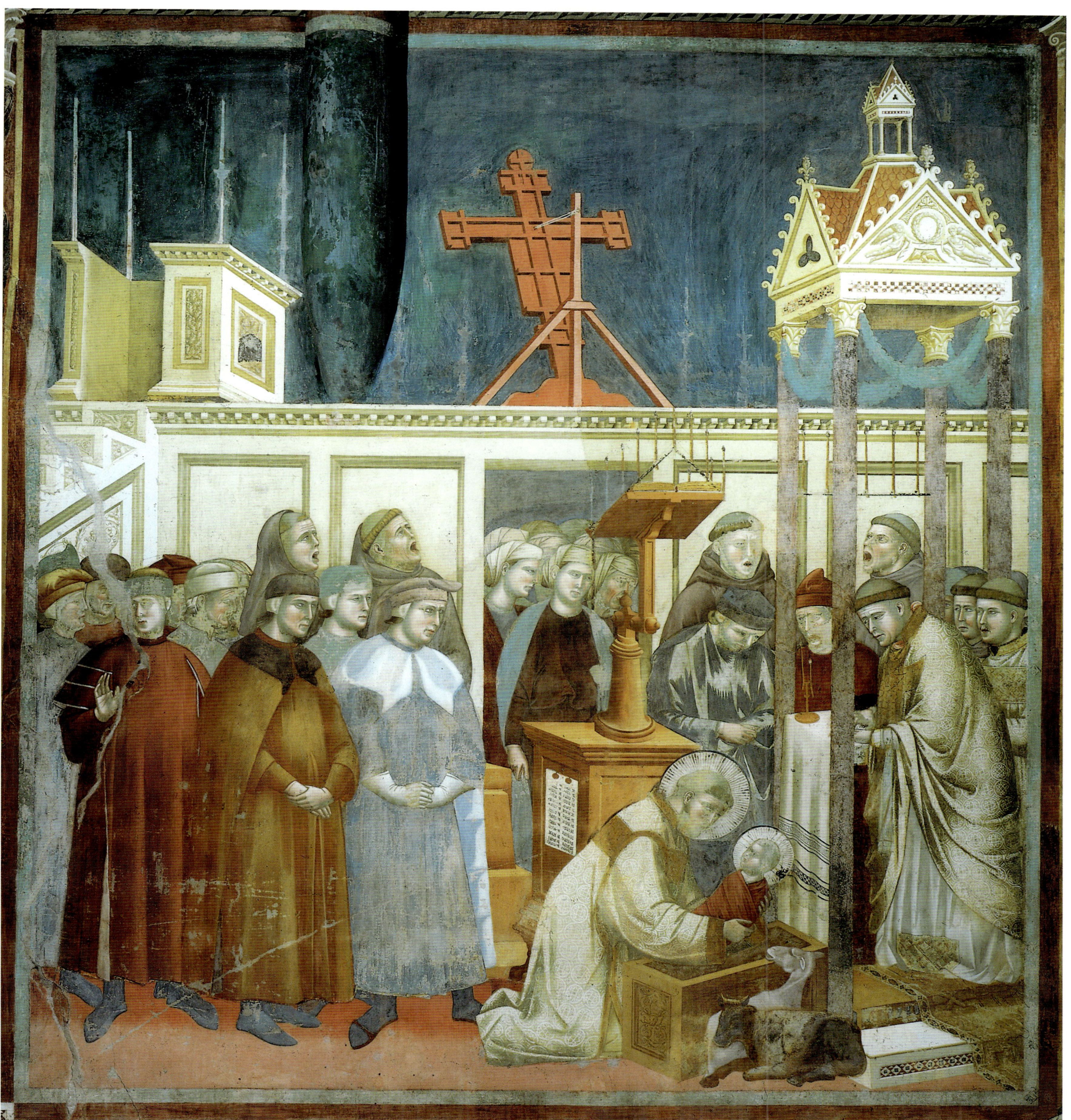

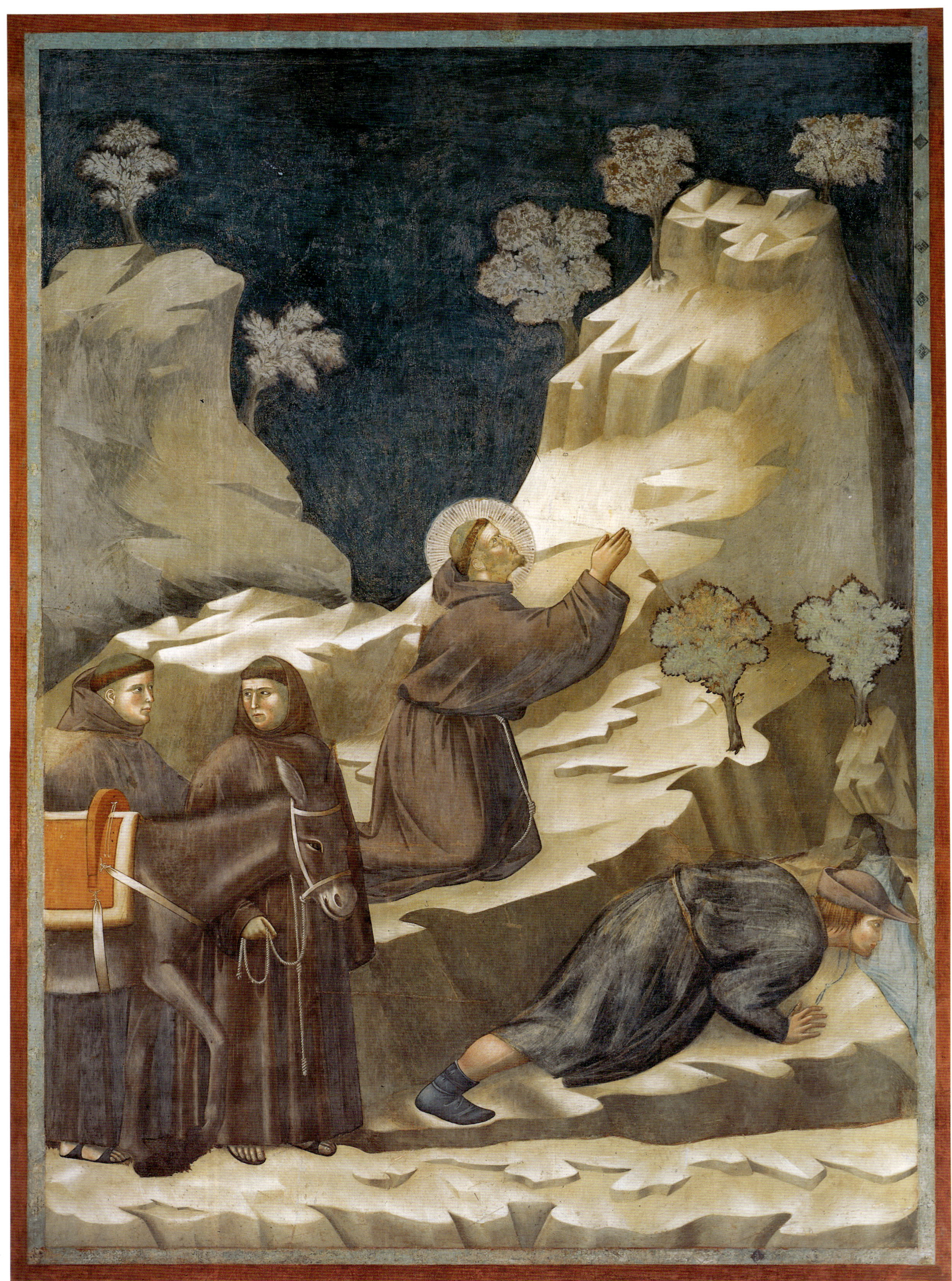

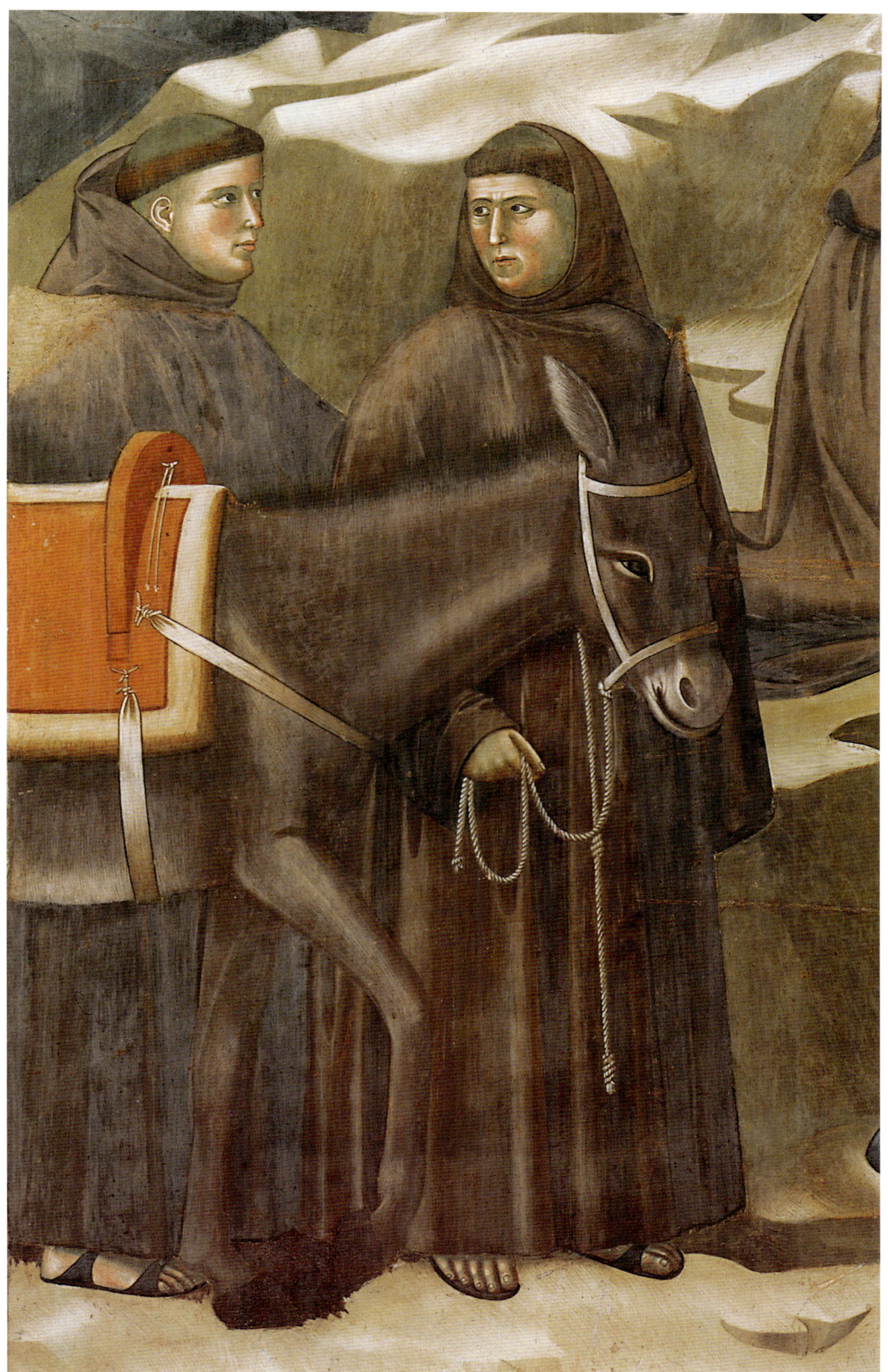

28, 29 *The Miracle of the Spring* (and detail), 14th
picture of the Legend of St. Francis, before 1300
Fresco
Basilica superiore di San Francesco, Assisi

The farmer, to whom Francis lent his mule as a mount,
was tormented by thirst. Water comes bubbling out of
the rocks in answer to the Saint's prayer. Giotto shows
Francis praying fervently. The farmer, almost dying of
thirst, collapses at the spring. As so often in Giotto's
representations, figures – here the two Franciscans –
comment on the scene with their glances and so
anticipate the reaction of the viewer. The earthquake of
autumn 1997 badly damaged the entrance wall, upon
which this fresco is situated.

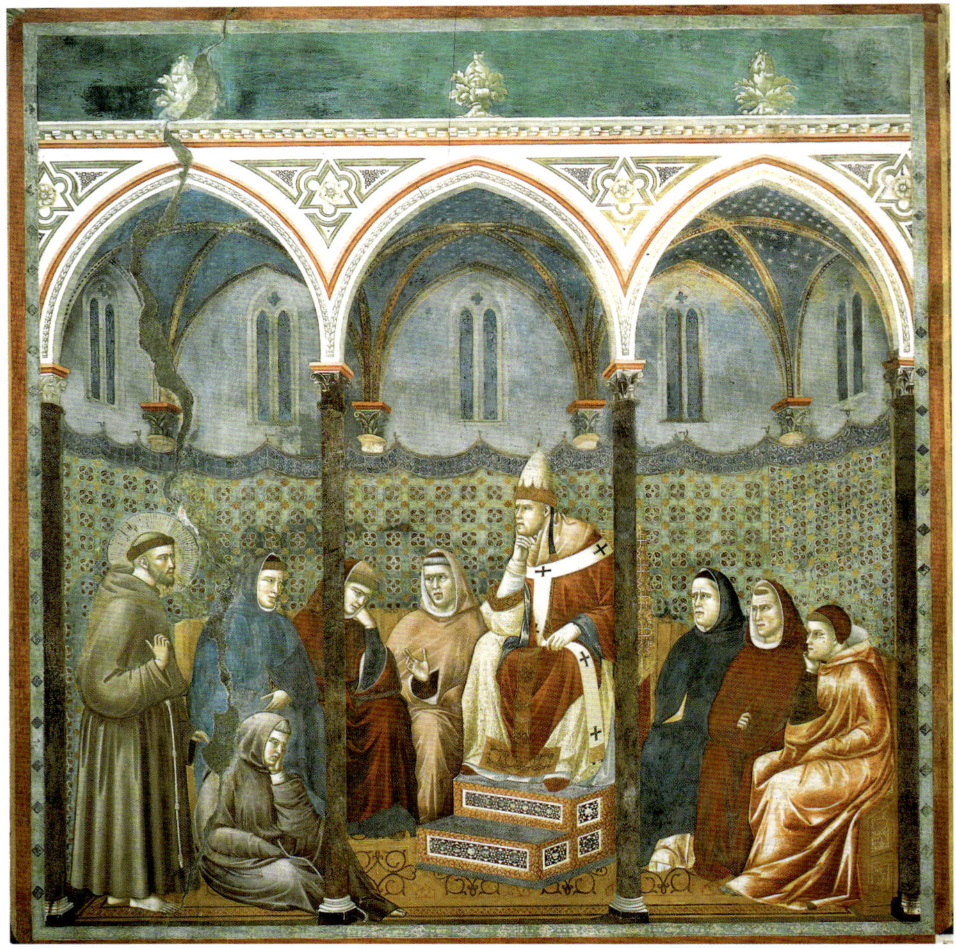

30 *Preaching before Pope Honorius III*, 17th picture of the
Legend of St. Francis, before 1300
Fresco, 270 x 230 cm
Basilica superiore di San Francesco, Assisi

Francis wanted to surprise Pope Honorius III with a well-
prepared sermon; however, he lost the thread of what he
was saying and had to improvise. His address captivated
everyone and convinced them that the spirit of God
spoke through him. Giotto expresses this through the
different reactions of those listening, reflected especially
in the lively facial expressions. The magnificent Gothic
hall in which the scene takes place emphasizes the dignity
of the pope and rhythmically articulates the group of
figures.

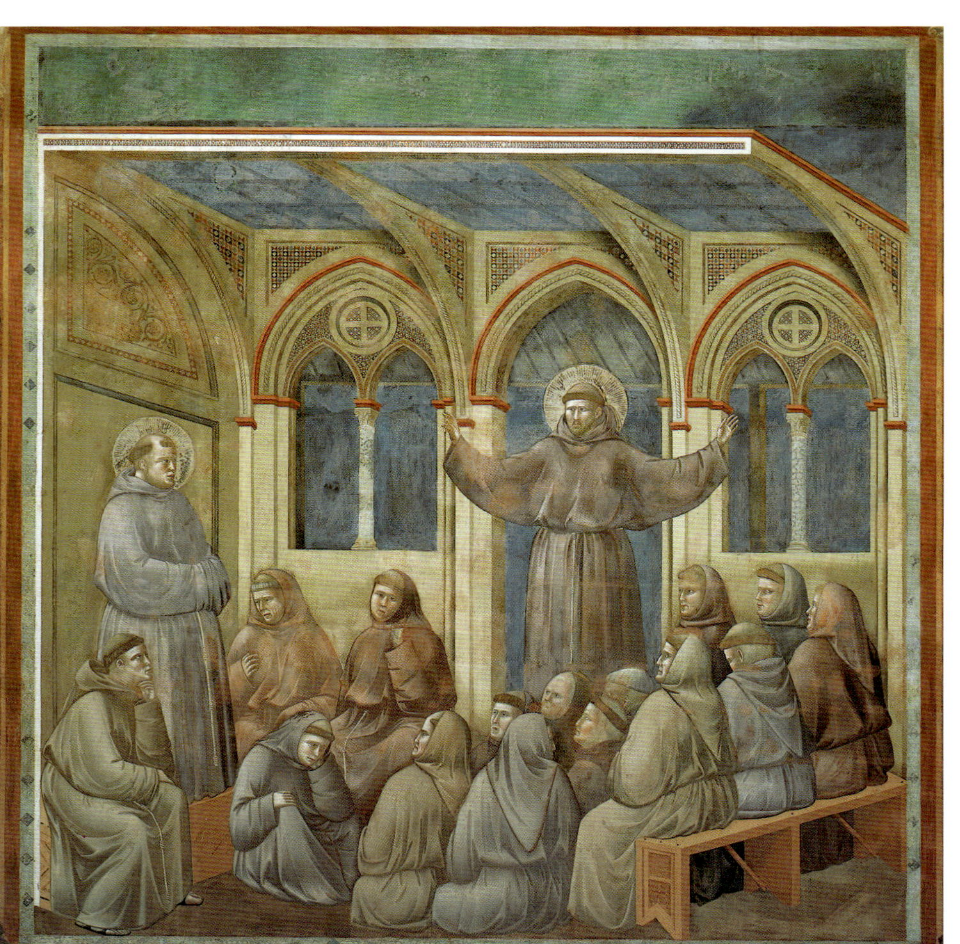

31 *The Apparition at Arles*, 18th picture of the Legend of
St. Francis, before 1300
Fresco, 270 x 230 cm
Basilica superiore di San Francesco, Assisi

During a meeting of the order, St. Anthony of Padua was
preaching in the cloister at Arles – Giotto shows a
generously proportioned Gothic room. Suddenly, Francis
appeared. Giotto depicts the saint with outspread arms –
the resulting shape of the cross alludes to his Christ-like
life. Only St. Anthony, who had just been speaking about
Christ, and one other member of the Order notice the
apparition. Giotto shows all the others listening with full
attention. The figures seen from the back are also
particularly impressive, the artist making the weight of
the bodies plain for all to see.

32 (opposite) *Preaching to the Birds*, 15th picture of the
Legend of St. Francis, before 1300
Fresco, 270 x 230 cm
Basilica superiore di San Francesco, Assisi

St. Francis came across a flock of birds that did not
fly away at his approach. He gave a sermon to the
expectantly waiting creatures, who only left the saint after
receiving his blessing. As so often, Giotto makes plain the
extraordinary nature of events through the reaction of a
secondary figure – in this case, through the Franciscan
friar, who raises his hand with a surprised expression on
his face.

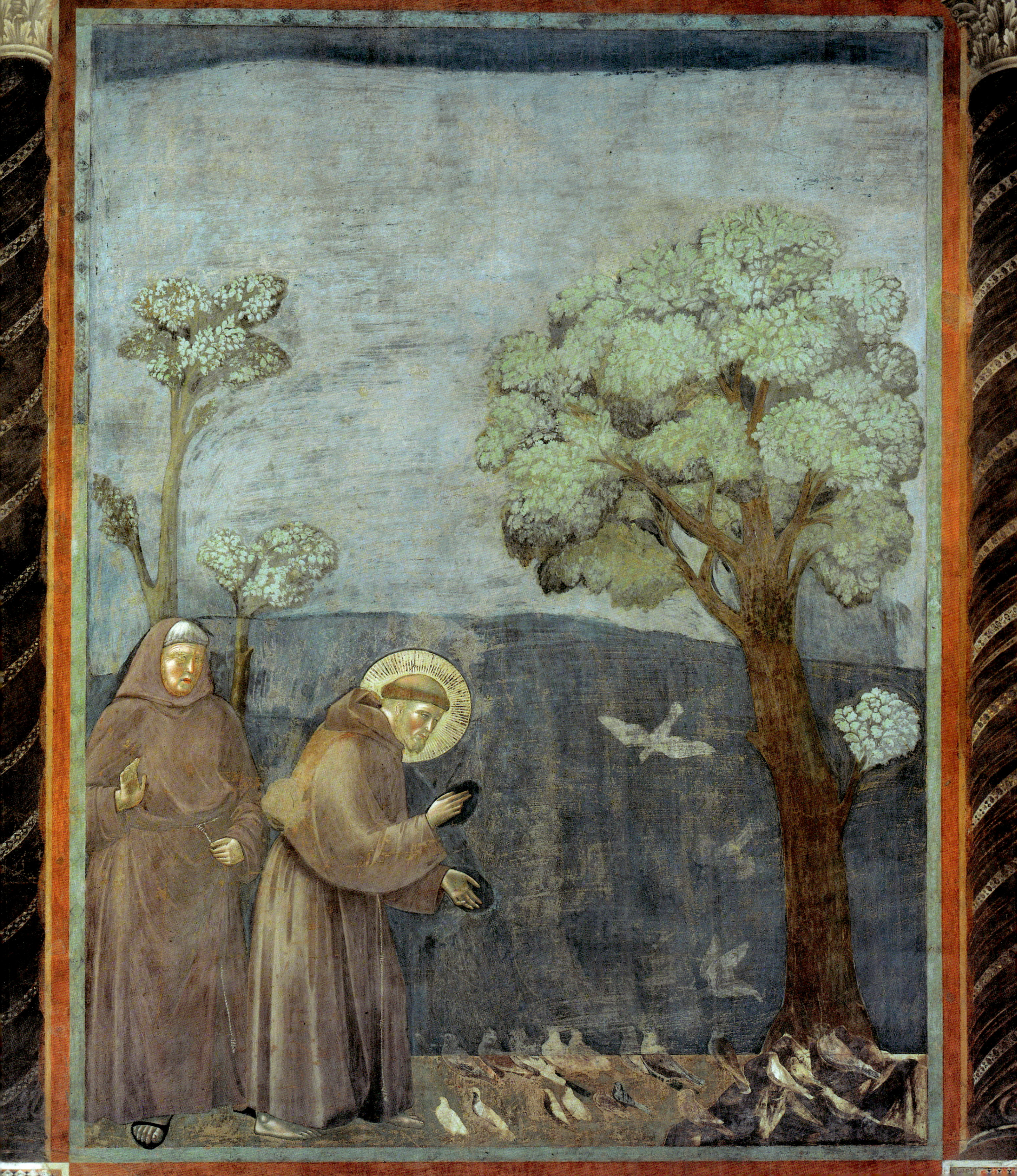

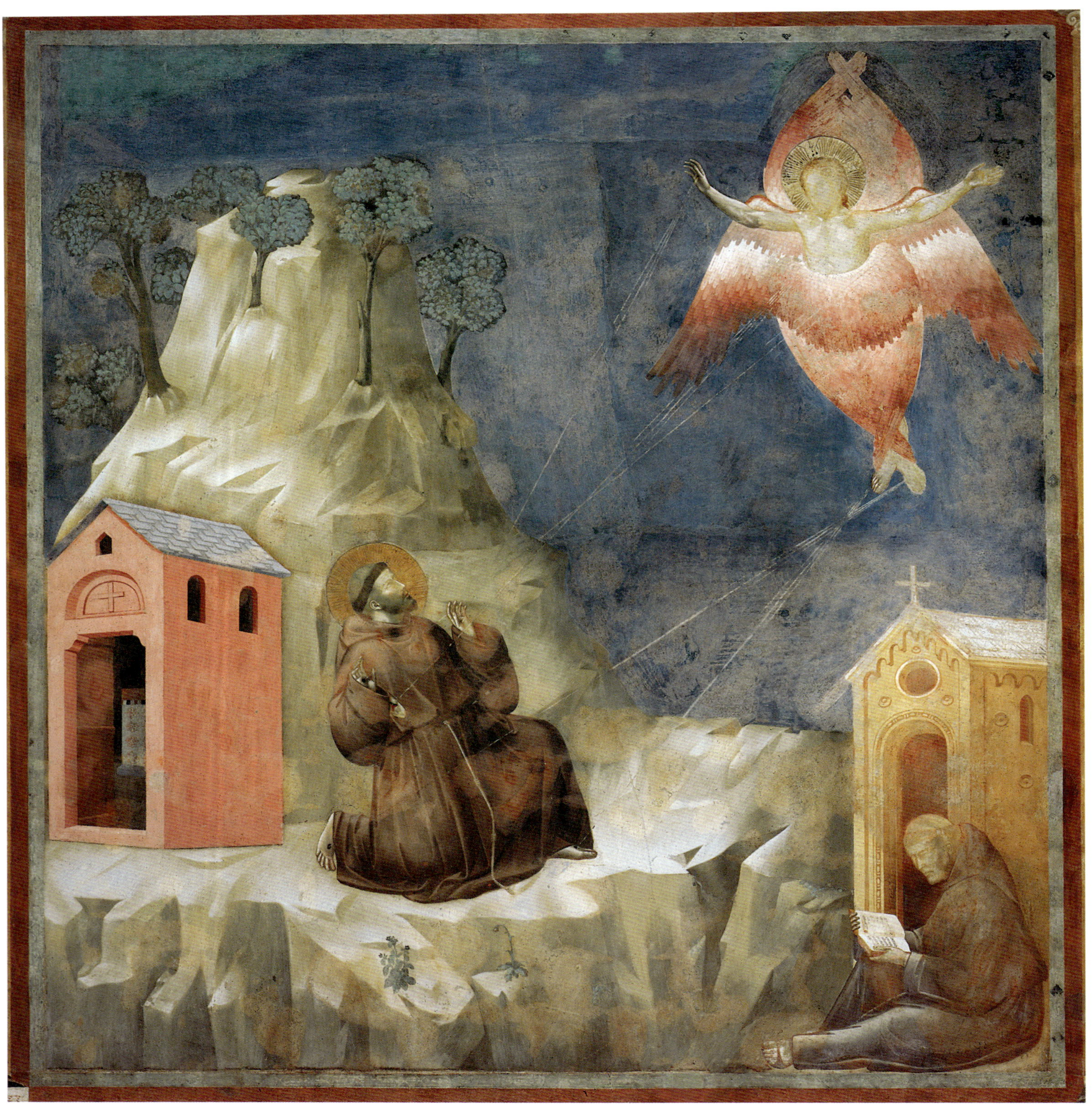

33 *Receiving the Stigmata*, 19th picture of the Legend
of St. Francis, before 1300
Fresco, 270 x 230 cm
Basilica superiore di San Francesco, Assisi

Giotto sets the event remote from the world, in the
isolation of the mountains and unnoticed by the reading
monk. Stigmatization is the high point in the life of the
saint. It marks him out for all to see as an imitator of
Christ. The Son of God appears to him, wrapped
around by angels' wings. Fine golden rays lead from his
wounds to St. Francis, and mark the latter out.

time, the rising sweep of rock harmonizes with
the vertical format of the painting, thus
illustrating the saint's petition for water. As in
the other frescoes, an exact knowledge of the
way people react is once more evident – details
such as the eloquent exchange of glances
between the two monks, or the greedy way in
which the farmer drinks, are particularly
impressive.

The figure of the drinking man also proves
that Giotto had continued to learn, not only
from antiquity, but also from contemporary

sculpture: this figure clearly reminds us of the
kneeling Mary Magdalene by Arnolfo di
Cambio at the fountain in Perugia.

In each of the twenty-eight individual
scenes the spatial and plastic, the artistic and
psychological qualities are important.
Developed from the Isaac frescoes of the
clerestory, these qualities account for the
particular, and previously unknown, vividness
of this series of pictures.

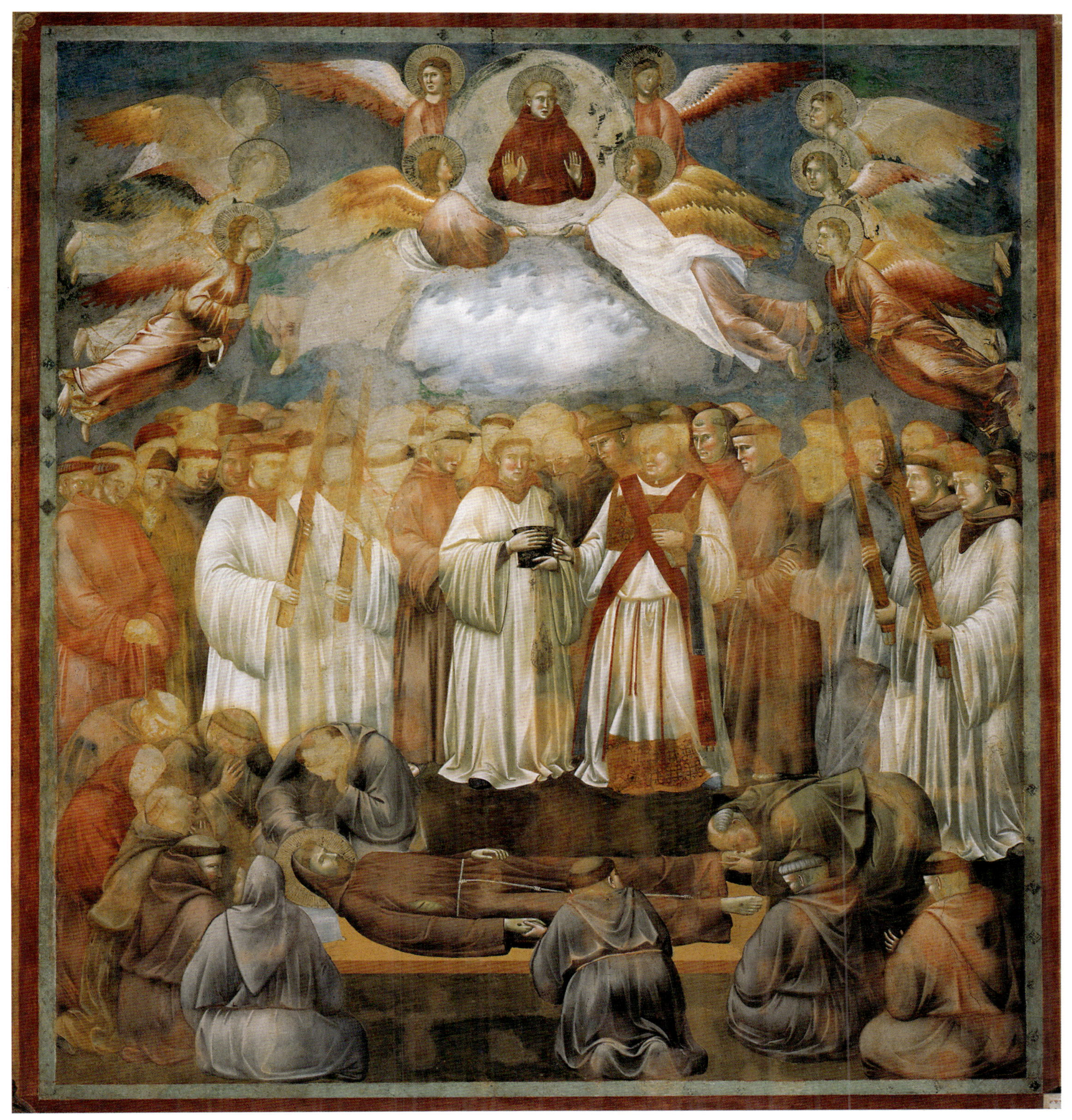

34 *The Death of St. Francis*, 20th picture of the
Legend of St. Francis, before 1300
Fresco, 270 x 230 cm
Basilica superiore di San Francesco, Assisi

When Francis felt close to death, he had himself brought
to a small church. He died there in the presence of his
Brothers. The death of the saint and his ascending soul
are here linked to the requiem mass to create a solemn
representation peopled with many figures. This fresco is
followed by a further eight pictures "peopled with many
figures", which are often dated several years later than the
other scenes.

Early Evidence of Giotto's Panel Painting

36 (opposite) *Crucifix*, ca. 1300
Tempera on wood, 578 x 406 cm
Chiesa di Santa Maria Novella, Florence

In contrast to earlier representations of Christ on the Cross, such as those by his teacher Cimabue, Giotto emphasizes the earthly heaviness of the body: the head sinks deeply forward and the almost plump body sags. The human side of the Son of God is made clear. Mary and John look down sorrowfully from the horizontal ends of the cross at the dead Lord.

In the Dominican church of Santa Maria Novella in Florence there is a large painted wooden crucifix (ill. 36). It is first mentioned in a document drawn up in 1312 – the will of the Florentine citizen Ricuccio. In it, the son of Puccio da Mugnaio donates a sum of money to the church, in order that a candle may be lit at all times "in front of the crucifix painted by the splendid artist by the name of Giotto di Bondone."

The large crucifix corresponds to the traditional form, like the one seen from the rear in the *Celebration of Christmas at Greccio* (ill. 27), and with which we are also familiar from older examples, such as the cross in Santa Croce created by Cimabue. However, the way in which it is painted displays the same break with tradition that characterized the frescoes in the nave of San Francesco at Assisi. The Christ painted by Cimabue is distinguished by an elegant, Gothic sweeping line. In Giotto's portrayal, on the other hand, the fine gradations of light and shade and the new type of colored shadow emphasize a different image of Christ – Christ appears more natural, more human. The fact that Giotto took into consideration the viewpoint of those who have come to worship also contributes to this effect, for the body's proportions are only "natural" when seen from far below. It is possible that Giotto found his way to this naturalness by intensively studying the early sculptures of Nicola Pisano, which are strongly influenced by antiquity.

The second panel work which belongs to this phase of Giotto's development also betrays signs of his having studied sculpture – in this case contemporary Florentine sculpture. Unfortunately, only the middle panel of the altarpiece from San Giorgio at Costa has survived (ill. 35). Yet the Virgin Mary and the frontally seated Child, his hand raised in benediction, do remind us of sculptures by Arnolfo di Cambio – here, in particular, of his Madonna for the cathedral at Florence, which is now housed in the Museo dell' Opera del Duomo.

Following a second visit to Rome, during which he was presumably able to work for Pope Boniface VIII, Giotto's figural language changed once again. The bodies of the figures in the paintings on the great altarpiece of the Franciscan church at Pisa (ill. 37), now housed in the Louvre, do not appear as compact as those in the preceding works. The figures have become slimmer, daintier and move in a more elegant fashion (ill. 38) than, for example, the Child delivering the blessing in the altarpiece from San Giorgio in Costa (ill. 35). This way of fashioning bodies and movement, which brings to mind several of the frescoes from the Legend of St. Francis at Assisi (cf. ill. 20), led researchers to attribute this work to Giotto's assistants rather than to the master himself. Even the inscription

35 (right) *Virgin Mary* from San Giorgio in Costa
Tempera on wood, fragment, ca. 180 x 90 cm
Galleria degli Uffizi, Florence

The Madonna and Child sit in front of a sumptuous bright carpet on a Gothic architectural throne. Angels peer over the backrest. The positions and the gestures of the figures are related to one another clearly and concisely. The Christ Child sits on his mother's left knee and raises his hand in benediction in front of her heart.

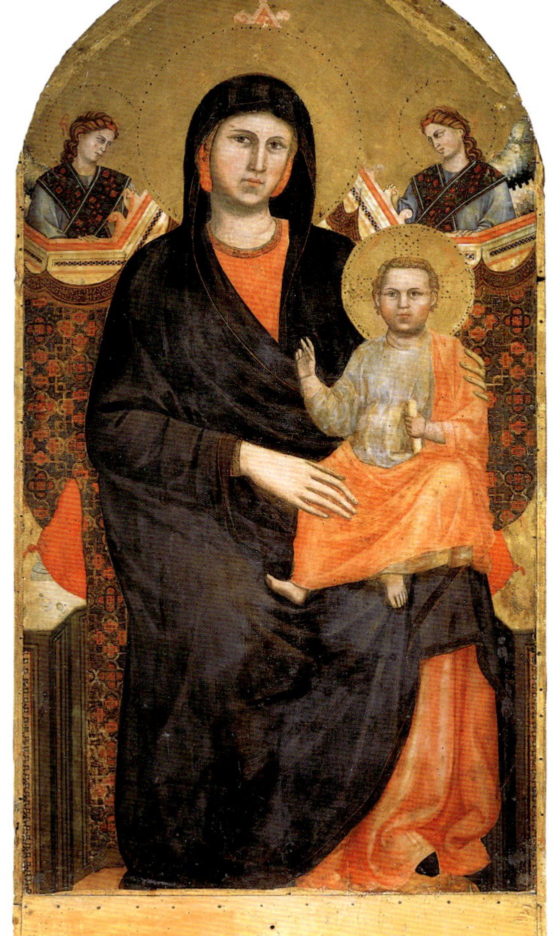

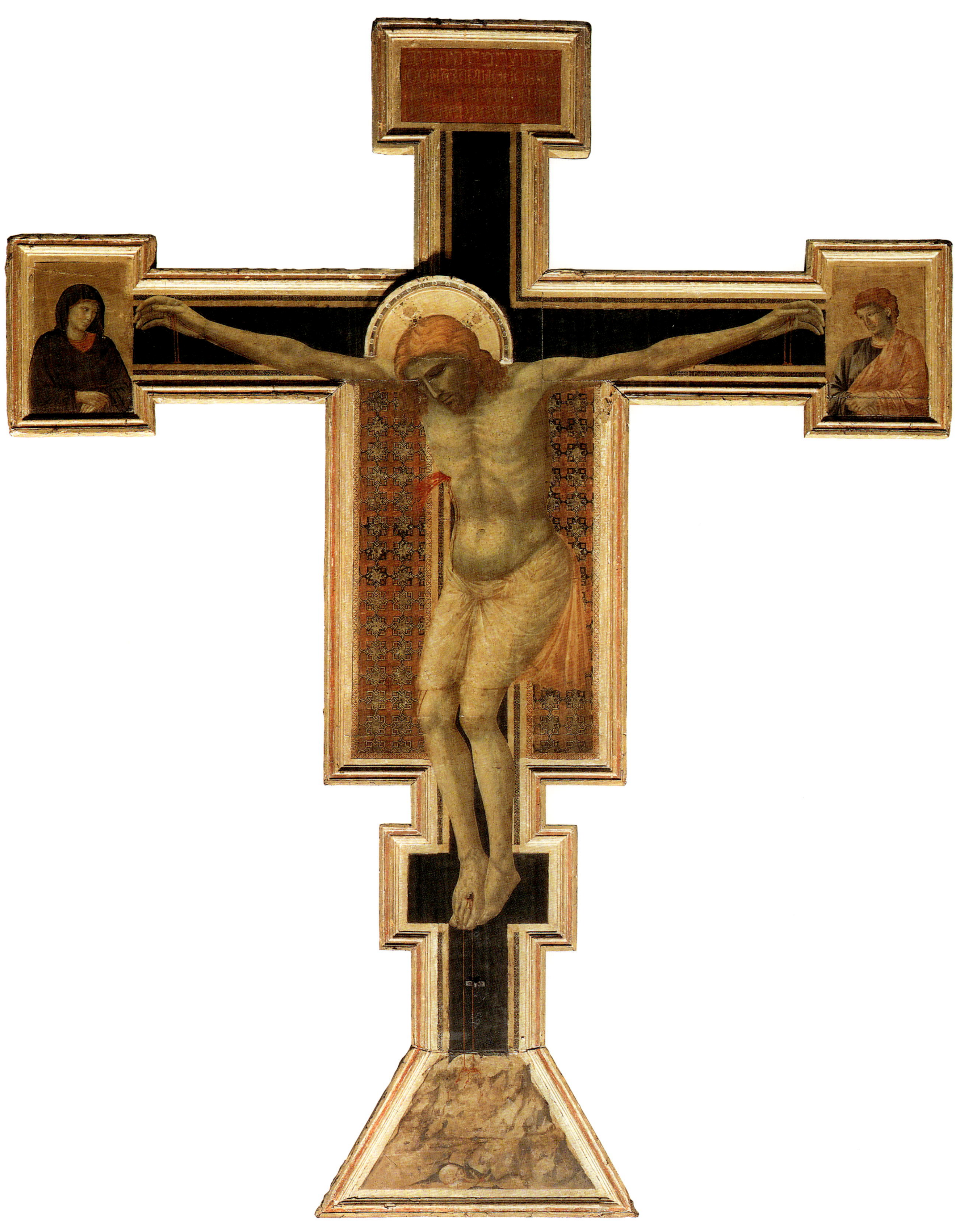

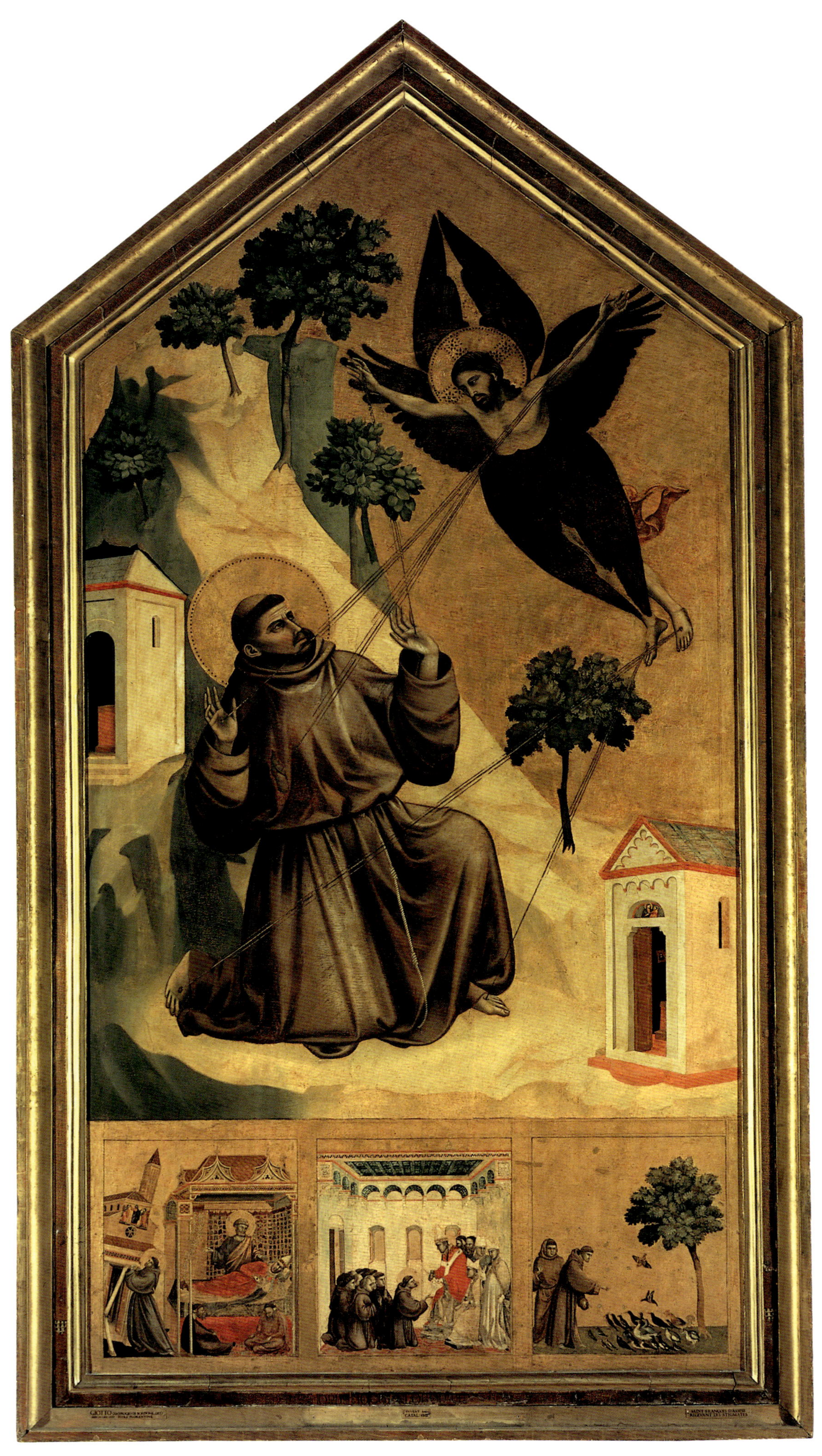

37 *St. Francis receiving the Stigmata*, ca. 1300
Inscribed: OPUS JOCTI FLORENTINI
Tempera on wood, 314 x 162 cm
Musée du Louvre, Paris

The exceptional vertical format of this panel, in which
the towering rock narrows the scope of the action, is
striking. The kneeling saint seems startled and raises his
hands. Christ appears to him, enveloped by angels' wings.
The intense gaze between the two figures seems to allow
the message that Francis has completely taken Christ to
himself and then received the stigmata to take physical
shape.

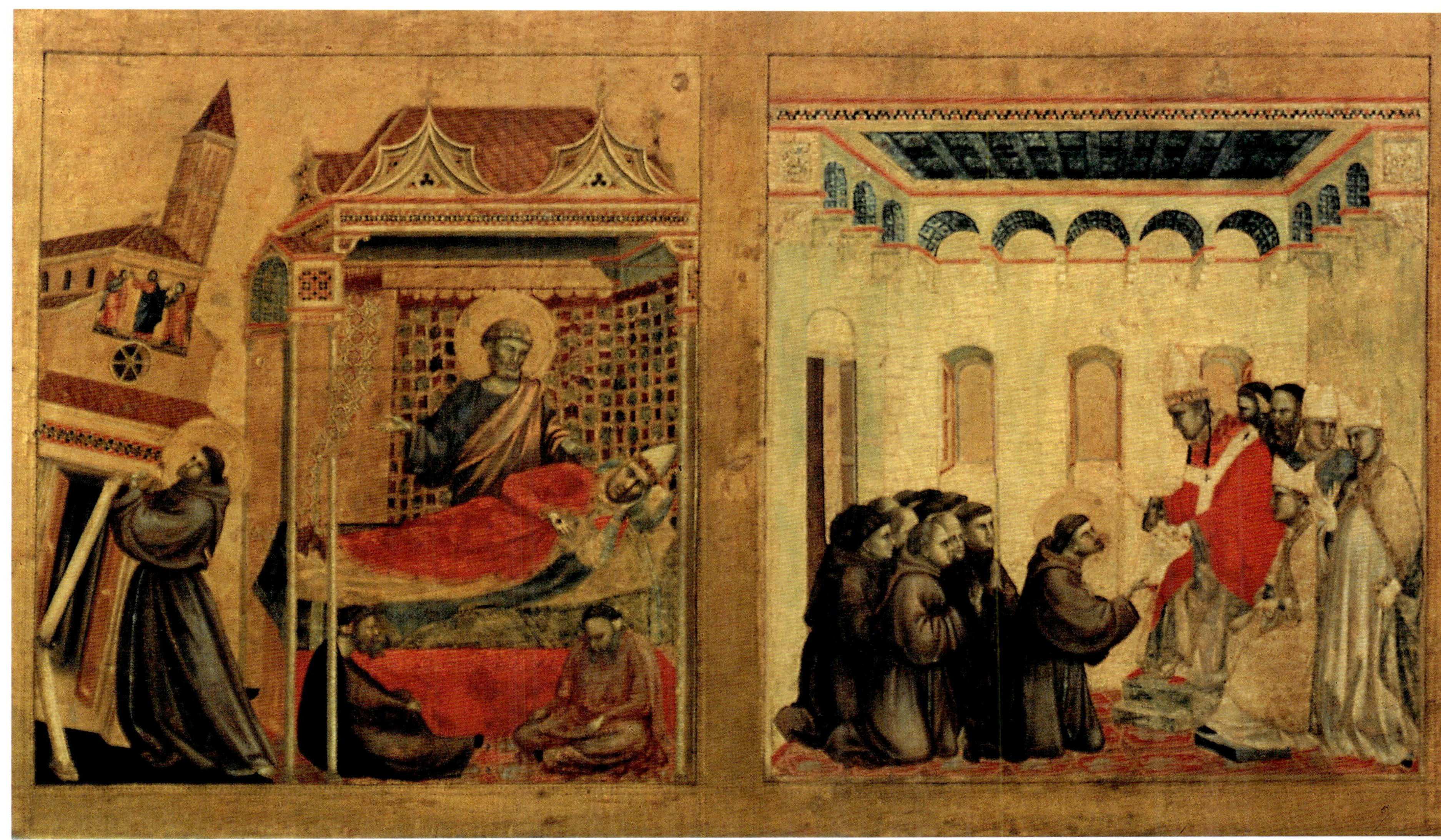

on the frame of the main panel showing *St. Francis receiving the Stigmata*, which refers to Giotto as the artist responsible: OPUS JOCTI FLORENTINI did nothing to change this opinion.

But in this panel, at least, the confidence with which space is represented, the clear composition of the figures, and the intensity of gaze speak in favor of Giotto himself having made a major contribution. Is it not conceivable that Giotto had been inspired with new ideas by his return visit to Rome, and that he was also able to incorporate the elegant Gothic sculptures of Giovanni Pisano, the son of the aforementioned Nicola Pisano, in his own work?

The contemporary chronicle of Riccobaldo Ferrarese (1312) refers, among other things, to a visit by Giotto to Rimini: Giotto is said to have painted in the great Franciscan church there. Since this church was later turned into a burial church for Sigismondo Malatesta and his family, all early frescoes have been lost, apart from a few fragments, which are similar to the art of Giotto. And the great influence Giotto's painting had on the development of the arts at the beginning of the Trecento in this city on the Adriatic is plain to see in numerous works.

The Franciscan church, however, does contain a large painted crucifix, which probably belonged in this church from the beginning, and which, in Giotto's overall output, can be attributed to the same period in which he created the Louvre panels.

These panel paintings were probably all executed around 1300 – shortly before or shortly after. The intensity of gaze of the figures is common to all. This is something we first noticed in the Isaac frescoes, and it characterizes the dramatic presence of the figures. Also common to the panel paintings is the visible effort made by the artist to achieve a naturalness, a new, more refined quality of painting, and a logically consistent depiction of space.

The differences between them reflect Giotto's study of such different sculptors as Arnolfo di Cambio and Giovanni Pisano. It appears as if Giotto in this way worked out a range of possibilities on which he could fall back at any time in the future, and which gave him the confidence to paint large-scale figures and spaces at his next workplace in Padua.

38 *Dream of Pope Innocent III* and *Confirmation of the Rule of the Order* (detail ill. 37), ca. 1300

Together with the *Preaching to the Birds* these two little panels form the predella of the altarpiece, which shows the stigmatization of St. Francis. The left-hand panel depicts the dream of Innocent III: Francis appears to the pope as the most important pillar of the Lateran basilica, which is on the point of collapse. Here, and particularly on the right-hand panel, we can discern a logically consistent depiction of space, in which the figures act in a "flowing" sequence of movements. This conception of the figures refers to the miniature-like depictions of Justice (*Iustitia*) and Injustice (*Iniustitia*) on the *dado* level in the Arena Chapel at Padua.

THE ARENA CHAPEL – GIOTTO'S FIRST MATURE MASTERPIECE

39 (right) *The Last Judgment,* Donor with church (detail ill. 41), 1302–1305

The nobleman Enrico Scrovegni offers the three Marys the church that he has donated. He is supported in this by a cleric, whose robe hangs over the real architecture. Giotto is attempting, by means of this illusionistic element and the portrait-like depiction of the donor, a realism which will draw the viewers into the picture.

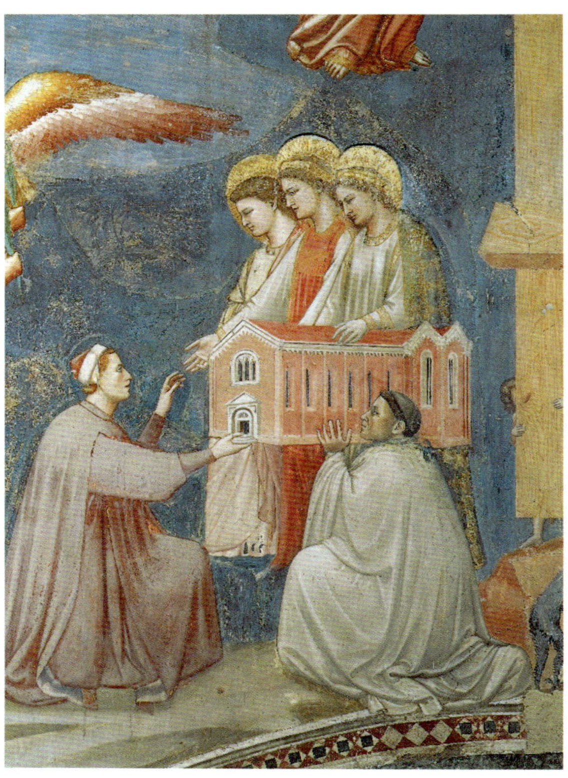

40 (opposite) Arena Chapel
View towards the east
Cappella degli Scrovegni, Padua

The view towards the choir shows the triumphal arch wall with its fictitious chapels below the depictions of the *Betrayal of Judas* and the *Visitation.* Above the *dado* level of painted marble Giotto articulates the walls using broad ornamental bands and narrower, horizontal strips. In so doing it becomes clear how he harmonizes the painted divisions with the existing architecture – to which the row of windows along one side belongs.

Enrico Scrovegni of Padua, ambitious son of the rich Reginaldo, whom Dante Alighieri had consigned to hell as a usurer in his "Divine Comedy", was planning to build a palace and a private chapel. To this end, in the year 1300, he purchased a large piece of land in the area around the Roman amphitheater – known as the Arena.

Of these impressive buildings, only the single-nave church remains. Constructed using clear, simple forms, it is referred to mostly as the "Arena Chapel" after its location, or as the "Scrovegni Chapel" after its donor (ill. 39). The redemption of his father and the saving of his own soul were his foremost considerations when making this donation. The church was therefore dedicated on 16 March 1305 to Saint Mary of Charity.

Today, it is Giotto's frescoes in the interior of the chapel which reflect the honor of the donor most of all,

and it is the fact that he is portrayed on the side of the Blessed at the *Last Judgment* that has recorded his face for posterity (ill. 39).

The frescoes in the Arena Chapel have always been considered as Giotto's first mature masterpiece, and at the same time as an important milestone in the development of western painting. The sometimes severe formulations arising from his attempts at renewal have here grown into a confident style, which portrays image, figures and space in relation to the picture surface in a new form. Contemporary chronicles verify the attribution to the Florentine master, and motifs borrowed from a Paduan antiphonary – a book of hymns from the Latin Mass decorated with miniatures – from the year 1306 widely support the dating, as do the recognizable influences of the great Sienese *Maestà* by Duccio (1309). We can assume that the church was completely decorated with frescoes at the time of its consecration. Only the choir was finished some time later by other artists from Giotto's school.

On the barrel vault a dark blue, star-studded sky spans the nave of the church, whose walls are articulated by painted decorative bands. In contrast to the Upper Church at Assisi, which is much wider, this small church interior would not have supported any feigned projecting architecture, which is why the painted bands here look more like flat wall arches and cornices (ill. 40).

The church is entered from the west, the side on which the sun goes down, and where, in accordance with an old tradition, there is a depiction of the *Last Judgment* (ill. 41). The way this large fresco is divided into registers is also traditional. But if we look at Giotto's invention in detail, then his novel attempts at visualizing different spheres, as well as abstract beliefs, become particularly apparent. Let us give a few examples here. In the center of the representation, Christ is enthroned as supreme Judge in a rainbow-colored mandorla. The deep, radiant gold background, the style of painting, and the delicate substance give the impression that the heavens have opened in order to reveal the powerful, extremely solidly modelled figure of Christ. Different levels are likewise alluded to when the choirs of angels disappear behind the real window,

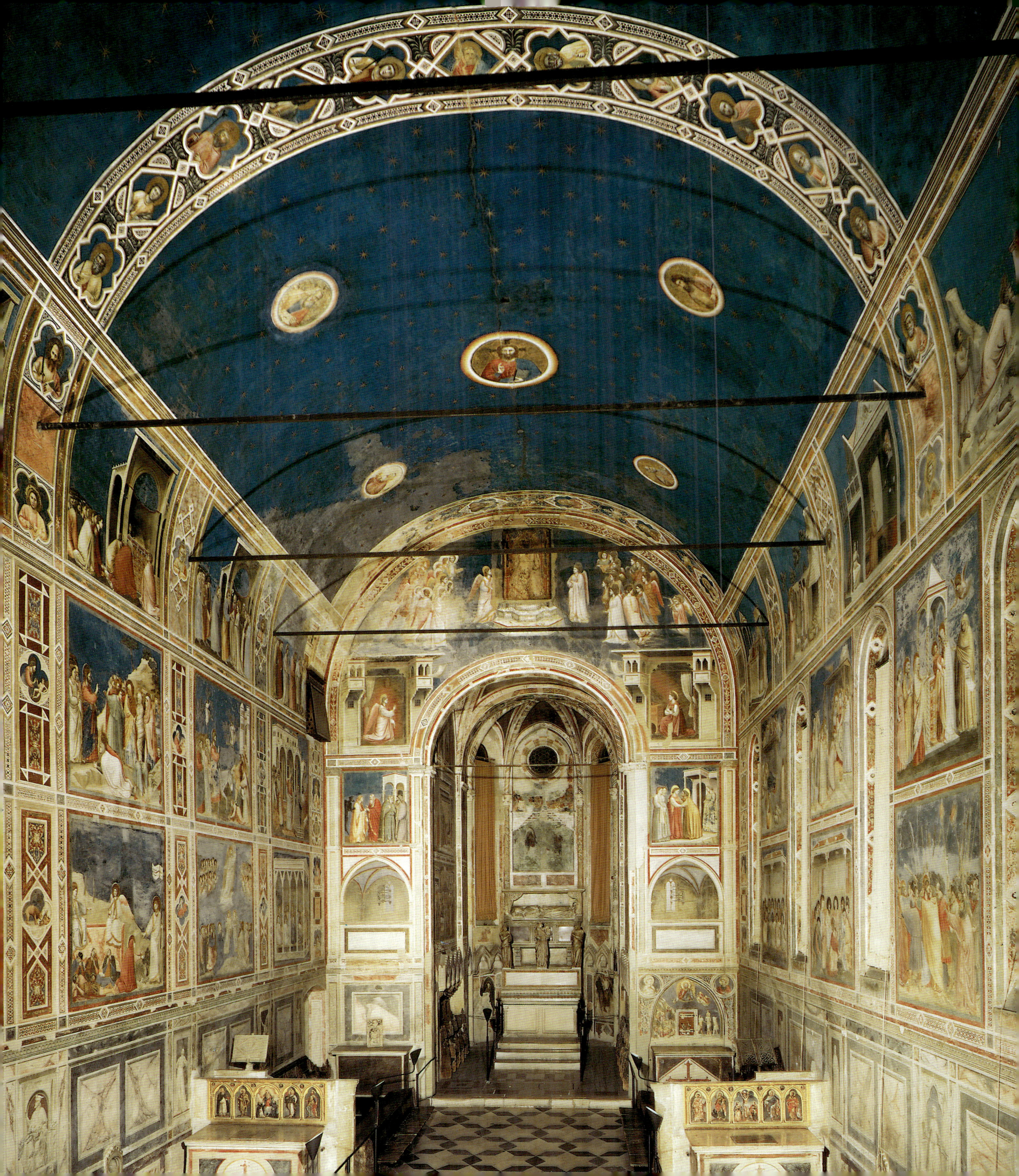

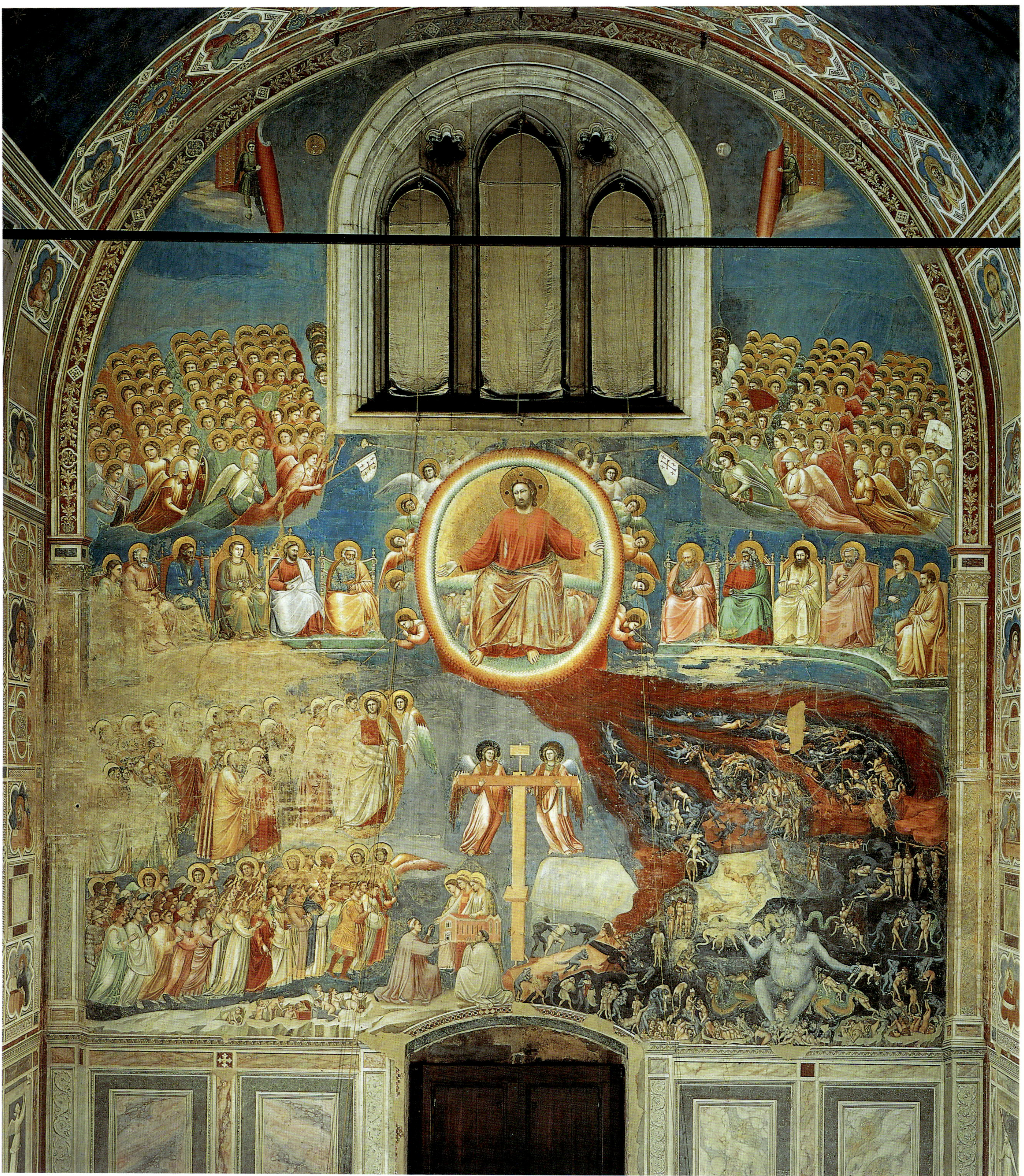

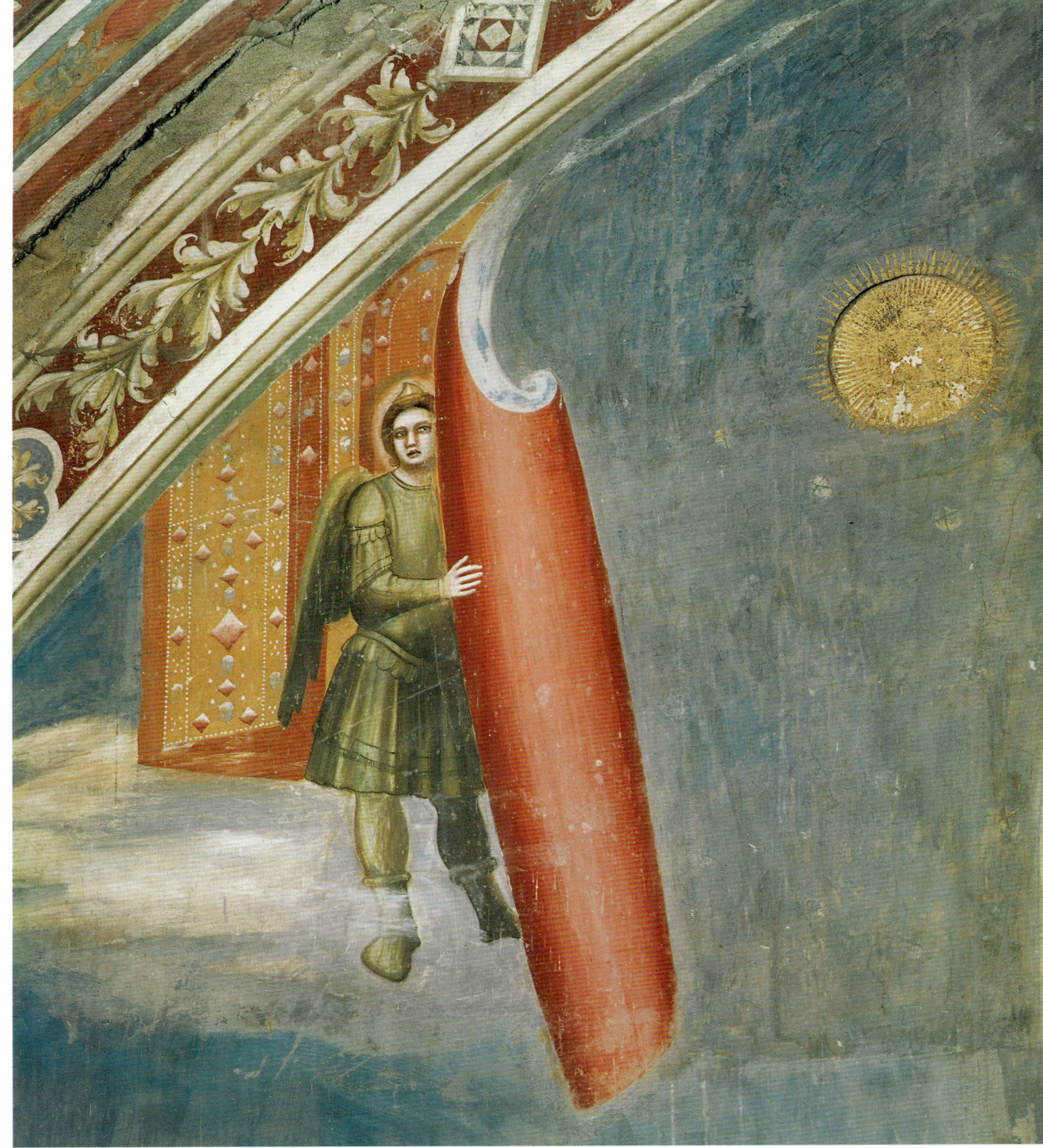

or when the celestial watch in the upper area of the
picture rolls back the firmament (ill. 42), behind which
the golden-red doors of the heavenly Jerusalem shine
forth. The black and red maw of hell, which seems to
anticipate Dante's "Inferno", is different again in its
impact (ill. 45).

The way in which Giotto establishes a connection
between the present-day world of the faithful and the
world beyond all time, the world of the Last Judgment,
contains another interesting detail. The donor
Scrovegni, still alive at the time, kneels next to those
being resurrected and offers "his" church to the three
Marys, assisted by a priest. The latter is portrayed in a
most lively manner: his robes hang – painted quite
illusionistically – over the arch of the portal (ill. 39).

The border between painted and real space appears
to have been breached here. This same intention was
already pursued in the feigned architecture of the
Legend of St. Francis at Assisi, and it also characterizes
the representation of God the Father at the top of the
triumphal arch wall above the entrance to the choir (ill.
46). The heavens have opened and ranks of angels
surround God the Father on his throne. Amongst the
angels, who move elegantly, the depiction of God, with
his delicately shimmering, bright robes and his hieratic
face, gives the impression of his belonging to a different
sphere.

This particular effect is also the result of a different
painting technique: God the Father is not painted as a
fresco on the wall, but in tempera on a wooden panel.
This "door" was presumably opened during the
mystery plays performed to celebrate the Feast of the
Annunciation, in order that the dove of Annunciation
could fly out. The representation of the *Annunciation*

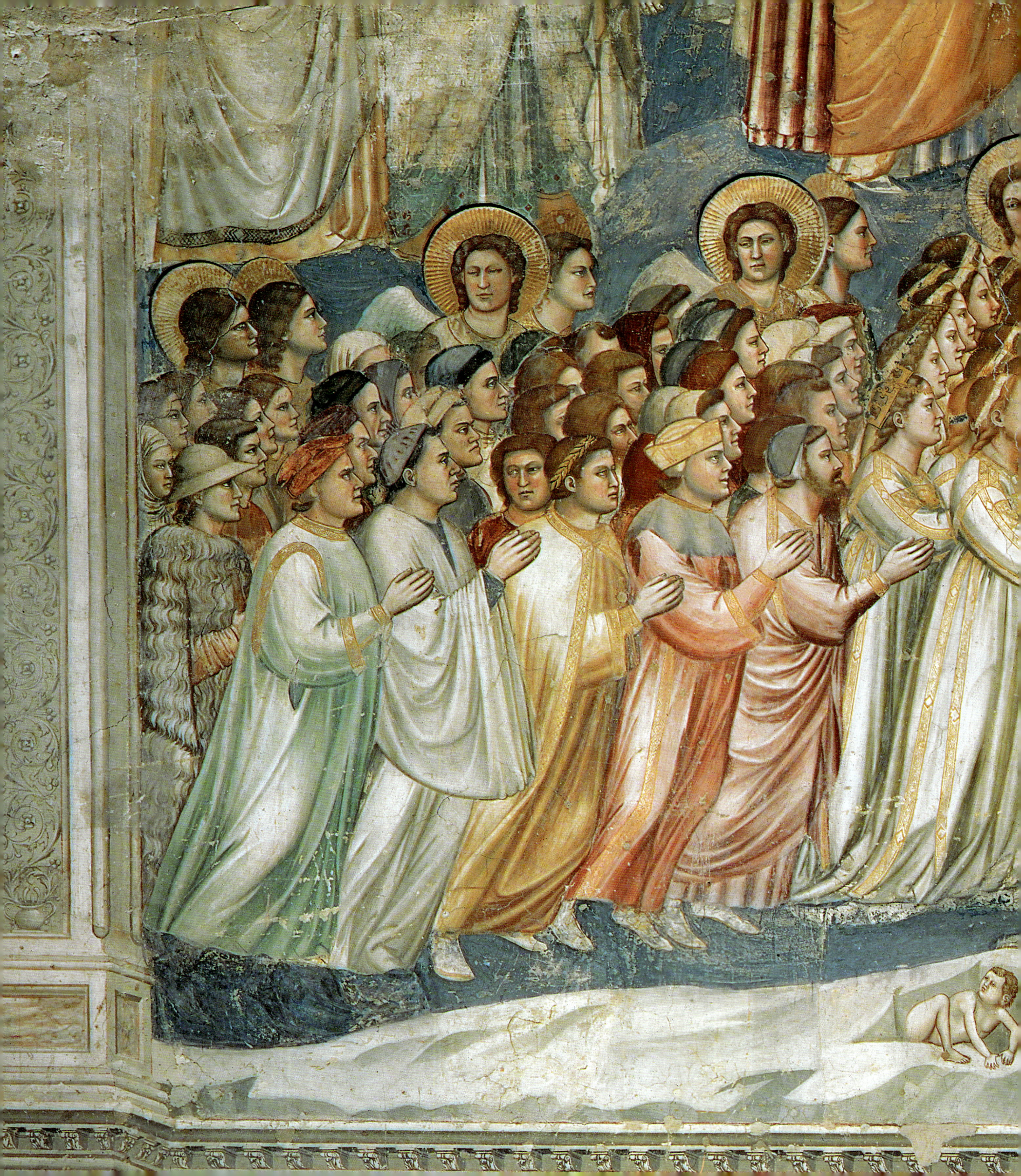

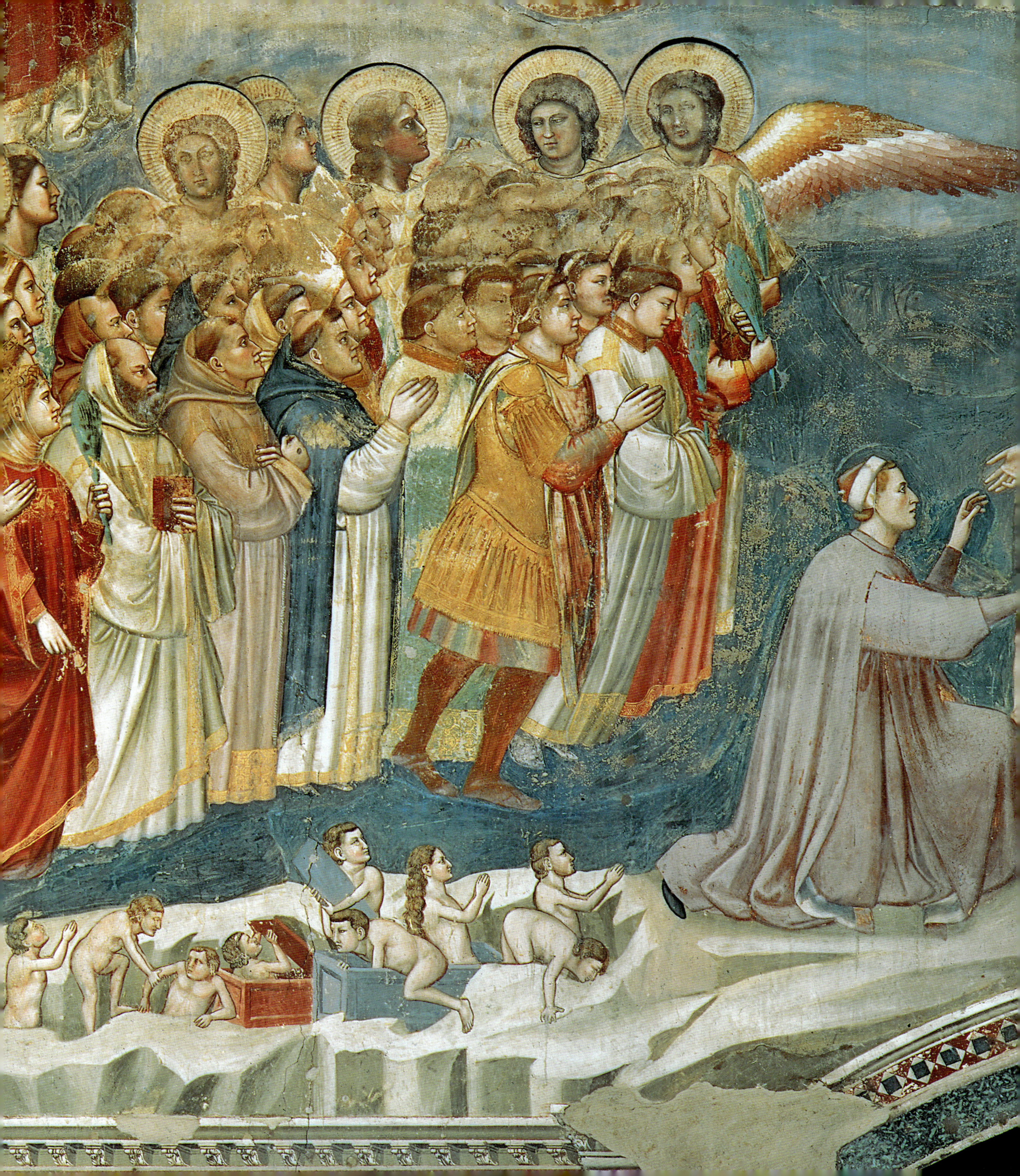

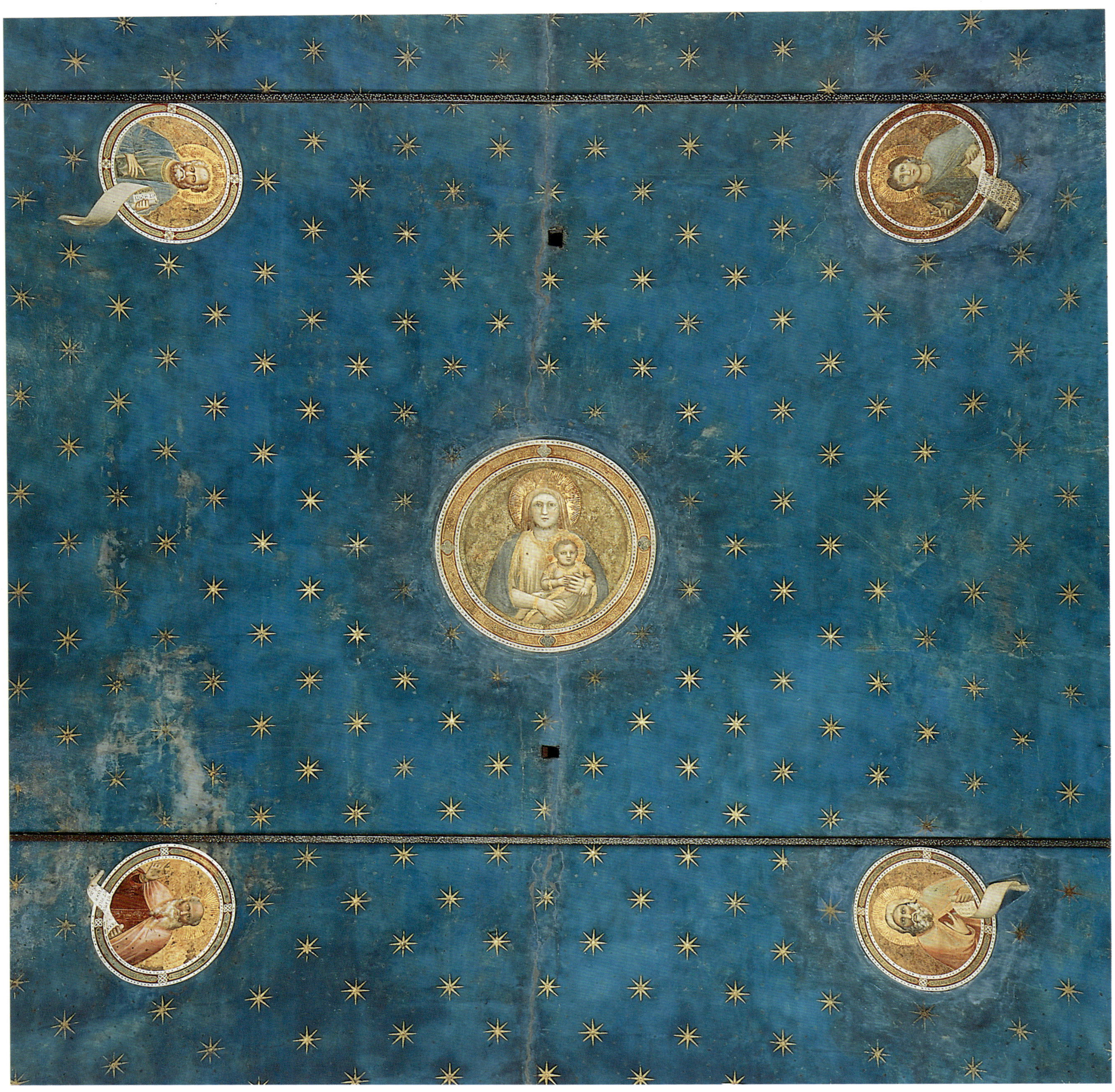

44 (above) Vault, 1302–1305
Fresco
Cappella degli Scrovegni, Padua

The Virgin Mary and the Christ Child are depicted in the
western heavens of the barrel vault, surrounded by four
prophets. It seems as if the figures look down from the
circular opening in the heavens. The scrolls of the
prophets, which seem to unfurl down into the real space,
further heighten this impression.

45 (opposite) *The Last Judgment,* Hell (detail ill. 41),
1302–1305

The Prince of Hell, a giant monster, is enthroned on a
dragon. He grabs the damned and eats them. The
torments of the naked people, which are being
administered by shadowy creatures, are depicted in great
detail.

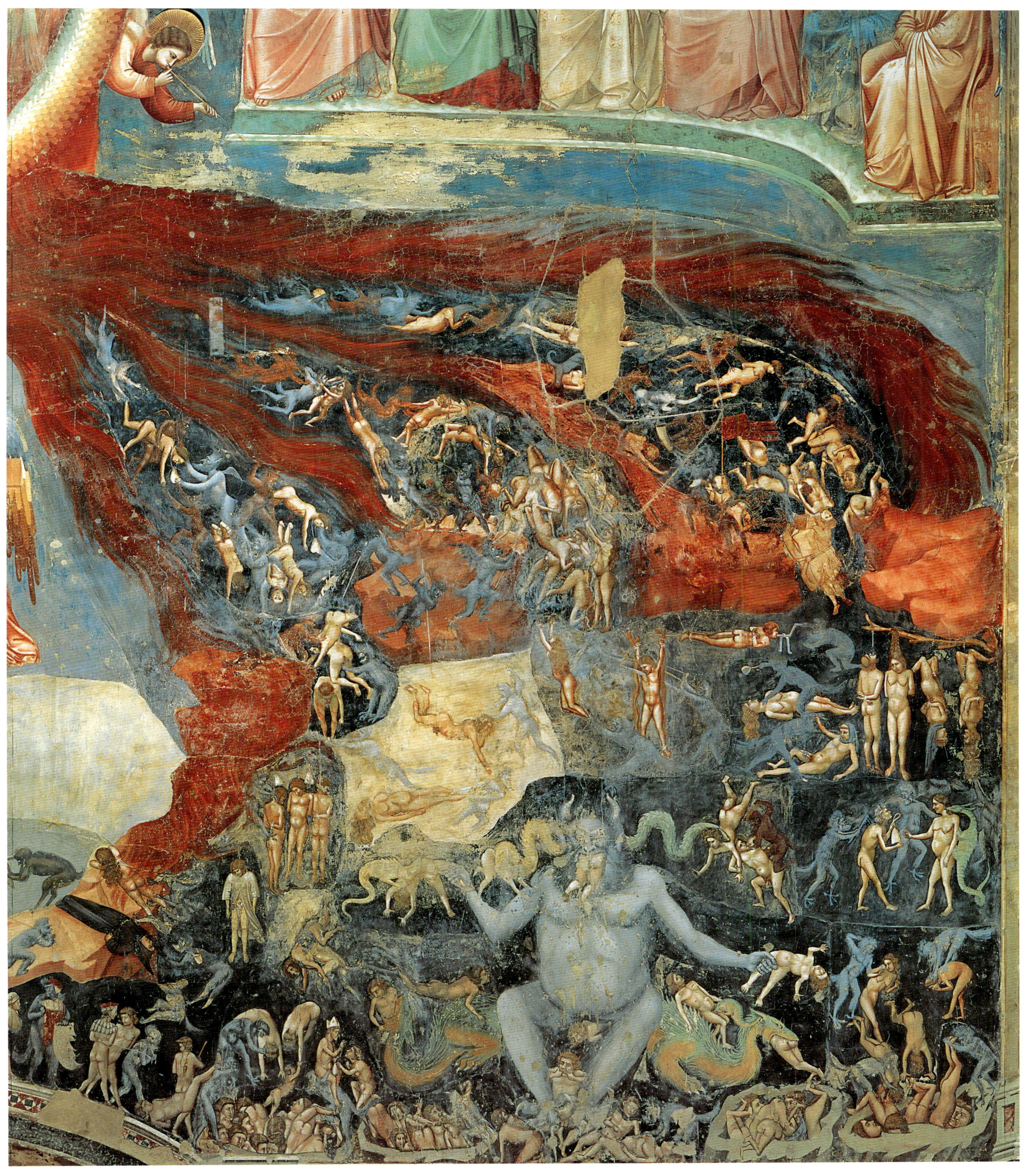

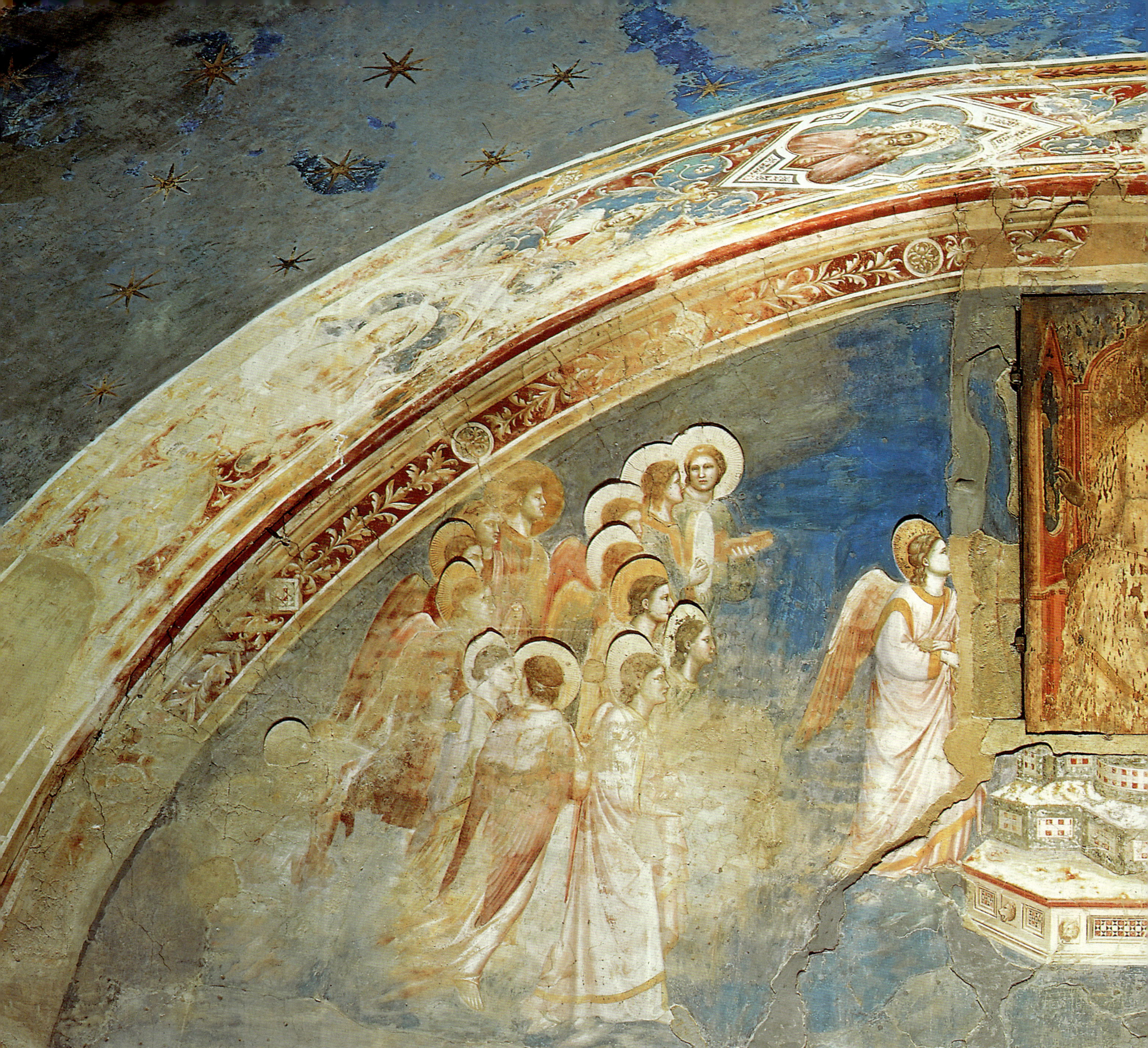

46 *God the Father encircled by Angels* (detail ill. 40),
1302–1305

A circle of angels surrounds the throne of God the Father.
The delicate beings are moving to the music
enthusiastically provided by smaller angels on the outside
edges. The small musicians and the angels looking at one
another seem especially vivid. The two angels next to the
throne of God have the effect of leading the eye into the
austere, almost motionless center. The depiction of God
himself is painted on a wooden panel. This was
presumably used as a door and opened on the occasion of
the mystery plays, which marked the Feast of the
Annunciation, to let out the dove of the Holy Spirit.

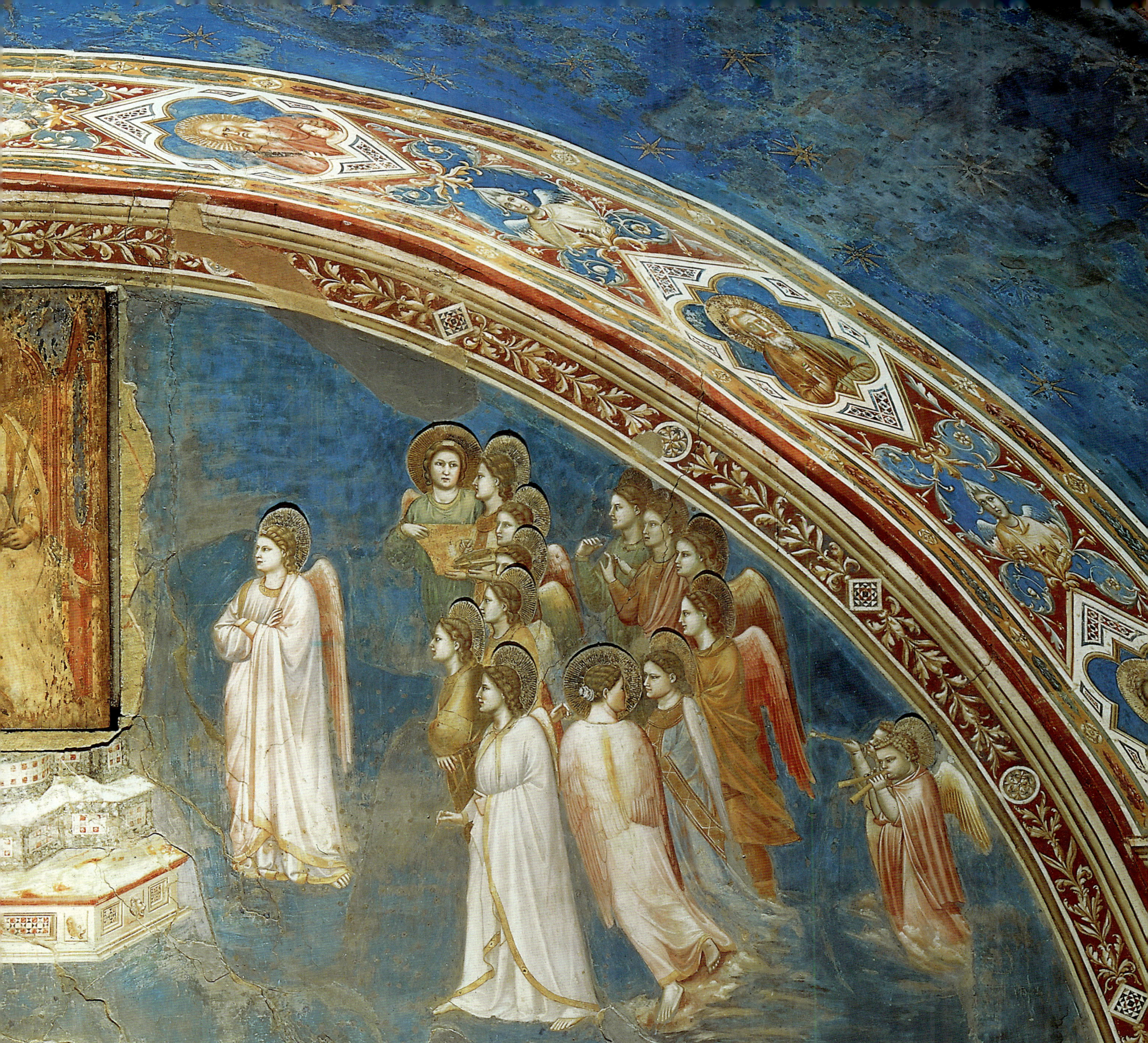

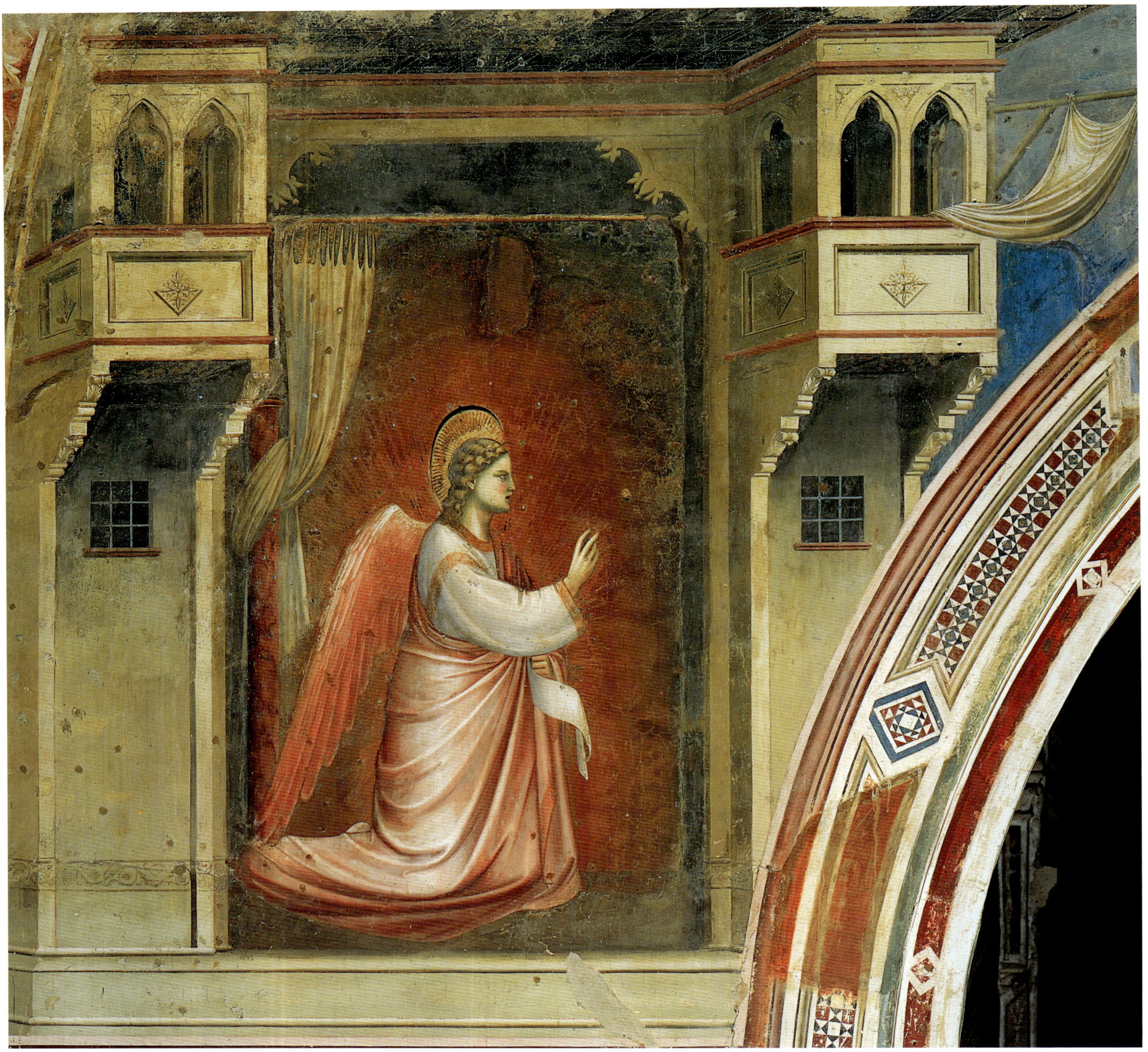

47, 48 *Annunciation* (details ill. 40), 1302–1305

Mary and the Angel of the Annunciation kneel in a narrow building to the left and right of the triumphal arch. Its jutting balconies are so aligned perspectively that they absorb the real architecture that lies between them, and the triumphal arch thus seems to convey the angel's greeting.

directly below it is an indication of this (ills. 47, 48). In a magnificent way, Giotto here combines the real architecture of the church interior with feigned, painted architectural elements to create a meaningful unity. To the right and left of the arch, the angel and Mary kneel in their respective buildings. It is only through the connecting architecture that tension is maintained within the depiction of the *Annunciation*, even over this great, daring distance and separation of figures, and that God the Father – at the top of the triumphal arch – is also included in the action. As far as

form and content were concerned, Giotto was even here entering new territory.

Vaulted by a starry sky with the two centers of Christ and Mary (ill. 44), the *Last Judgment* in the west and the *Annunciation* in the east, witnessed by God, frame the nave of the church. In between the two, the story of Mary is narrated on the upper register of the walls – beginning with scenes from the lives of her parents, Joachim and Anne – and the youth of Christ and the story of his Passion are narrated on the two lower registers. To a great extent the representations follow the

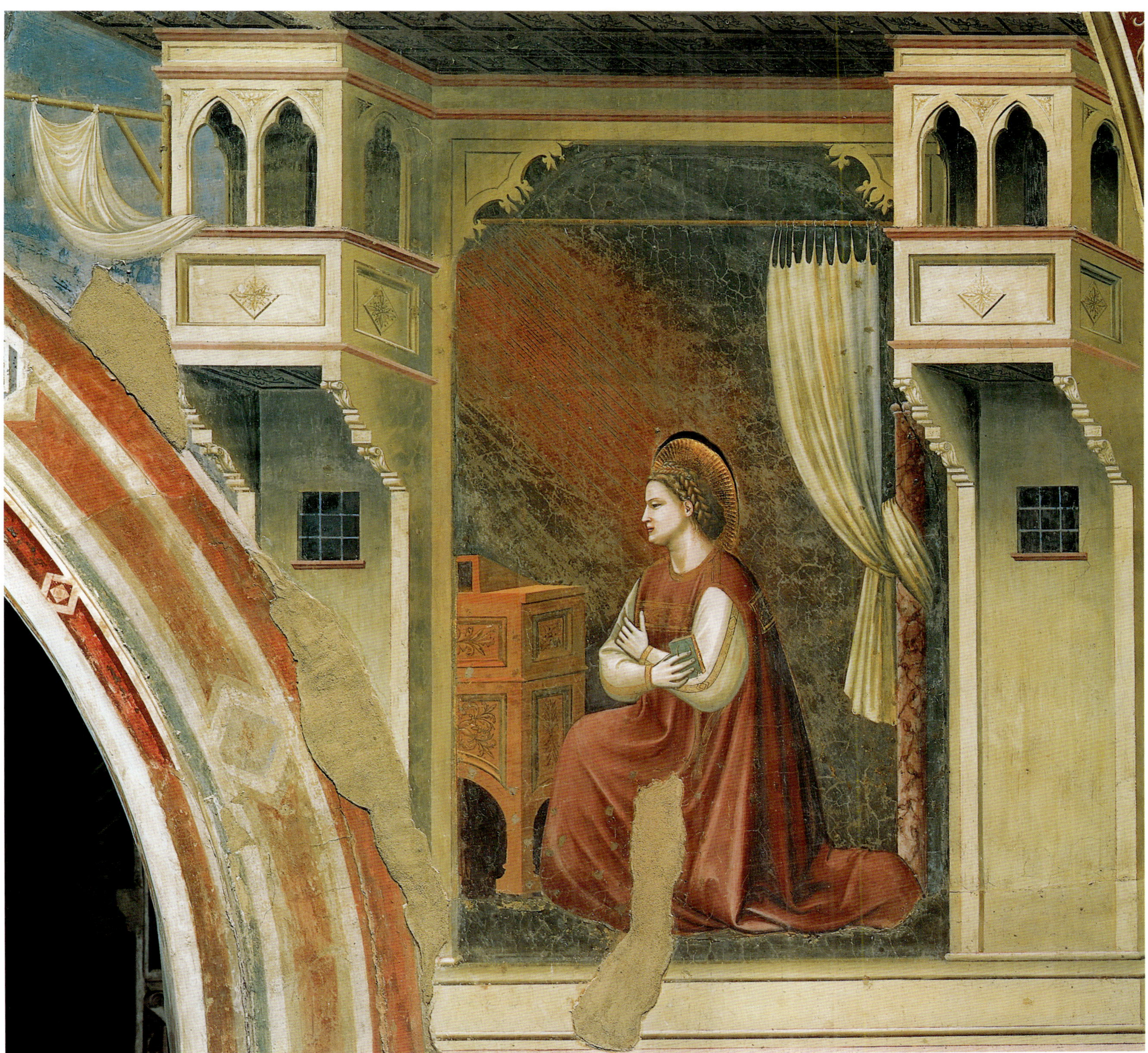

"Legenda aurea", a collection of legends of the saints, written by Jacobus da Voragine in 1264. The narrative cycles rest on a painted *dado*. This complements the pictorial program, and proves to be one of the inventions with which Giotto renewed art, even in what is supposed to be only a secondary setting.

Two very realistically painted, multi-colored panels of marble alternate respectively with depictions of figures. The personifications of the Vices on the one side, and of the Virtues on the other, appear here as marble sculptures brought to life. However, they are not made of stone (ills. 49 – 62). This kind of tone-on-tone painting (*grisaille*) is just as novel as the view into a painted sacristy, which Giotto displays above the marble *dado* on either side of the triumphal arch (ill. 63). Here, painted and real space once again merge into one. Using a very clear perspective – with a common vanishing point – Giotto depicts two views of an interior space with cross-rib vaulting, whose dimensions are suggested by the lamp which hangs from the ceiling.

Since the Arena Chapel has no windows on one wall,

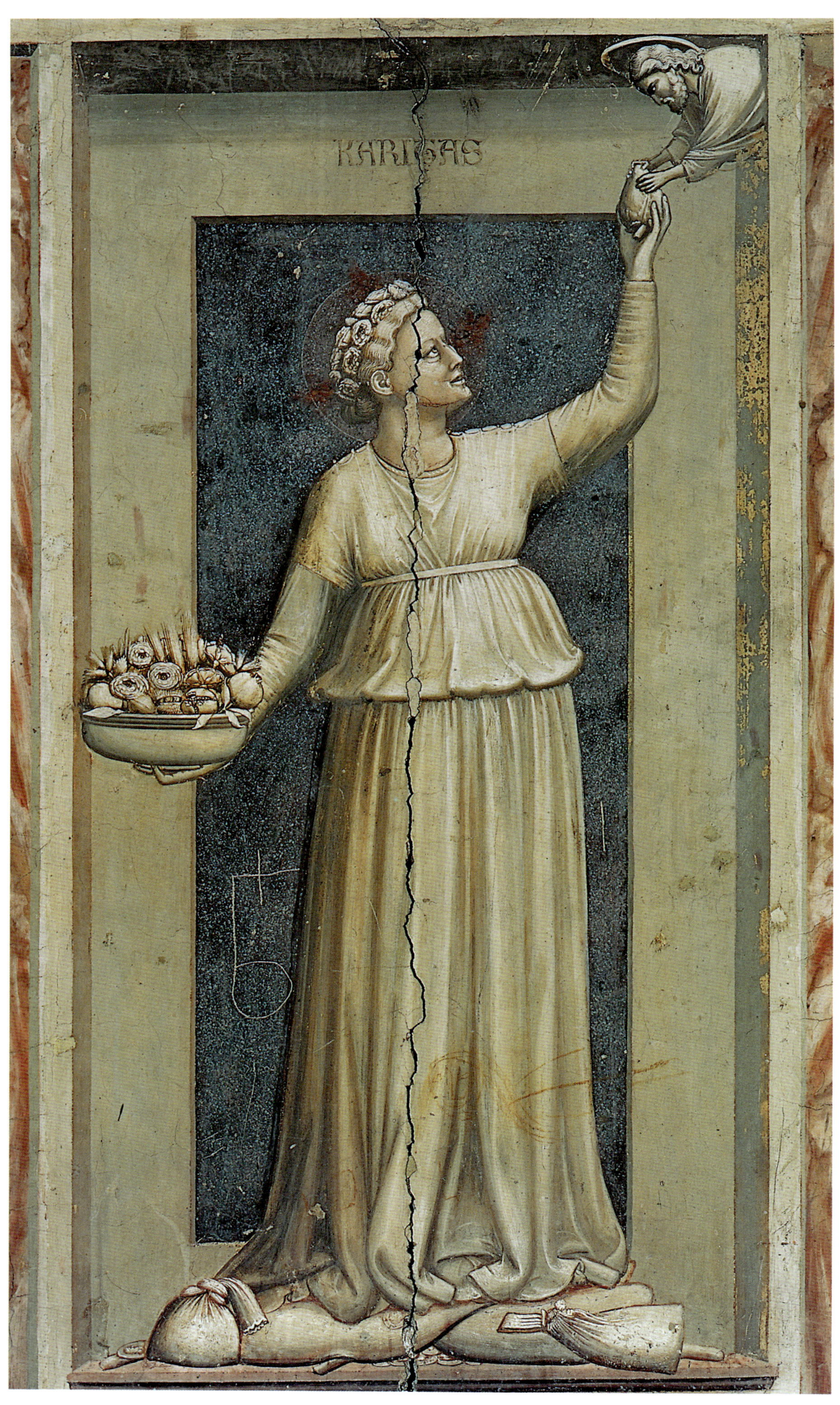

49 (left) *Charity*, 1302–1305
Fresco
Cappella degli Scrovegni, Padua

Among the multi-colored, painted marble slabs of the
dado level, illusionistically depicted niches open up, in
which Giotto has painted, as stone statues, the Virtues on
one side of the chapel and the Vices on the other.
Charity (*Caritas*) holds a basket of wonderfully painted
fruit in the one hand, and with the other receives a heart
handed to her by God the Father.

50 *Hope*, 1302–1305
Fresco
Cappella degli Scrovegni, Padua

Hope (*Spes*) is portrayed as winged female figure,
receiving a crown from God the Father.

51 *Faith*, 1302–1305
Fresco
Cappella degli Scrovegni, Padua

Faith (*Fides*), is showing the viewer a cross-staff and
scroll. Of all the Virtues and Vices depicted, this one
seems most like a statue.

52 *Justice*, 1302–1305
Fresco
Cappella degli Scrovegni, Padua

Justice (*Iustitia*), is enthroned on a wide Gothic seat. She
holds punishment and clemency on scales in her hands.
Peaceful life develops under her reign – this is displayed
in the scene on the pedestal of her throne.

53 *Prudence*, 1302–1305
Fresco
Cappella degli Scrovegni, Padua

Prudence (*Prudentia*) sits at a broad writing desk. A quill
in her hand, she gazes into a mirror, which symbolizes
knowledge.

54 *Fortitude*, 1302–1305
Fresco
Cappella degli Scrovegni, Padua

Fortitude (*Fortitudo*) is positioned as a woman in armor
against the dark marble and behind her raised shield. She
raises her weapon forcefully, prepared for attack, in order
to defend virtue.

55 *Temperance*, 1302–1305
Fresco
Cappella degli Scrovegni, Padua

Temperance (*Temperantia*) is a female figure who stands
very casually in her niche. She very calmly wraps a ribbon
around the hilt of a sword.

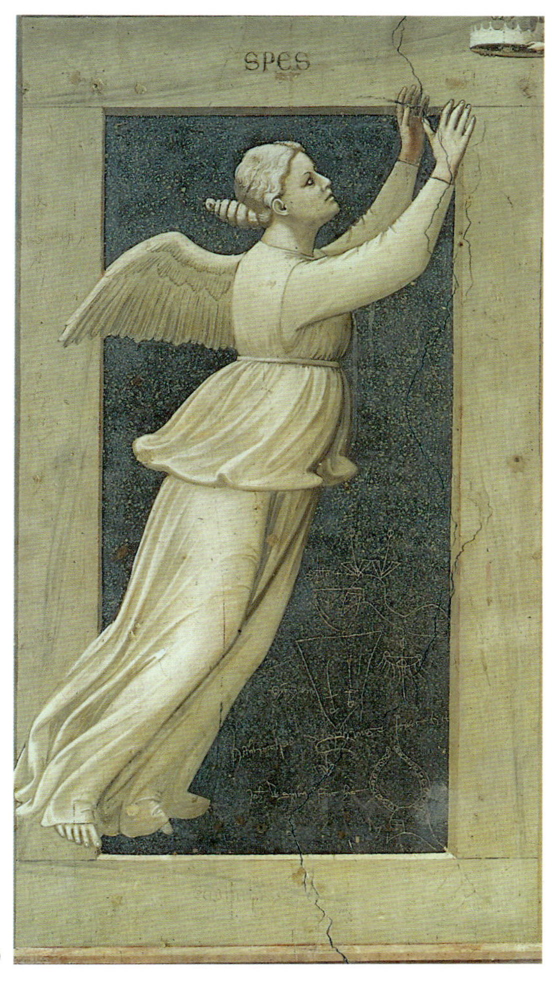

50

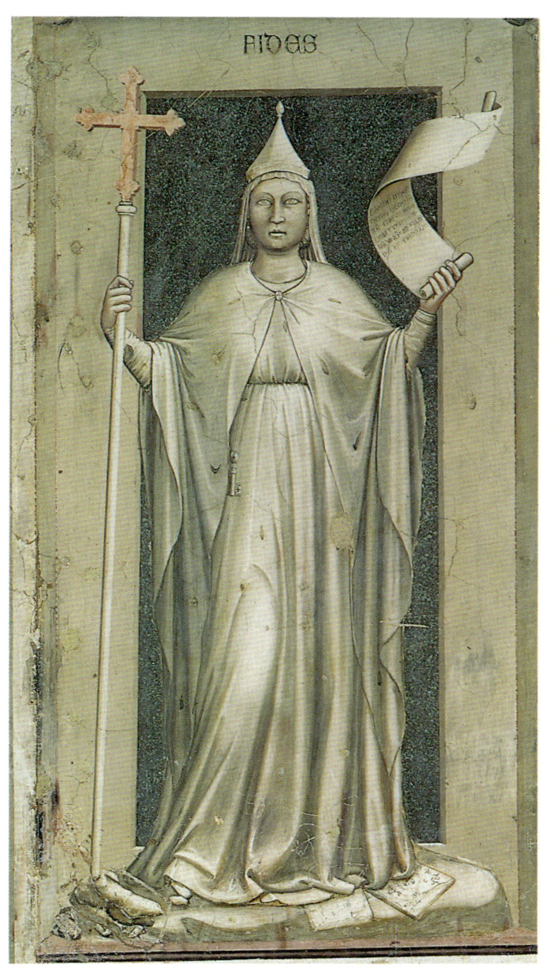

51

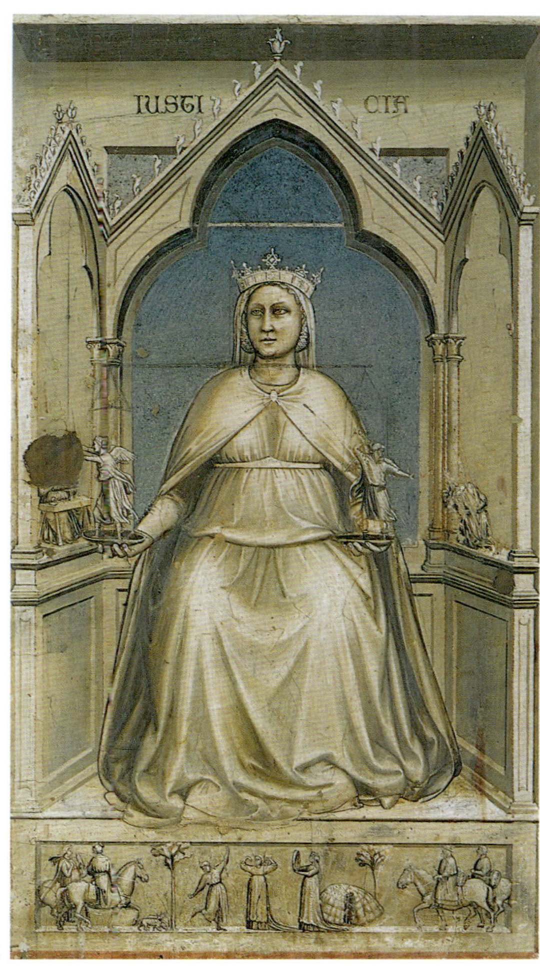

52

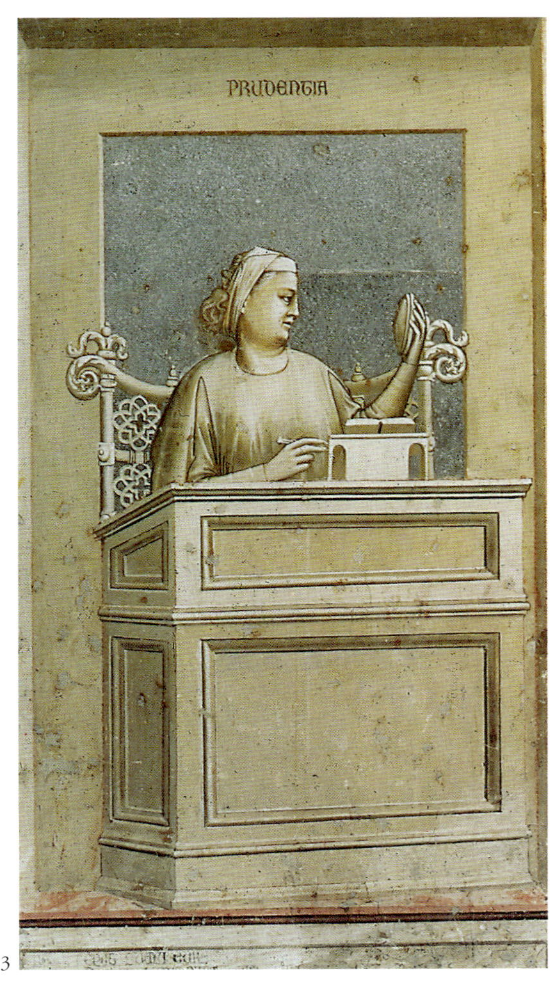

53

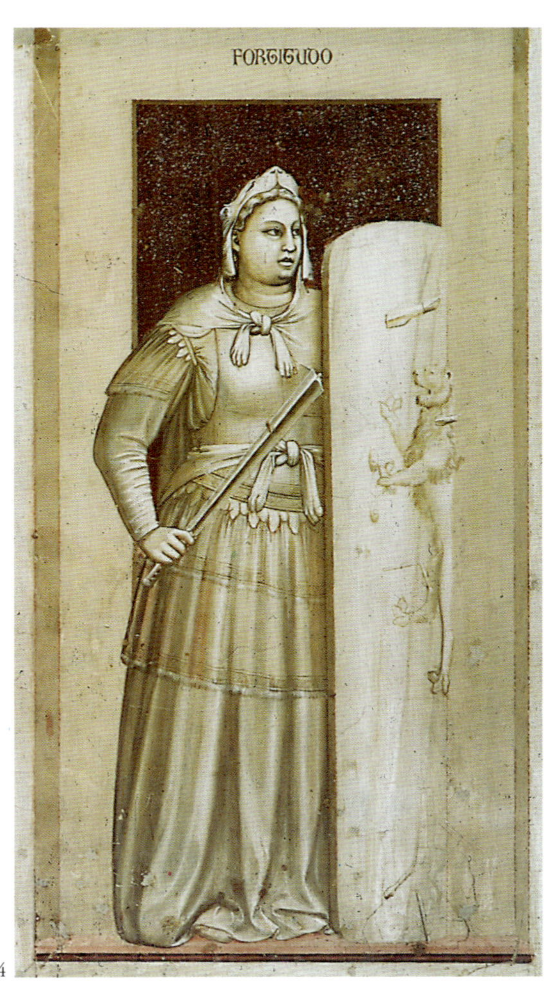

54

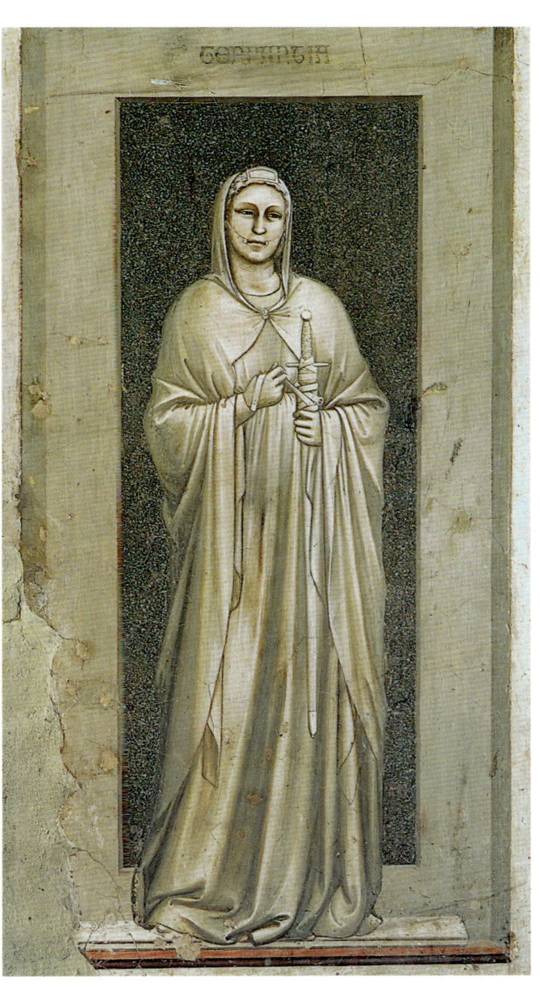

55

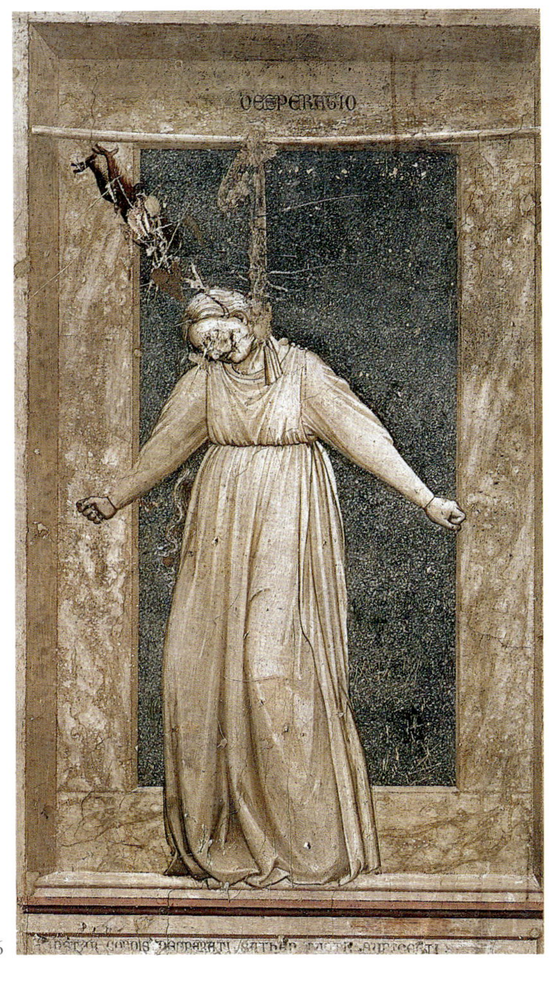

56

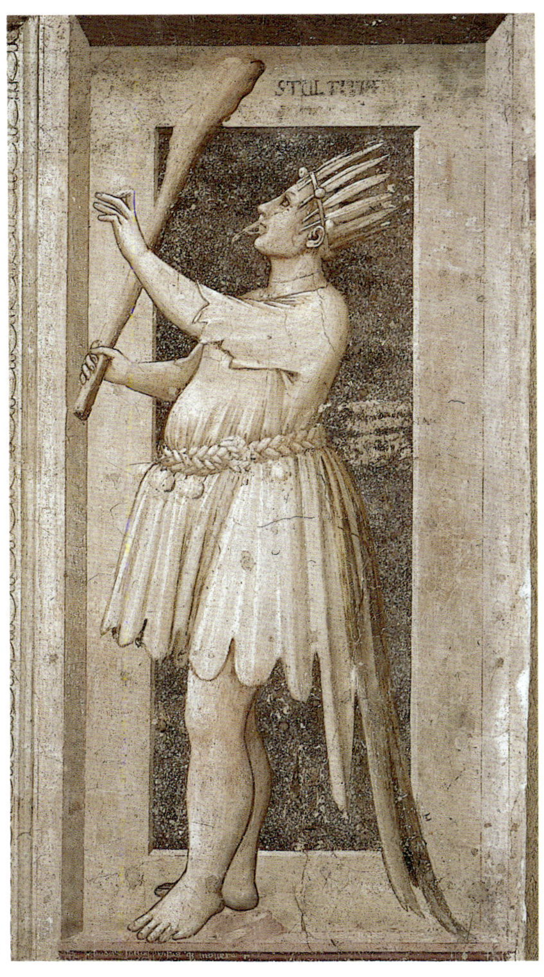

57

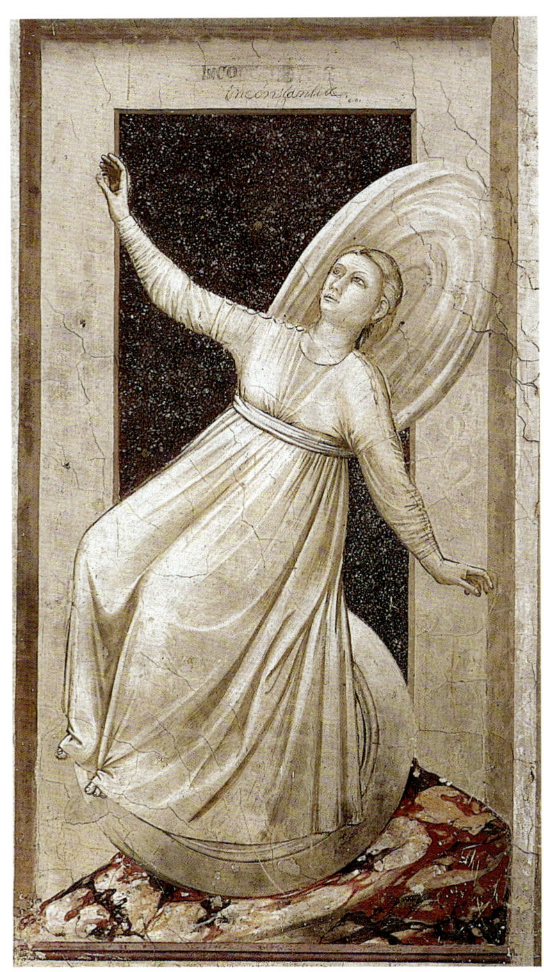

58

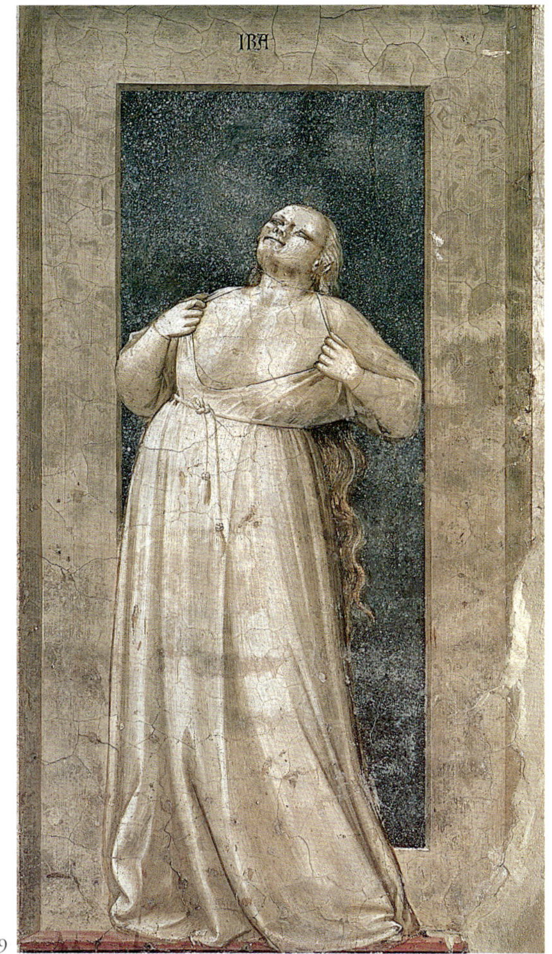

59

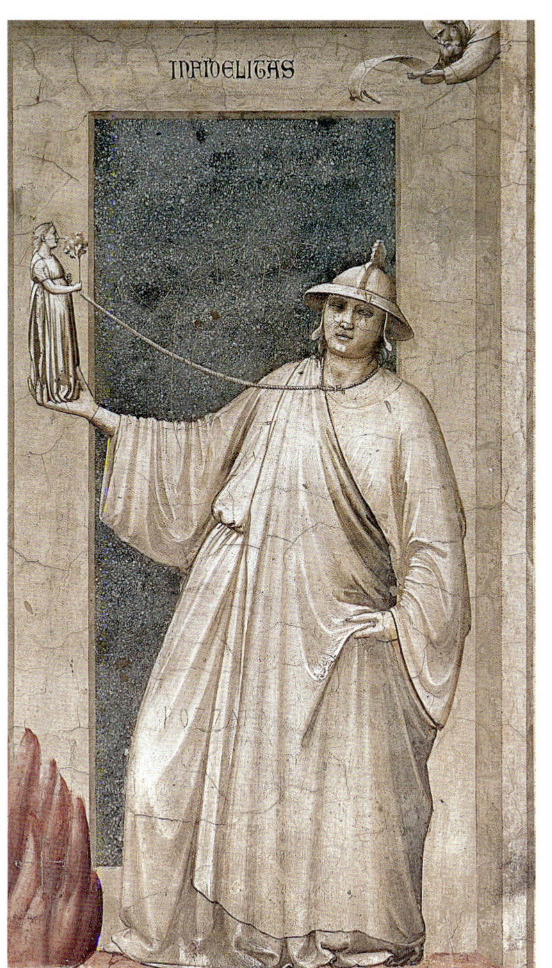

60

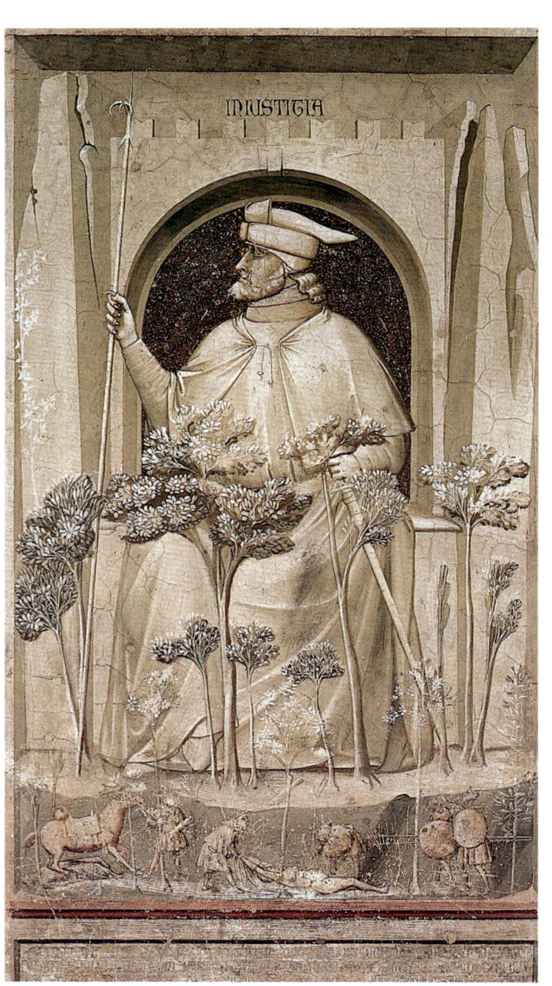

61

56 *Despair*, 1302–1305
Fresco
Cappella degli Scrovegni, Padua

Despair (*Desperatio*) appears as a female suicide – a
demon has taken hold of her soul. Giotto here uses the
painted marble niche in a most impressive fashion in
order to display narrative details, such as the way the
beam and the rope are fastened.

57 *Foolishness*, 1302–1305
Fresco
Cappella degli Scrovegni, Padua

Giotto characterizes the vice of *Stupiditas* particularly
through the body forms: Foolishness stands in her niche,
plump and ungainly. In addition, her fool's cap and
costume indicate her mental state.

58 *Inconstancy*, 1302–1305
Fresco
Cappella degli Scrovegni, Padua

With her rolling disc, Inconstancy (*Inconstantia*) is
situated on a sloping surface. Giotto gives a clear
impression of unsteadiness through this device alone.
Through the gesture of trying to regain balance, the
leaning posture, and the robe that flies up, he
characterizes yet more strongly a permanent sense of
movement, a constant swaying backwards and forwards.

59 *Anger*, 1302–1305
Fresco
Cappella degli Scrovegni, Padua

This woman, the personification of Anger (*Ira*), tears her
robe, full of rage. Her face also appears quite distorted by
the violent inner emotions.

60 *Idolatry*, 1302–1305
Fresco
Cappella degli Scrovegni, Padua

Idolatry (*Infidelitas*) appears tied to the strings of a
heathen idol, which he is carrying in his own hand.

61 *Injustice*, 1302–1305
Fresco
Cappella degli Scrovegni, Padua

Injustice (*Iniustitia*) is personified by a man who rules in
an impenetrable fastness. The consequences of the rule of
injustice are abuses, which can be seen in the foreground.

62 (right) *Envy*, 1302–1305
Fresco
Cappella degli Scrovegni, Padua

Envy (*Invidia*) is depicted as an ugly old woman with
enormous ears, horns and a snake crawling out of her
mouth. She holds a sack of money in one hand, and the
inner fire of jealousy burns at her feet.

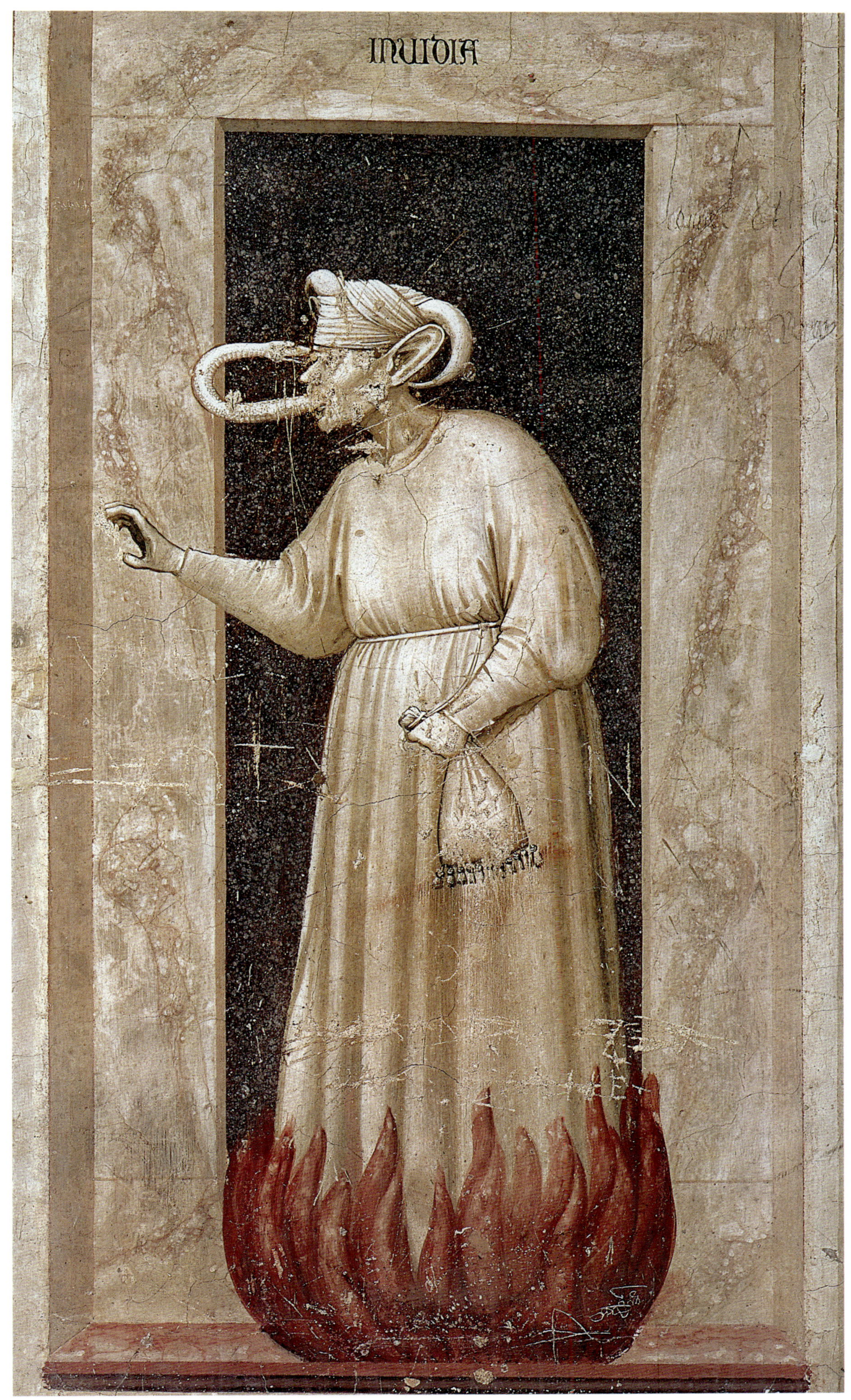

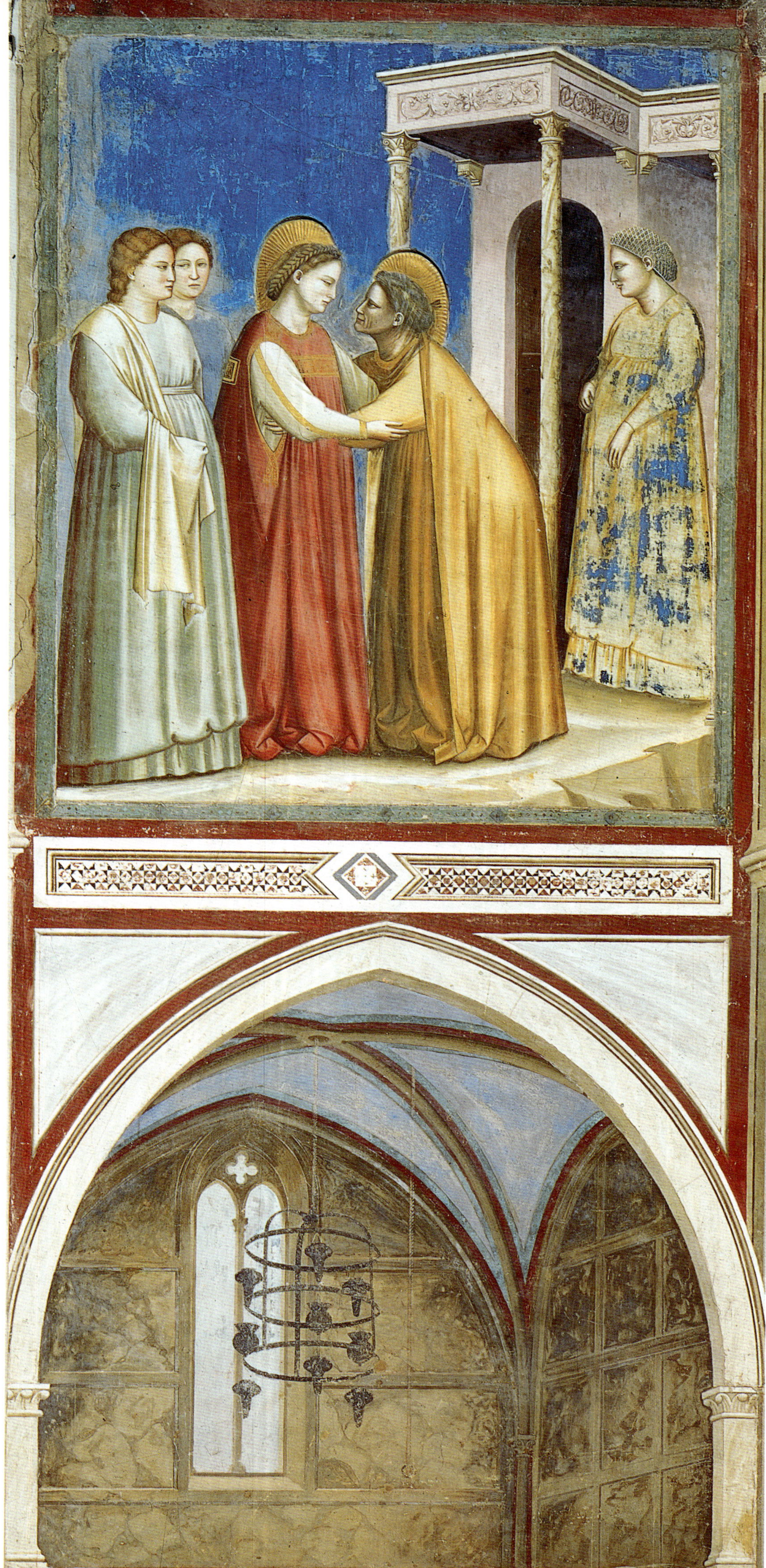

63 (left) *The Visitation*, 1302–1305
Fresco
Cappella degli Scrovegni, Padua

The pregnant Mother of God and her two companions
visit Elizabeth, who is expecting John the Baptist. The
two women embrace in front of the portico. As so often,
Giotto places the intensity of the encounter in the
exchange of glances. Beneath this fresco the wall,
decorated with painted marble, appears to open up:
Giotto here shows us a view of a chapel with cross-rib
vaulting and a narrow Gothic window. A chandelier
hangs from the vertex of the vault defining the depth of
this unusual, illusionistically painted space.

64 *Rejection of Joachim's Sacrifice*, 1302–1305
Fresco, 200 x 185 cm
Cappella degli Scrovegni, Padua

The elderly Joachim is denied entry to the temple, as he
has remained childless. The architecture reinforces the
priest's gesture of rejection, to which the saint replies with
a saddened look. The sheep, as a sacrificial animal that
has become superfluous, has a particularly touching
effect.

65 *Joachim among the Shepherds*, 1302–1305
Fresco, 200 x 185 cm
Cappella degli Scrovegni, Padua

Sad and introverted, Joachim arrives among the
shepherds. Using the contrast between the lively sheep,
the dog that greets him, and the knowing glances of the
shepherds, Giotto elucidates his state of mind in the
voluminous, closed form of the saint.

66 *Annunciation to Anne*, 1302–1305
Fresco, 200 x 185 cm
Cappella degli Scrovegni, Padua

The miraculous encounter takes place in an obliquely set,
box-like room. An angel appears in the window opening
and announces the birth of her daughter Mary to the
praying Anne. Giotto illustrates the intimacy of the scene
using the domestic objects, and particularly the contrast
between interior and exterior – a maid sits spinning
outside in front of the door.

67 *The Sacrifice of Joachim*, 1302–1305
Fresco, 200 x 185 cm
Cappella degli Scrovegni, Padua

In the open countryside, Joachim has sunk to the ground
and catches sight of an angel, who indicates to him that
his sacrifice has been accepted. Color is used to establish a
connection between these two figures, illustrating the
miraculous nature of events. As so often, Giotto also
employs a figure here who comments on the action – the
praying shepherd. In his coloring, he is closer to the rocks
and the animals. He too recognizes the hand of
benediction in the sky.

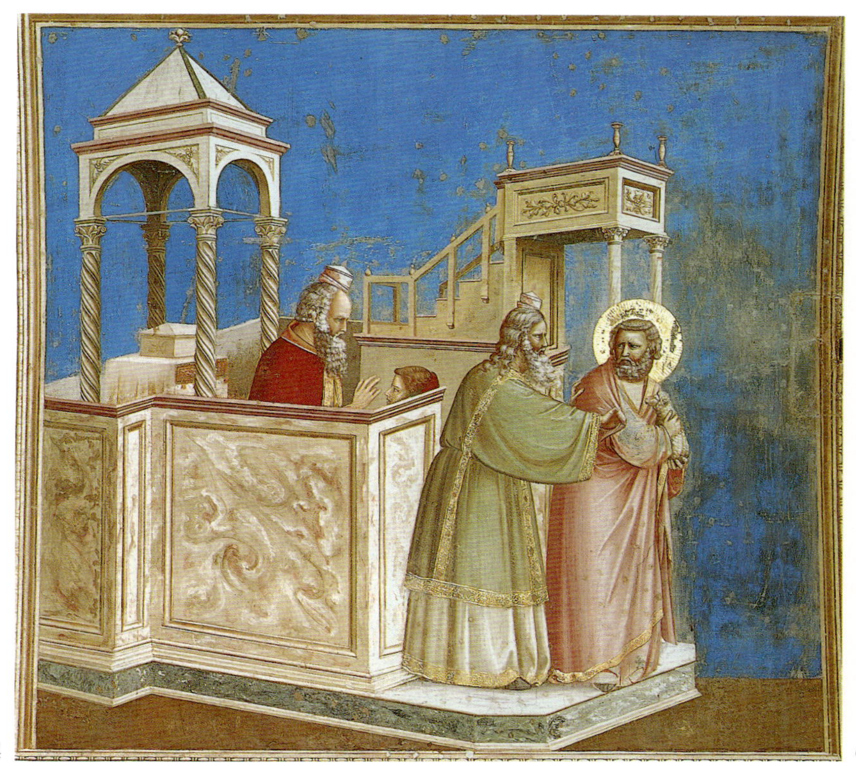

64

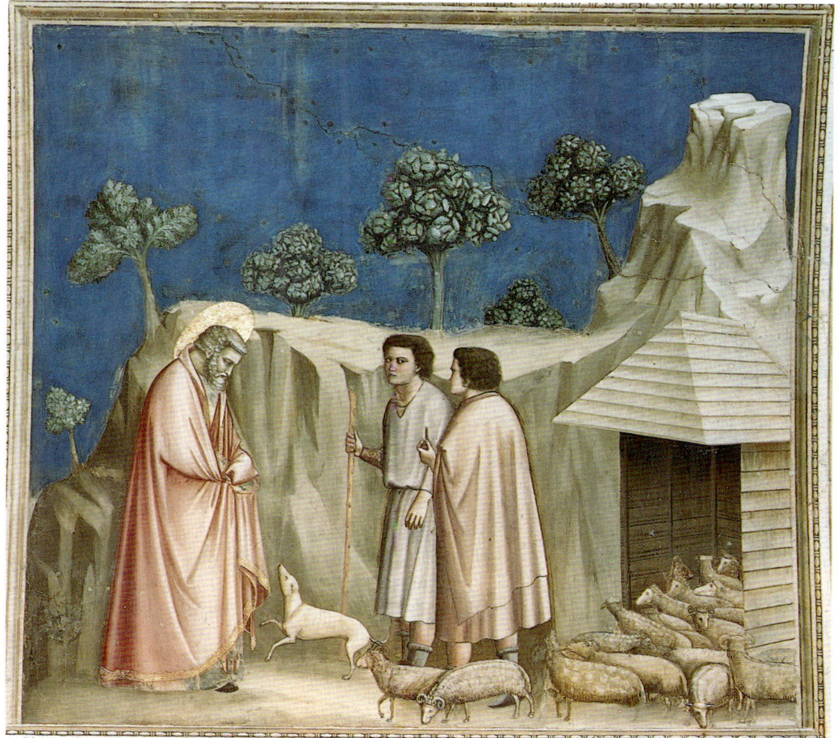

65

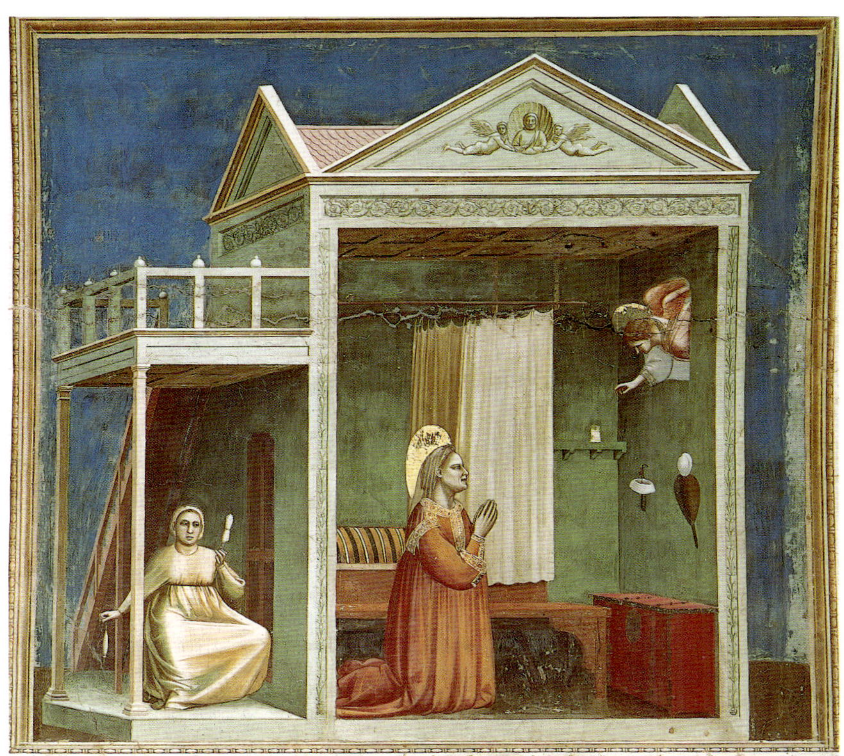

66

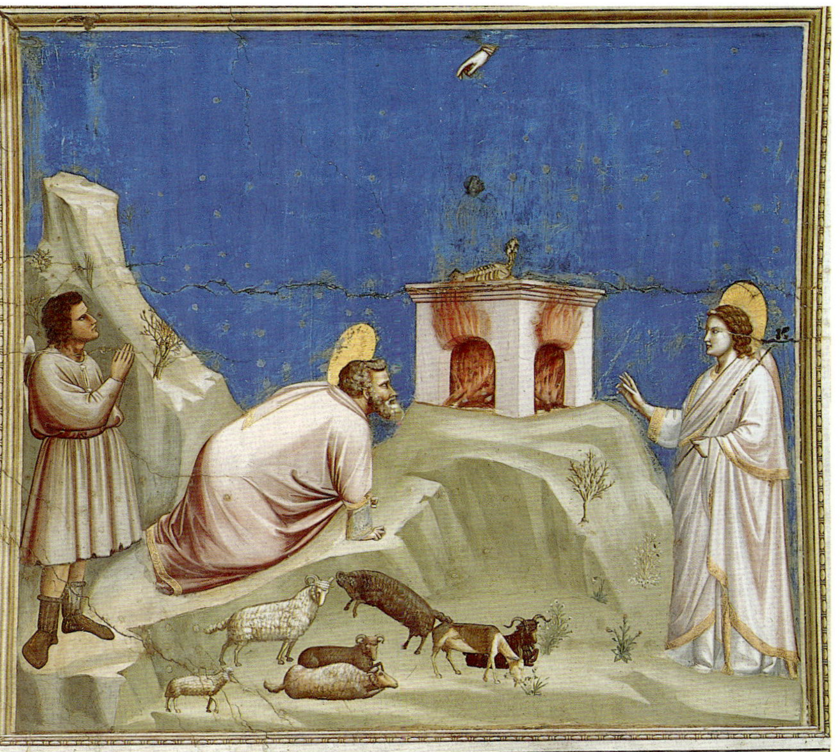

67

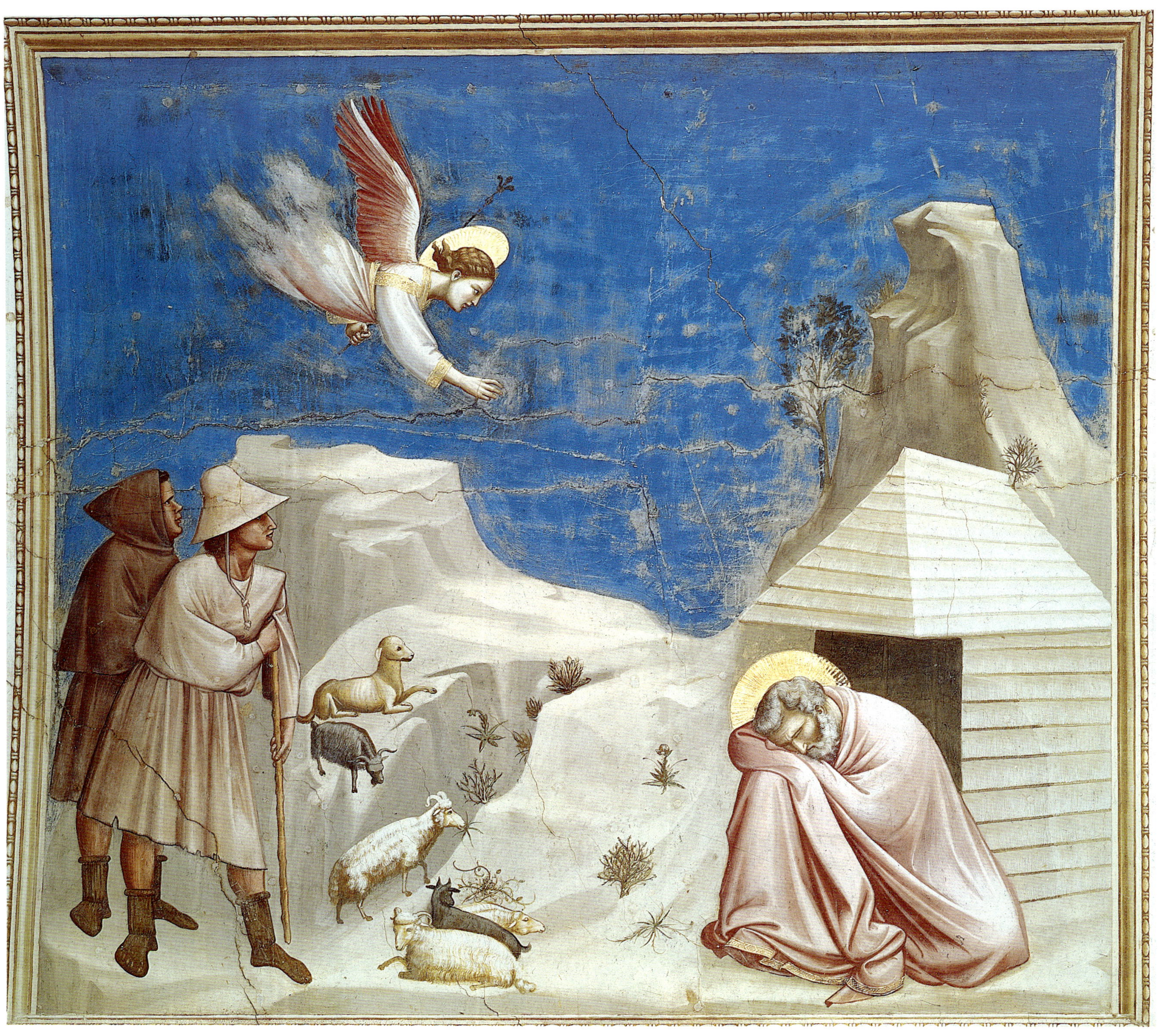

68 *The Dream of Joachim*, 1302–1305
Fresco, 200 x 185 cm
Cappella degli Scrovegni, Padua

Joachim is slumped in the shelter of the hut and the rock,
asleep. The shepherds watch over him and their flock.
One of them appears to see the celestial phenomenon –
an angel bringing Joachim tidings of his impending
fatherhood. Tremendous tension is created along the
diagonal between the angel and Joachim, allowing us to
comprehend what is happening.

and six narrow, tall ones on the other, the picture fields
could not be distributed symmetrically over the two
wall surfaces. That is why the frescoes here are smaller
in size than those in the Legend of St. Francis at Assisi
(200 x 185 cm compared to 270 x 230 cm), and why
they have been articulated in a different, more stately
rhythm.

Giotto and his assistants painted from top to bottom.
Since the painting was executed *al fresco*, moist plaster
had to be applied only to a surface of sufficient size to
be decorated in one day. We can assume that

preliminary drawings were made for individual picture
fields, so that Giotto could leave the execution of the
secondary figures, the backgrounds and the decorative
bands to members of his workshop. Without assistants
and specialists, it would not have been possible to
realize such an extensive decorative program in the
short space of two to three years. Even if expert art
historians believe they can identify individual assistants
on the basis of stylistic characteristics, both in Padua
and in the later frescoes for the Lower Church at Assisi
and the Florentine church of Santa Croce, each of these

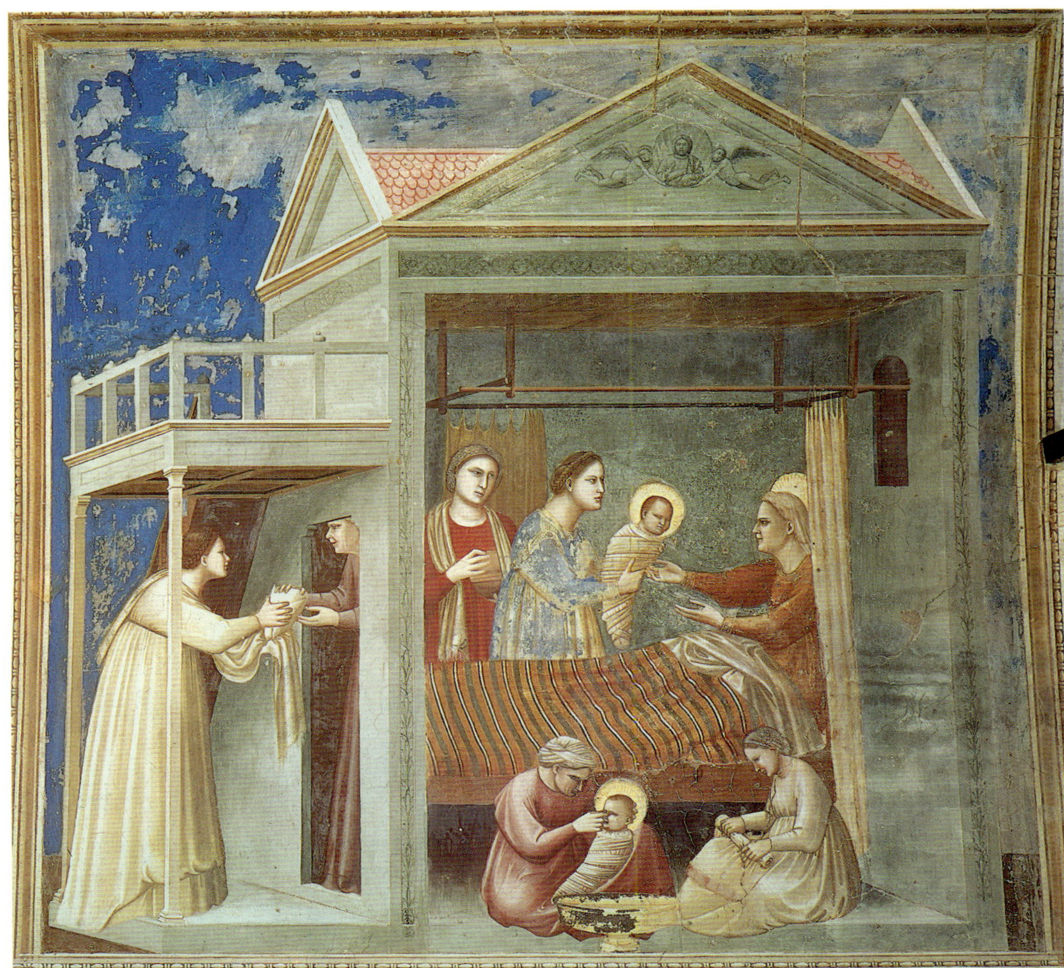

69 *Meeting at the Golden Gate*, 1302–1305
Fresco, 200 x 185 cm
Cappella degli Scrovegni, Padua

Anne and her companions have gone to meet Joachim.
The spouses encounter one another on the bridge in
front of the Golden Gate of Jerusalem, certain that they
will now become parents. Everything around them seems
to be affected by this – from the arches of the
architecture, which appear to echo the posture of the
couple, to the faces, which reveal very different responses.

70 *Birth of the Virgin Mary*, 1302–1305
Fresco, 200 x 185 cm
Cappella degli Scrovegni, Padua

The birth of the Virgin takes place in the same house as
the annunciation to Anne. In the small room, somewhat
too narrow for the figures, Anne sits up in bed and is
handed the baby in its swaddling clothes by a nursemaid.
The child appears for a second time in the idyllic scene in
front of the mother's bed. As in the Annunciation scene,
Giotto also shows the view of the building from outside.
He does not divide interior and exterior, but connects
them using the two women.

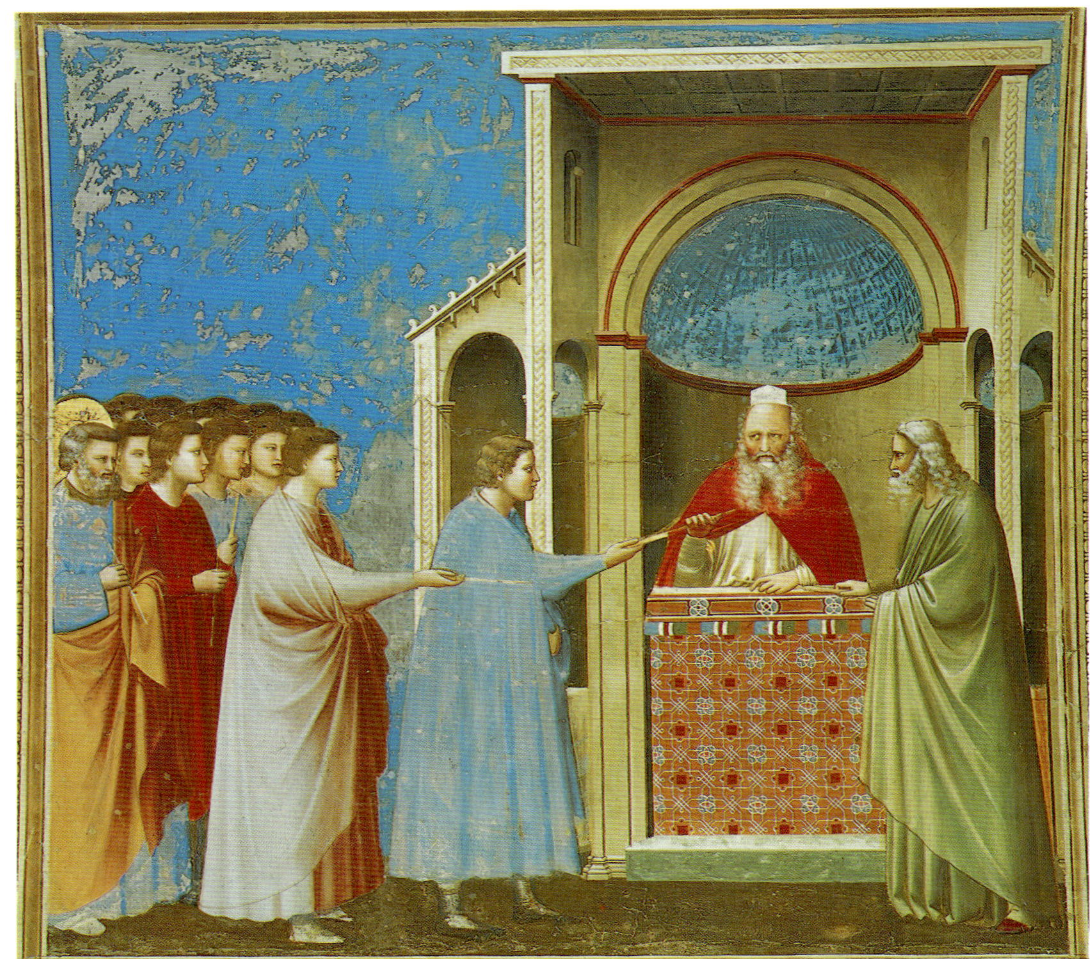

71 *The Bringing of the Rods*, 1302–1305
Fresco, 200 x 185 cm
Cappella degli Scrovegni, Padua

Having been educated at the temple, the Virgin Mary
was to become betrothed. However, since her parents had
dedicated her to the Lord, her future husband was to be
decided upon by a miracle. He whose rod brought forth
blossom would marry the Virgin. The fresco shows the
choir of a church, at whose altar the high priest stands,
receiving the rods. Attentive and excited, the young men
hand over their rods. Only Joseph stands somewhat
hesitantly on the extreme left. The legend tells us that he
considered himself too old for the Virgin.

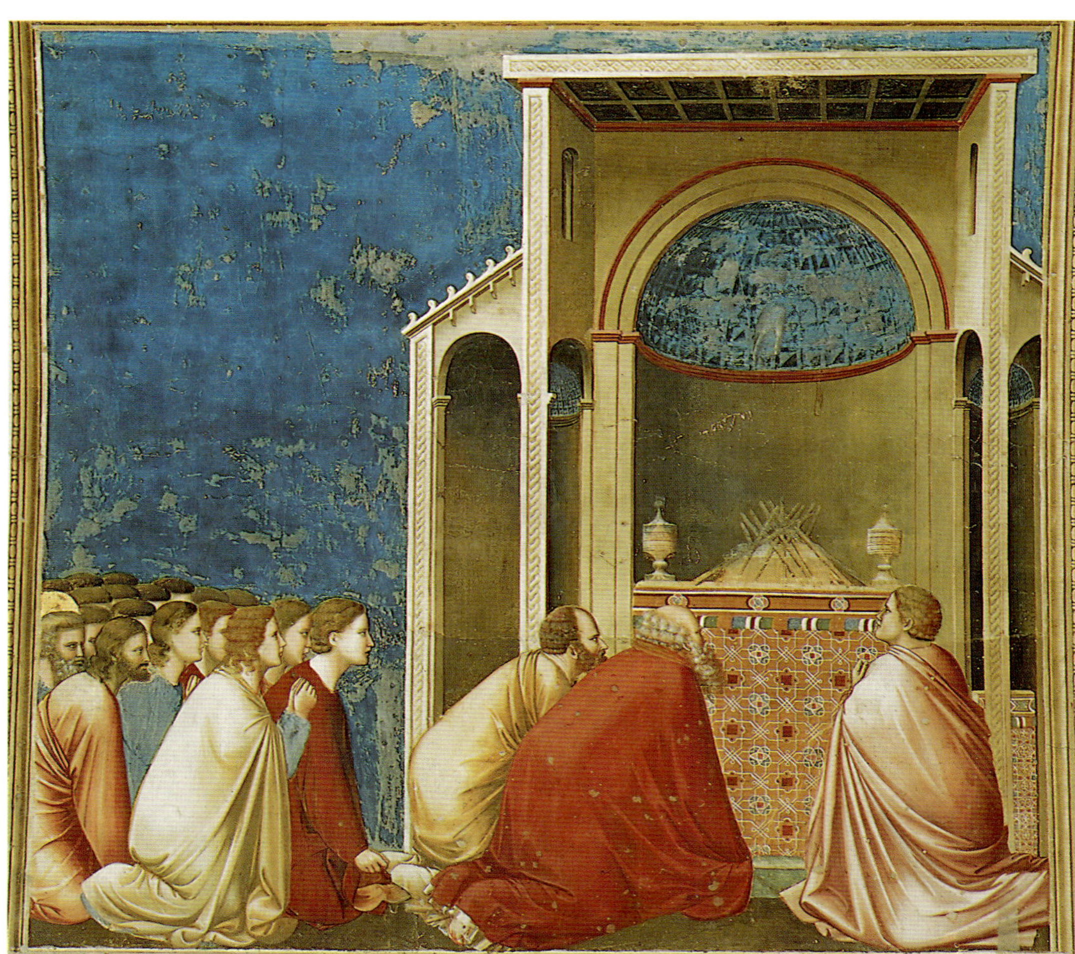

72 *The Wooers Praying*, 1302–1305
Fresco, 200 x 185 cm
Cappella degli Scrovegni, Padua

The men and the high priest kneel before the altar in rapt
attention. They are praying for the miracle, which will
decide who will marry the Virgin Mary. In front of the
cupola of the apse of the church we can make out –
somewhat indistinctly – the Hand of God, pointing: one
of the rods will blossom.

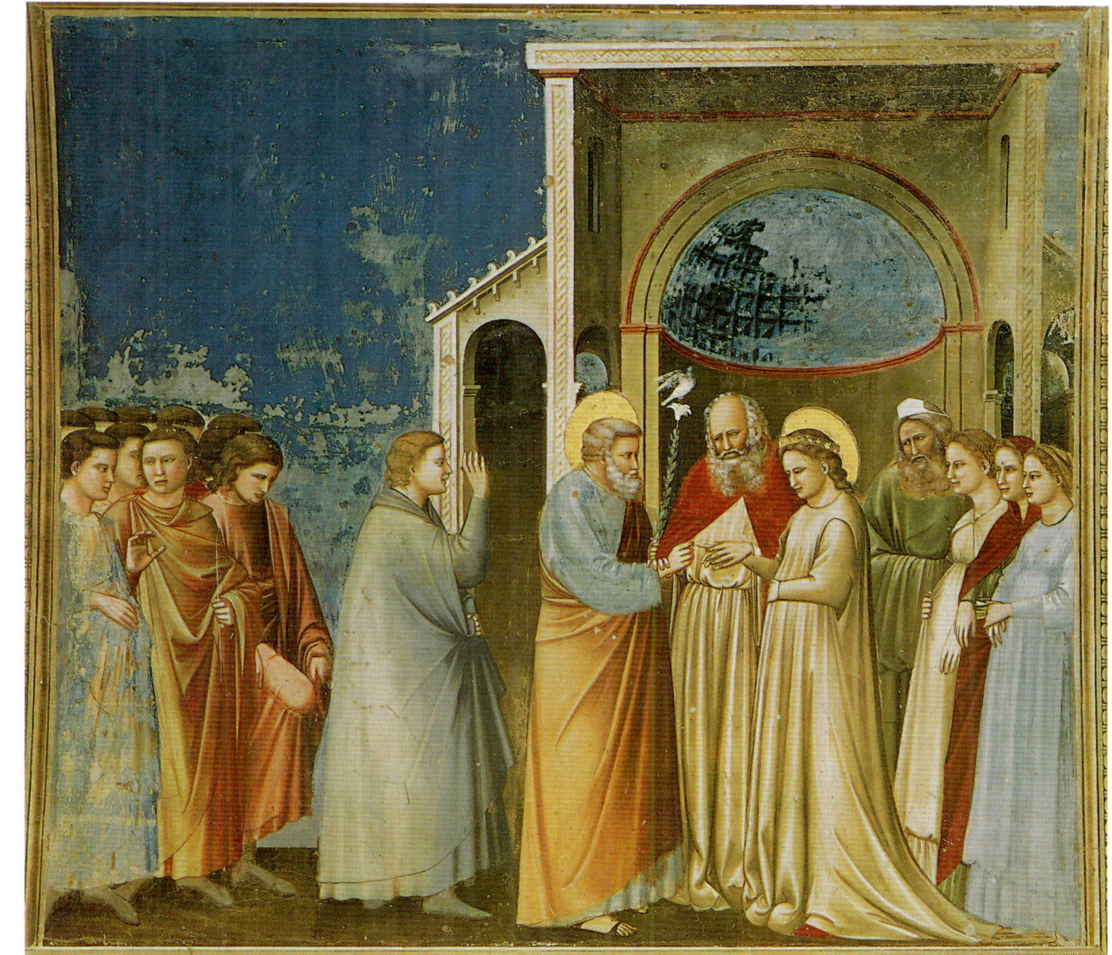

73 *Marriage of the Virgin*, 1302–1305
Fresco, 200 x 185 cm
Cappella degli Scrovegni, Padua

After these two preparatory scenes, which are seldom
depicted, the marriage of the Virgin Mary now takes
place in front of the temple, whose architecture is shown
here for the third time. The high priest carefully moves
the Virgin's hand towards Joseph, who would like to place
the ring on her finger. Mary's gaze is lowered. She rests
one hand on her stomach, alluding to her impending
pregnancy.

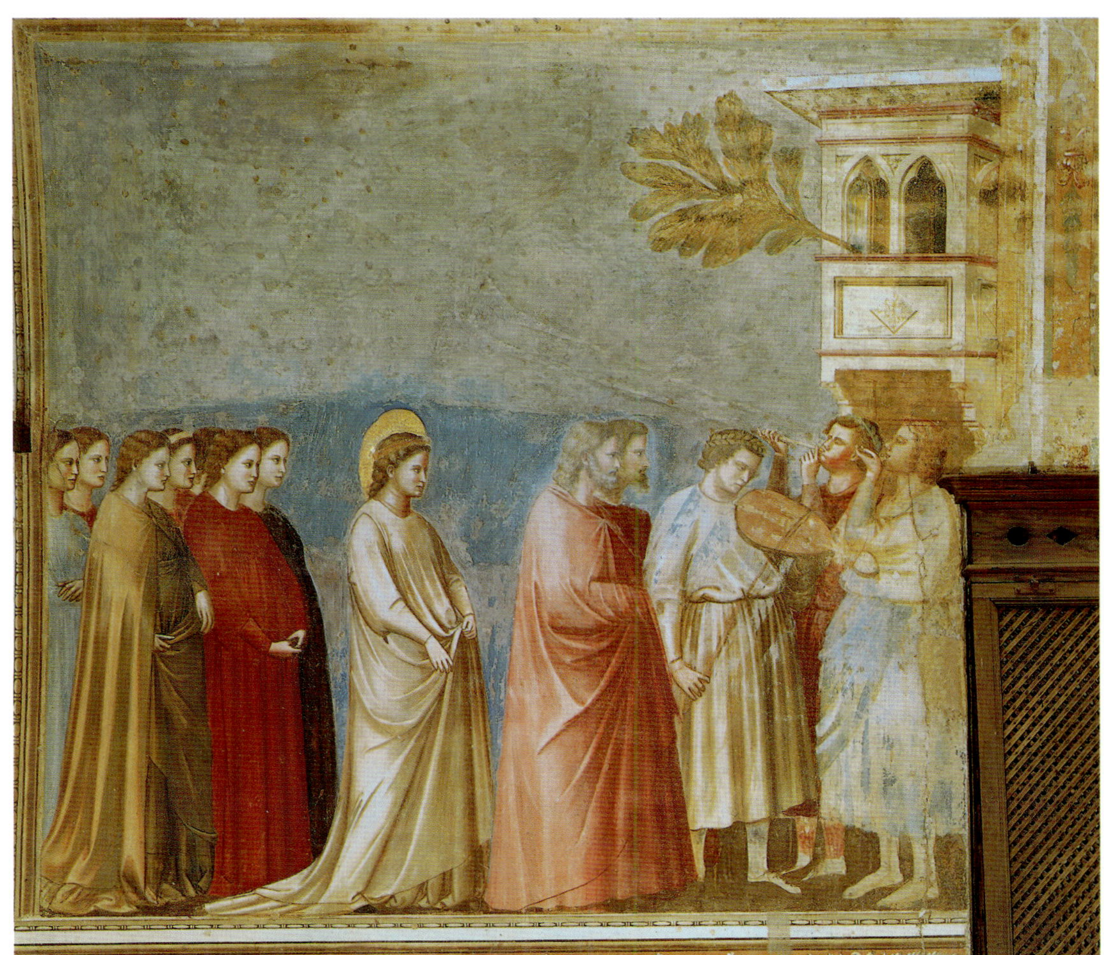

74 *Bridal Procession of the Virgin*, 1302–1305
Fresco, 200 x 185 cm
Cappella degli Scrovegni, Padua

Mary walks in front of her companions and is led to the
house of her parents, where she is received by musicians.
This group alone lends a cheery air to the sombre
procession. The bay window of the house, from which a
palm leaf juts out as an allusion to the imminent birth of
the Lord, appears again in the representation of the
Annunciation. In this way Giotto incorporates the *Bridal
Procession of the Virgin* into the sequence of the narrative.

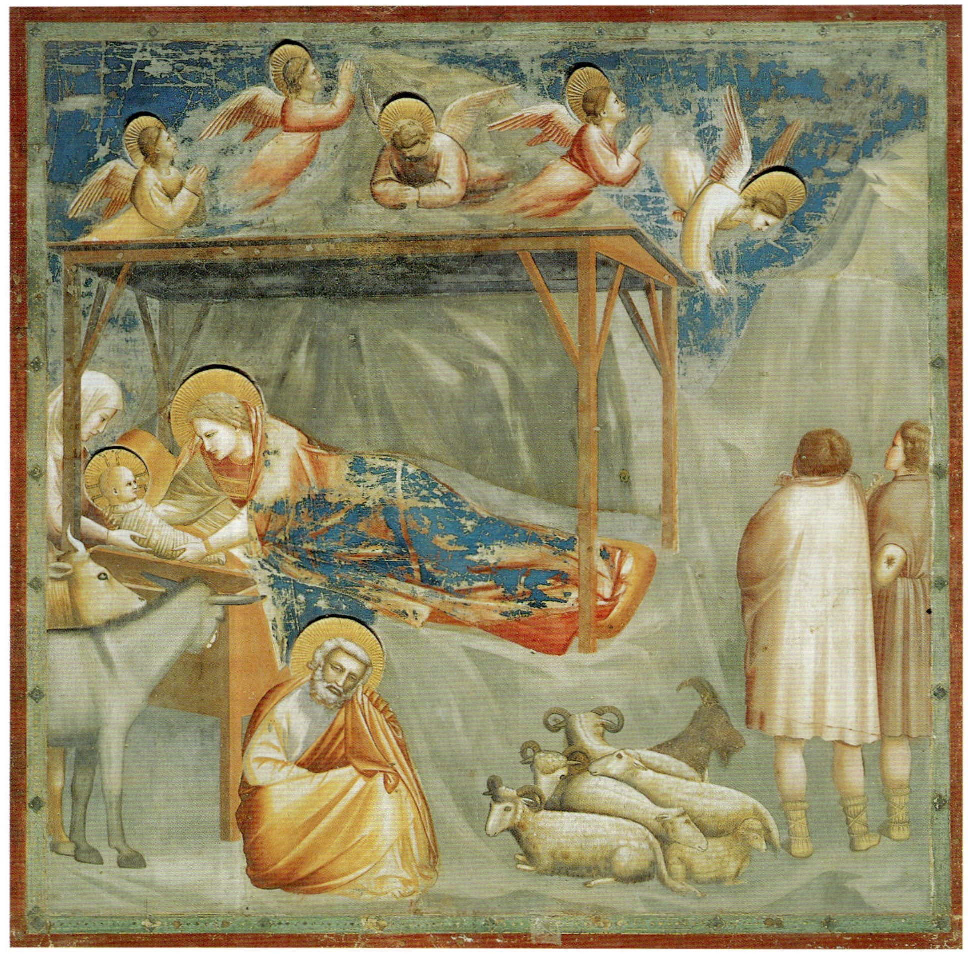

75, 77 (left and opposite) *Nativity*, 1302–1305
Fresco, 200 x 185 cm
Cappella degli Scrovegni, Padua

The simple shelter under which the Virgin and her Child
seek refuge is situated in the middle of a bleak rocky
landscape. Mary turns on her side on the bed in order
to receive the new-born baby from the arms of a midwife
– a natural and spontaneous gesture, which is captured
by the way mother and child look at one another.
Although on the periphery, this exchange of glances
seems to be the actual center of the portrayal, which is
expanded to include the scene of the Annunciation to the
shepherds.

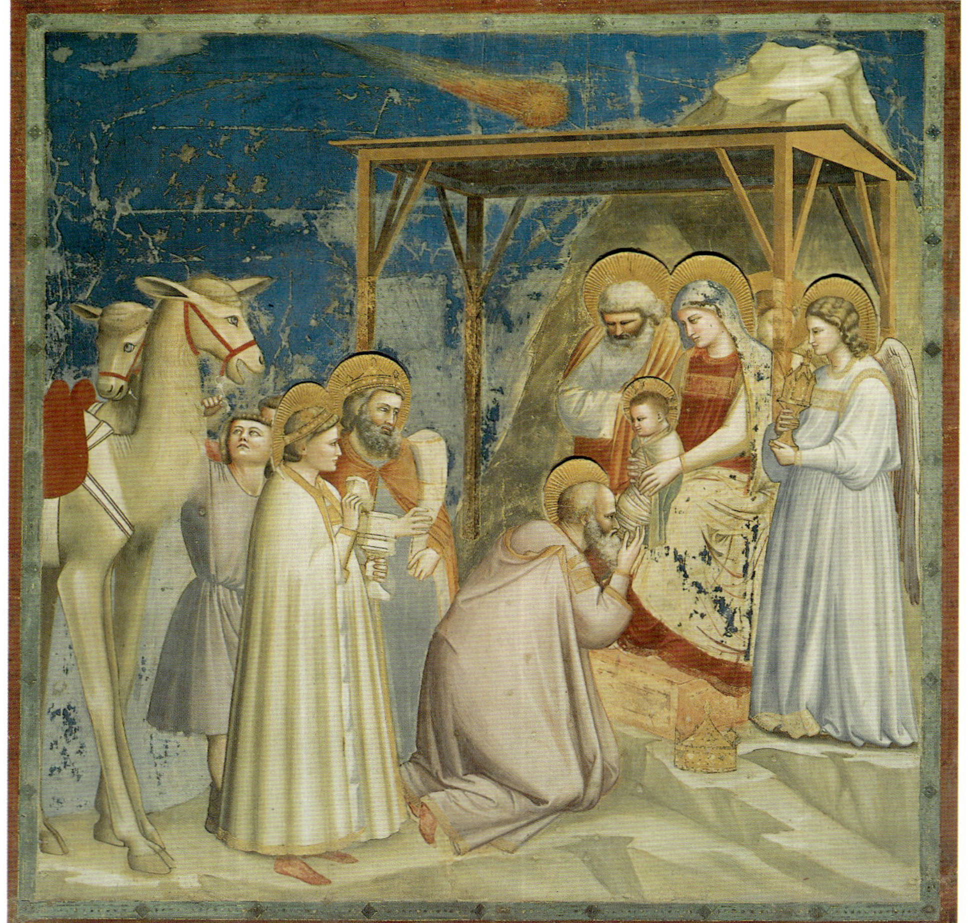

76 *Adoration of the Magi*, 1302–1305
Fresco, 200 x 185 cm
Cappella degli Scrovegni, Padua

With camels and gifts the three kings have followed the
comet along the narrow rocky path to the stable at
Bethlehem. On the fresco, this stable really does seem
to be the end of the road. The oldest king has taken off
his crown, and kneels before the baby Jesus. All present
watch what is happening quietly and reverently. Only
one vividly depicted secondary figure, the camel driver,
prefers to attend to his animals. Giotto uses this contrast
to increase the effect of the main scene.

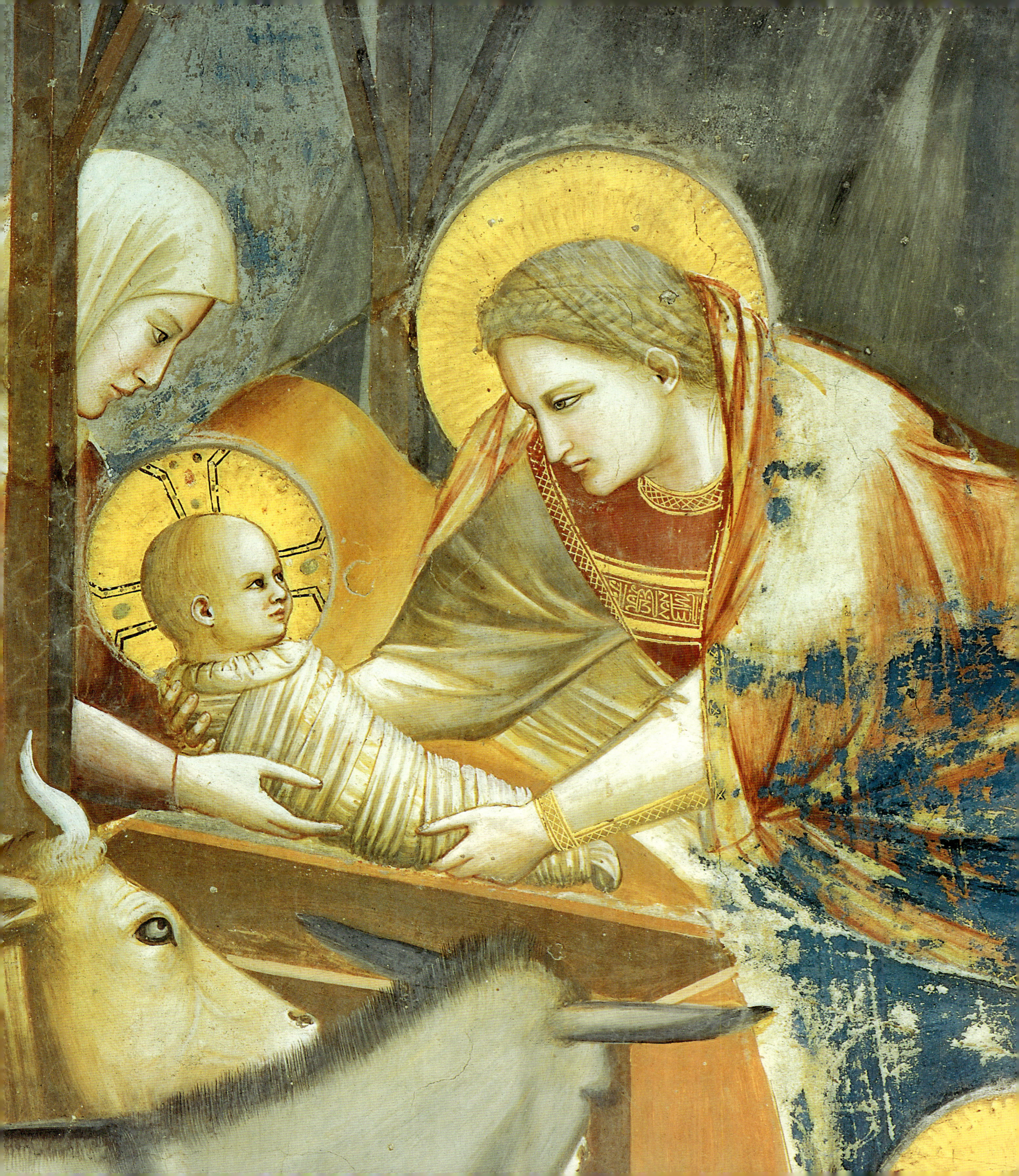

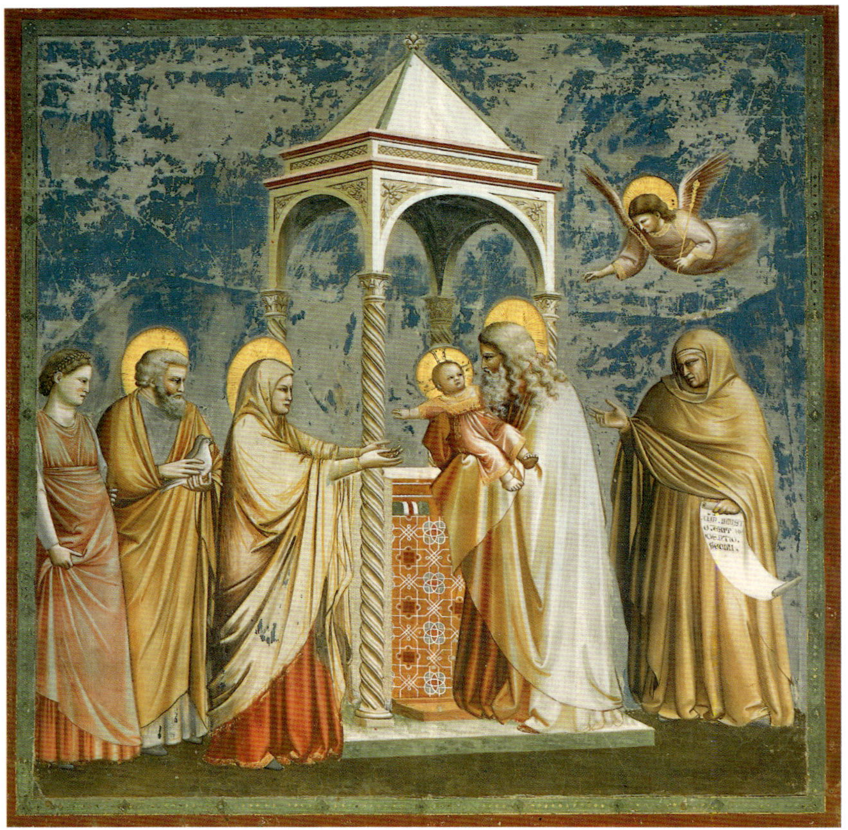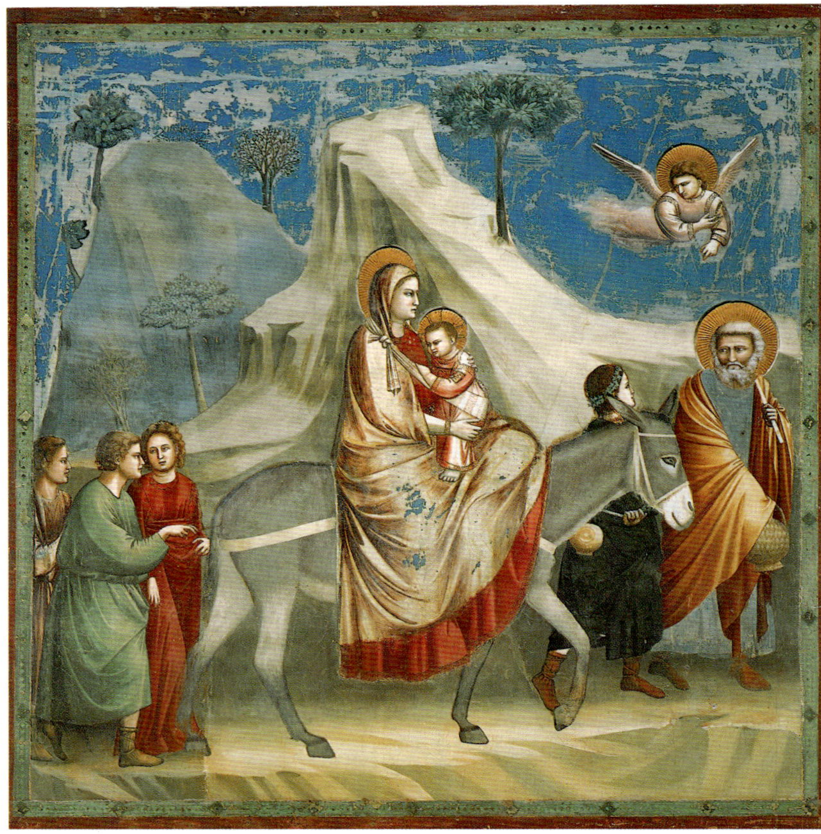

78 (above left) *Presentation of Christ at the Temple*,
1302–1305
Fresco, 200 x 185 cm
Cappella degli Scrovegni, Padua

The baby Jesus wriggles in the arms of a priest, at whom
he is looking, and reaches out for his mother, who
approaches with open arms. These three figures are
supported by the architecture behind them, and thus
solemnly united as a group.

79 (above right) *Flight into Egypt*, 1302–1305
Fresco, 200 x 185 cm
Cappella degli Scrovegni, Padua

On a narrow rocky path, the procession seems to move
past the viewer. Equipped with everyday objects,
everyone is in motion, looking at one another and talking
to one another – only the Virgin Mary sits still and
unmoving. The statuesque nature of her upright position
is further reinforced by the rock behind. Although the
child is as natural as can be, the central figures in the
picture thus stand out from their surroundings and have
a sublime effect.

paintings nevertheless appears as a unified whole,
showing the hand of the master and bearing the stamp
of his talent for invention.

The individual scenes are composed in such a way
that each stands as a picture in its own right, and yet
each contains an impetus which passes from story to
story in succession. Thus the narrative begins at the top
left-hand of the south wall with the *Rejection of
Joachim's Sacrifice* (ill. 64), which occurred because of
his childlessness. Here we are dealing with a true
opening picture: the closed architecture of the temple
introduces the first idea of solidity, while Joachim's dual
movement brings this scene to a close, on the one hand,
and on the other paves the way for the rest of the series,
which finds a premature conclusion in the last picture
of this register, the *Meeting at the Golden Gate* (ill. 69).

The action is also driven forward by the repetition of
buildings. Thus the temple of the opening picture
reappears in the fresco *Presentation of Christ at the
Temple* (ill. 78), and the *Annunciation to Anne* and the
Birth of the Virgin Mary take place in the same
architectural structures (ills. 66, 70). The protruding
bay window, towards which the *Bridal Procession of the
Virgin* progresses in a very lyrical atmosphere, is also a
feature of Mary's residence in the next picture (ills. 48,
74). The three preceding pictures, which deal with the
subject of Mary's marriage (ills. 71–73) take place in
similar architectural structures, as do the *Last Supper*
and the *Washing of the Feet* (ill. 86). However, the
repetition of spatial situations conveys more than the
progressive flow of the narrative, it also indicates the
respective scene of the action in a particular way. The

clearly defined locations make the events appear very
natural. And, to a greater extent than in the Legend of
St. Francis, the precise siting lends the action an
immediate and intelligible dramatic presence.

This presence is carried by the actors, by the
differentiations in the depiction of their encounters and
of the way they express their feelings. Thus, his offering
having been rejected, Joachim returns to the shepherds
(ill. 65). Wrapped up in shame and sorrow, he neither
perceives the joyful greetings of the dog or the
innocently natural sheep, nor the knowing looks of the
two shepherds. Could the feelings of rejection of the old
man be portrayed any more vividly?

Having made an open-air sacrifice (ill. 67), an angel
announces to Joachim in a dream that he will become
a father (ill. 68). Now, Giotto portrays him as being
completely at one with his surroundings. Joachim
sleeps in front of the sheltering hut and the animals lie
around or graze in undisturbed peace. Even the
shepherds, who are not bareheaded here as in the first
encounter, and who do not look at one another, radiate
an air of contemplation and calmness. They give the
impression they are watching over the solemn moment
of the Annunciation.

Two pictures earlier, Anne had been informed, also
by an angel, of the happy event of her pregnancy (ill.
66). The *Annunciation to Anne* takes place in a house.
As in the Isaac frescoes in the Upper Church at Assisi
(ills. 12, 13), Giotto here shows a room, which we see
both from without and within. The angel appears in the
narrow window opening and turns to the kneeling
Anne.

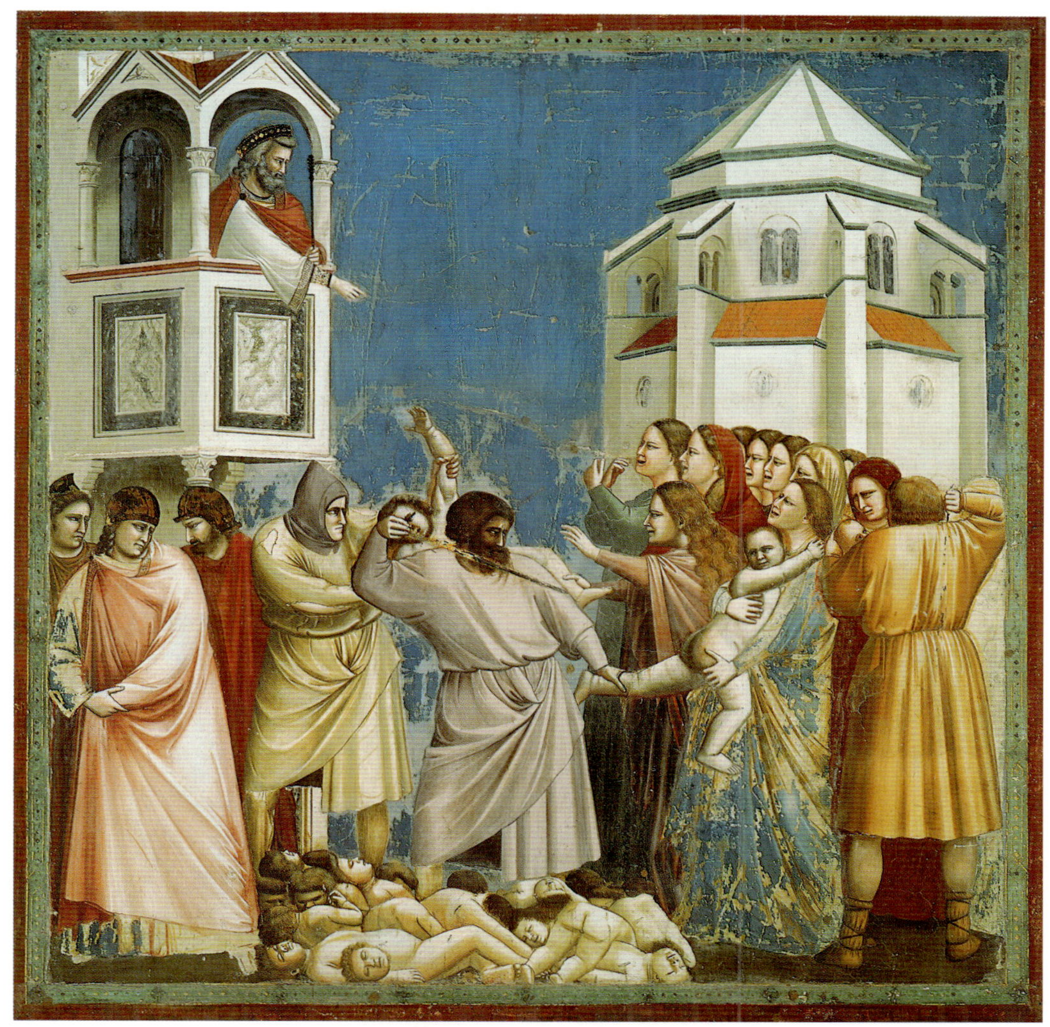

80 *The Massacre of the Innocents*, 1302–1305
Fresco, 200 x 185 cm
Cappella degli Scrovegni, Padua

A great number of slaughtered children lie on the ground.
A soldier stands over the corpses and, at the command of
King Herod (who appears in the painting himself),
snatches a baby boy from his mother. The women
scream, weep and try to protect their children. The men
on the other side turn away, crushed and ashamed.

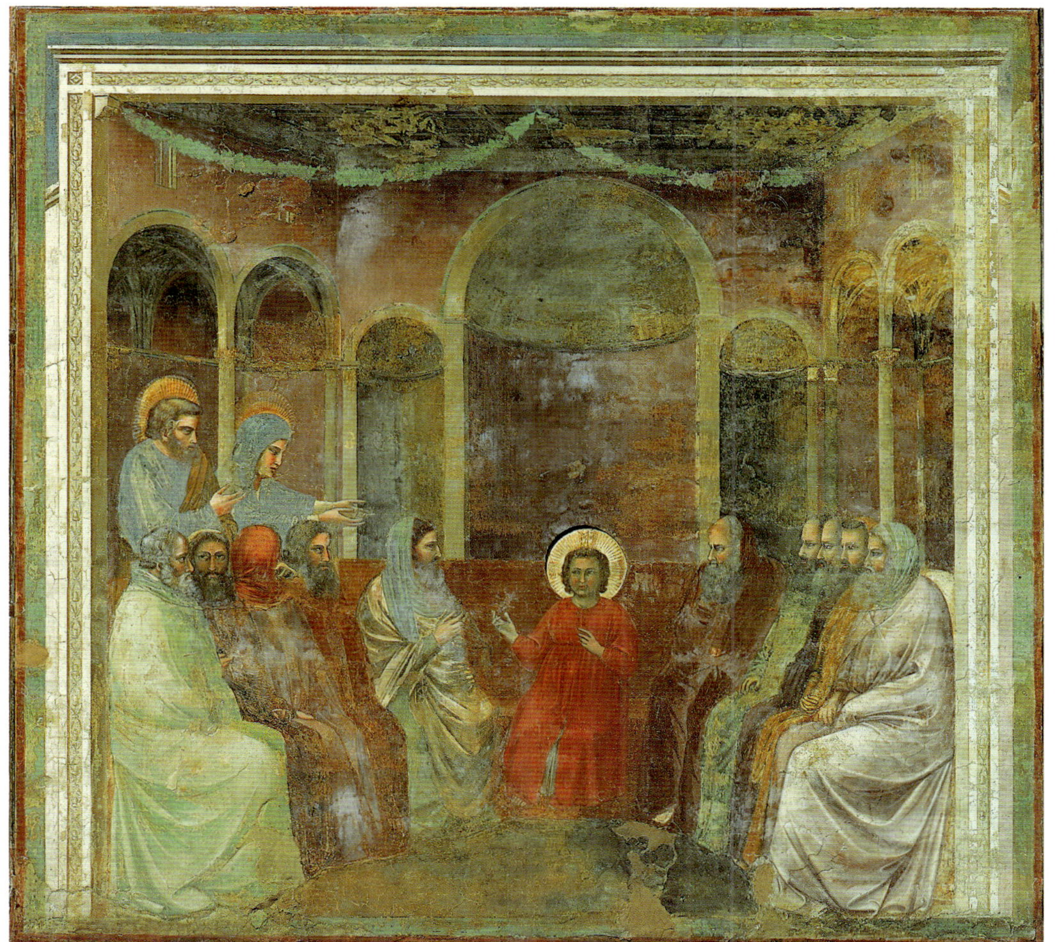

81 *Teaching in the Temple*, 1302–1305
Fresco, 200 x 185 cm
Cappella degli Scrovegni, Padua

In a rich red robe, the little twelve-year-old Jesus sits in
the temple and holds a discussion – as his gesture quite
clearly indicates. The arches of the architecture seem to
echo the young boy's speech and at the same time to
concentrate events on him. The scribes listen closely and
in doing so show quite different reactions. Only one of
them is completely distracted by the appearance of the
worried parents.

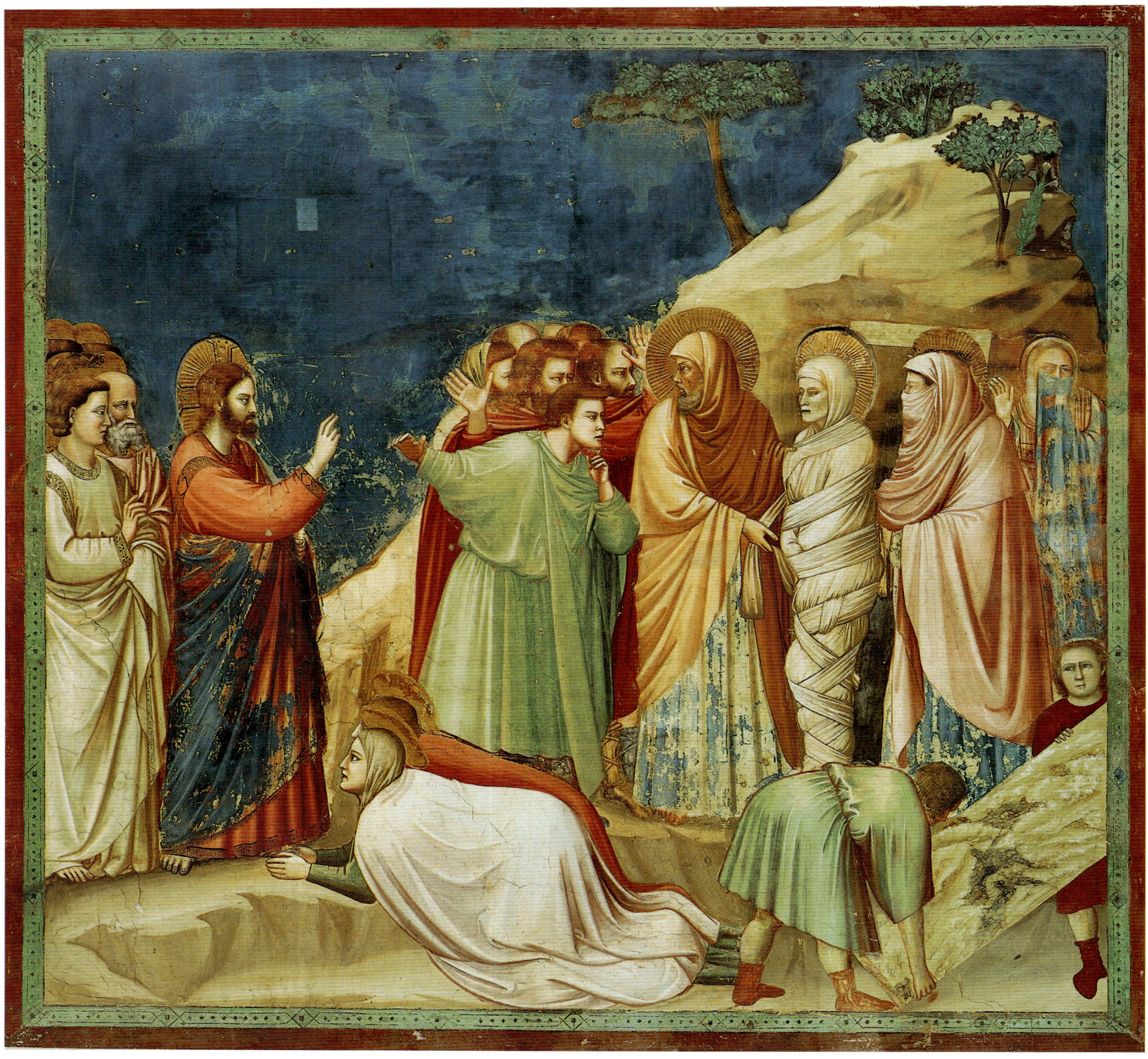

The two elderly spouses recognize one another and their good fortune in their *Meeting at the Golden Gate* (ill. 69). It is the final picture of the upper register and, at the same time, an allusion to an event which is yet to come: the *Birth of the Virgin Mary* (ill. 70). The maid, who in the *Annunciation to Anne* sat with the spindle below the balcony, here leans inquisitively towards the main event and holds Anne's cloak. In the next fresco, this very same companion will appear anew under the balcony of the house, fetching a vessel.

In the last fresco of the upper register the composition is concentrated on the encounter between Joachim and Anne: Joachim is accompanied by a shepherd, who is partly cut off in the fresco. On the one hand, Giotto uses this completely new device in painting to create the impression that the succession of pictures, intersected by the framework, would unfold before our eyes in one continuous procession. On the other hand, a figure cut short in such a manner increases the dynamics within the picture field and makes us focus on the action at its center.

Even the verticals of the architecture and the golden

82, 83 *Raising of Lazarus* (and detail), 1302–1305
Fresco, 200 x 185 cm
Cappella degli Scrovegni, Padua

This scene is composed with the heightened effect of the gaze and gesture of Christ in mind. The rhythm of the individual gestures and the reactions of those present clearly show the energy which emanates from Christ, which startles the onlookers and wakes Lazarus from the dead. This energy carries on like an arrested wave into the narrative details: the arrangement of the folds in Lazarus' winding sheet or in the hitched up cloak of the disciple next to him are touched by it, as are the precisely characterized faces.

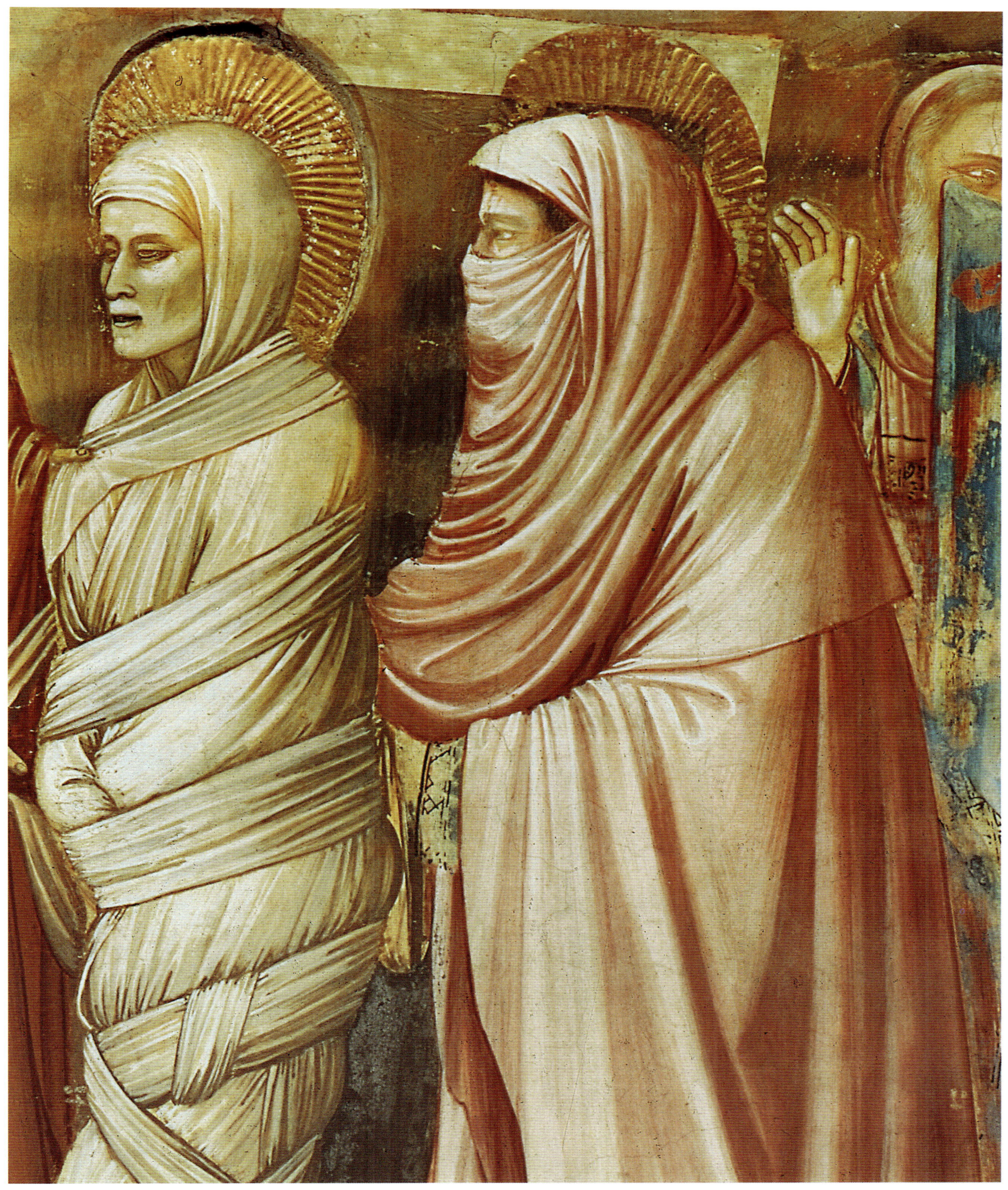

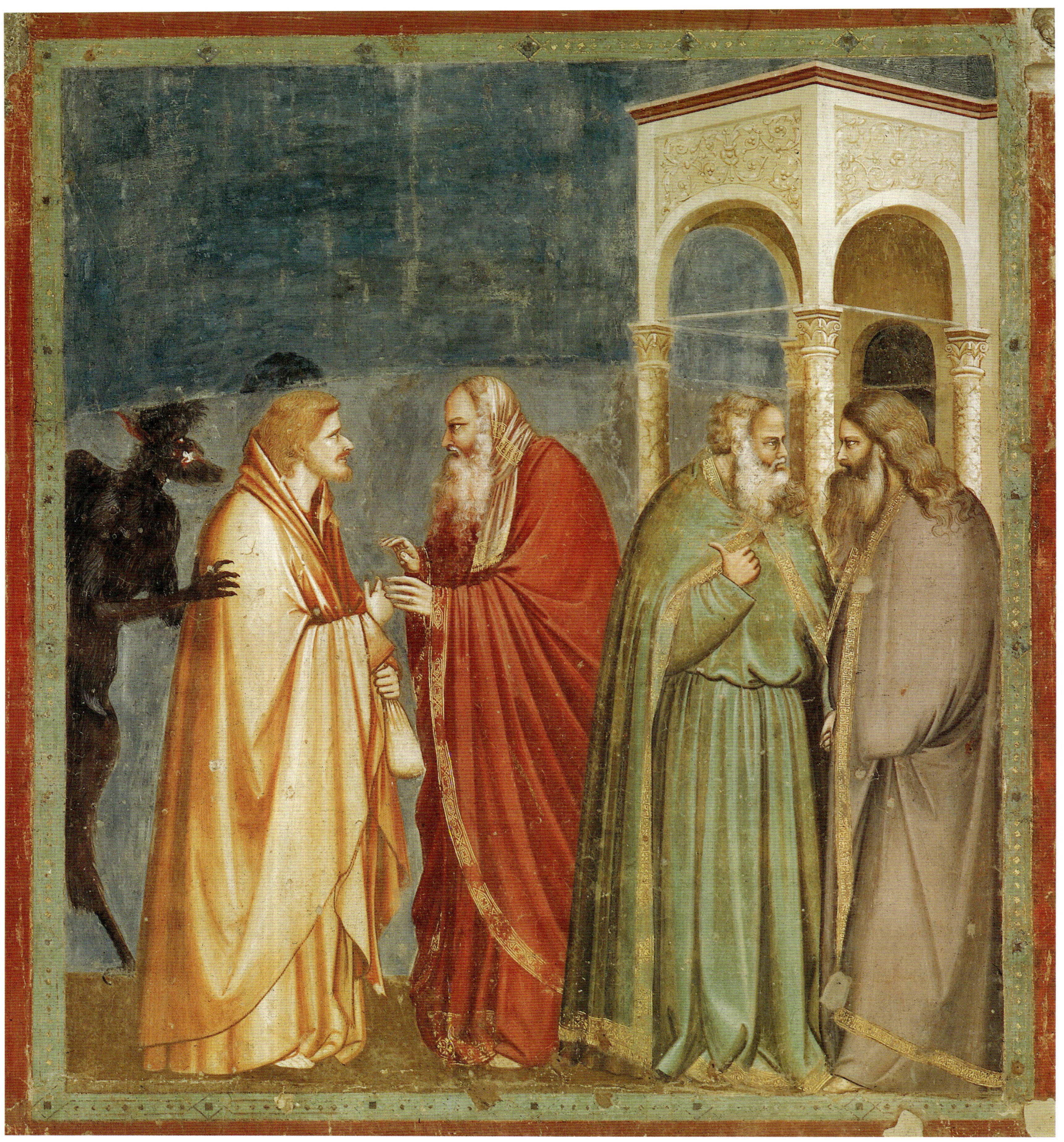

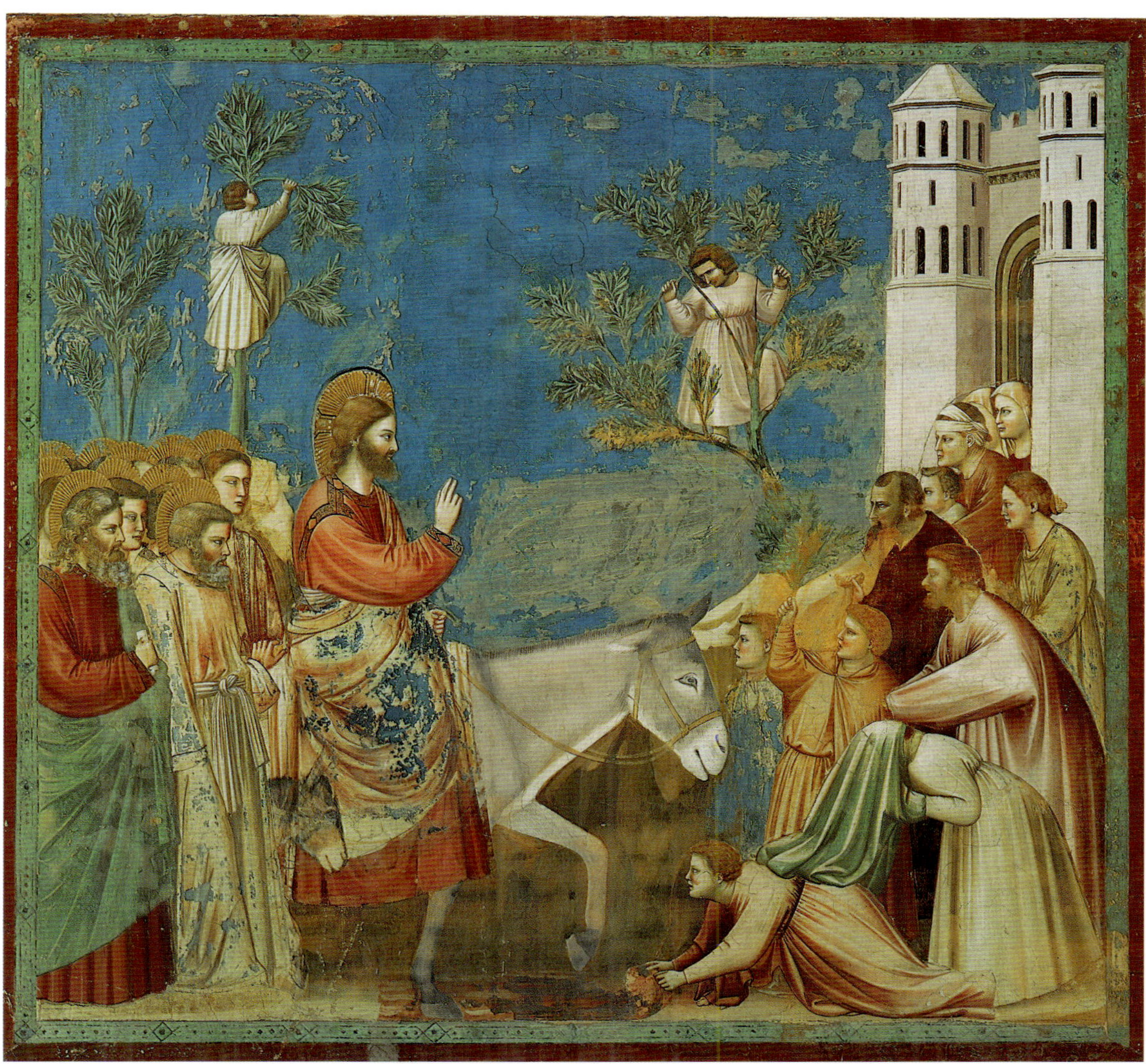

85 (right) *Entry into Jerusalem*, 1302–1305
Fresco, 200 x 185 cm
Cappella degli Scrovegni, Padua

84 (opposite) *Judas' Betrayal*, 1302–1305
Fresco, 200 x 185 cm
Cappella degli Scrovegni, Padua

This scene, very seldom depicted, is displayed on the triumphal arch wall. The scribes, who were whispering in the preceding scene, *The Driving of the Traders from the Temple* (ill. 96), persuade Judas to betray his master. Judas, with the Devil at his back and holding a sack of gold, exchanges a knowing glance with the Pharisee.

85 (right) *Entry into Jerusalem*, 1302–1305
Fresco, 200 x 185 cm
Cappella degli Scrovegni, Padua

Accompanied by his disciples, Christ enters Jerusalem mounted on an ass. The people come to meet him in front of the city gate – we can recognize the Golden Gate on the right of the painting. To honor their Lord, some of them spread their clothes out on the ground. Giotto plainly demonstrates how events are progressing through the various stages of disrobing on the one side, and the movement of the donkey on the other. Movement and counter-movement give us the origin and the end of the procession.

arch of the city gate respectively illustrate and mirror the way the couple lean towards one another. The two meet on a bridge, on the border between the outside world and the security of the city. They embrace with great tenderness and kiss one another. The way in which the volumes of the figures fuse underlines the tenderness of the moment, in which the faces also melt, as it were, into one another (ill. 1).

The story of Mary's parents begins with a painful rejection and concludes with this intense encounter. The sensitive portrayal of their meeting already contains the germ for the start of the next narrative, which commences with the *Birth of the Virgin Mary* (ill. 70) and which leads to the youth of Christ (ills. 75 – 85) by way of the *Bridal Procession of the Virgin* (ill. 74).

The same intensity and sensitivity with which Giotto was able to portray a moment of loving consent and of God-given knowledge is also used to depict tense confrontation, as in the fresco *The Arrest of Christ*, in which Judas' kiss signifies betrayal rather than affection (ill. 87). Judas embraces his Lord and each looks the other in the eye. It is precisely in this gaze that the greatest tension lies, since it contains an absolutely clear signal of what will follow (ill. 88). At the same time, a

moment of almost supernatural calm arises here in the midst of the excited tumult – time seems to have stopped for the duration of this gaze. The overall composition is aimed at accentuating this motif: heads in profile, gestures, the turning and twisting motions of the figures in the painting are all aligned towards this place of rest.

This dramatic, tension-filled scene is situated directly below the *Presentation of Christ at the Temple* (ill. 78). This ordering demonstrates that the path that Christ must follow can be revealed not only across a register, but also in the connections from top to bottom. For both events represent a turning point in the story: the *Presentation of Christ at the Temple* is preceded by the frescoes depicting the happy events of the *Nativity* and *The Adoration of the Magi* (ills. 75, 76). The *Flight into Egypt* and the *Massacre of the Innocents* follow (ills. 79, 80). The peaceful scene of the *Washing of the Feet* (ill. 86) prepares the way for the *Arrest of Christ* (ill. 87), while the more violent scenes showing *Christ before Caiaphas* and the *Mocking of Christ* come after it (ills. 89, 90).

Following the confrontation with Judas, Christ's facial expression changes. His countenance appears

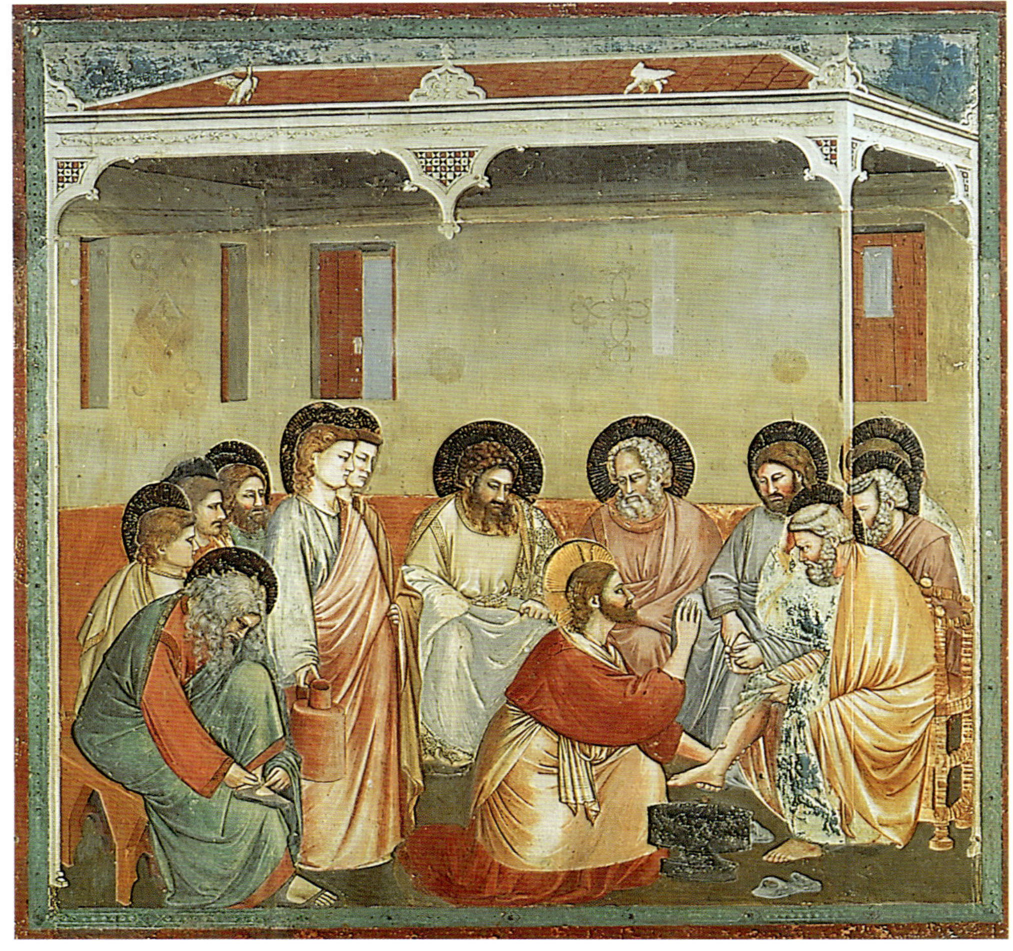

86 *The Washing of the Feet*, 1302–1305
Fresco, 200 x 185 cm
Cappella degli Scrovegni, Padua

The washing of the feet takes place in an open room.
This event is portrayed in a most lifelike manner: one
disciple is busy putting his sandals back on, another is
scratching his foot, and Peter is gathering up his robe to
prevent it getting wet. In spite of the many narrative
touches, Giotto still concentrates his depiction on the
exchange between Christ and Peter. The latter puts his
hand to his head, obviously unable to believe what his
Lord is telling him.

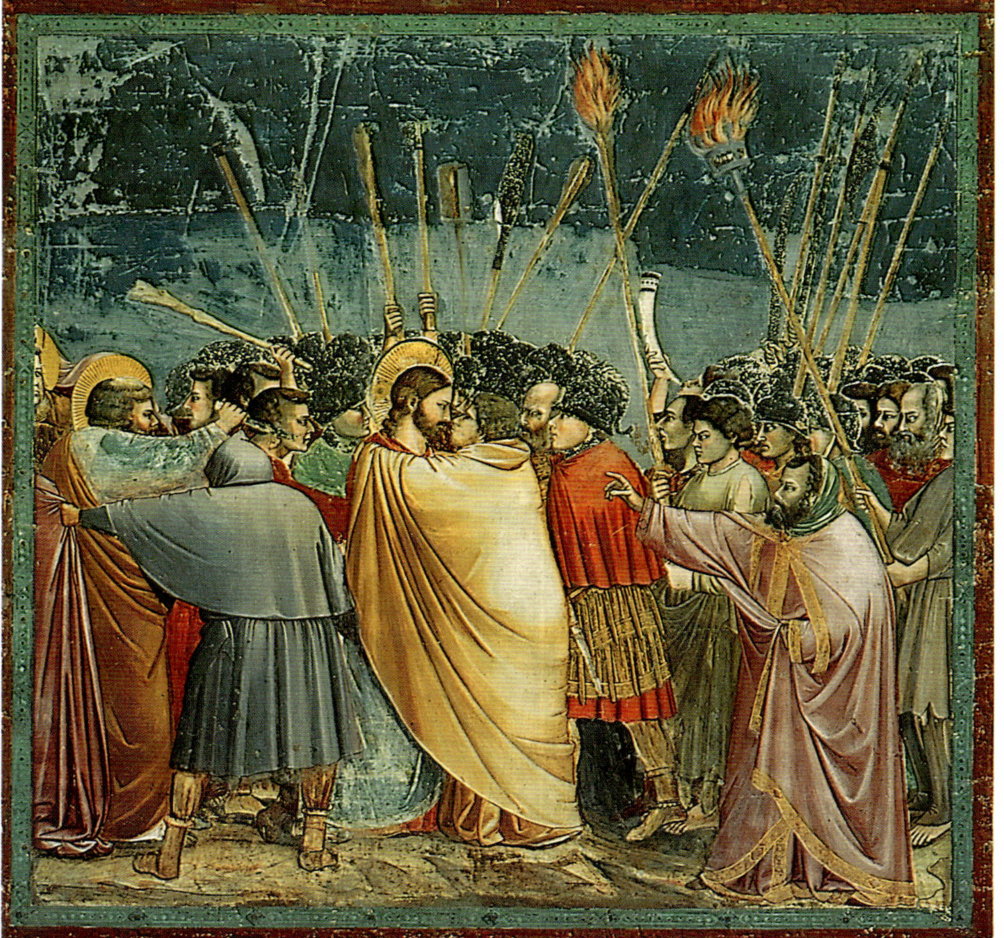

87 *The Arrest of Christ*, 1302–1305
Fresco, 200 x 185 cm
Cappella degli Scrovegni, Padua

This dramatic scene takes place at night. Torches shine
out among the sticks and halberds against the blue of the
sky. The throngs of people crowd into the center, towards
Christ, who is betrayed by Judas' kiss. Every movement,
even that of Peter as he cuts off the ear of an attacker, and
every gaze heightens the tension of the central
confrontation.

88 (opposite) *The Arrest of Christ* (detail ill. 87),
1302–1305

With the force of his body Judas presses against Christ,
who appears to disappear beneath the traitor's cloak. This
expresses the inevitable outcome of this overwhelming
confrontation. Surrounded and hemmed in by numerous
faces, the profiles of Christ and Judas almost collide. The
two look at one another – the one with dignity and
seriousness, the other full of malice. The whole drama of
the event is captured in this infinitely long exchange of
glances.

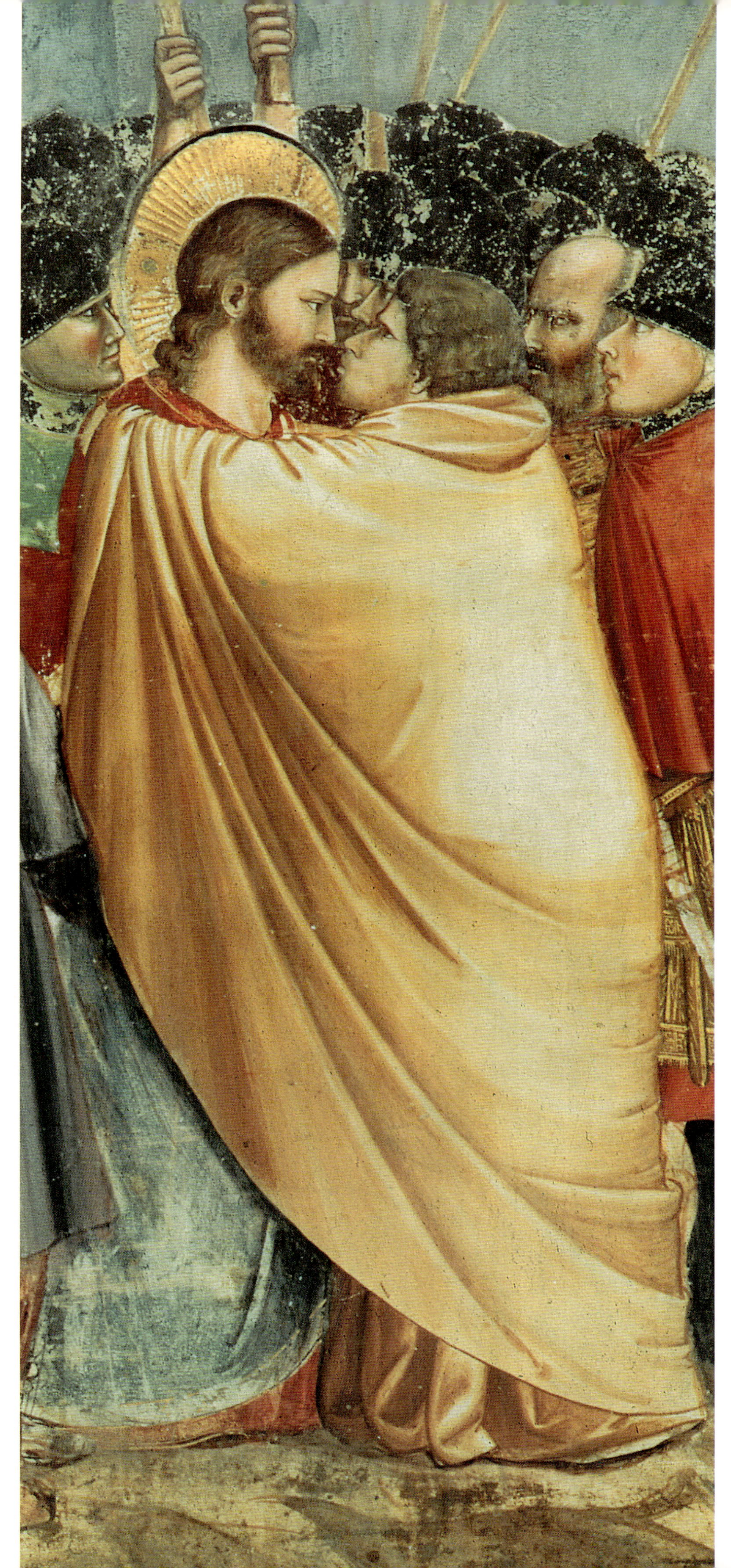

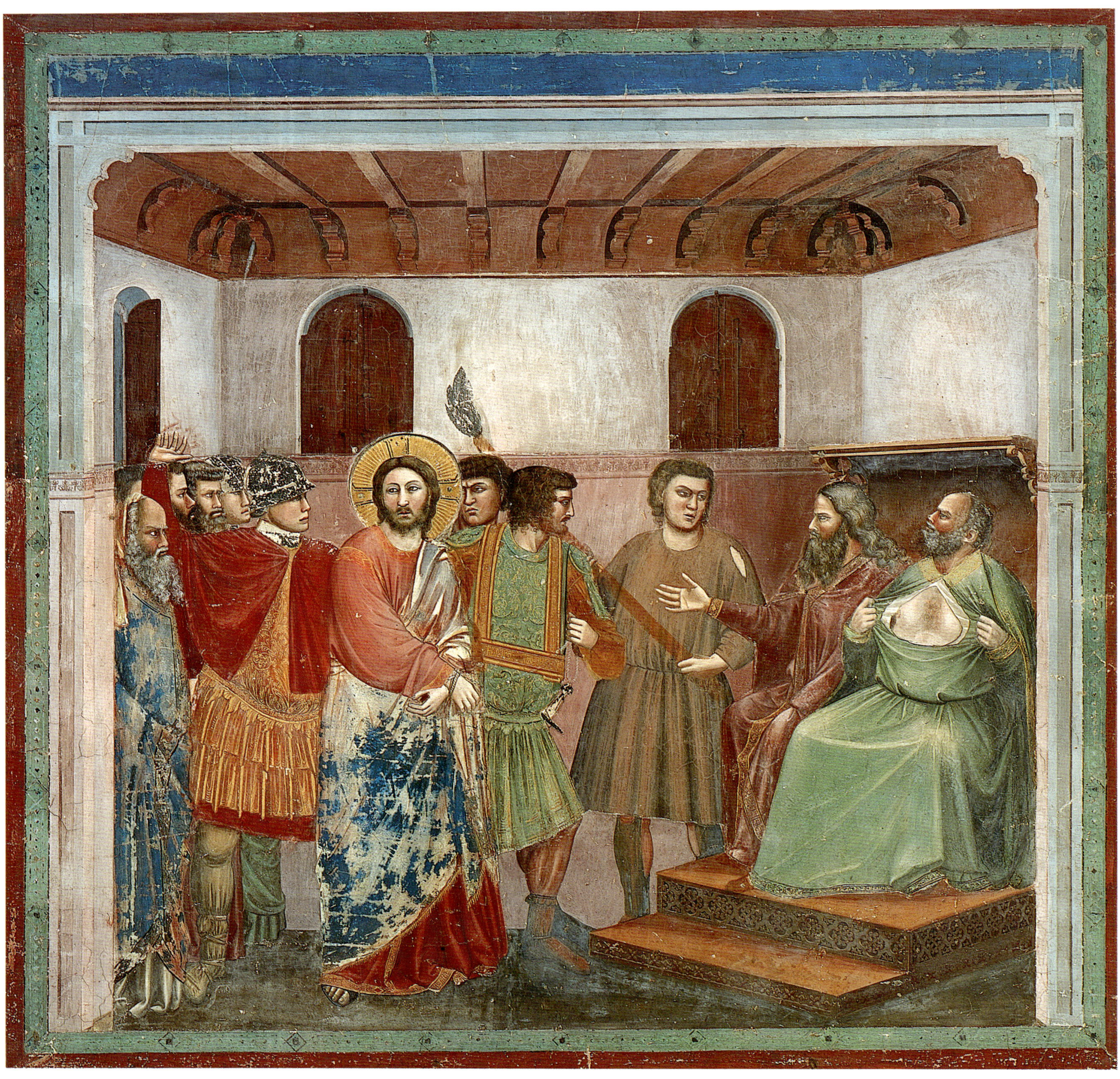

89 *Christ before Caiaphas*, 1302–1305
Fresco, 200 x 185 cm
Cappella degli Scrovegni, Padua

The scene takes place in an enclosed, darkened room.
One torch is lit and only one window is slightly open.
Caiaphas' seat is raised up. He tears his robe in anger,
while the soldiers bring Christ in. In the previous frescoes
Christ appeared in profile or half-profile. Here his face is
shown frontally. In this way Giotto illustrates a change –
Christ seems to have lost all his vigor.

more abstracted – perhaps most visibly in the *Mocking
of Christ* (ill. 90). Christ sits untouchable amidst the
obtrusive soldiers, who are exaggerated in a caricature-
like way. He lets everything happen to him passively,
and shuts his eyes. In a representation so rich in detail
the extent to which the gestures mark the individuality
of the figures becomes clear, as does the fact that
encounters and gazes constitute the main content of the
pictures.

Whether in the embrace of Mary and Elizabeth and
their understanding look in the fresco *The Visitation*
(ill. 63), Christ's gesture of benediction towards the
expectant faces in the *Entry into Jerusalem* (ill. 85), or
the outraged gesture of the Lord, accompanied by the
careful consideration of the disciples and the anxious
flight of the children, in the *Driving of the Traders from
the Temple* (ill. 96), Giotto everywhere displays a rich
palette of human emotions.

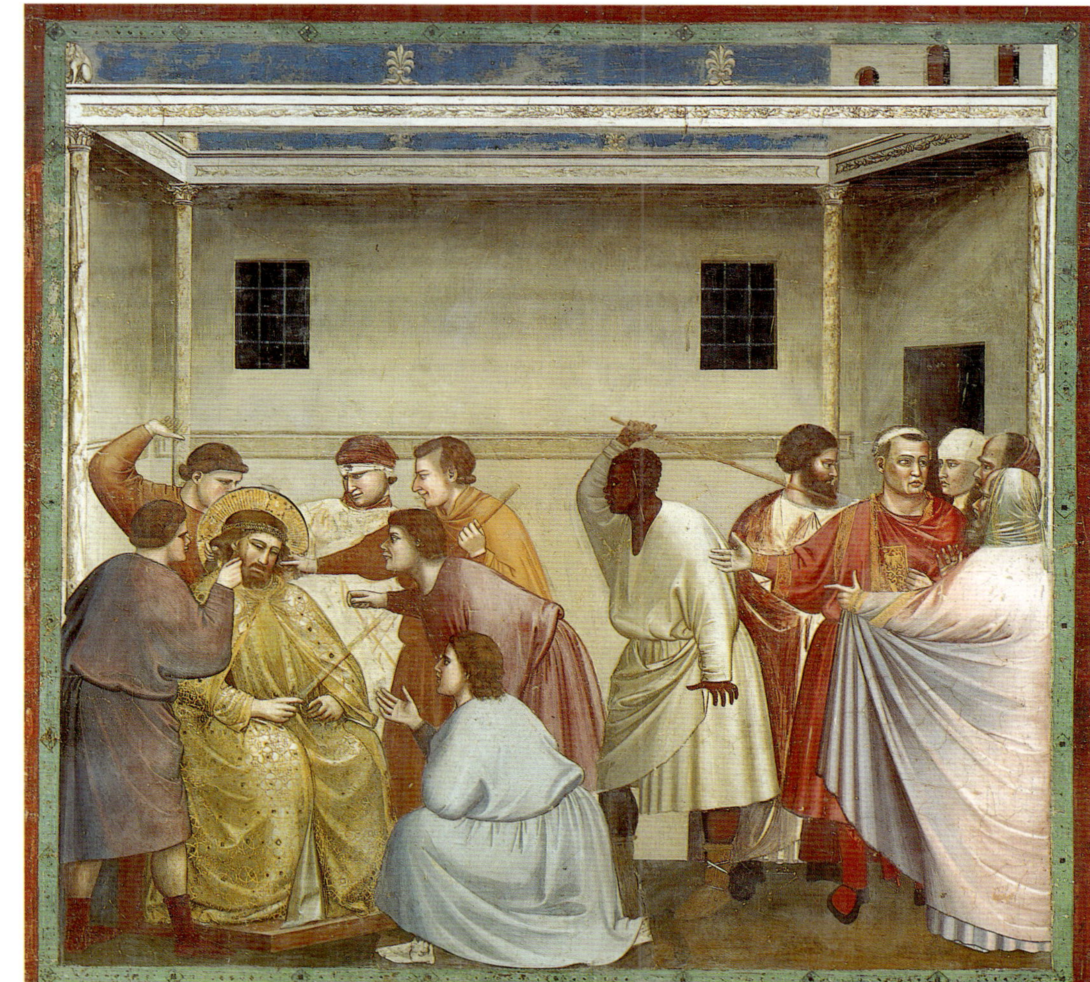

90 *The Mocking of Christ*, 1302–1305
Fresco, 200 x 185 cm
Cappella degli Scrovegni, Padua

The contrast between the caricature-like figures and the introverted Christ, who has had the royal mantle wrapped round him in mockery, could not be greater. Two completely different worlds are depicted in the one picture. As in all the scenes which follow his arrest, Giotto also shows Christ here as a changed character: submissive and lacking all vitality.

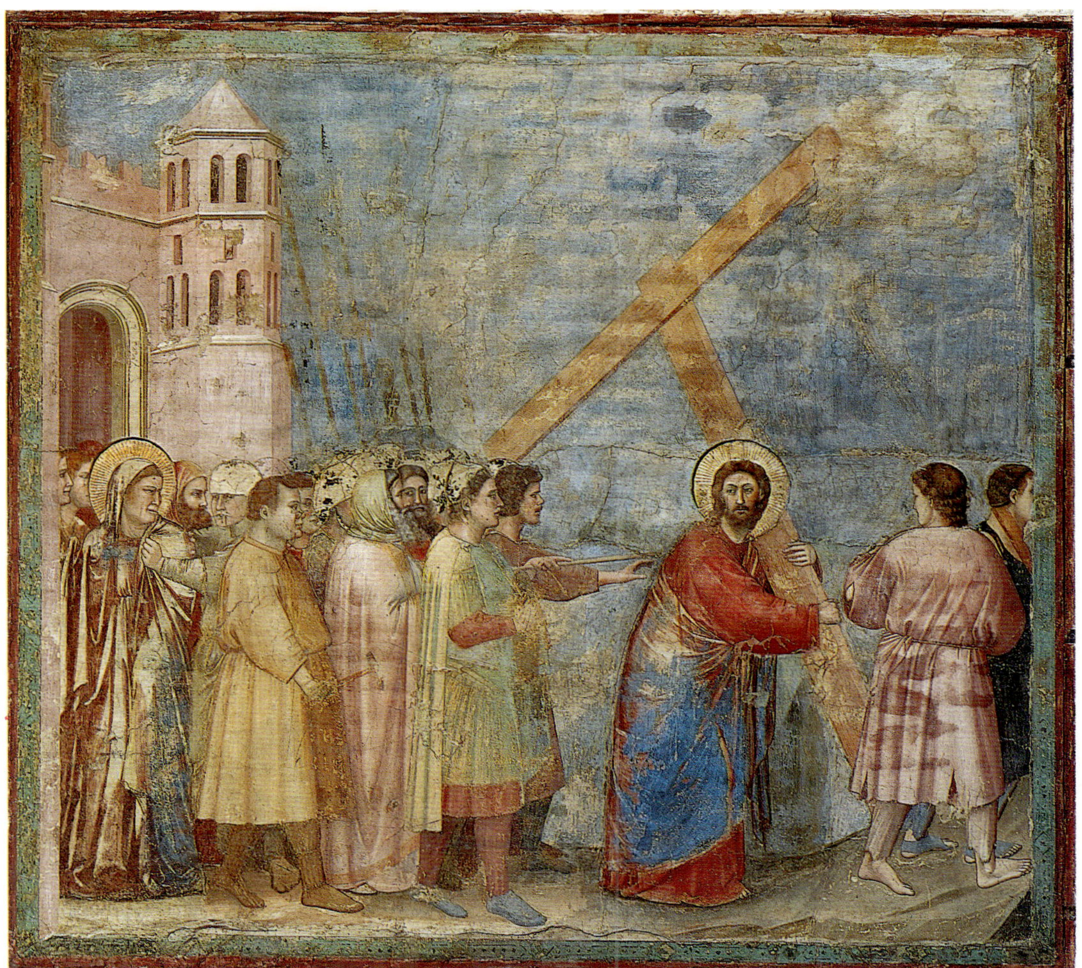

91 *The Carrying of the Cross*, 1302–1305
Fresco, 200 x 185 cm
Cappella degli Scrovegni, Padua

The crowd of people has left Jerusalem en route to the hill of Calvary by the Golden Gate. Some push the unhappy mother back, others drive Christ onward. The latter appears isolated to the right of the center of the painting, thus illustrating the loneliness of his journey. At the same time, Giotto creates the impression of a procession using the two truncated figures on the right edge of the picture.

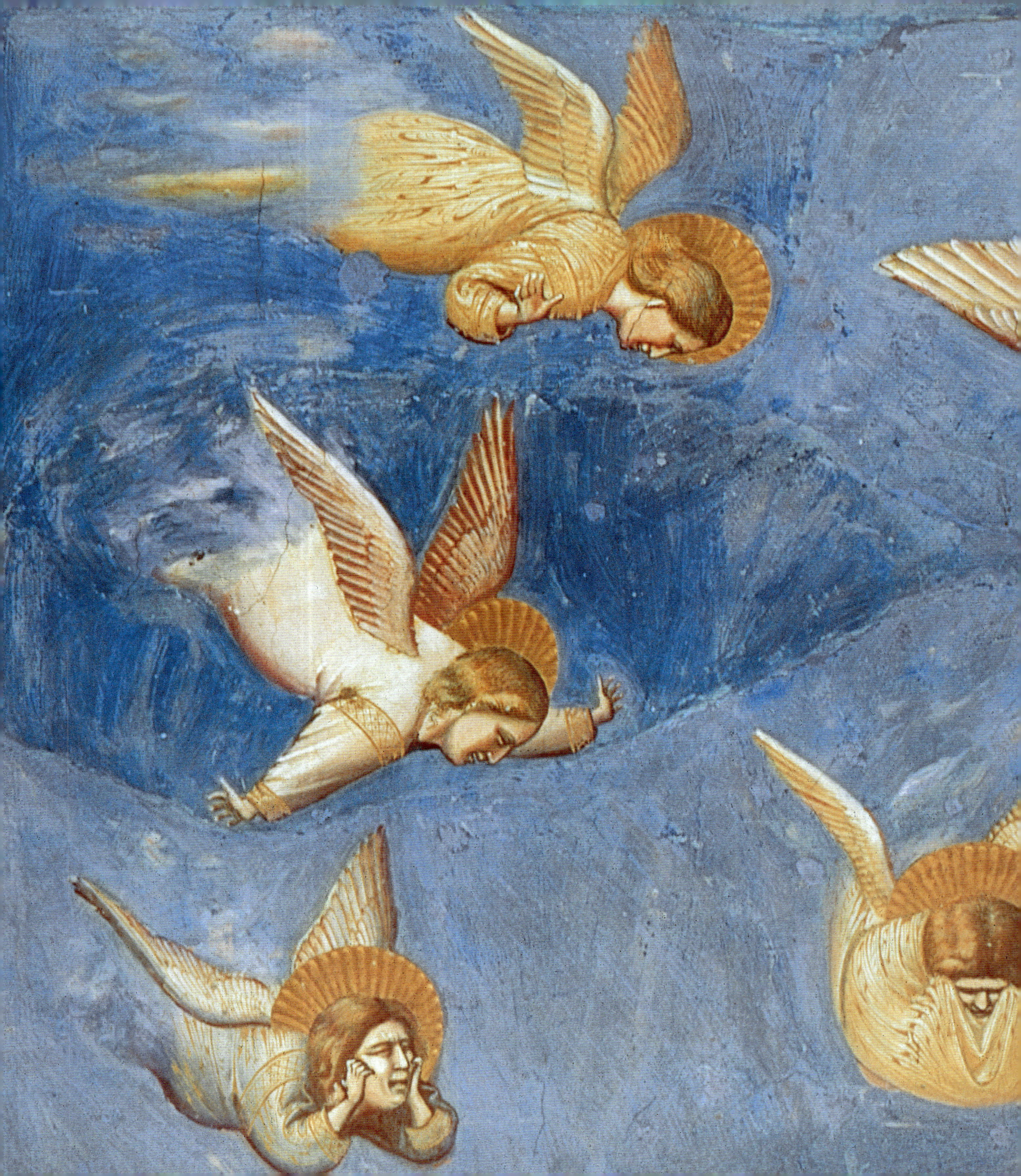

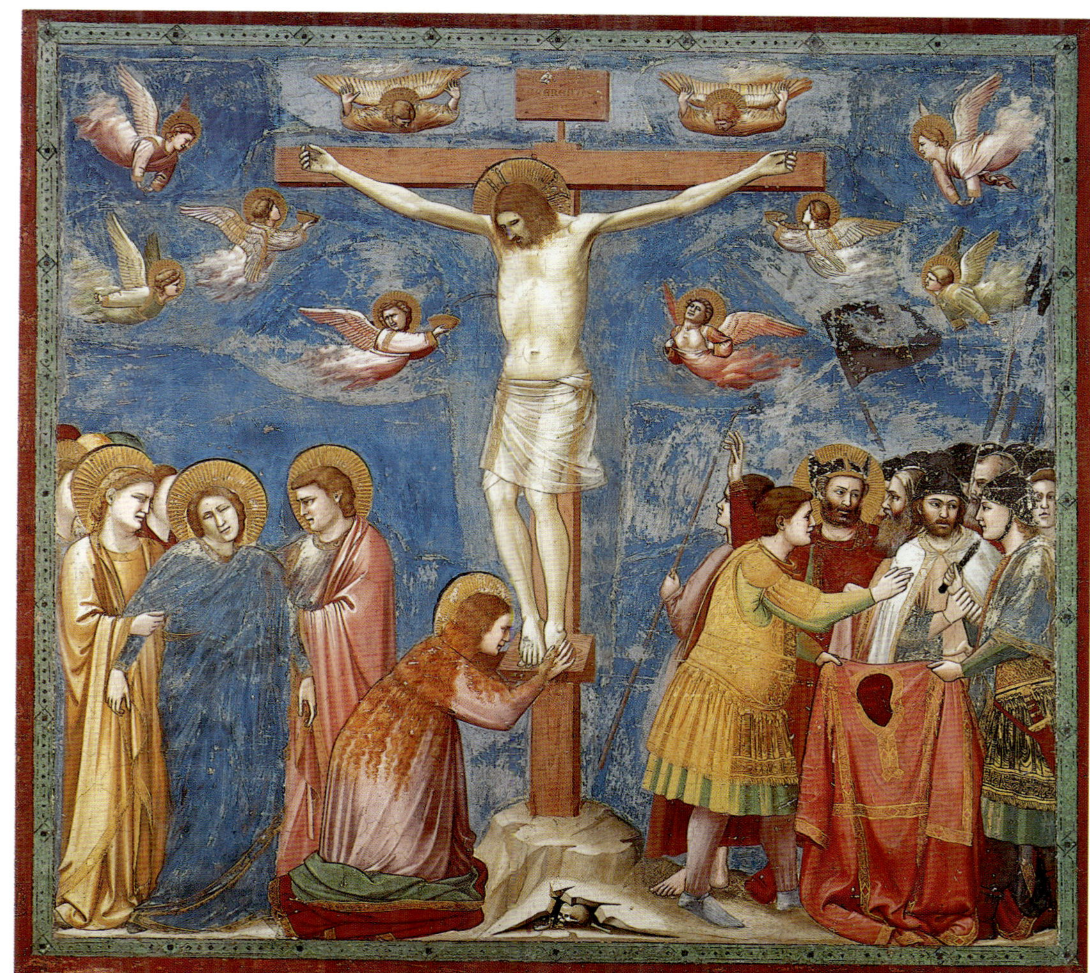

93 *The Crucifixion*, 1302–1305
Fresco, 200 x 185 cm
Cappella degli Scrovegni, Padua

The crucified Christ towers over the two groups of
figures. Angels swarm around him with a great variety of
reactions of grief and pain. Mary Magdalene has fallen at
his feet, her cloak has slipped unnoticed from her
shoulders – her delicately painted, superb head of hair is
now her only adornment. His mother, the Virgin Mary,
collapses in a faint, while on the other side the soldiers
fight over Christ's mantle. The centurion has recognized
Christ and is attempting to point him out to the others.

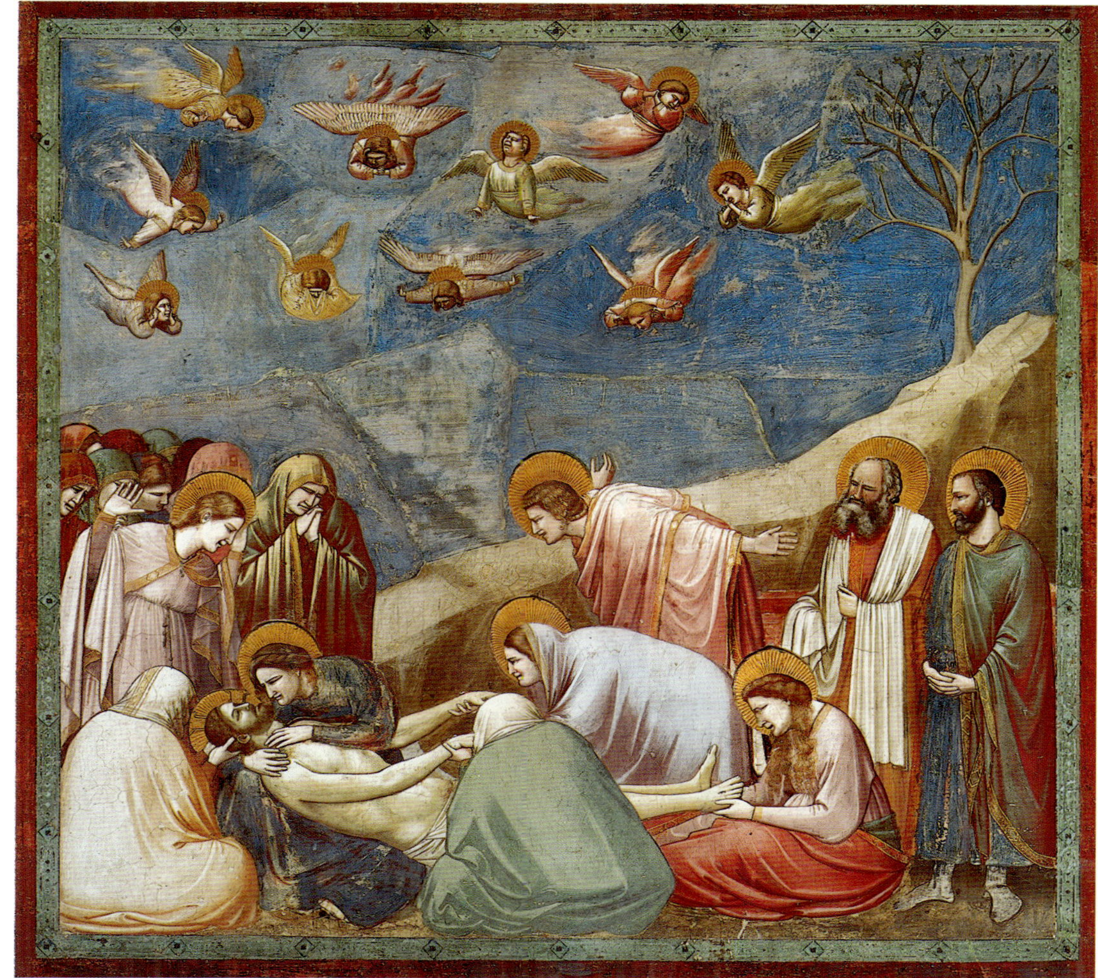

92, 94 (opposite and right) *Lamentation*, 1302–1305
Fresco, 200 x 185 cm
Cappella degli Scrovegni, Padua

With varied gestures, indicating individual degrees of
sorrow, the women and John approach the body of
Christ. Their gestures seem to pave the way for the most
intense impression of grief, the embrace and gaze of the
mother. At the same time, the gestures of the women and
of the disciples, which are reflected once more by the
angels, appear like a development of the mother's sorrow,
which is concentrated on the moment of the most
intimate encounter.

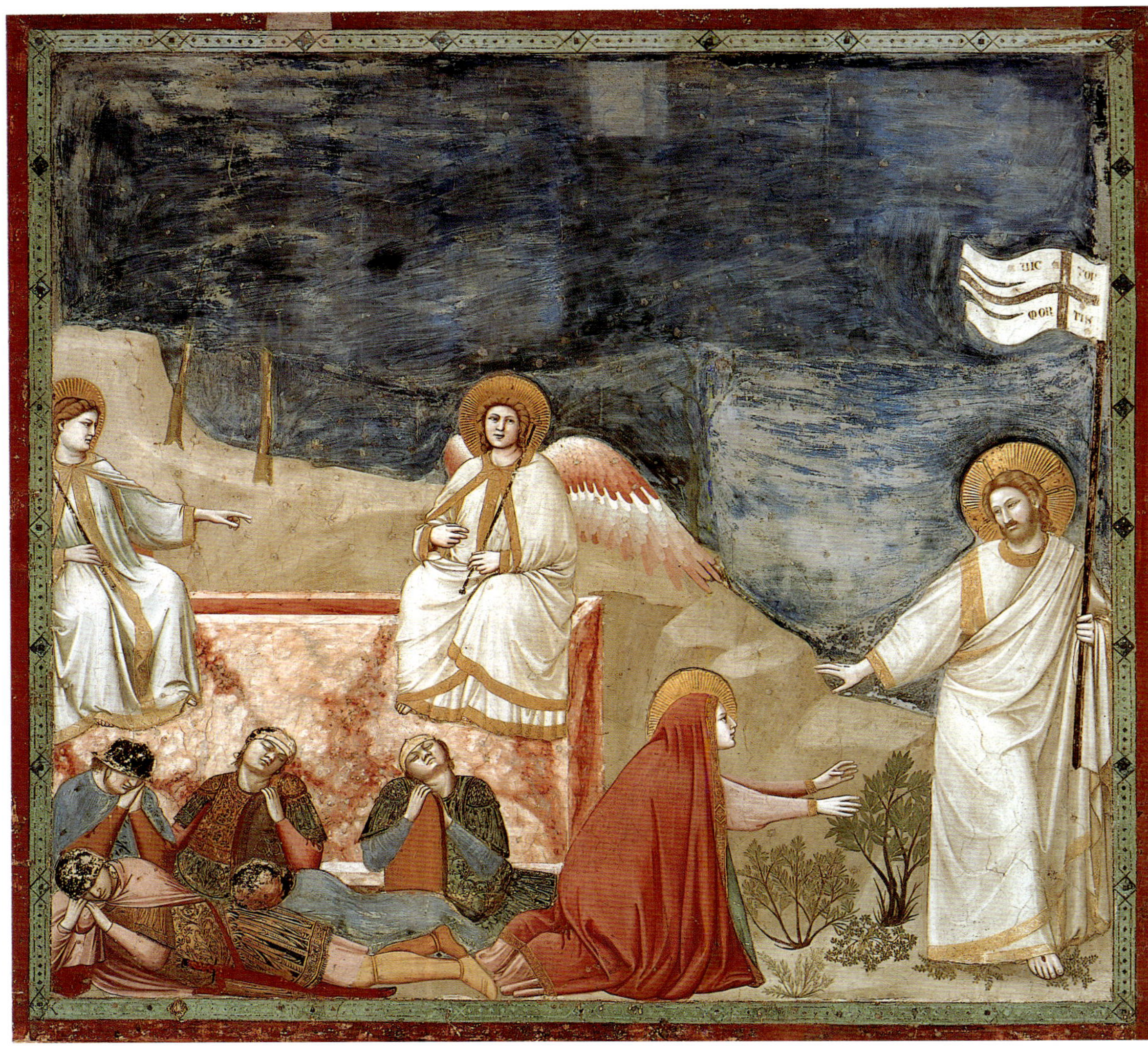

95 *Easter Morning*, 1302–1305
Fresco, 200 x 185 cm
Cappella degli Scrovegni, Padua

Mary Magdalene recognizes Christ on Easter morning in
front of the open tomb. She attempts to speak to her
Lord and to touch him. He refuses, with the words
"Touch me not". Giotto depicts the in-between status of
Christ – no longer of this world, but not yet of the next
world – through the wavering posture and the delicate
coloring. The contrast with Mary Magdalene and the
sleeping soldiers heightens this impression.

Even if Giotto does not yet depict the extensive
landscapes and the deep interior spaces of the
Renaissance, his mountains, temples and houses are
nevertheless no longer the simple suggestions of these
found in older painting. From the rocks and the
architectural structures, which accompany the
respective events and provide a rhythmic articulation,
he builds pictorial stages on which the heavyweight,
sculpturally modelled figures claim their space.

Through their facial expressions and gestures the
figures in the Arena Chapel paintings present a
spectrum of feelings and moods never seen before. The
meeting of eyes between Judas and Christ, the one
looking on mildly, the other fanatically fixed in his gaze,
is an example which says it all (ill. 88). Another is the
meeting of glances of mother and child in the *Nativity*,
which expresses love and awe (ill. 77). There are almost
no earlier representations in which the baby Jesus
thrashes about on the arm of the High Priest in such a
lifelike manner (ill. 78), or in which musicians devote
themselves so completely to their playing as in the
Bridal Procession of the Virgin (ill. 74). We are distressed
by the violent grief of the mothers whose children are
being slaughtered on Herod's orders (ill. 80), or by the
pain of Mary as she embraces her dead son (ill. 94).

These facial expressions and gestures have been
observed exactly from nature. This serves to create a
vivid picture of the events portrayed. The viewers
empathize with the sorrow, the pain or the joy – and
they no longer do so, as was the case in earlier art,
because of the subject matter, which is moving in itself,
but because of the emotions portrayed in the painting.
It is Giotto's particular skill that the solemn and
wonderful nature of the story being told is always there
to be seen and experienced. Responding to what it
recognizes as natural, guided by figures viewed from
behind and by gestures, our view follows the rhythm of
each composition to its center. There, time stands still
for a moment, as in the *Arrest of Christ* (ill. 87), *Christ
before Caiaphas* (ill. 89), and particularly clearly in
the *Raising of Lazarus* (ill. 82) – the ever-present
"sacredness" is glimpsed in these moments.

96 (opposite) *The Driving of the Traders from the Temple*
and *Pentecost*, 1302–1305
Fresco, 200 x 185 cm
Cappella degli Scrovegni, Padua

The narrow bands that articulate the walls have a similar
effect to *Cosmati* work on marble thrones. Marble with
grotesque and floral elements, such as can be found on
portals of the period, and derived from antique models,
characterizes the broad bands. Narrative representations
on the one hand, and angels and prophets on the other,
are depicted in the quatrefoils and multifoils respectively.
They both complement the pictorial program and
convey the impression that we are able to glimpse a layer
lying further behind.

In the upper picture field we can see Christ driving out
the traders with a violent gesture. The latter start with
fright, the animals jump free, the children seek the
protection of the disciples, and the scribes whisper to one
another perfidiously. The span between the scribes and
the touching gesture with which John presses a child to
his side emphasize Christ's actions.

In the representation below this, Pentecost is being
celebrated in a structure set obliquely in space, and
whose Gothic arcades permit a view of the interior. The
disciples have gathered, and rays from the Holy Ghost
descend upon them. Their faces show astonishment and
transfiguration.

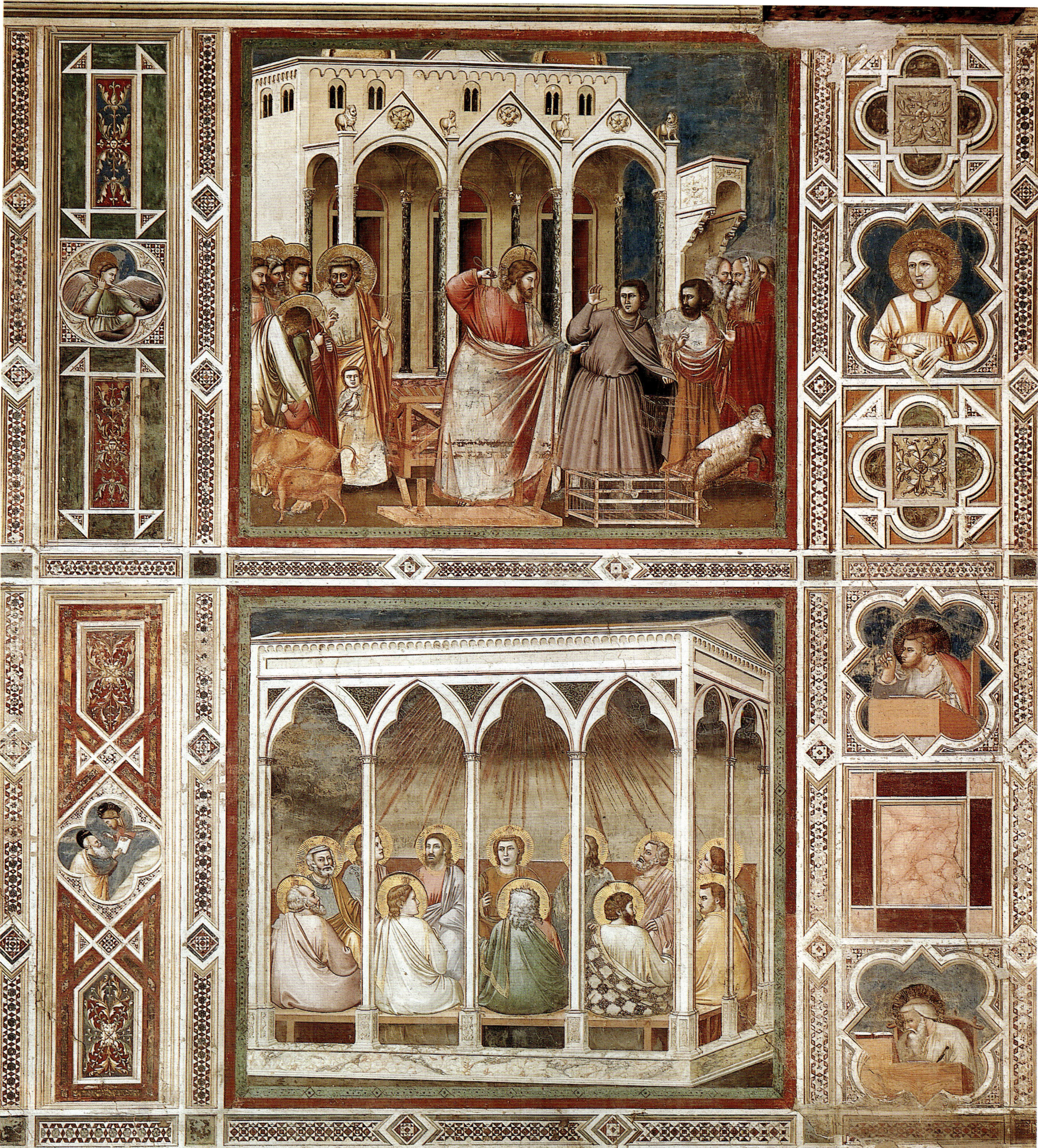

Highlights of Giotto's Panel Painting

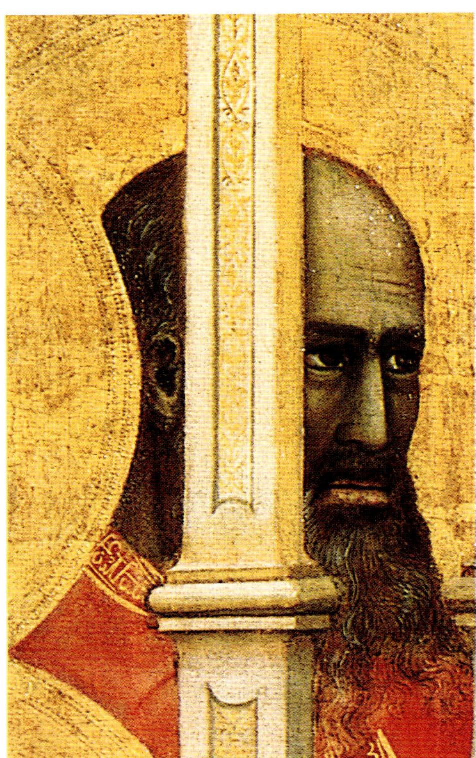

97, 98 *Ognissanti Madonna* (and detail), ca. 1309
Tempera on wood, 325 x 204 cm
Galleria degli Uffizi, Florence

This representation of the *Maestà*, with its novel
conception of the subject and its delicate style of
painting, worked through with gold, numbers among
the high points in Giotto's panel painting. Here, the
natural portrayal and the solemnity of the mother and
child are intensified in a special way. The clear
perspectival composition, in which the clearly directed
gaze of the surrounding figures is included, makes the
Child's gesture of benediction appear as the focal point,
both optically and as regards content. The way in which
Giotto creates the opportunity to heighten the
expression is illustrated by this detail, which shows the
saint directly next to the Virgin's throne. Separation –
through the end of the throne – and closeness – through
the gaze – are combined here in a single arc of tension.

The attribution of the large painting of the Madonna
from the Florentine church of the Ognissanti (All
Saints), now housed in the Uffizi Gallery, derives from
a written notice from the early 15th century. The panel,
described as the *Ognissanti Madonna* after the church in
which it was originally installed, has the same strength
of representation as the frescoes at Padua, and is
therefore dated by art historians as having being
painted in the first decade of the 14th century (ill. 98).

From the moment we look at the wooden panel
painted in tempera we are fascinated by the gleaming
solemnity of the paintwork. A fine web of golden
edgings on the robes, of halos, and of decorative
elements blends the golden hue of the background with
the representation as a whole. Both the delicate shades
of violet and pink, the warm green and red, and the
flesh colors of the figures thus take on a brilliant luster,
which allows the panel to shine with incomparable
splendor.

Giotto turns to a type of picture known as the Maestà
– the Madonna surrounded by saints and angels –
which is especially well-known because of the Maestà
by Duccio, begun in 1308, the one-time altarpiece of
the cathedral at Siena, and through the great fresco in
the Sienese Town Hall, completed by Simone Martini
in 1315. These two examples of mature Sienese art have
a relatively wide format: the numerous saints kneel and
stand in rows to the left and right of the Virgin's throne.
There they could be said to lead a "life of their own" –
some look into the center of the picture, others look at
one another, and yet others direct their gaze out of the
picture. Giotto's panel, on the other hand, is vertical in
format (325 x 204 cm) and thus approaches the size
and proportions of an older type of portrayal of the
Madonna. This aspect is made particularly clear in the
Uffizi Gallery in Florence, where the *Ognissanti
Madonna* is exhibited next to Duccio's *Rucellai
Madonna* and the *Madonna S. Trinità* by Cimabue,
both of which were executed in the 1280s.

Even the two older masters do not show the Virgin
Mary and Child alone, but closely surrounded by
angels. Nevertheless, Giotto transformed the
representational style of the Maestà decisively. It is the
same innovative step that we saw in the example of the

Isaac frescoes at Assisi, compared to those of Cimabue
and his followers. Giotto's panel differs from the two
masterpieces by his predecessors in the new firmness of
its structure and in its spatial proportions.

An architectural throne, set in perspective, gives the
Virgin and Child space. The luxurious decoration and
the filigree Gothic ornaments of the construction caress
the central figures and separate them from their
surroundings. A marble step, which is decorated with
Cosmati work, just like the cabinet of the throne, leads
up to the principal figures and so provides a natural
basis for their raised position within the picture.

An angel kneels at either side of the step, left and
right (ill. 100). We can recognize the space occupied by
their strong, softly-modelled bodies very clearly by the
way in which they either overlap or provide a glimpse
of the steps behind. They do not hover like Cimabue's
angels, and do not appear to have been simply applied
to a flat surface like those of Duccio, but kneel with lifelike gravity. In one hand the angels hold a vase
containing a lily and red and white roses, the symbols
of Mary's grief and of her purity. They look up at her.
In order to overcome the distance, they bend their
backs slightly and tilt their heads backwards. Doing so
lends their gaze a certain directness and focus. And all
the figures – the standing angels and the saints – are
aligned with the center in this way.

The intensity of these gazes reflects the perspective
layout of the picture as a whole and concentrates
adoration on the Virgin Mary and the Christ Child. It
is exactly this feature which distinguishes the *Ognissanti
Madonna* from all other Maestà representations by
Giotto's younger and older contemporaries. The
elevation of the central figures thus becomes almost
completely natural, beyond all representative function
and symbolic perspective, which Giotto – quite
the child of his time – does not eschew, but does
modify.

The modelling of the central figures contributes a
great deal to the interplay of solemnity and naturalism:
Mary gazes out of the picture, her head imperceptibly
held to one side. An extremely thin, transparent veil
frames her delicate features, over which lies her cloak,
of thicker material and in traditional dark-blue. It

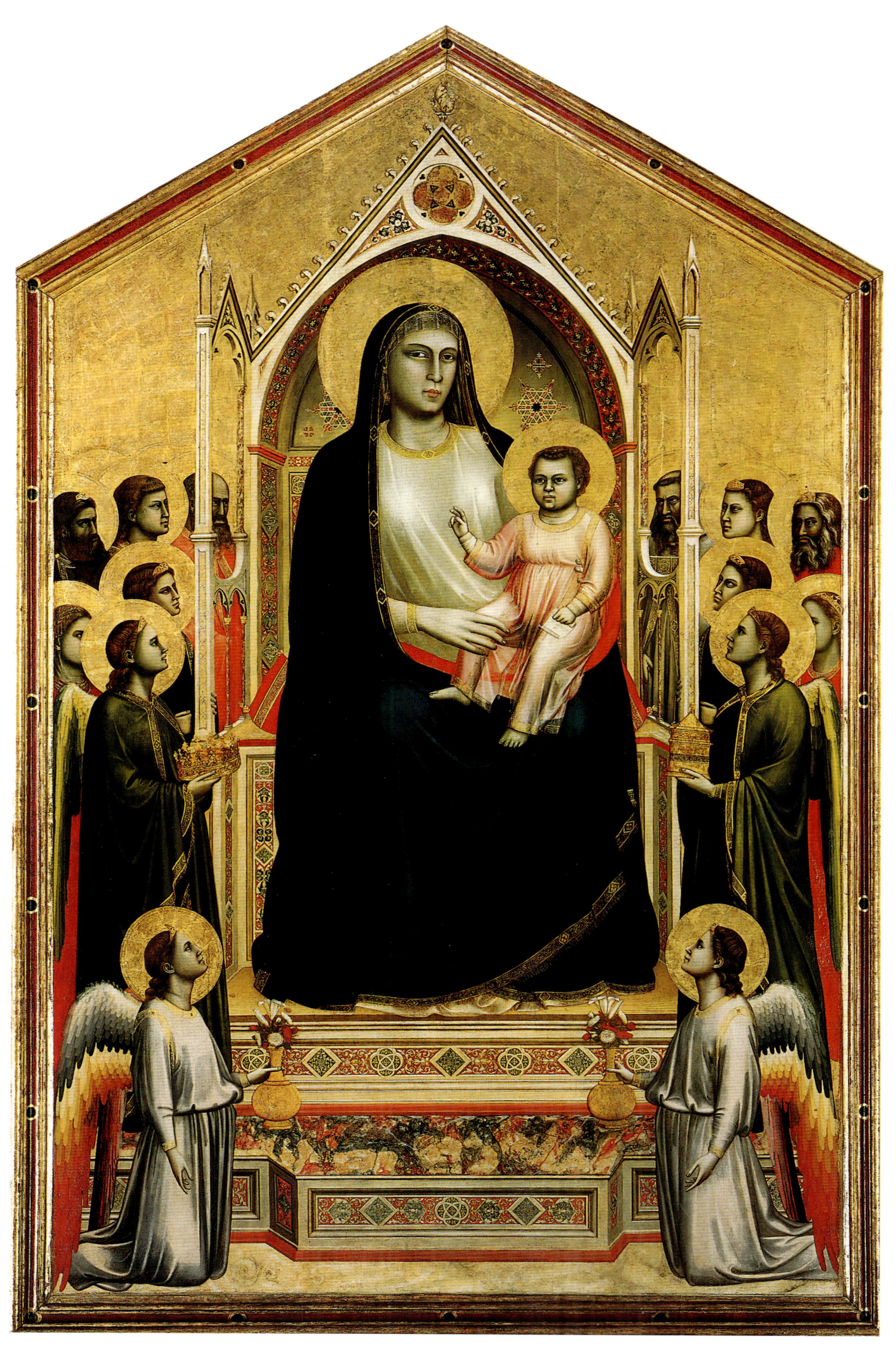

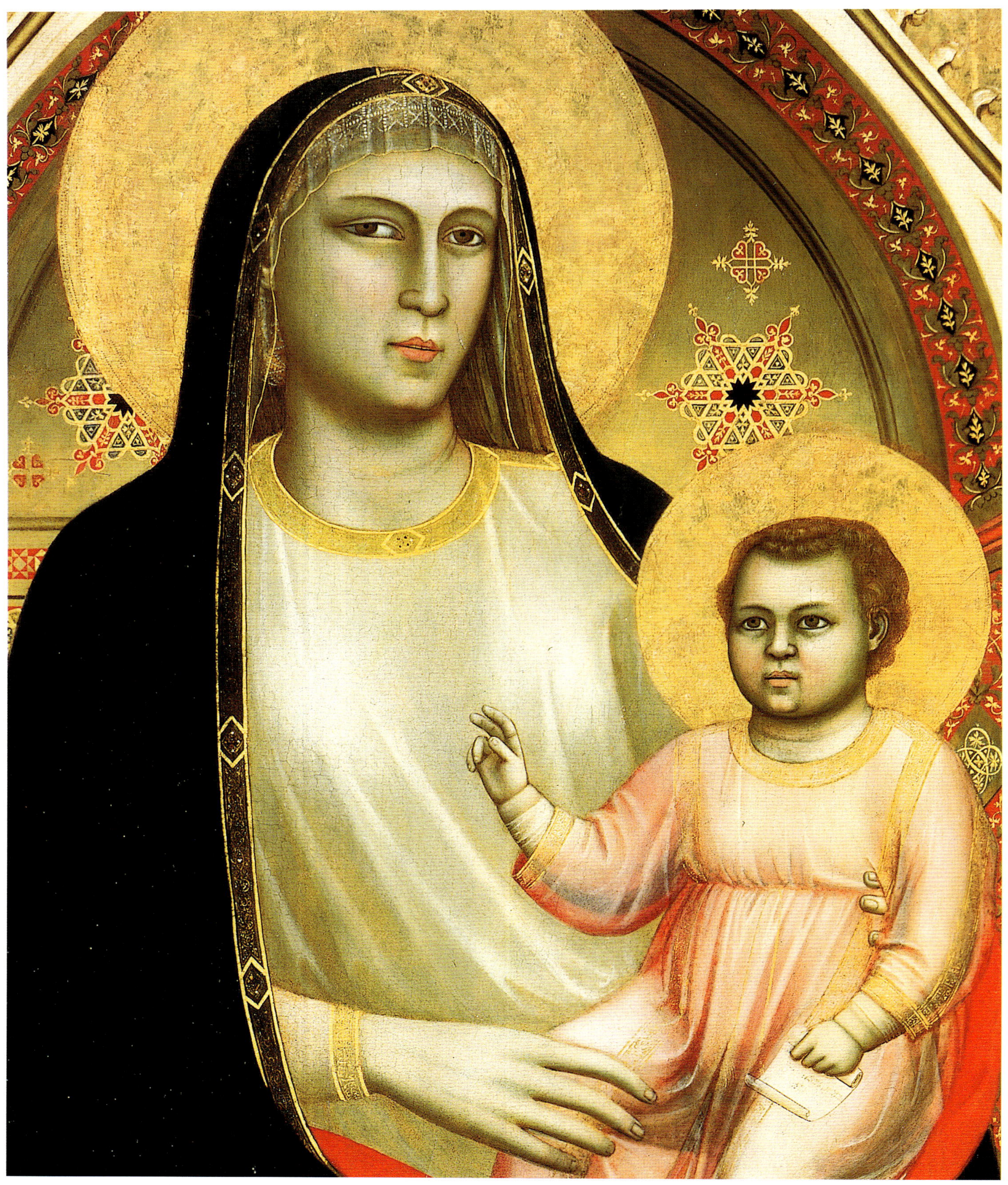

99 (above) *Ognissanti Madonna* (detail ill. 98), ca. 1309

In an incomparable fashion Giotto uses the most delicate
style of painting to achieve a great closeness to nature of
appearance. We believe we can feel the delicacy of the
see-through material over the Virgin's head, just as we
can see her breast, even down to the nipple, through the
softly flowing fabric of her robe. This utmost naturalness
of the maternal and the feminine heightens the sublimity
of her gaze precisely by way of contrast.

100 (opposite) *Ognissanti Madonna*, kneeling angel
(detail ill. 98), ca. 1309

The flowers that this angel presents to the Madonna have
here been painted from nature, probably for the first
time since antiquity. The delicate and lifelike way in
which they are painted is comparable to the basket of
flowers and fruit of *Charity* in the Arena Chapel.

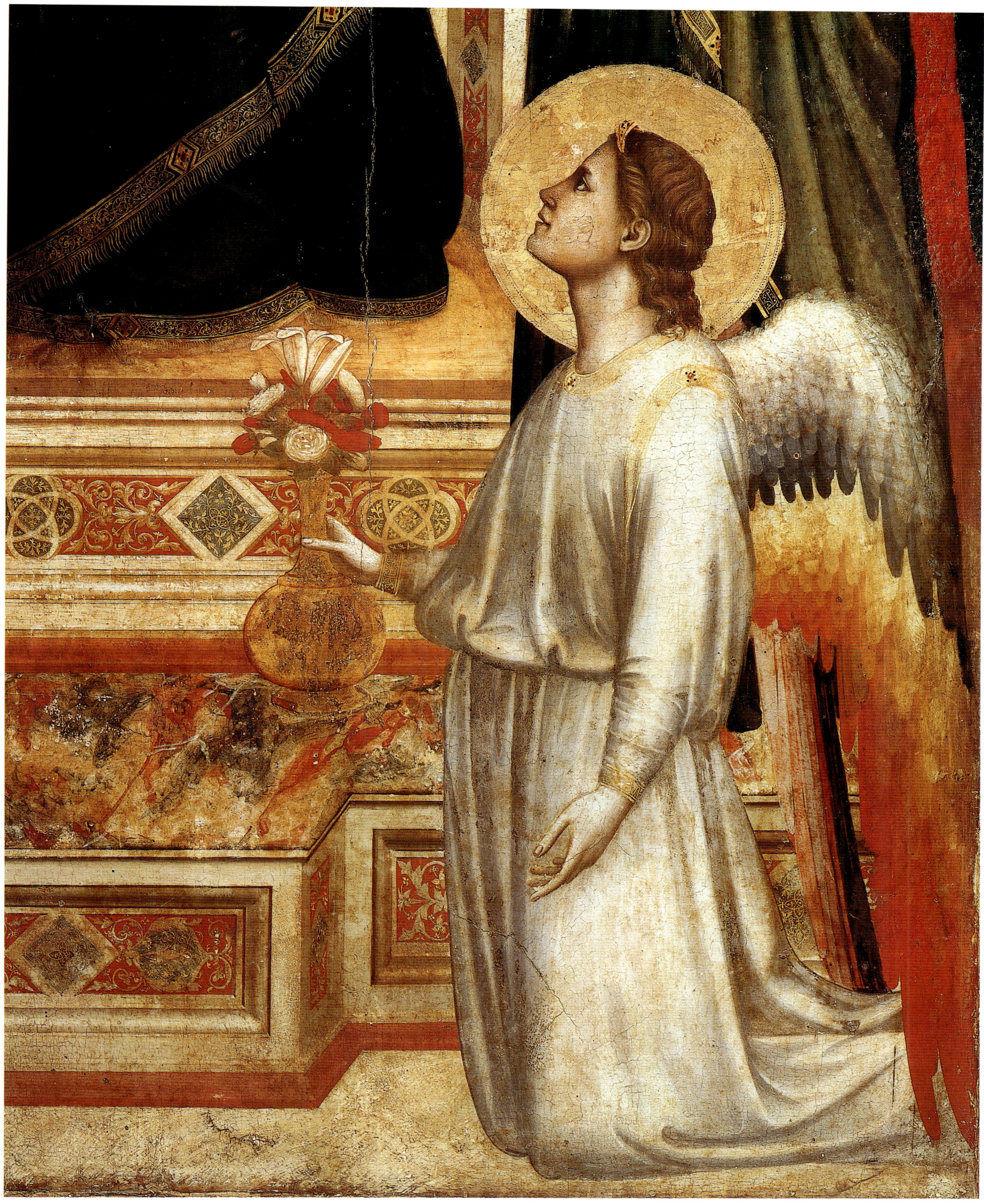

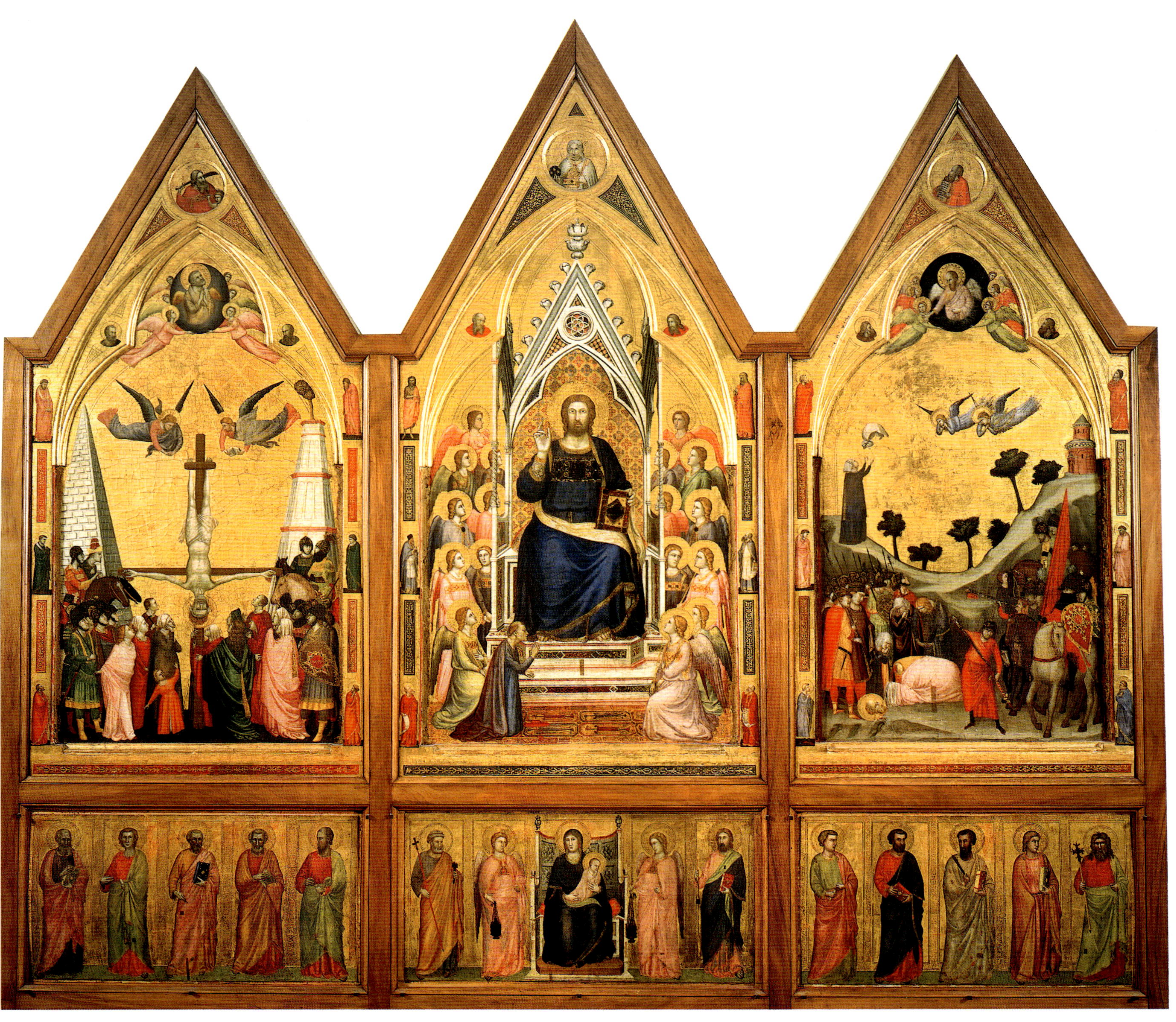

101 *Stefaneschi Altar*, side showing Christ, 1313
Tempera on wood, 220 x 245 cm
Vaticano, Pinacoteca Vaticana, Rome

The golden background and the rich coloring of the very
delicate painting allow the side showing Christ to shine
with particular splendor. Christ, delivering benediction,
is enthroned in the center and surrounded by a host of
angels. The side panels are devoted to the martyrdom of
St. Peter on the left and St. Paul on the right. The
representation of the Virgin Mary and Child on the
predella emphasizes the central axis of the altarpiece.
Apostles surround Mary.

shrouds the entire figure and emphasizes the weight of
the seated Madonna. The Christ Child sits on her left
thigh. The mother supports the child, with her hand in
the same position as in Duccio's representation – but
how different, how much more natural and casual she
appears here.

The Virgin Mary has lifted up her cloak with one
hand, so that the Child is set against the brilliant red of
its lining. The thin, immeasurably delicate outer
garments of the Child alternate between white and pink
as if to reflect this color. Although he is a plump infant,
this Christ Child is imbued with complete seriousness
– here too a natural way of looking at things is
combined with the religious subject matter in a quite
new fashion. Unmoving, Christ gazes with alert eyes

into the distance and raises his tiny hand in
benediction. This gesture is the central point of the
whole composition – and also the point at which
almost all lines of perspective meet.

The Virgin's cloak is drawn back between Mother
and Child as if to separate them from the outside world
and as if to receive the Child, and the fine, precious
gauzy material of Mary's undergarment underlies the
central gesture. The material is almost transparent,
revealing the mother's breast in all its naturalness. The
unapproachable Madonna, adored by choirs of angels
and saints, is at the same time also a living, earthly
mother with her robust child.

Only a few years after the creation of the Florentine
Maestà, Cardinal Jacopo Stefaneschi placed the

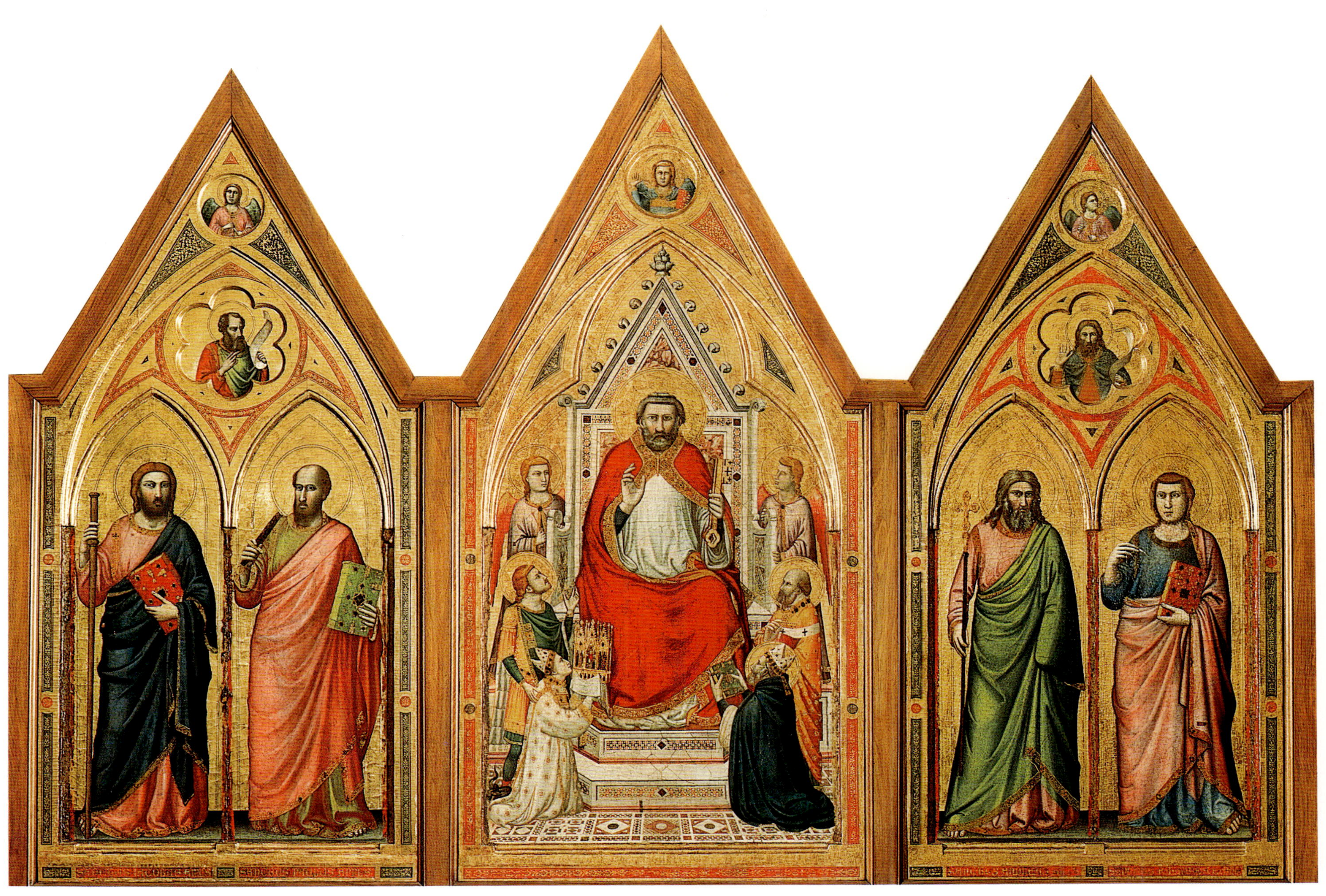

commission for a large altarpiece with Giotto (ills. 101, 102). Stefaneschi, who came from a very respected Roman family, may have heard of the magnificence of the *Ognissanti Madonna* and so have become aware of the Florentine artist. He may also have been informed of Giotto's abilities by his distant relative Enrico Scrovegni; besides which, he was most likely familiar with the frescoes at Assisi, for the election of a pope, at which Stefaneschi was present, had taken place in Perugia, which is very close to Assisi. At the time at which Giotto was given the commission, probably in 1313, the papal seat, and therefore the residence of the cardinals, was no longer in Italy, but in Avignon in France. This remained the case until 1376, although the Roman cardinals in particular were fighting for a

return from "exile" to their traditional seat in Rome. Because of this situation, the donation of an altarpiece which was to be installed in the most important papal church of St. Peter's in Rome, the building that preceded the current St. Peter's, takes on a political significance. His donation underlines the determination of Stefaneschi and of the other Roman cardinals to return, and expresses his concern about the memorial church of St. Peter.

The triptych, painted on both sides, is currently housed in the Pinacoteca at the Vatican. According to the findings of the latest research, it probably originally stood in the old cathedral of St. Peter's on the canon's altar in front of the southern triumphal arch wall. Today, the three panels, painted front and back, have a

102 *Stefaneschi Altar*, side showing Peter, 1313
Tempera on wood, 220 x 245 cm
Vaticano, Pinacoteca Vaticana, Rome

This side of the triptych, with Peter, the prince of the Church, enthroned at its center, is constructed as if it were the cross-section of a church with a five-aisled nave: below the arcades of the side aisles the apostles James and Paul are standing on the left, with Andrew and John on the right.

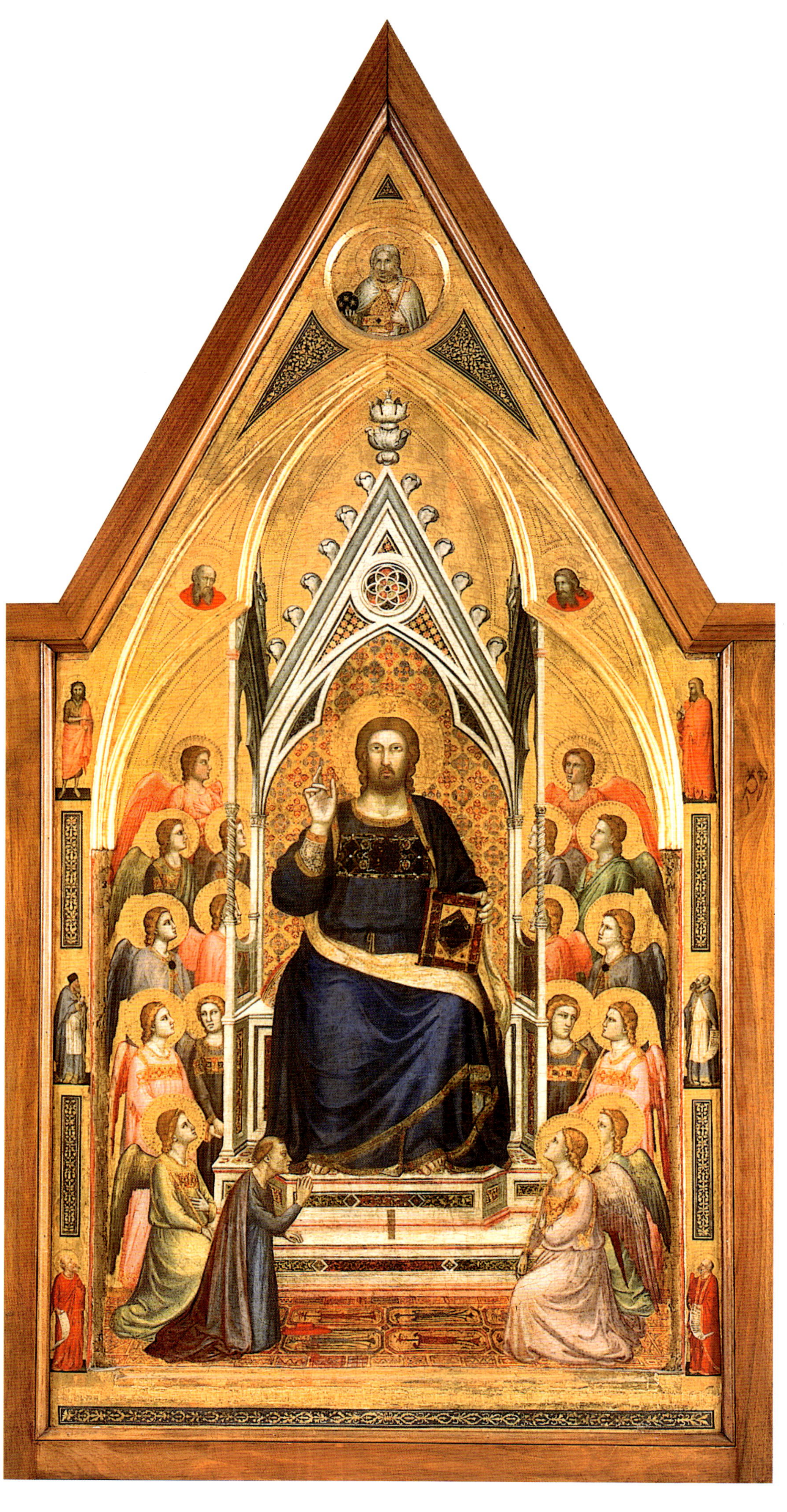

103 (left) *Stefaneschi Altar,* side showing Christ, middle panel (detail ill.101), 1313

Surrounded by a heavenly host, the enormous Christ is enthroned in solemn majesty on a richly decorated Gothic throne. As if given a place among the circle of angels, the donor Cardinal Stefaneschi kneels before the throne on the marble floor, which is laid out in perspective. He is clothed in a simple robe and has reverently laid aside his cardinal's hat. Unlike the angels, the cardinal bends forward as if he wanted to kiss the feet of the Lord.

104 (opposite) *Stefaneschi Altar,* side showing Peter, middle panel (detail ill. 102), 1313

Peter sits, surrounded by angels and saints, on a simply constructed throne inlaid with *Cosmati* work. His right hand is raised in blessing, and in the other he holds the keys of his office. Before him, kneeling on the luxurious marble floor, laid out in perspective, are the hermit-saint Peter of Morrone to his right, and the donor Cardinal Stefaneschi, offering him the altar, to his left.

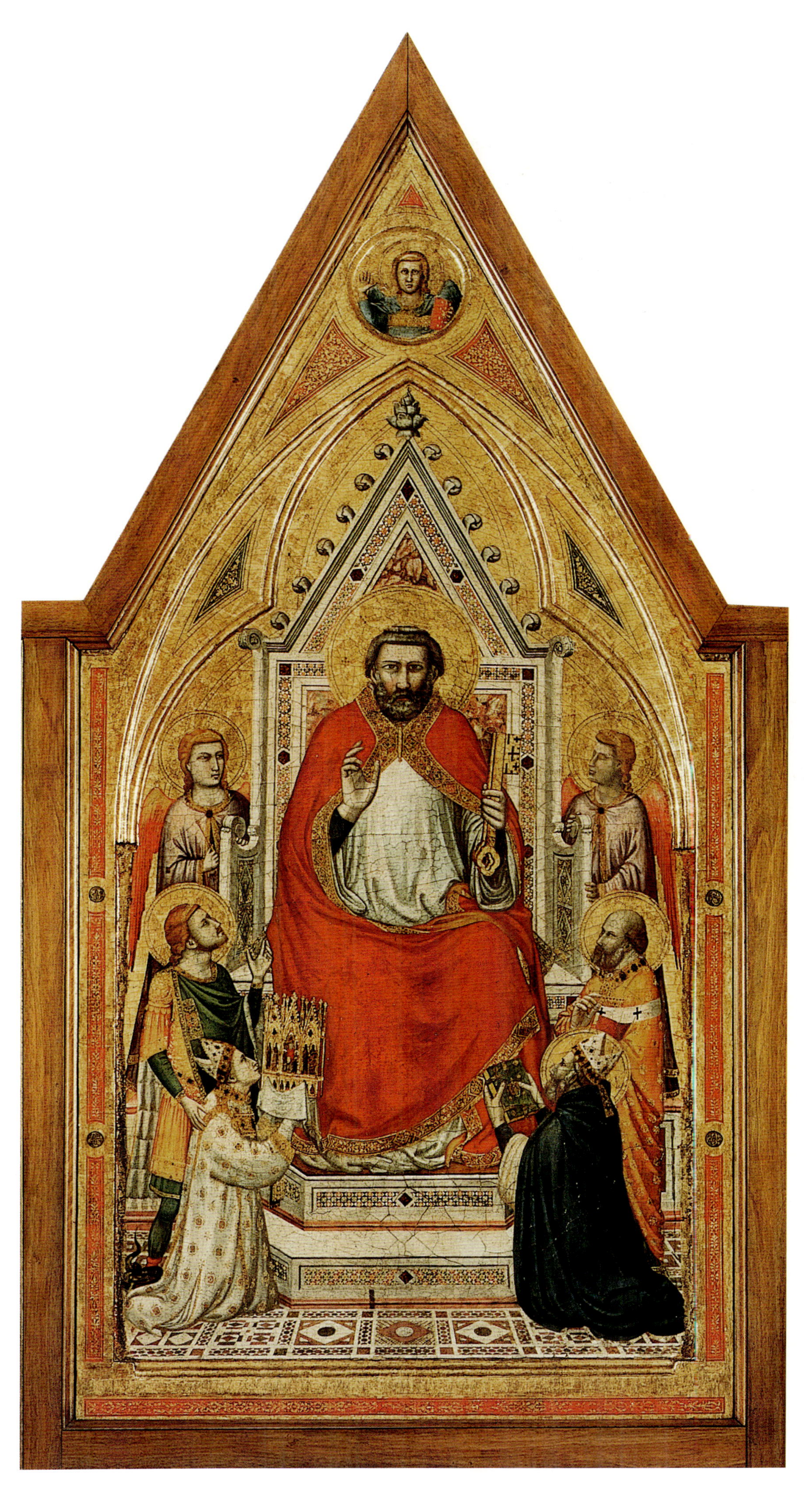

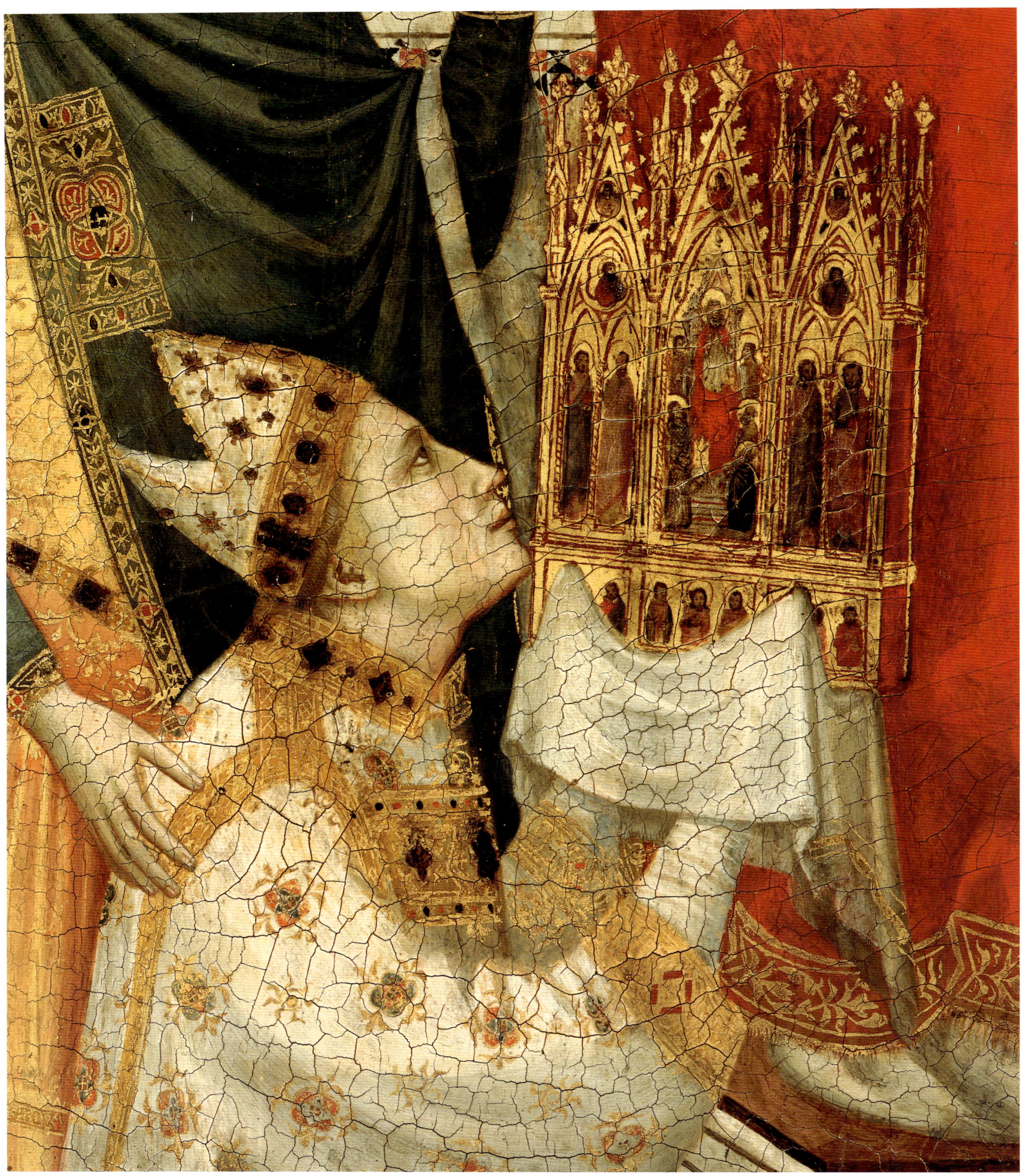

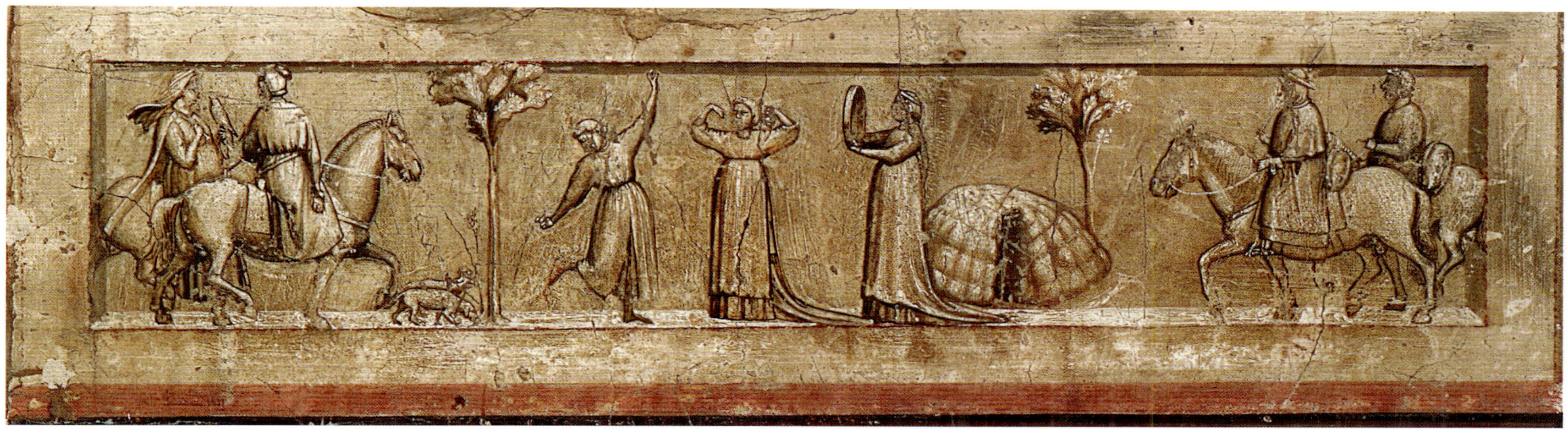

total width of 220 cm and a height, in the middle axis, including predella, of 245 cm, although the side panels are a few centimeters shorter and narrower than the middle panel. All three panels are, therefore, extremely tall in size, and the compositional solution to this is a masterpiece in itself. The original framework and some of the predella panels have been lost over the years, but what remains is astonishing enough and worth seeing.

One side of the triptych can be clearly made out at first glance and from a distance – it appears more monumental than the other side with its host of small figures. The central panel, with its gold background, is dominated by St. Peter (ill. 104). Again we see a style of painting similar to that in the *Ognissanti Madonna* (ill. 98), which adds luster to materials.

However, the use of perspective to structure the picture seems more logically consistent here, and thus the space in which the action takes place seems more generous – airier – than in the Florentine panels. The geometrical patterns of the marble floor lead into the picture space. If we think back to the sometimes very narrow pictorial stages in the frescoes at Padua (ill. 79), or to the floors of the interior spaces in some of the representations at Assisi, which often fell away obliquely (ill. 23), then the advancement in portraying the spatial dimension becomes most apparent. Giotto uses the development in perspective in two ways: firstly, to add weight to the center. With no background architecture to enclose him, the powerful figure of St. Peter stands out optically like a statue against the back of the throne, which lies parallel to the picture plane. In contrast to the *Ognissanti Madonna*, this reinforces the symbolic perspective. It is meant to be an exhortation for the popes, who understand themselves as successors to the throne of St. Peter, to be present in Rome. Giotto uses the figures assembled round the throne to prevent this dominant central figure from bursting the bounds of the picture. In spite of the narrow format, they are arranged in a circle and they have room to move freely and unhindered.

Two angels stand on the throne's high podium. They look "round the corner" at Peter from behind. Their wings reflect the red of his cloak most beautifully – they are thus assigned completely to the holy figure. On one side, the side of the papal keys, a saint stands in front of the throne. He is dressed in a papal vestment and recommends to Peter a second, kneeling saint, who wears the dark cloak of a hermit. This recluse can be identified from contemporary miniature representations as Celestine V, or Peter of Morrone.

The programmatic intentions of the painting's commissioner are closely linked to this hermit-saint. Following a long period of disagreement among the college of cardinals, the latter elected the hermit Peter of Morrone pope in 1294, at a time when the papacy was going through a difficult phase characterized by apocalyptic premonitions. Only a few months later, Celestine V, revered as "the angel-pope", the name by which he has gone down in history, resigned office. His successor, Boniface VIII, has been suspected ever since of having forced this unusual abdication, and of being responsible for the early death of the hermit. Cardinal Stefaneschi had a special connection with these two popes. He became a cardinal under Boniface, and remained on the side of those who defended him following his death in 1303. On the other hand, Stefaneschi dedicated a written work to the life of Celestine – it is possibly this codex that the saint is offering to Peter. In addition, the cardinal followed the process of canonization of the hermit in 1313 and kept a written record. The fact that the latter was ultimately canonized not as pope, but as the hermit Peter of Morrone, allowed his resignation to appear in a positive light and also reconciled the Christian world with Boniface VIII, who could now be considered the legitimate and innocent successor to the papal office. Thus, Stefaneschi had a double reason for having this hermit-saint portrayed in the year he was canonized.

The donor himself, in the ceremonial robes of a cardinal, kneels on the other side. Jacopo Stefaneschi was cardinal of the Roman church of San Giorgio at Velabro, and so it is St. George who here recommends him to Peter. We can clearly make out the fine, shining golden armor of the saintly knight and the small dragon, the symbol of St. George, which writhes at his feet.

107 *Stefaneschi Altar*, side showing Christ: *Martyrdom of Peter* (detail ill 101), 1313

Peter has been nailed to the upside-down cross between a pyramid and the so-called *Meta Romuli*, the symbol of Rome and the Vatican. Soldiers and mourners throng towards the cross, while the saint's soul is already departing. Exact observation – the saint's hair hangs downward; sensitivity – a woman tenderly embraces the cross; and the most delicate brushwork – the green cloak of the figure with her back to us gleams sumptuously – characterize this composition.

It is unusual for the donor, still living and doubtless portrayed from life, to appear among the saints (ill. 104). That the donor was depicted at Padua on the side of the Blessed at the *Last Judgment* was remarkable enough (ill. 41). However, there, the priest who accompanies him creates a link with the faithful in the church, and the proportional differences in size, at the same time, produce a certain distance between Scrovegni and the events portrayed. Stefaneschi, on the other hand, appears to be on an equal footing with the saint – almost equal, for Giotto does create barely perceptible differences and distances to the center. Thus Stefaneschi kneels further to the side than St. Peter of Morrone, and is completely covered behind by St. George. Moreover, he cannot look directly at Peter. For he kneels – as he would in St. Peter's cathedral, and like the canons who have come to worship – in front of the altar he donated, which, in the picture, he lifts up towards Peter with both hands.

Reproducing the real situation in the picture is another remarkable step towards depicting the sacred situation in a way which makes it seem actual and natural. The miniature painted altar can also be understood in this sense (ill. 105). We are familiar with paintings in which models of churches or precious books are handed over – the donor Scrovegni with his Arena Chapel is one example. But Giotto goes even further here. If we look closely, we will recognize the St. Peter side of the altar, which means that the donor appears for a second time with his model of the altar. We are confronted here with an early picture-within-a-picture representation such as would reappear only in the early Renaissance.

The delicate style of painting demonstrates how natural the subject matter is, and converges with the opportunity of accurately constructing space. This is not the mathematical perspective of the early Renaissance, but an empirical perspective based on experience. Giotto incorporates it in his new pictorial invention and adapts it to the natural qualities of the representation. It is through this very synthesis that he stands on the threshold between the Middle Ages and the modern era.

On each of the side panels of the St. Peter side of the altar two saints stand below a double arcade (ill. 102). The overall view gives the impression that we are looking in cross section at a church with a five-aisled nave. In comparison, the other side, the side showing Christ, is constructed of three such divisions (ill. 101). It appears more slender and more delicate, somehow more solemn and less real. Here, the side panels are devoted to the martyrdoms of the principal saints of the church for which the altar was created: Peter and Paul. These depictions contain many figures, in keeping with the central panel. There, Christ sits, his right hand raised in benediction and his left leaning on the Holy Scriptures, on a delicately structured Gothic throne. He is surrounded by a circle of angels, just as the supreme judge is surrounded by the heavenly host in depictions of the Last Judgment. The apostles and prophets who stand in the borders along the edges as witnesses and

observers also follow this pattern, as do the images in the spandrels of the panel: as representatives of the Old Testament, Moses and Abraham look down from left and right on the Christ of the Apocalypse in the center. In this context, the martyrdoms on the side panels are an aid to petitionary prayers, and serve as a testament to faith. If we interpret this side of the altar with reference to the Apocalypse, then the appearance and proportions of the enthroned Christ are no longer so displeasing in comparison to St. Peter on his throne on the other side as many researchers consider them to be. They are the expression of a completely different sphere and of a different subject.

Here, too, the figure of the donor creates the link with the immediate present. The cardinal kneels bareheaded – he has placed his hat on the richly decorated floor – and in simple robes before the steps of the throne. He bends forward, as if to kiss the Savior's foot. This same actualization is achieved in the side panels by the extremely lively depictions.

It is precisely the exceptional format of these narrative side panels that makes them perhaps the most exciting compositions in Giotto's œuvre. The crucifixion of St. Peter takes place on the left-hand panel against a golden background (ill. 107). The upside-down cross has been erected between two tall pieces of architecture. These make the panel, which is already slender enough, seem even more narrow, the space seem reduced, and the wealth of figures seem dramatically compressed. Yet all those portrayed still appear to be able to move freely and have the opportunity to turn to face the cross with the most varied expressions of grief.

The depiction of the beheading of St. Paul, which is supposed to have taken place in the open countryside, is structured differently (ill. 108). There is a greater division of the composition into fore-, middle-, and background. Events in heaven and on earth are both linked to, and separated from, one another by a rocky landscape. At a time when landscapes were not yet part of an artist's repertory, the impression of depth created by these rocks is very remarkable indeed. Giotto had already had his first experience of depicting landscapes in the frescoes at Assisi – for example in the *Miracle of the Spring* (ill. 28) – and in the Arena Chapel – in the *Dream of Joachim* (ill. 68), for instance. The landscape here is also directly related to the action, just as it was in these frescoes: a wedge of rock in the foreground divides the figures into two groups. Grieving women and soldiers full of consternation have gathered around Paul. His torso is still on its knees, while his severed head already lies on the ground. On the right, the soldiers withdraw. Cold-blooded and unmoved, the executioner sticks his sword back in its sheath. Clothed in striking red, this henchman stands right in the foreground, almost on the central axis. He embodies the inevitability of events and, therefore, becomes the compositional base of a spiral that winds its way upward, linking earth and heaven.

The rocky landscape, which rises to the left, leads from the executioner to the maid Plantilla. She also

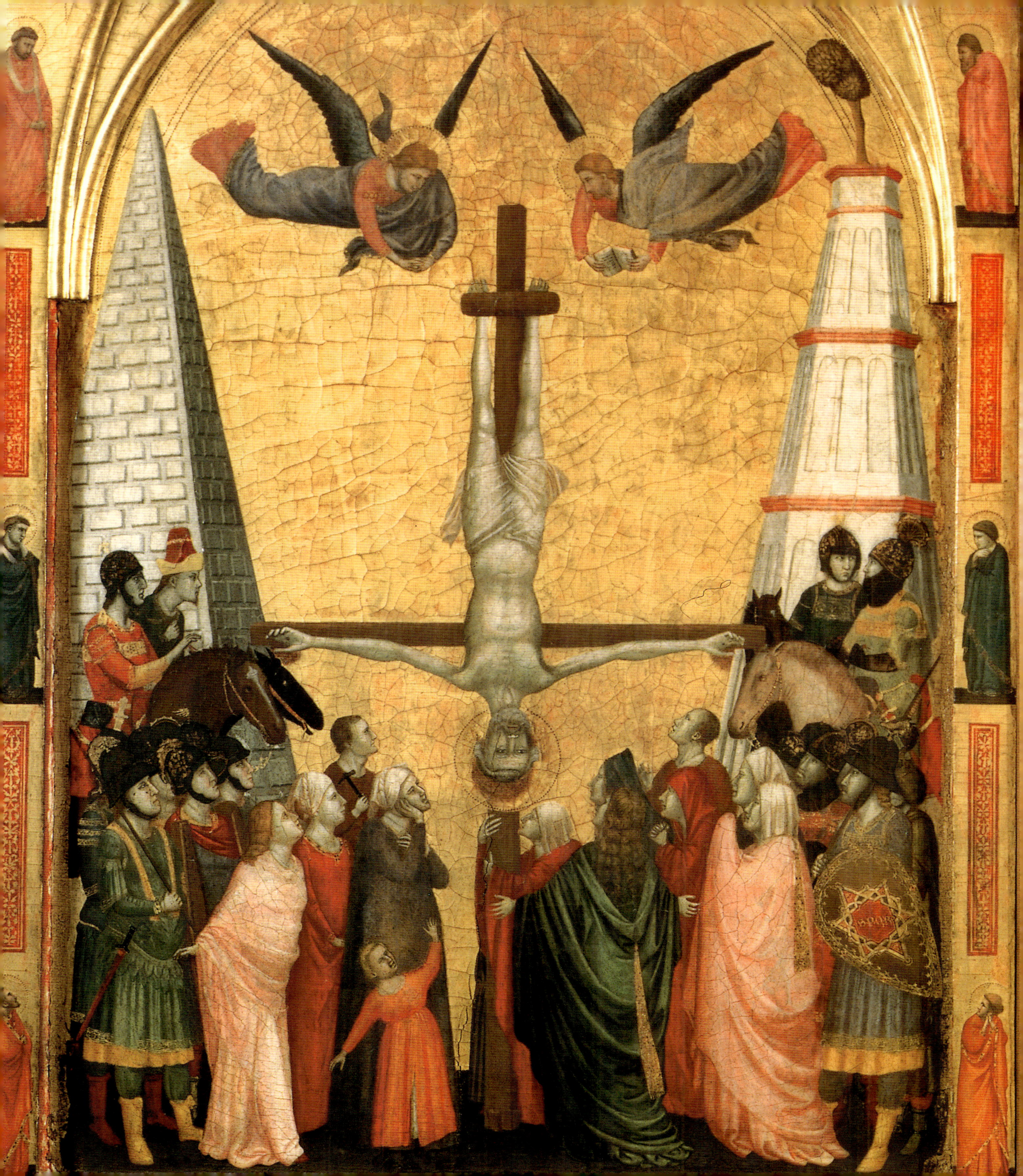

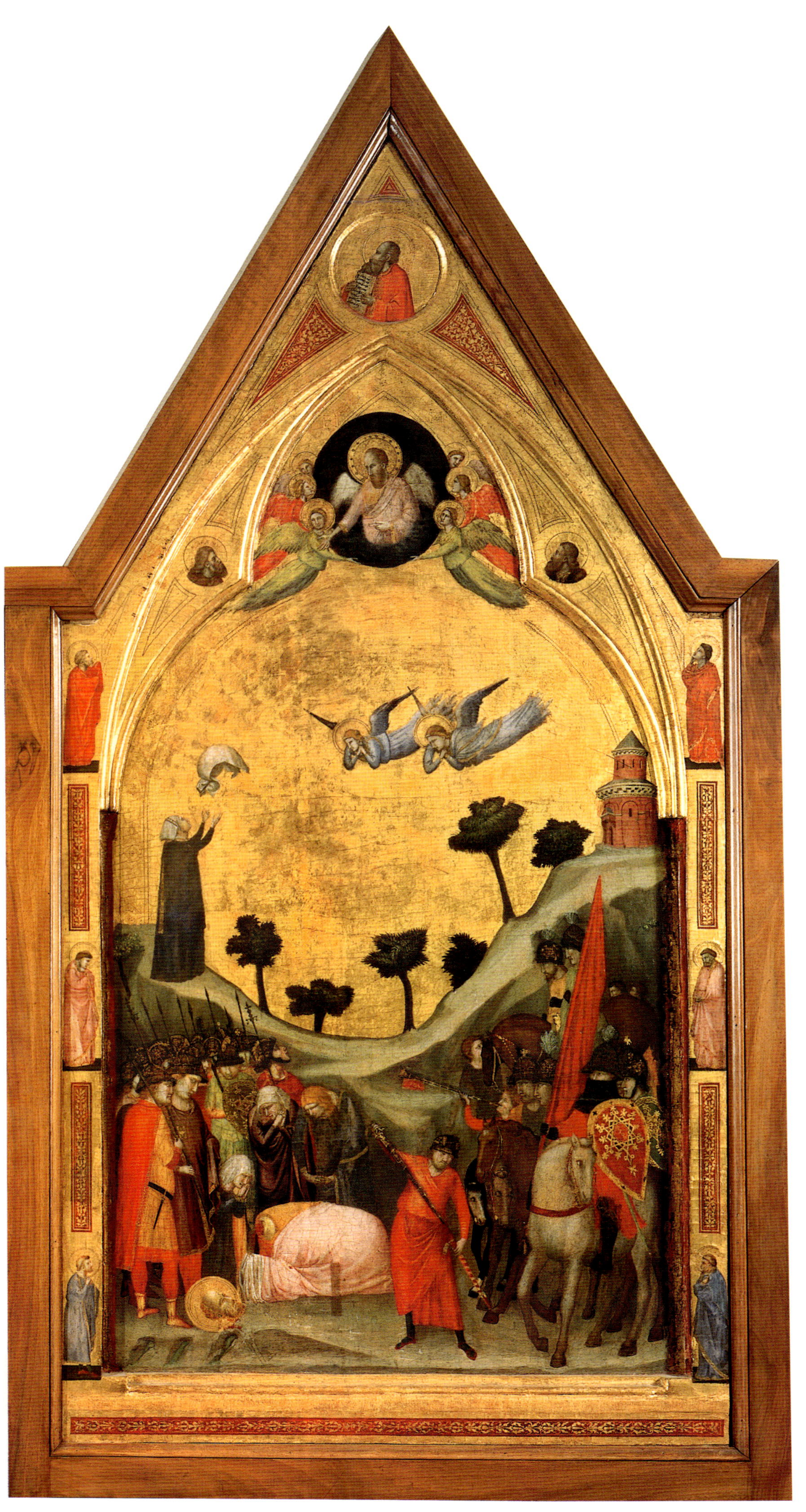

108, 109 *Stefaneschi Altar*, side showing Christ:
Martyrdom of Paul (details ill. 101), 1313

Against the golden background an amazingly deep
landscape stretches out, representing the place where the
apostle Paul was beheaded: on the hill on the right we
can recognize the lighthouse of Ostia. Opposite this
tower, a maiden is thrown the cloth used to catch the
saint's blood by his spirit. In the foreground, we see the
executioner in the center of the picture, separating the
group of mourners around the beheaded man on one
side, and the retreating soldiers on the other.

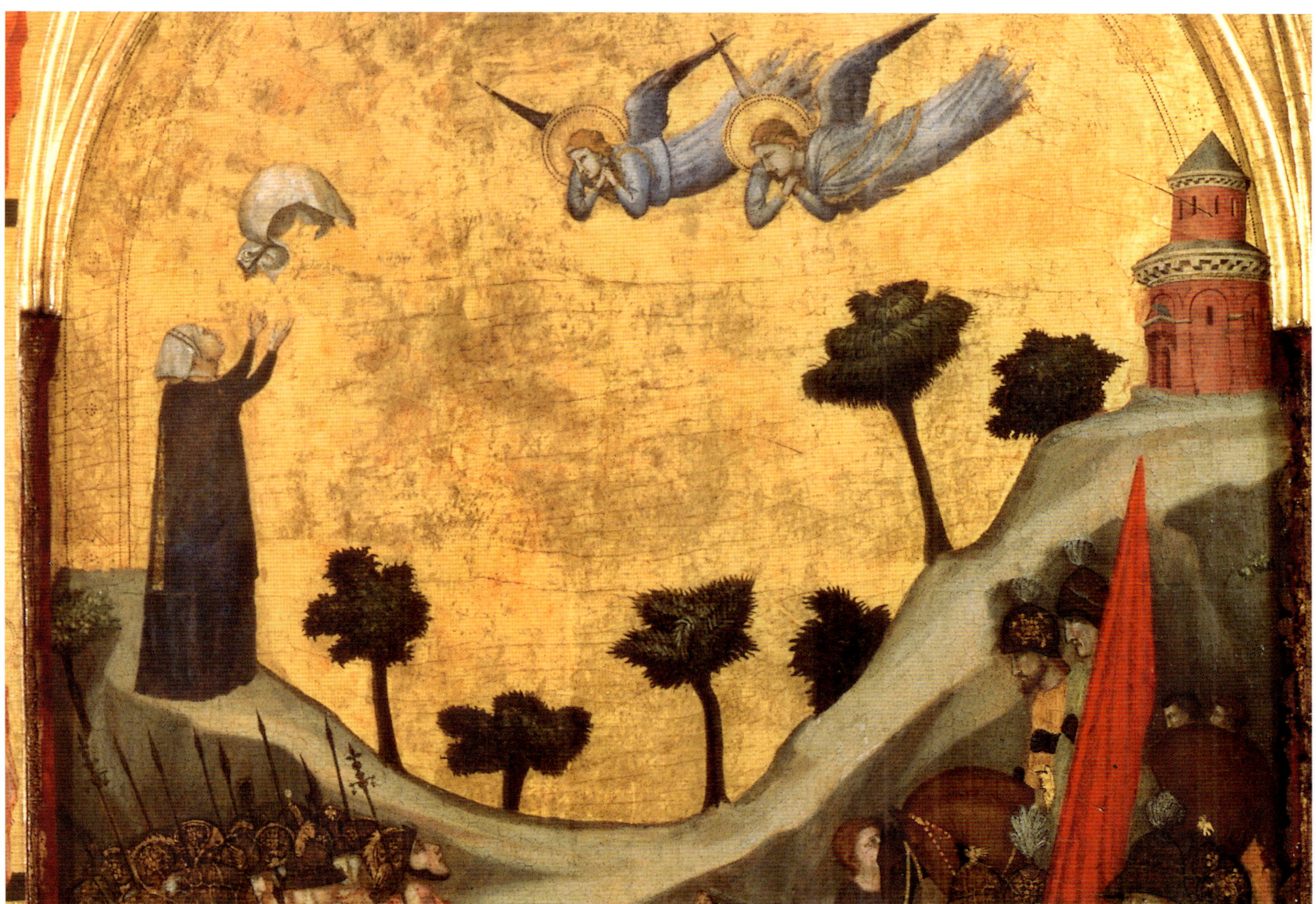

appears among the mourners, directly next to the beheaded man. Now she stands high above them. The winged soul of the saint throws the cloth used to catch his blood back to her as a sign of comfort. She is perhaps one of the most touching and poetic figures in the whole composition.

In comparison with his earlier works, the better development of space and the more logical use of consistent perspective are new to all the panels of the triptych. Even the figures move differently here, although their gestural language has the same essential features as it did in the frescoes at Padua. They are, on the whole, more slender, not so heavy, and so they are in keeping with the unusually lustrous and delicate style of painting. However, the ability of the figures to move is as little new to Giotto's work as are their miniature-like qualities. These features can already be found in some of the representations of the Virtues in the Arena Chapel – especially on the podium of the thrones of Justice (ill. 106).

The sumptuous way in which this altarpiece has been painted, however, achieves a rich gloss of bright coloring, which did not occur previously in Giotto's works. An example of this is the female figure with the shimmering green cloak and the long, loose hair, standing in front of St. Peter's cross. It is possible that Giotto was inspired by his contact with Sienese artists to paint in a more miniature form and with a richer coloring. But perhaps this development also derives from corresponding impulses from Rome or from his involvement with a very different artistic medium, one new to Giotto – the mosaic. The glittering stones of the latter could have prompted Giotto to make the colors also shine more brilliantly on wood. In any case, the renewed study of the art of antiquity and the design of the giant *Navicella* mosaic will have given Giotto new inspiration for understanding and depicting space, which he could then translate into the medium of paint in the Stefaneschi triptych.

THE GREAT MOSAIC IN ROME

110 *Tondo with angel*, ca. 1310
Mosaic, diameter 65.5 cm
S. Pietro Ispano, Cappella Simoncelli, Boville Ernica,
Rome

Although heavily restored, this fragment of the *Navicella* conveys an impression of the splendor of the original mosaic.

A written obituary for Cardinal Stefaneschi, stored in the Vatican library, mentions among his donations not only the magnificent altarpiece, but also a mosaic that he likewise commissioned from Giotto, and for which he paid 2,000 gold florins.

The giant mosaic was originally situated on the eastern porch of the old St. Peter's basilica and occupied the whole of the wall above the entrance arcade facing the courtyard. It measured approximately 13.5 x 9.5 m, and depicted on its uninterrupted surface St. Peter walking on the waters. Unfortunately, this extraordinary work has been destroyed in the course of its history. During the construction of the new St. Peter's in the 17th century it was moved several times to a different location, resulting in smaller and greater losses. First, the inscription disappeared, and only two fragments of the framework survived – an angel in the Vatican Grottos, restored almost beyond recognition, and another equally heavily restored angel in the church of St. Peter at Boville Ernica (ill. 110). Even greater losses among the figures followed – especially that of Peter – until the mosaic was finally installed inside the church in 1628 to protect it from the effects of the weather. Prior to this, Francesco Berretta was commissioned to make an exact copy in paint (ill. 111). But the mosaic did not stay for long even on the interior façade of St. Peter's. Another change of location, its ultimate loss and a Baroque reproduction mark the further fate of the work up till 1674.

Today it is the Baroque version of the *Navicella* that we see in the entrance area of St. Peter's. The mosaic was already called the *Navicella*, or "little ship" when a copy appeared in the church of St. Peter in Strasbourg in 1320, or when it was drawn by Parri Spinelli about 80 years later (ill. 112). From the 14th century on, many pilgrim guides mentioned it by this name. People were impressed by the large boat, which dominated the scene, and whose sail, filled by the storm, loomed over the horizon. Such a natural representation of a seascape and of a ship in trouble was known only from ancient works of art, if at all. Together with the mosaic's brightness, the effect must have been overwhelming – enthusiastic reports of the *Navicella* by worshippers testify that this was so.

During the Renaissance, the great historian Leon Battista Alberti emphasized the way the figures were depicted and placed this alongside works from antiquity as an example in his teachings. He praised the vividness of the eleven disciples in the boat, who look on anxiously as their companion Peter strides across the water to Christ. Using posture, gesture and facial expression, Giotto, according to Alberti, let the disciples express their fear in diverse and individually different ways.

In the Gospel of St. Matthew (chapter 14, 24 – 32), the evangelist relates how the disciples feared for their lives on the lake of Gennesaret. Their boat in distress, the Lord appears to them on the water, and they take him for a spirit. Only Peter is trusting enough to dare to climb out of the boat and walk across to Christ. The apostle is seized by doubt, and he threatens to sink into the waters. Christ immediately puts out a hand to save him. The story can be read as an incitement to unwavering faith, and its representation at one of the most important places in Christendom can be seen as a parable of the situation of the church: the ship of the church pitches and rolls and even the pope, Peter's successor, has doubts. Salvation can only be found in faith in Christ. But the pope had left Rome and was residing under the influence of the French king at Avignon. Was this why the ship of the church had begun to sway? And did Cardinal Stefaneschi wish this donation to be understood not only as a general exhortation to unwavering faith, but moreover as an appeal for the return of the pope to Rome? We may presume so.

Since Giotto, in Florence in December 1313, arranged for his household items to be collected from his Roman landlady, he must have been in Rome for some time before that. The stylistic characteristics that emerge from the copy made on canvas by Berretta also suggest that the mosaic be dated between the Paduan frescoes and the Stefaneschi altar, i.e. between 1305 and 1313. The expanse of the landscape, the expressiveness and the mobility of the figures exceed the possibilities seen in Padua and have some influence on the representations on the altarpiece.

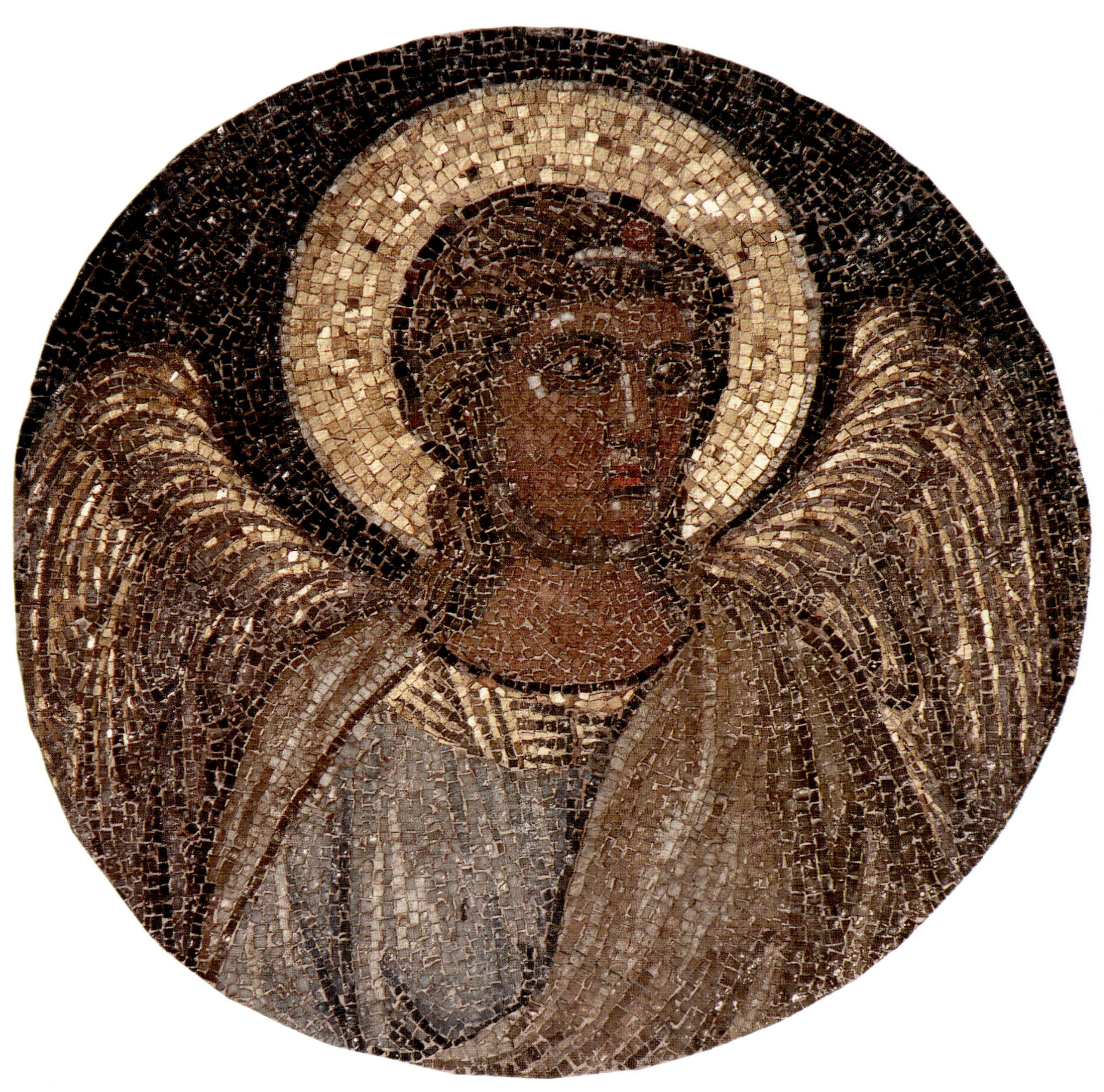

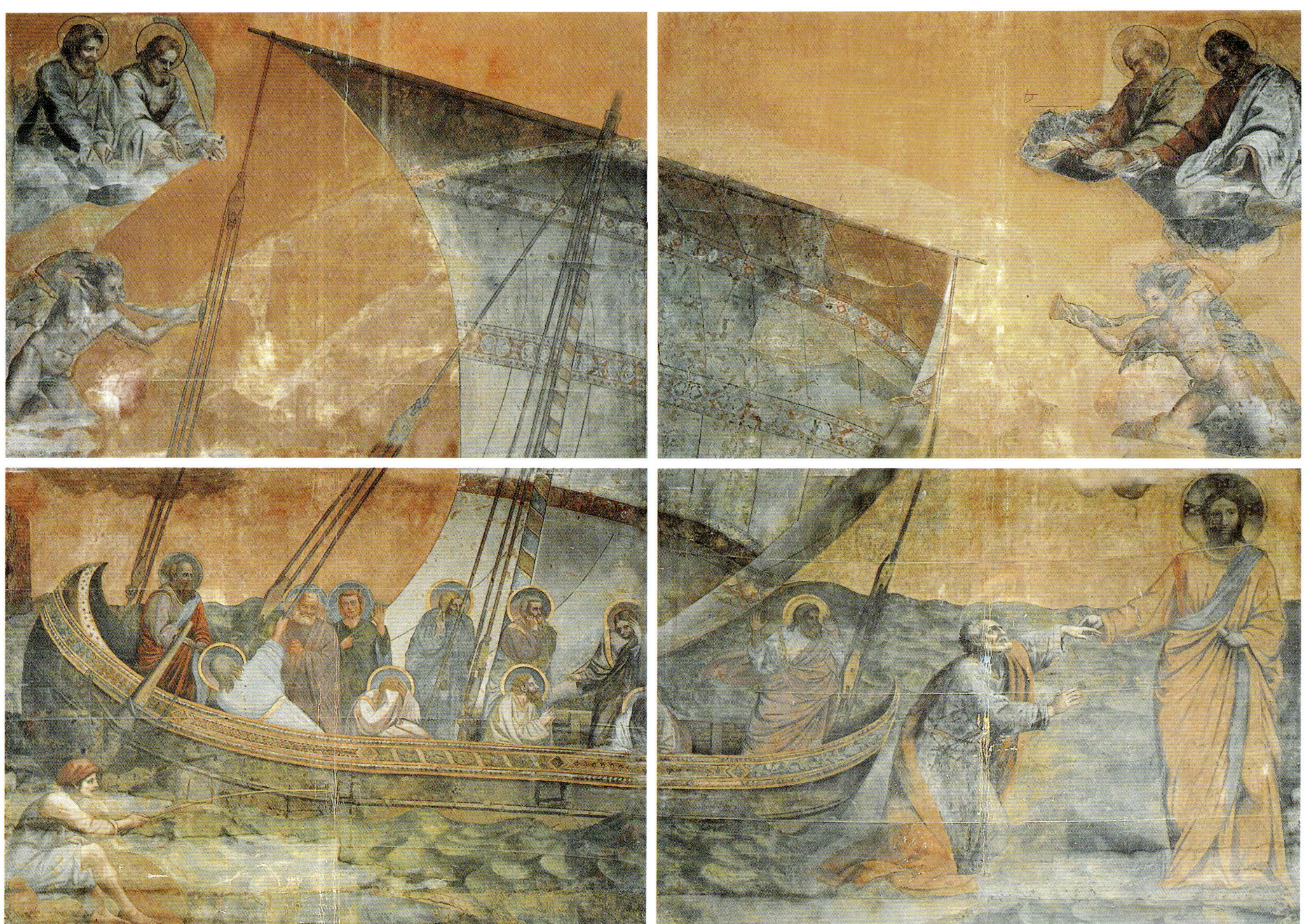

111 Francesco Berretta
Navicella, 1628
Canvas, 740 x 990 cm
Vaticano, Rev. Fabbrica di S. Pietro, Rome

Francesco Berretta made a copy on canvas of Giotto's
mosaic before it was cut down from the wall and moved
to another place. Although the framework, the figure of
Peter and large parts from around the edges had already
been lost at this stage, we can still make out the
monumental composition of the mosaic – the great ship,
in which Peter's companions, full of fear, watch the
events on the water.

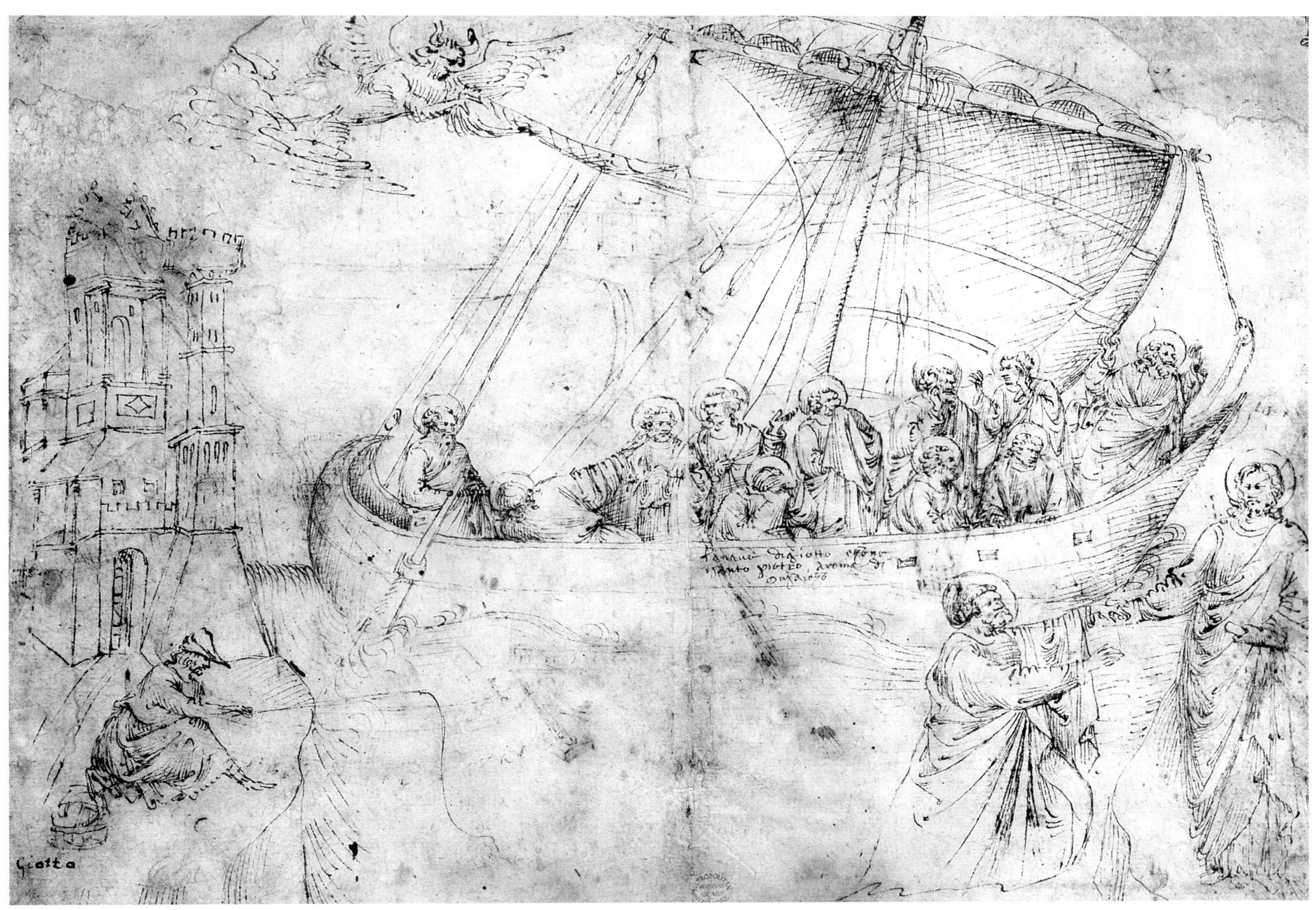

112 Parri Spinelli
Navicella, ca. 1400
Drawing: pen on paper, 27.4 x 38.8 cm
Metropolitan Museum of Art, Hewitt Fund, New York

Parri Spinelli made a drawing of Giotto's mosaic when it
was still in its original position. He emphasized what
seemed to him to be the essential features: the great sail
filled with wind, the anxious disciples, and Christ, saving
Peter from the waters. Moreover, he reproduced in detail
the architecture of the harbor and the peaceful angler on
the left-hand edge of the picture. This peripheral scene
was soon lost during the many removals of the mosaic.

Back in Florence – the Decoration of the Peruzzi Chapel

113 Peruzzi and Bardi Chapels
Church of Santa Croce, Florence

The two chapels, which Giotto decorated for the two Florentine banking dynasties, lie next to one another in the Franciscan church. On the left, we can see into the Bardi Chapel and can make out the vault with its representations of the Franciscan virtues; to the right, in the Peruzzi Chapel we can see the scenes from the life of John the Evangelist. It is clear that Giotto composed these latter paintings in relation to the view from outside the chapel.

At the end of 1313, Giotto was back in Florence and winning new clients there. He was once more working in a Franciscan church, in the great Minorite church of Santa Croce, for which he was to continue creating works right up until the end of his life. According to a statement made by the Florentine artist Lorenzo Ghiberti (1378–1455), Giotto painted four of the chapels here. Several noble Florentine families are also said to have commissioned panel paintings from him, with which they endowed the altars in Santa Croce. But only two chapels and one altarpiece which can confidently be attributed to Giotto have survived the ravages of time – the Peruzzi and Bardi chapels, and the *Baroncelli Polyptych* (ills. 113, 147).

The construction of the Peruzzi Chapel, the second chapel of the right-hand transept, was made possible by the influential banker, Donato di Arnoldo Peruzzi, who left additional money for this memorial chapel in his will in 1299. It was probably his grandson Giovanni di Rinieri Peruzzi who donated the murals honoring John the Evangelist and John the Baptist, which were the first works created by Giotto in Santa Croce.

The juxtaposition of the two John cycles is unusual, and researchers believe it contains a mixture of religious and secular iconography: John the Evangelist was the donor's name-saint; John the Baptist was patron saint both of the city of Florence and of St. Francis, to whom Santa Croce is dedicated. In his family's memorial chapel the banker Peruzzi, therefore, has realized a program which connects his own memory and that of his family with the religious background of the Franciscans and the fate of the city, in which the Peruzzis were one of the most influential families. It is, in a manner of speaking, an act of obeisance towards the most important order of the day and towards the city of Florence, the ecclesiastical and the secular powers, so to speak. An act of obeisance, however, which at the same time elevated himself and his family.

In the entrance arch to the chapel, busts of prophets appear in six-lobed traceries. The vault is decorated with the symbols of the four evangelists, and there are further representations of the Apocalypse on the window wall, such as the Lamb of God at the top of the window arch.

The Apocalypse is a fixed component in the Franciscan body of thought, and at the same time stands in relation to the subject of the Resurrection, which appears fitting for a memorial and sepulchral chapel. John the Baptist, as a forerunner of Christ, alludes to the Resurrection. Following the death of Christ, John the Evangelist preaches of the kingdom of God and prophesies the second coming of the Lord in his *Vision of John the Evangelist on Patmos* (ill. 119). The banker who commissioned the works eschewed the emphasis on poverty usual in Franciscan churches. Instead, the realism of the representations, as well as the effects of the miracles, which Giotto illustrates in the faces and gestures of his figures, suggest a new feeling of self-determination even within city life.

Naturalism and realism, and his use of these to incorporate the miraculous into individual experiences of the world, were already characteristics of Giotto's earlier works. This was the basis on which he developed his art in the Peruzzi Chapel. The overall layout here demonstrates the logical consistency he used in further development of the kind of spatial structure with which we are familiar from the architectural framework of the Legend of St. Francis at Assisi. The perspective is based on a viewpoint just outside the chapel (ill. 113).

On the walls inside there are three scenes each from the life of the Evangelist and of the Baptist opposite one another above a simple *dado* of painted marble. In each case, two of the paintings, which are framed by ornamental bands, take up the whole width of the side wall, the third filling the lunette above. At the bottom, the *Ascension of John the Evangelist* and the death of the Baptist in the representation of *Herod's Banquet* (ills. 122, 118), and the *Raising of Drusiana* as well as the *Birth and Naming of John the Baptist* (ills. 120, 117) correspond with one another; at the top, it is the *Vision of John the Evangelist on Patmos* and the *Annunciation to Zachariah* (ills. 119, 114).

Giotto did not paint these pictures onto moist plaster as was usual, but onto dry plaster – another experiment with new materials following on from the mosaic. Unfortunately, due to this technique, the murals, which were painted over in the 18th century and restored in the 19th, have not survived very well. Much of the

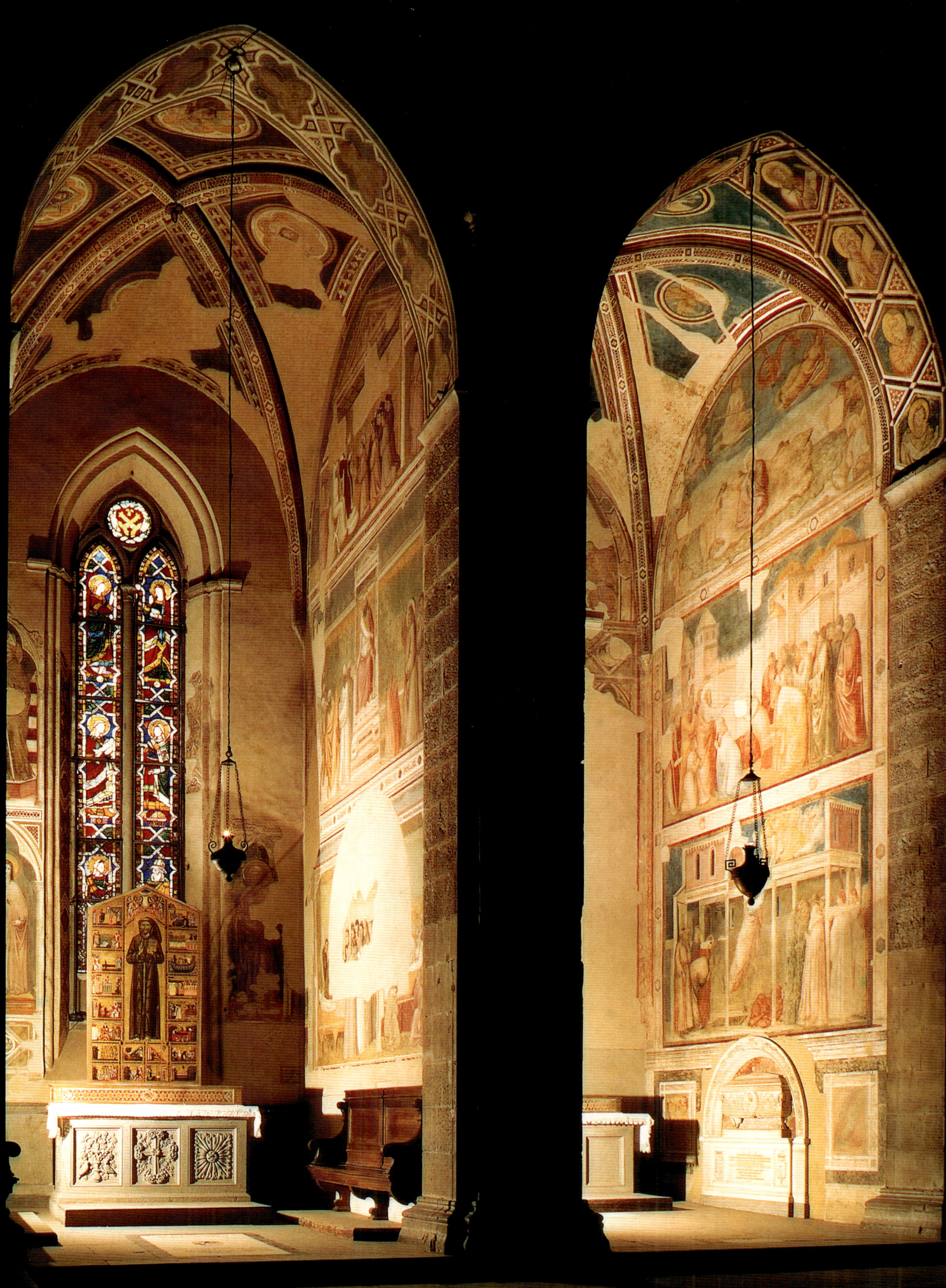

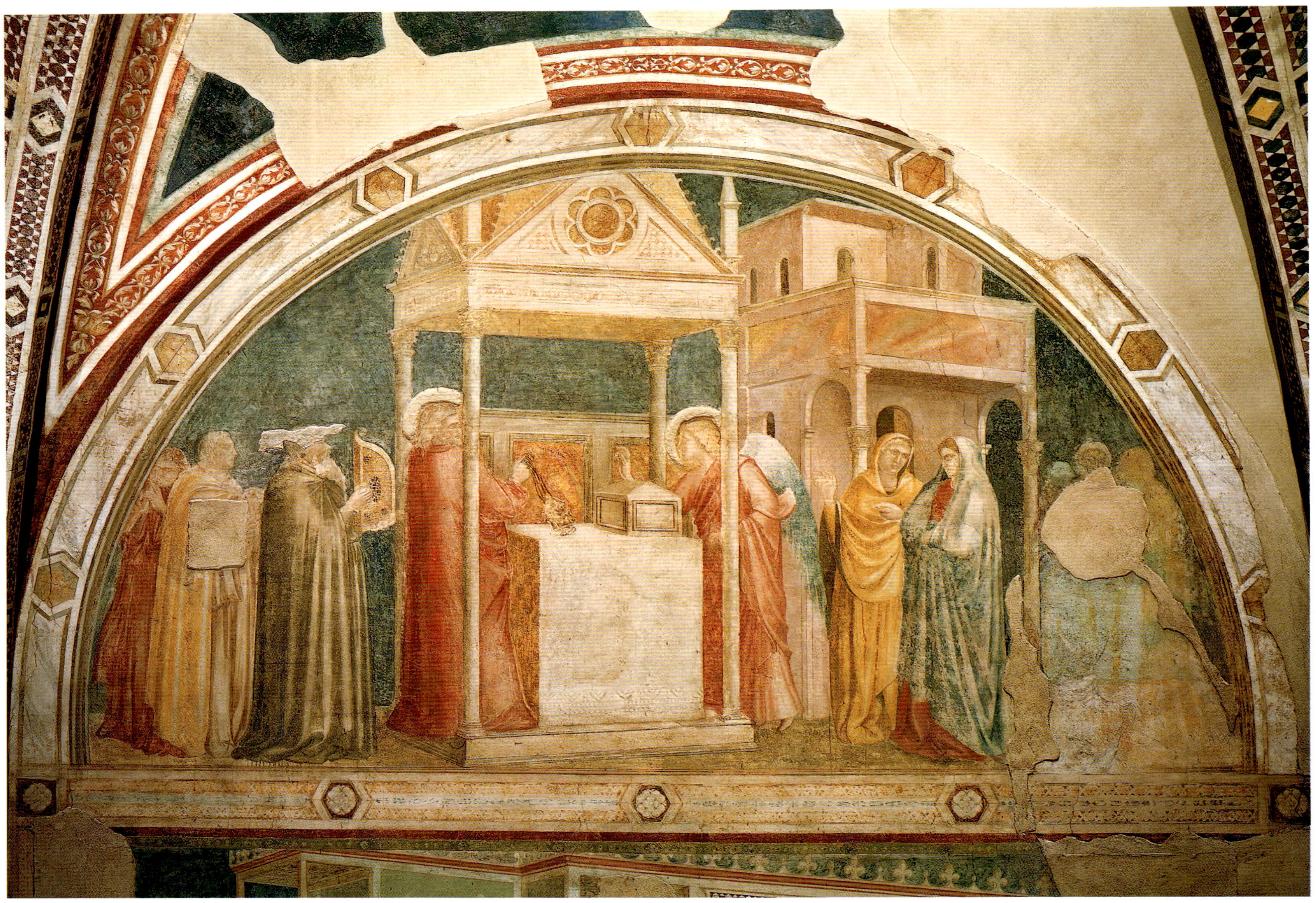

surface has been lost, so that the quality of the painting is more to be guessed at than assessed. However, we can make out clearly the composition, the shaping of figures and the formation of space.

The scene in the lunette depicting *Vision of John the Evangelist on Patmos* follows on from the landscape in the *Navicella* (ills. 111, 119). The Evangelist is sitting on the island in the middle of an extensive seascape, whose spatial qualities can only really be appreciated by a spectator standing outside the chapel. John is lost in thought and yet quite attentive to the apocalyptic phenomena around him – we are reminded of the *Dream of Joachim* at Padua (ill. 68). John's inner visions have taken on form. They seem to rotate around a central point, around the ear of the Evangelist, which is turned upwards. Because of this, John gives the impression of being wide-awake, completely in the grip of these manifestations.

While this scene is clearly centered, the scene in the lunette opposite, the *Annunciation to Zachariah*, is subdivided by its two pieces of architecture (ill. 114). The figures, the procession of musicians and the

gossiping women, move in a particularly realistic manner here, one could almost say in an everyday manner. This makes Zachariah's shock at the appearance of the angel, whom the others obviously do not see, all the more dreadful. It is precisely this contrast that makes the sudden intervention of a celestial being comprehensible, even to the spectator.

In the scene below, two interior spaces open out before us (ill. 117). In contrast to the comparable representation at Padua, the *Birth of The Virgin Mary* (ill. 70), the architecture has been moved closer to the edge of the picture here, so that we do not see as much of the outside of the building, and the rooms are more extensive. The figures move more easily here. We have already observed this change in relation to the Arena frescoes in the Stefaneschi altarpiece, but now it has been translated to the more monumental scale of wall painting.

In contrast to the quiet world, greatly characterized by the women around Elizabeth as she lies in childbirth and around the speechless patriarch Zachariah, the situation is loud and dramatic in *Herod's Banquet* (ill. 118). Different pieces of architecture match the

114, 115 *Annunciation to Zachariah* (and detail), ca. 1313/14
Mural
Chiesa di Santa Croce, Cappella Peruzzi, Florence

Zachariah shrinks back before the angel, who prophesies the birth of a son. The musicians on one side, and the women on the other, do not seem to notice any of this. The depiction of the women in particular reveals a change in the way figures are fashioned compared to the Arena Chapel. Although comparable in volume, these women move in a more lithesome fashion.

Giotto has also further developed the depiction of space. Thus the buildings disappear behind the painted frame of the lunette, creating the impression that the view has been truncated.

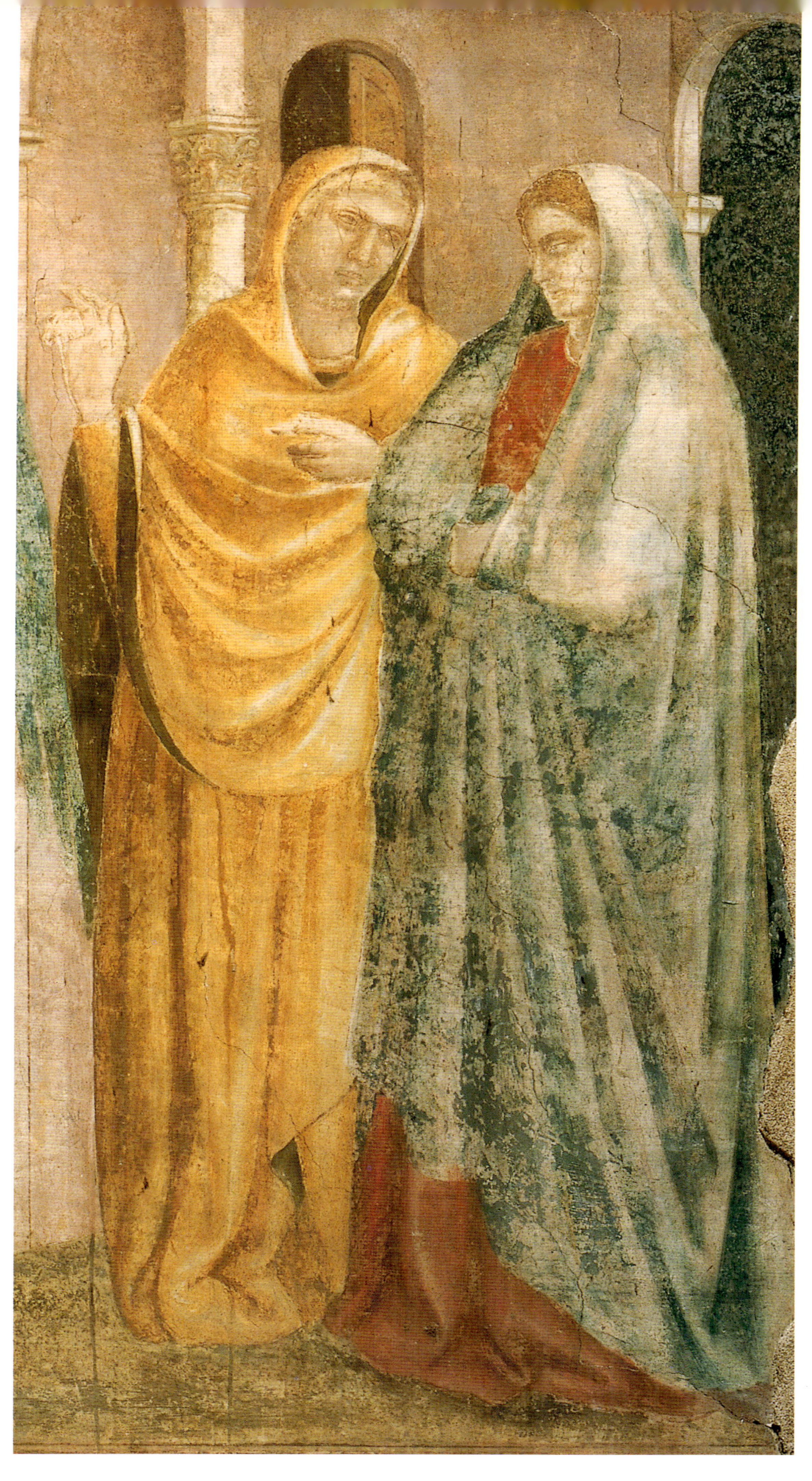

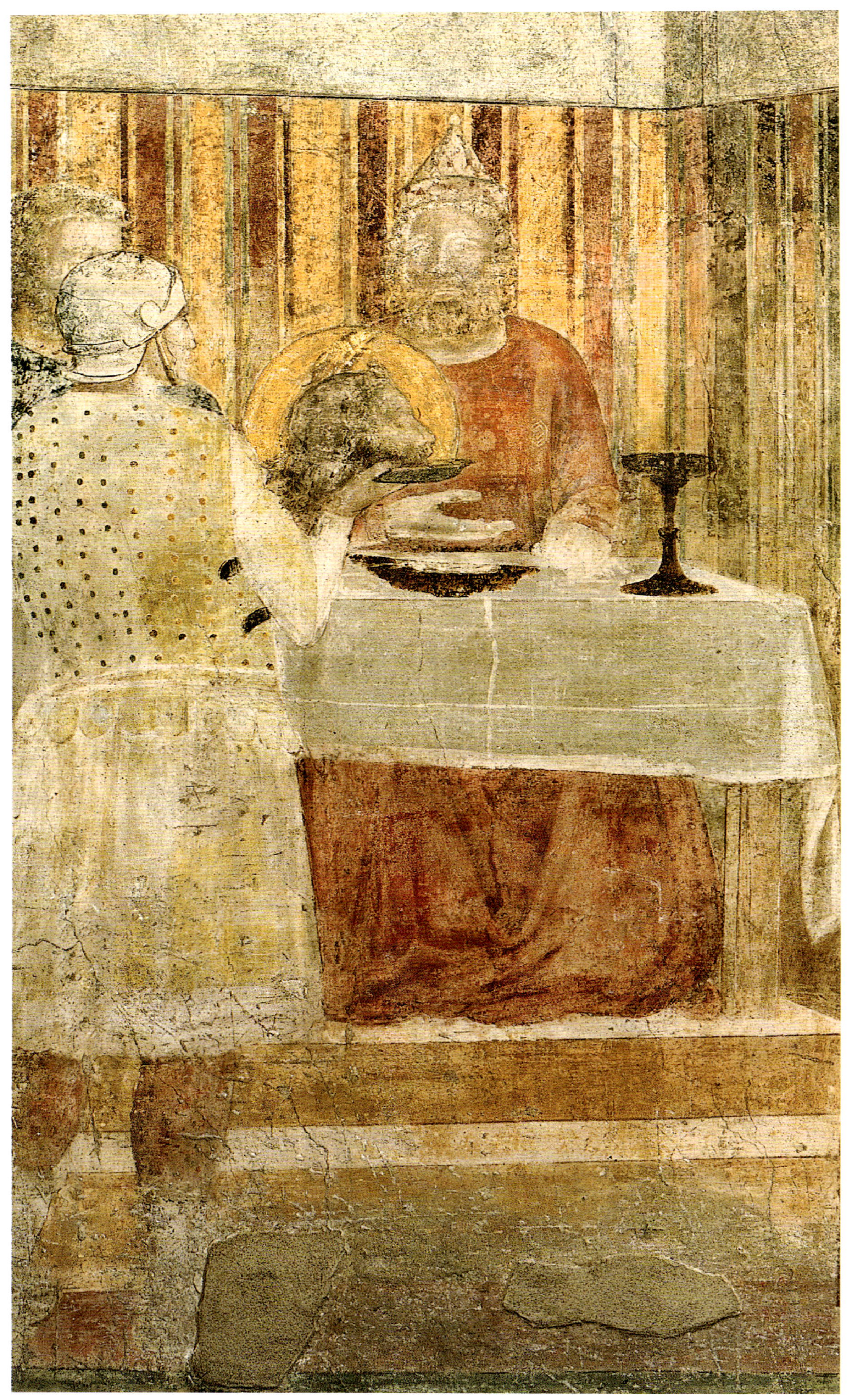

117 (opposite, above) *Birth and Naming of John the Baptist*, ca. 1313/14
Mural
Chiesa di Santa Croce, Cappella Peruzzi, Florence

This picture field contains two scenes, which Giotto unites by way of the architecture and the domestic environment common to both. On the right, we can see Elizabeth, John's mother, in labor, and on the left, his father, who is writing his name on a tablet. The world of this house is characterized by women: by women in expensive clothing, who appear considerably more urban than the women in the frescoes at Padua.

116, 118 (left and opposite) *Herod's Banquet*, ca.1313/14
Mural
Chiesa di Santa Croce, Cappella Peruzzi, Florence

The banquet takes place in a splendid open hall, decorated with small marble figures. John the Baptist is beheaded at the request of the dancing Salome. In contrast to the festiveness of the scene, Giotto increases the brutality of the events through the gestures, culminating in the encounter between Herod and the henchman, who hands him the severed head as if it were a dish of fare. Even although the surface of the faces is badly damaged, this moment of horror and outrage is still clear: plates, hands, dishes and head form an alarmingly brutal unity, over which soldier and king look at one another.

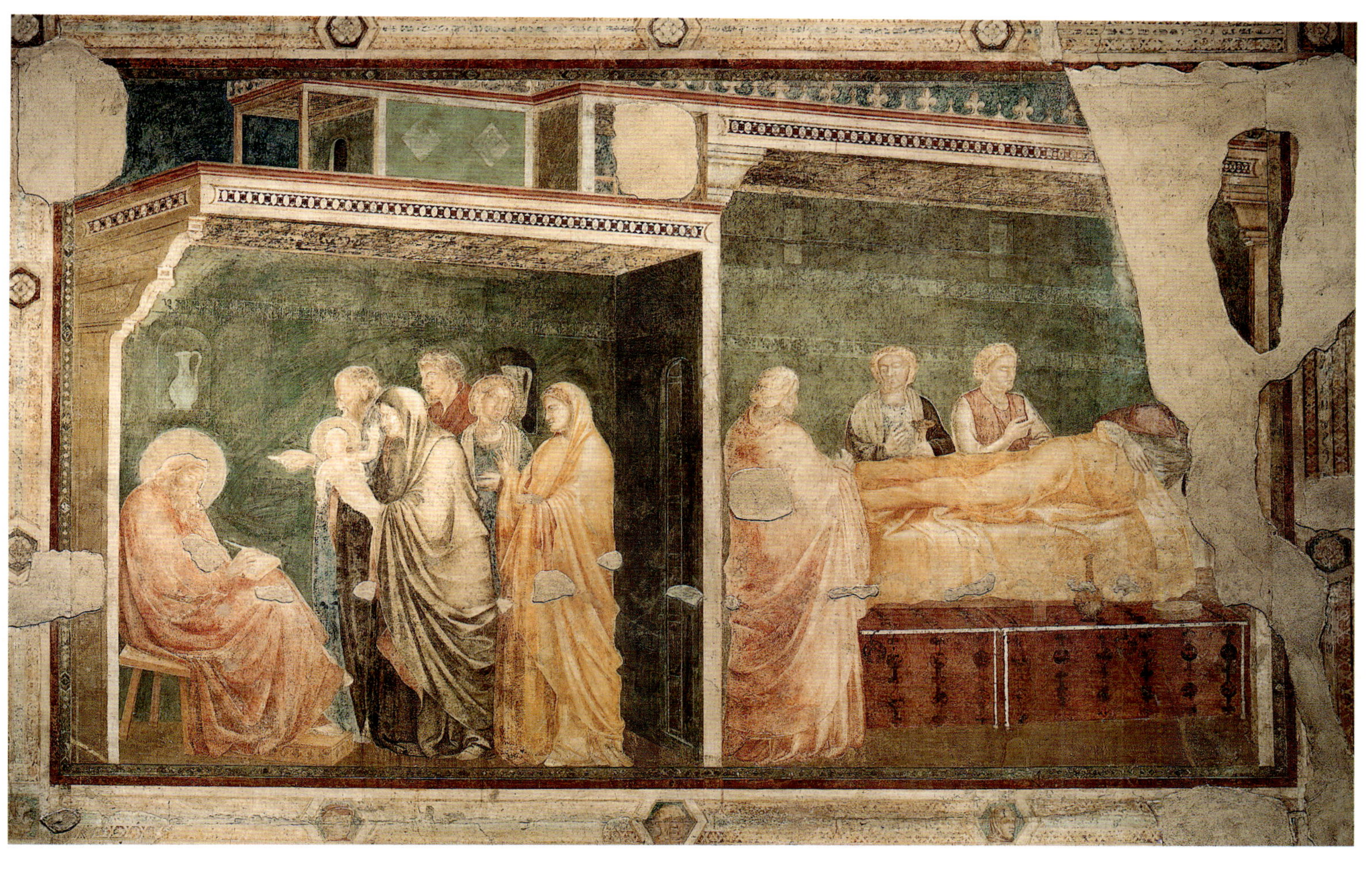

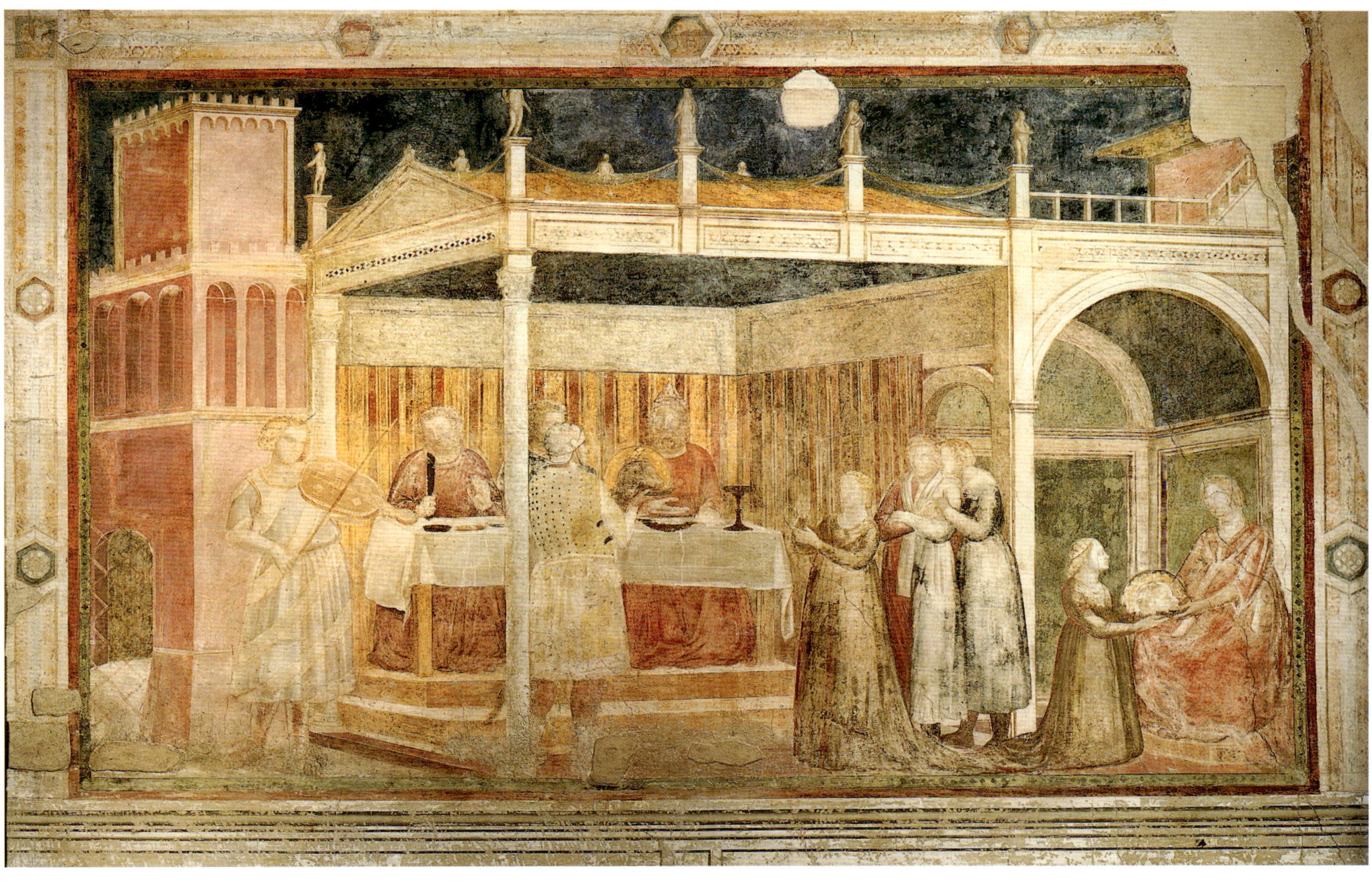

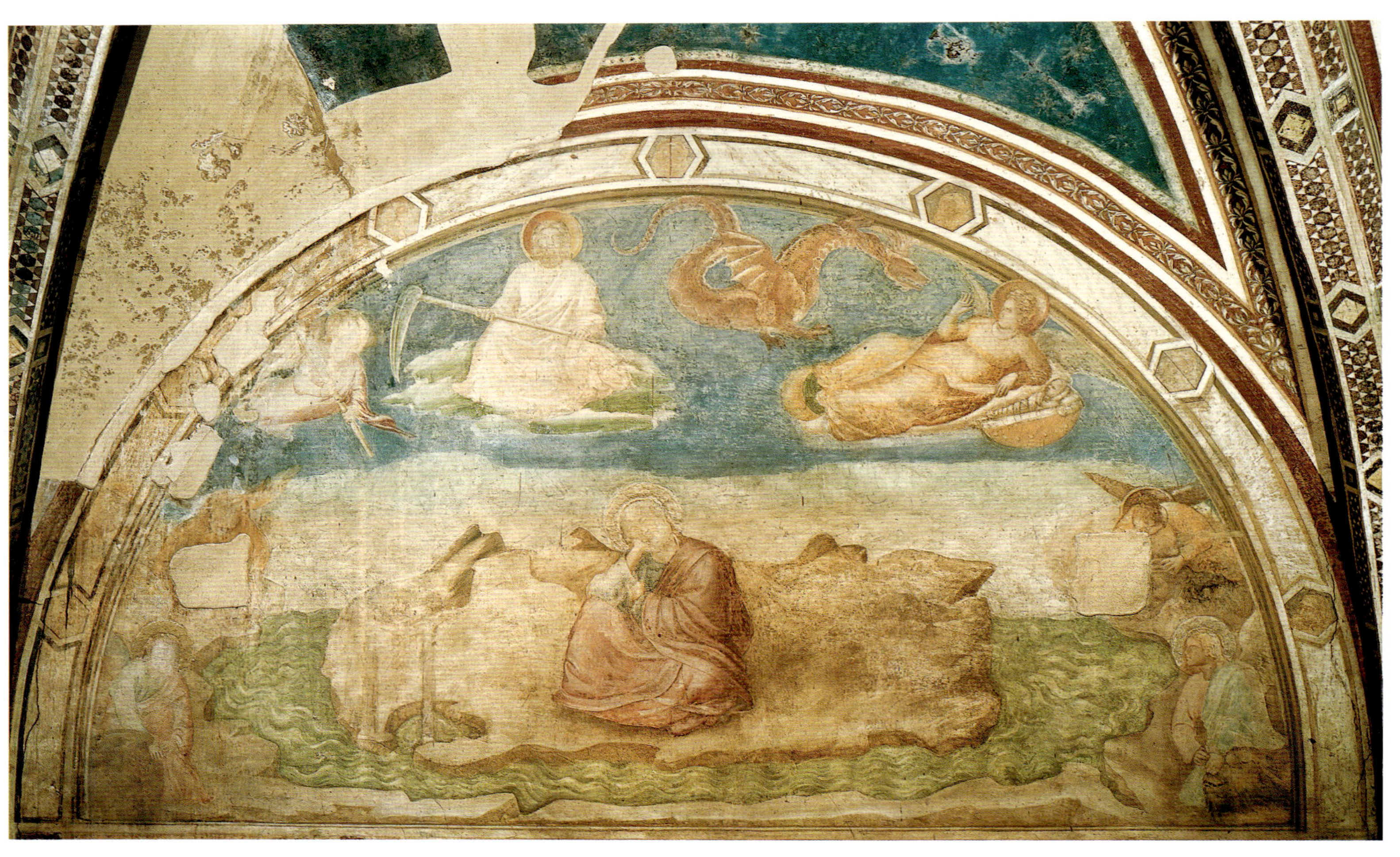

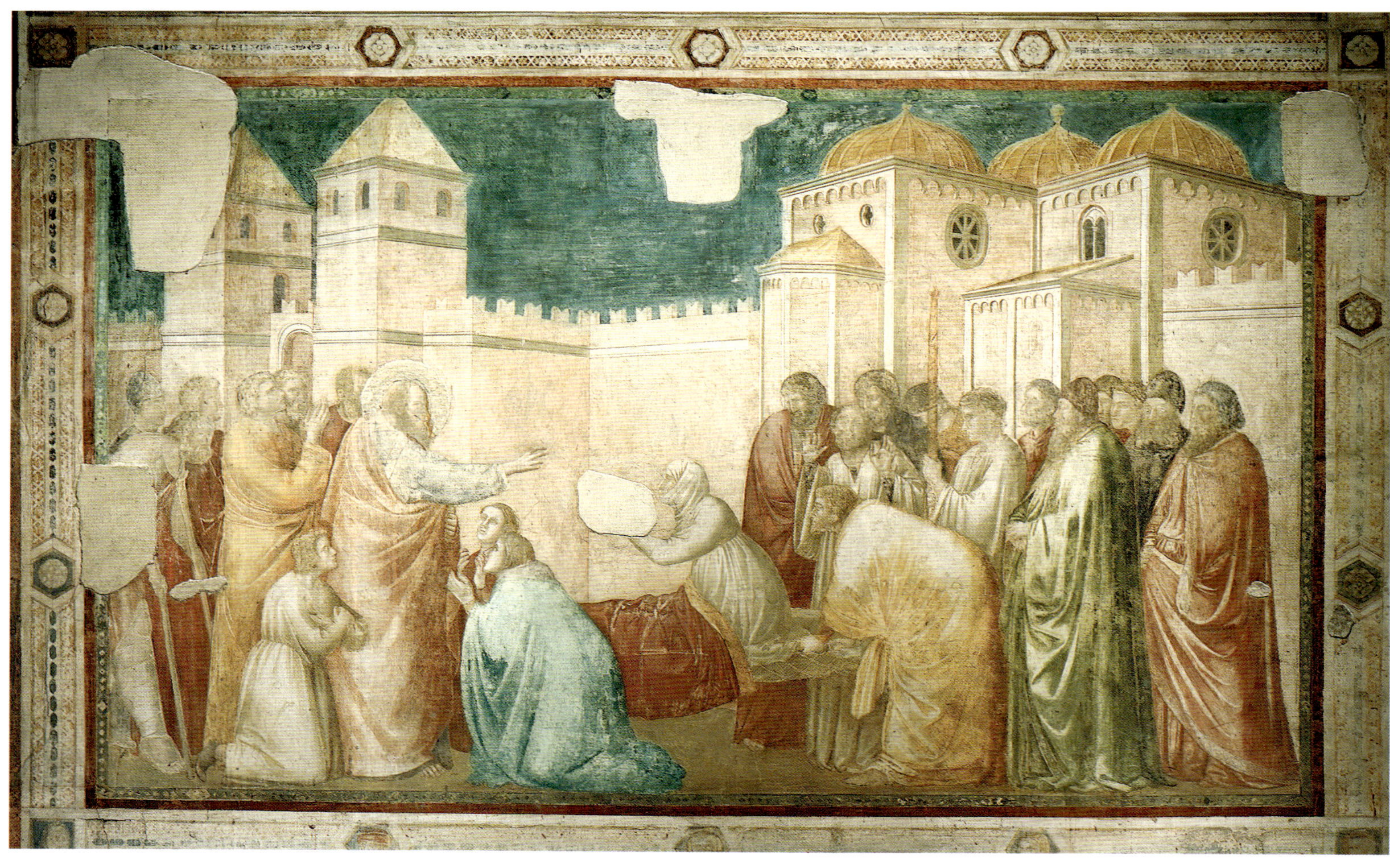

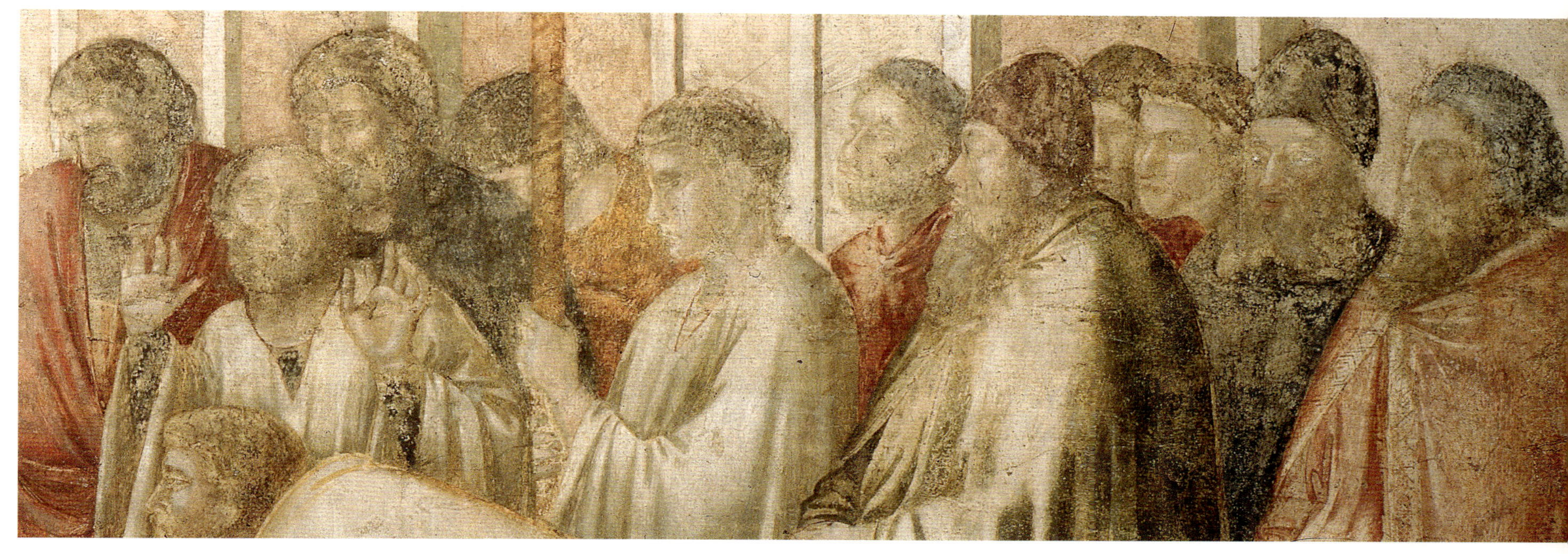

character of each of the individual scenes. The unfriendly tower on the far left contains the unseen torso of the Baptist. In the center of the bright banqueting hall are the head of the murdered man and Herod. And on the extreme right, in a small, closed room, Salome hands her mother Herodias the terrible trophy.

The musician connects tower and banqueting hall. Salome dances to his music, watched lecherously by two figures. The posture and gestures of these three figures express delightful arousal and form a sharp contrast to the uniformed figure that also stands in front of the table. This soldier hands John's head to Herod. We can unfortunately no longer make out the expression on the king's face, but can still recognize the drama of the situation. The plate, Herod's hand, the hand of the soldier, and the dish containing the head of the Baptist are layered one on top of the other. Only the golden rays of the halo protect and transfigure the noble head, seen in profile, which is being brutally presented here as a dish to eat (ill. 116).

Herod's Banquet brings the series of three paintings on the left-hand wall to a close, thematically and formally. Especially in this representation, it is striking how mobile and "correctly" proportioned the small figures are in relation to the architecture. This has led to the supposition that Giotto's assistants were at work here. Surely this type of representation was intended to heighten our recognition of everyday city life. While the surface is too badly damaged to allow a conclusive evaluation of the degree of involvement of the workshop, the figural language and the heightened drama of the composition nevertheless do appear to correspond very closely to the rest of Giotto's output.

The diverse palace architecture in this final picture from the life story of the Baptist, and to a greater extent the architecture in the *Ascension of John the Evangelist* on the wall opposite (ill. 122) illustrate yet again that the artist was mindful of the view from outside the chapel. The perspective of the church building only becomes plausible when seen from the entrance, and only from there can we discern the layout of the choir recesses as well as the construction of the open hall of the church. People, citizens of the town, have made their way there. They are taken aback, are amazed, blinded or even thrown to the ground by an event which has overtaken them, the consequence of which – the open memorial slab – they see, and the effect of which they feel.

The ascension of the Evangelist takes place in their midst. The church building is open at the top. Christ appears, accompanied by his disciples, as if on a cloud – it is known that Michelangelo made sketches of this mural, and perhaps the cloud of figures around God the Father in the *Creation of Adam* in the Sistine Chapel derives from this representation. The celestial figures remain hidden from the sight of those present.

In a subtle way, Giotto uses the layout of the architecture to illustrate that we are dealing with a divine manifestation. The people only see its effect. This is also true of the ascending figure of the Evangelist, for he is wrapped in a halo of golden rays, which emanates from Christ and in which he is also being carried. The encounter between the saint and Christ is particularly intense: all of the tension lies in their exchange of glances, a gaze which is able to cancel out gravity. Christ helpfully grasps John's wrist with his right hand. Their two other hands do not yet touch. It is precisely by capturing this single moment in time that Giotto achieves a plausible representation of the ascension. The extraordinary and wonderful nature of this event is clearly expressed in the animated gestures of the people.

A miracle is also taking place in the middle picture on the right-hand wall. In front of the gates of the city of Ephesus, John the Evangelist raises a woman by the name of Drusiana from the dead (ill. 120). The city walls with entrance gate and church are depicted with magnificent clarity of perspective and structure. Many

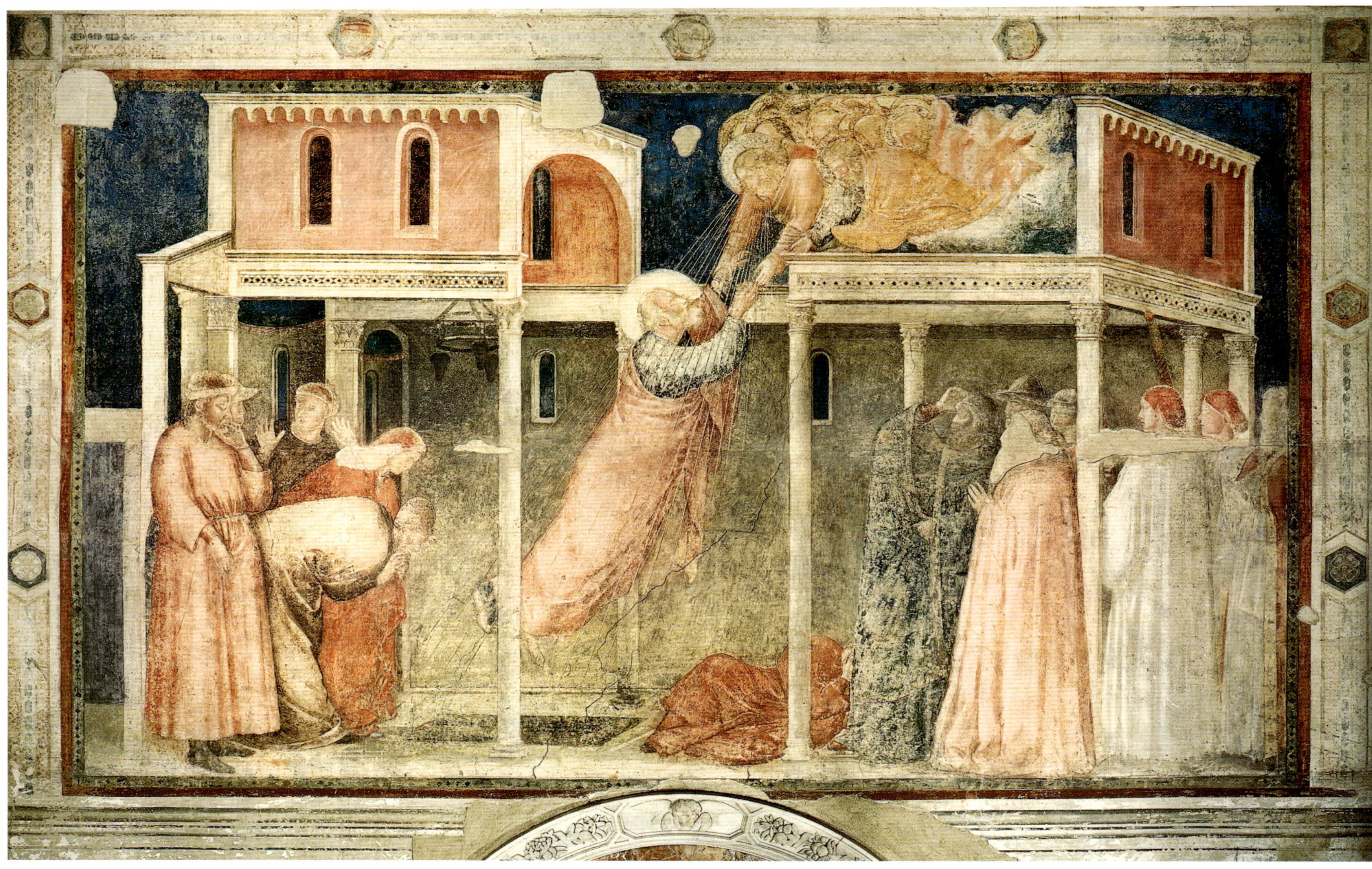

scholars assume that the representation of these buildings was inspired by the tales of merchants who had been to Asia Minor, and that the donor Peruzzi wanted to use it as an allusion to his own trade relations, which extended into these regions. Within the picture itself the architecture on the one hand connects the two groups of people, who stand facing one another, and on the other divides and structures them.

A large group of citizens of Ephesus was obviously accompanying Drusiana's funeral procession. The varied and yet closed appearance of this group corresponds to the architecture of the church, which acts as a backdrop. The Evangelist steps towards the townspeople. Surrounded by the praying, the pleading and the injured, his massive figure corresponds to the tower that looms up behind him. The gesture with which John stretches out his delicate hand, over the heads of those kneeling, towards Drusiana has an extremely powerful effect (ill. 126). As if magically drawn by the hand and the gaze of the Evangelist, the dead woman has sat up, is looking at the man who resurrected her and has stretched out both hands towards him. Unfortunately Drusiana's hands are

destroyed, but we can still sense that the sharp edge of the wall optically divides the two figures. It enhances the impression of an imagined spark passing between them. As in the *Ascension of John the Evangelist*, the miracle takes place through the intensity of gaze and can be experienced in the reaction of those present.

The introduction of a psychological element to the representation and the vividness of the figures can already be observed in the frescoes in the Upper Church at Assisi. The rhythmical articulation of the scene and the plastic modelling of the figures struck us in the frescoes at Padua. The intensity of gaze characterized the composition of the *Ognissanti Madonna* (ill. 98), and the mobility of the figures in a more extensive space marked the triptych in Rome. All of this knowledge seems to come together here in the narrative wall paintings in the Peruzzi Chapel. Building on this, Giotto dared to try out a new technique, unified the perspective throughout the whole cycle in a comprehensive fashion and again extended the spatial dimensions.

122, 123 *Ascension of John the Evangelist* (and detail), ca. 1313/14
Mural
Chiesa di Santa Croce, Cappella Peruzzi, Florence

Giotto illustrates the miracle of the ascension of John the Evangelist using the astonished, startled reactions of the group at the open tomb. The other group appears blinded and in the grip of a shock wave. The ascension takes place between these two groups: Christ, surrounded by heavenly hosts, appears above the building. He emits golden rays, which envelop the body of the evangelist. They transport the latter to a different sphere and seem like a materialization of the gaze with which Christ looks at John. We are given the impression that the energy, which overcomes gravity, lies more in the meeting of the eyes than in the coincidence of the gestures.

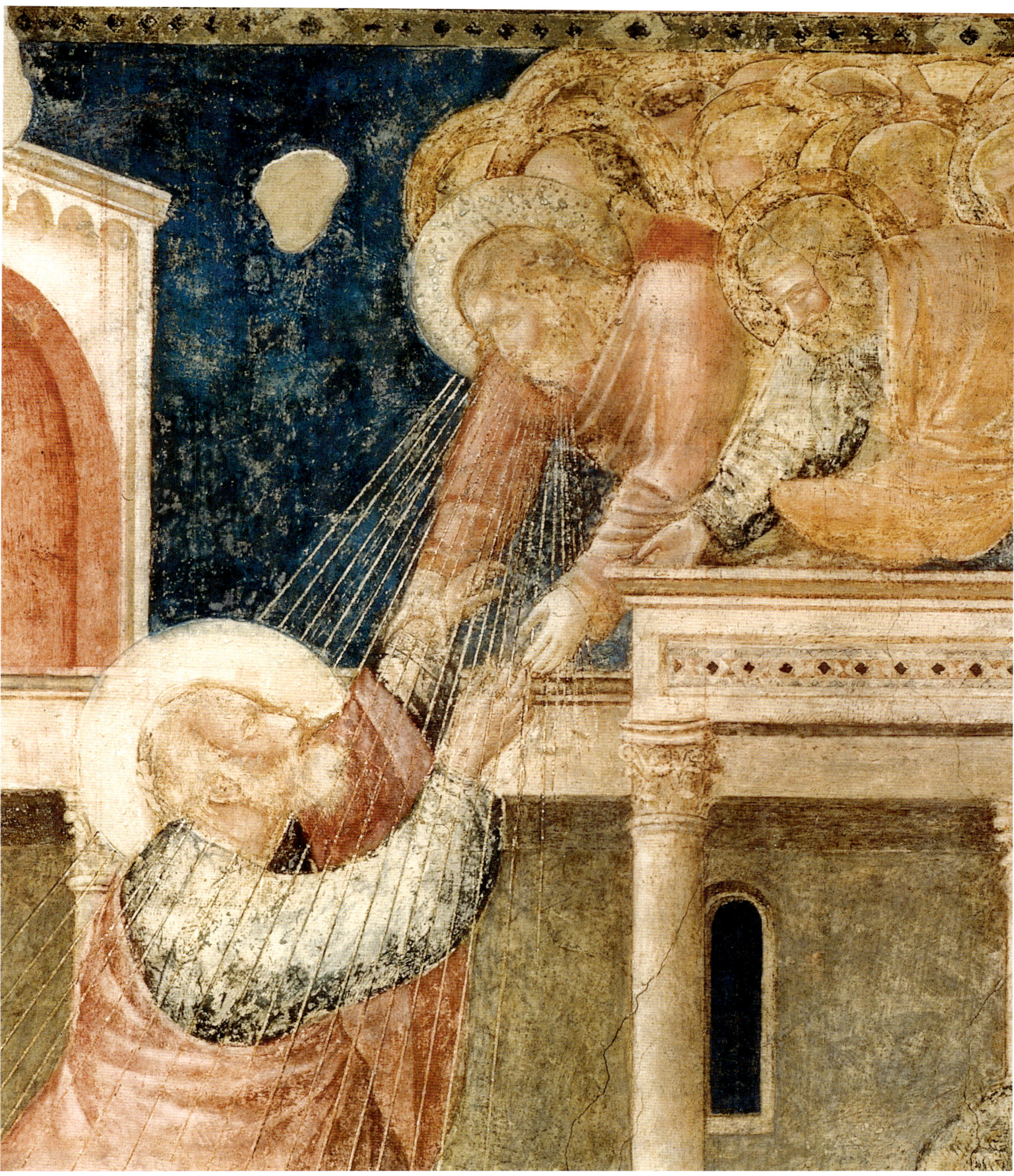

124 (left) *Raising of Lazarus* (detail ill. 82), 1302–1305

From the twisting motion of his body this Christ in the Paduan resurrection scene creates the tension and energy which is passed on to Lazarus via his scarcely bent arm and hand.

125 (center) Pupil of Giotto
Raising of Lazarus (detail ill. 127), ca. 1315

This Christ stands there firmly, but without vigor. His rigid gesture becomes purely symbolic and seems like a mixture of the Christ from the same scene in the Arena Chapel and the John of the resurrection scene in the Peruzzi Chapel in Florence.

126 (right) *Raising of Drusiana*, (detail ill. 120), ca. 1313/14

This detail clearly shows how Giotto reinforces the strength of the Evangelist's gesture by the way he turns his body, and how John's actions emanate from this motion, in a manner of speaking. The obstacle to be overcome, the praying people who have come up close to him, also increases the vigor of his gesture.

The Magdalene Chapel of the Lower Church at Assisi is a lateral chapel in the corner between the northern transept and the nave. Its fresco decoration takes different forms: medallions with half-length figures in the compartments of the vault, standing saints in the inside face of the entrance, narrative scenes on the walls and on the lunettes, and two portraits of donors on the end walls. Like Cardinal Stefaneschi in the Roman triptych, Teobaldo Pontano, Bishop of Assisi, had himself represented there twice: he kneels, first of all in bishop's vestments before the first bishop of the city, St. Rufinus, and then as a simple Franciscan monk before St. Mary Magdalene.

At the beginning and in the middle of this century the frescoes were cleaned and painstakingly restored. Since then some have held them to be work of the utmost quality from Giotto's own hand, others as the ambitious work of pupils.

Some point out that the relationship with the Paduan frescoes is evident here, that the three dimensional forms, which predominate in Padua, are here set free in paint, and that the way to the paintings in the Peruzzi Chapel is already marked out. To the other side, these appear more like copies of Giotto's frescoes at Padua: the noticeable widening of the composition arising from a knowledge of Giotto's later works such as the *Navicella*.

"Giotto or not Giotto" is the question which must be asked of large parts of the Lower Church frescoes and which we will look into here using one single example.

Since the arguments refer to the affinities with the Arena Chapel frescoes on the one hand, and to the "road to" the Peruzzi Chapel on the other, let us take a closer look at these connections.

If we compare the *Raising of Lazarus* from the Paduan cycle with that from the Magdalene Chapel (ills. 82, 127), then with our first glance we can at once recognize the common features which cause people to assume that this is the work of the master's own hand, or at least that a direct model exists – perhaps even the cartoon from Padua – or that this is a slavish imitation of the master. Two groups of figures stand facing one another in front of a rocky landscape. One is gathered around Christ, who raises his hand, the other surrounds Lazarus, who is wrapped in a shroud. Mary and Martha – at Padua they are lying down, here they kneel – mediate between the two groups, and two boys attempt to move aside the lid of the tomb in the rock. The simple pictorial motif, which is common to both frescoes, can first of all be described in this brief summary.

Let us now look at the differences, and begin by considering the Paduan fresco (ill. 82). Christ has stepped

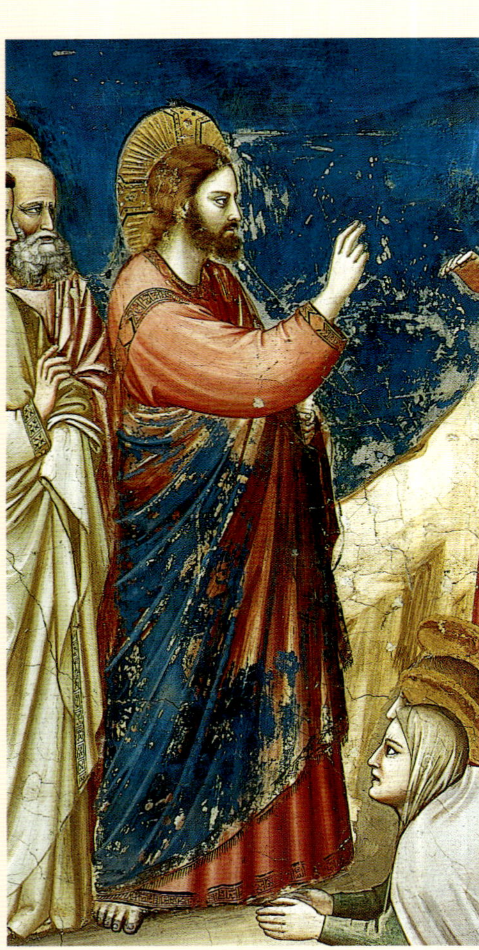

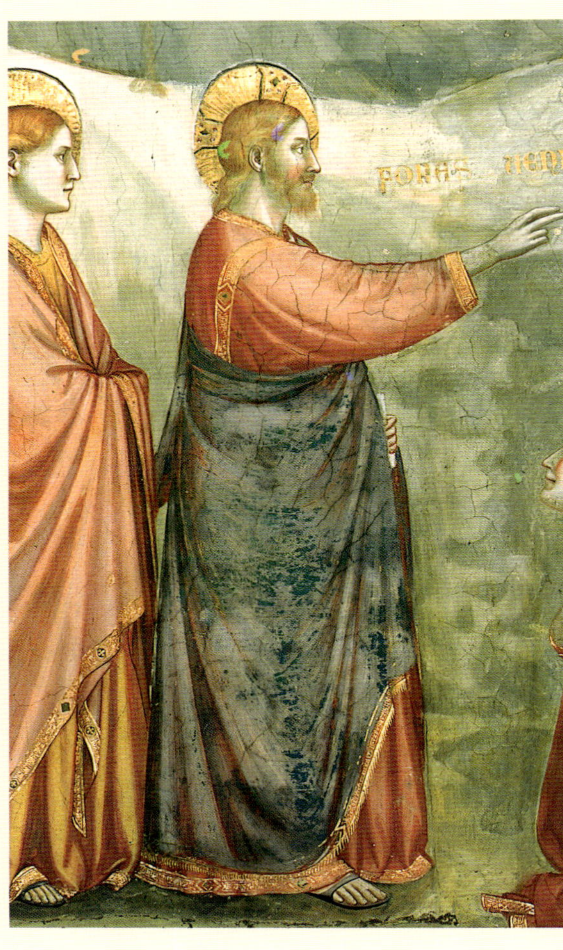

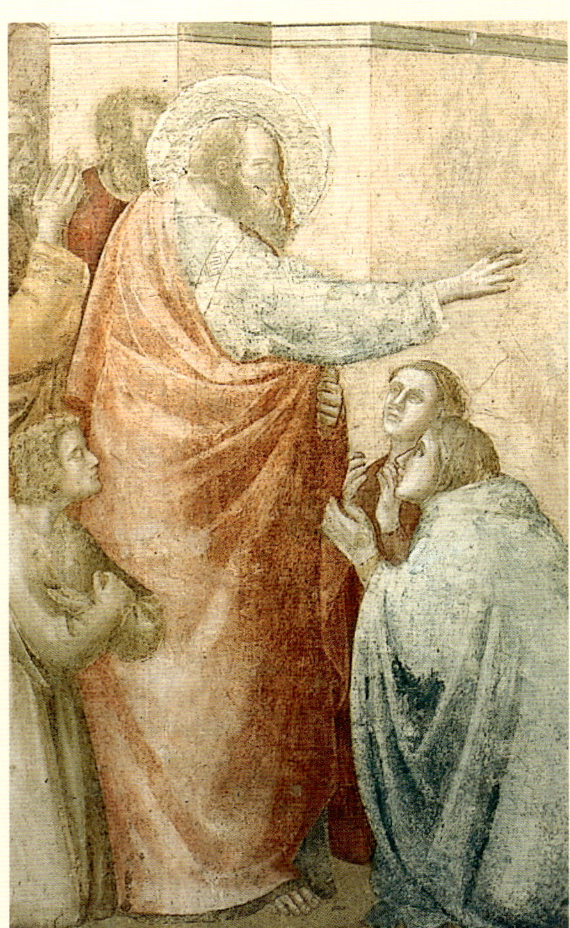

forward from the group that accompanies him. He stops, and lifts his hand, as if with the remaining sweep of his movement, just high enough so that he can still see over the top of it. This precise measure reinforces gesture and gaze, which is directed towards the pale, dead eye-sockets of Lazarus. The miracle takes place in the tension between these two, between the actor and the recipient; this incomprehensible event is all the action there is. The immense energy that emanates from the figure of Christ is answered by the gestures of the people in attendance around Lazarus, as if they sensed it earlier than the dead man, as if it coursed through their limbs. These people throw up their arms, put their hand to their chin in disbelief, or turn towards Christ, startled and horrified. These gestures respond to that of Christ as if in a rhythmic wave. They are so vivid as to illustrate the actuality of the miracle.

The situation at Assisi is quite different (ill. 127). There are only a few people gathered around Lazarus. The space occupied by all of the figures is clearly shown, not just by those in the foreground as at Padua. This is surely a development which can also be observed in the paintings in the Peruzzi Chapel.

At Padua the composition of the group of figures around Lazarus causes the latter to become almost freely isolated as the only protagonist opposite Christ. Thus the tension is developed just between these two: with direct aim, the life-giving power reaches the still motionless Lazarus. In the Assisi fresco those accompanying Lazarus stand closer to him; they attend to him, like the two disciples who create room for him to move. The event appears to have advanced a stage further. Lazarus has even already opened his eyes. He looks at Christ, who stands opposite him at a relatively great distance. This Christ has removed himself further from his companions than the one at Padua. He has stepped forward and is directing the great sweep of his gesture at Lazarus.

At Padua Christ's gesture and gaze stand out absolutely clearly against the blue sky. The descending line of the rock contrasts with the ascending gesture of the hand. Figure and gesture virtually become charged with tension. In contrast, Christ here remains completely enclosed by the rocky landscape. The edge of the rock takes up his gesture and reiterates it. There is no gestural rhythm in reaction to it – the figures seem calm and unmoved. The figure and gesture of Christ himself are lacking in vigor.

This is not due to the different format of the painting, but has its roots in the overall composition and in the way the figure of Christ himself is built up (ill. 125). Christ stands exactly parallel to the picture plane; no vigor develops from his apparel, or from a slight turning motion of the body as it does with the Christ-figure at Padua (ill. 124). His pointing movement does not have the energy capable of shooting through those present. Neither does it meet with any resistance from which any tension could develop. The women who kneel before Christ are too far away for this purpose. As if the artist himself did not really trust the strength of his figure, he inscribed the words of resurrection – "Foras veni Lazare" – above Christ's arm as an aid.

How different things are in the resurrection fresco in the Peruzzi Chapel (ill. 126). Without a doubt, John the Evangelist served as the model for the Christ at Assisi: the formation of his robes, gesture and profile setting are the same. But John tilts his head further forward, so that a tension develops from his voluminous body, which can be passed on by his hand.

In contrast, the Christ at Assisi simply stands there. Presumably, he was supposed to take on both the massiveness of the Evangelist and the solemnity of the Paduan Christ. The artist understood as little of either model as he did of the overall composition, which successfully introduces drama both in Padua and in Florence, despite the widely-structured space there.

At Padua and Florence Giotto brought to events an expressive sense of drama by showing the precise moment when the miracle takes place. He achieves this by using a composition based on tension. The representation at Assisi, on the other hand, strives towards balance. The concern of this artist seems to lie more with anecdotal narrative and the attraction of painterly contrasts.

In the middle of the second decade of the 13th century, on the occasion of his being confirmed in office in 1314, Bishop Pontano presumably commissioned this pupil of Giotto, and perhaps even others, to decorate his chapel. The same group continued to work in Assisi afterwards – certainly the artist of the *Raising of Lazarus* did. In some of the frescoes in the northern transept we can detect this feeling for the tasteful use of colors and for anecdotal content.

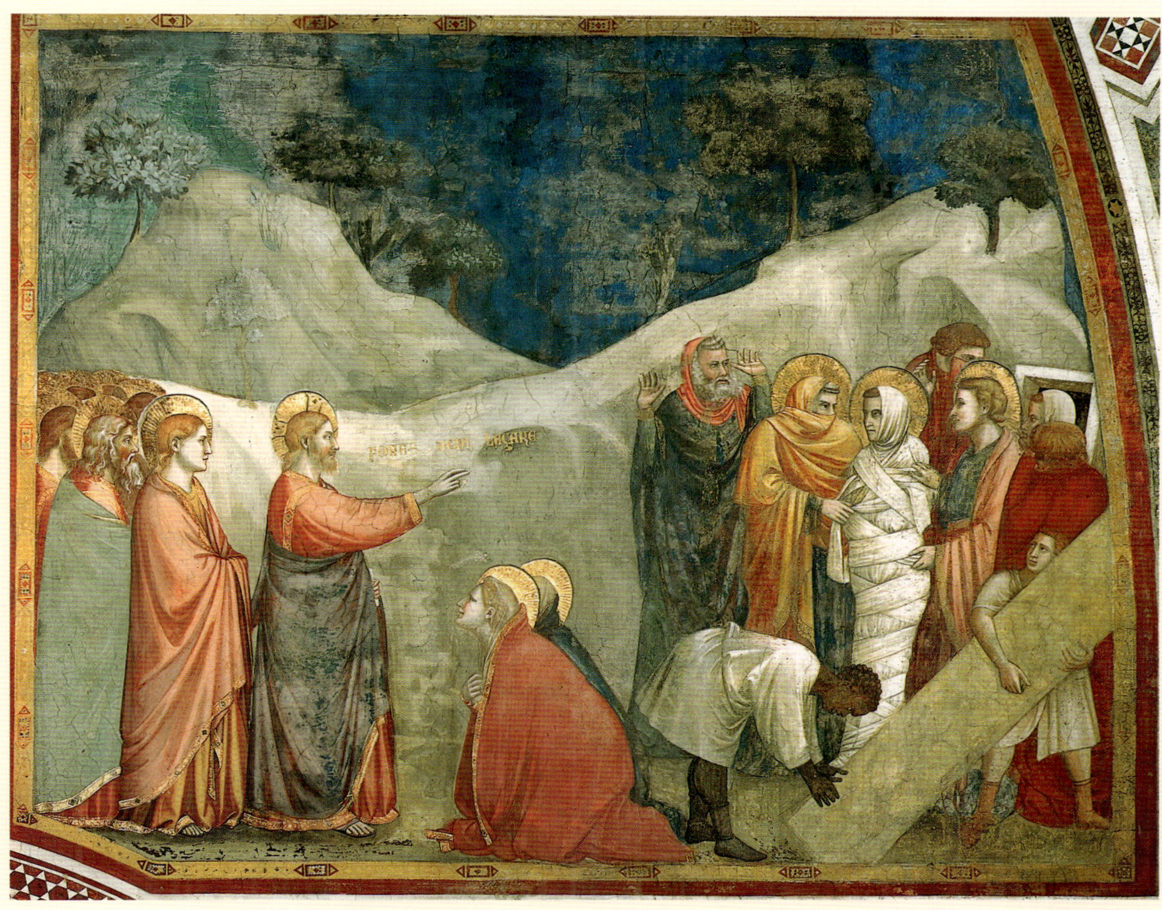

127 Pupil of Giotto
Raising of Lazarus, ca. 1315
Fresco
Basilica inferiore di San Francesco, Cappella della Maddalena, Assisi

At the request of Mary Magdalene and Martha, Christ, accompanied by his disciples, raises their brother Lazarus from the dead. The words of resurrection: "Foras veni Lazare' (Come forth, Lazarus) are written in golden letters on the rock face. Lazarus has opened his eyes and his grave clothes are already being removed.

THE ALLEGORIES OF THE ORDER – A FINAL HIGH POINT AT ASSISI

128 Crossing vault, 1316–1319
Fresco
Basilica inferiore di San Francesco, Assisi

Around the keystone with its representation of the Christ of the Apocalypse, the allegories of the three Franciscan virtues and *St. Francis in Glory* are painted in a radiant halo in the compartments of the vault.

In the crossing vault of the Lower Church of San Francesco at Assisi, Giotto created an impressive culmination, both of the paintings there and of Franciscan iconography. At the same time he once more expanded the pictorial possibilities open to him.

In the four compartments of the vault the three Franciscan virtues – Poverty, Obedience and Chastity – are pictured and explained by inscriptions on the arches of the wall (ill. 128). Since the work and the writings of St. Bonaventure, Francis has been conceived as the "angel of the sixth seal". For this reason these pictures are bound within a framework whose figurative elements allude to the Apocalypse and whose central motif is the apocalyptic Christ on the keystone of the vault.

Francis himself devoted his life to the imitation of Christ and was rewarded for doing so shortly before his death by receiving the stigmata, which made him even more like his Lord. In this respect the scenes from Christ's infancy in the southern, and those from Christ's Passion in the northern transept, belong to the overall program of the decoration, which culminates in the paintings in the crossing vault. Franciscans take a vow of poverty, obedience and chastity when they enter the order. In his testament Francis referred his brother monks specifically to these three virtues, which seemed to him immensely important for any life imitating the Lord's.

Here in the crossing they surround the picture field showing the transfigured founder of the order (ill. 129), which is located on the western compartment of the vault, that is to say, directly above the high altar. Francis is enthroned in the midst of a host of dancing and music-making angels. In pairs, the angels at the front pull the saint's precious seat through the radiant golden heavens. They pull him, as it were, from out of the depths of the vault. When looking at the four compartments of the vault we have to take into consideration the perspective and the effect of the curvature, which appear somewhat distorted on flat photographs. When composing these picture areas, Giotto considered the optical effect most thoroughly. While he positioned one father of the church and his scribe to the left and right of each vertex in the vault of

the Doctors of the Church in the Upper Church (ill. 15), and so brought the depth of the architecture into play as an element of tension between the figures, Giotto quite intentionally made use of the central dome here to represent a more extensive spatial structure. The period of almost twenty years of experience between the decoration of the two vaults is made clear by this juxtaposition.

In order to reach the Franciscan virtues, those that are willing must climb a high rocky plateau. Using this cliff, which rises up from the depths into the golden heavens, Giotto creates in each of these compartments of the vault a stage upon which the action takes place. The fact that there is any action at all, that the three virtues are not simply represented as personifications with the corresponding attributes, as they are in Padua, is a grandiose new invention, which was to become the accepted thing. In an allegorical pictorial narrative the rites of introduction to the sphere of activity of each respective virtue are portrayed: on the eastern compartment St. Francis is wed to Poverty (ill. 130), for poverty was supposed to be his constant companion; on the northern compartment the chaste are cleansed (ill. 134); and opposite this is the acceptance of obedience as a permanent yoke (ill. 133).

Poverty is a gaunt woman, dressed in rags (ill. 137). But behind her the most beautiful roses are growing, and a lily of purity blossoms among them. Even though this fresco is monumentally large, the way these Marian flowers are painted recalls the bunch of flowers in the *Ognissanti Madonna* (ill. 98).

Christ himself weds Francis to Poverty, and celestial witnesses support the alliance. The reactions of the world, on the other hand, are varied. While a young man on one side wishes to imitate Francis, rich people on the other side ridicule his life of poverty (ill. 131). Through these onlookers the allegory has an effect on contemporary life: the decision to live a life of poverty can be made at any time. As in the altarpieces or in the narrative cycles of paintings, contemporary spectators can identify with individual figures in the picture. It is precisely this mixture of allegorical content and vivid reality that is new. It is comparable to the way that eternity is glimpsed within the here and now of the

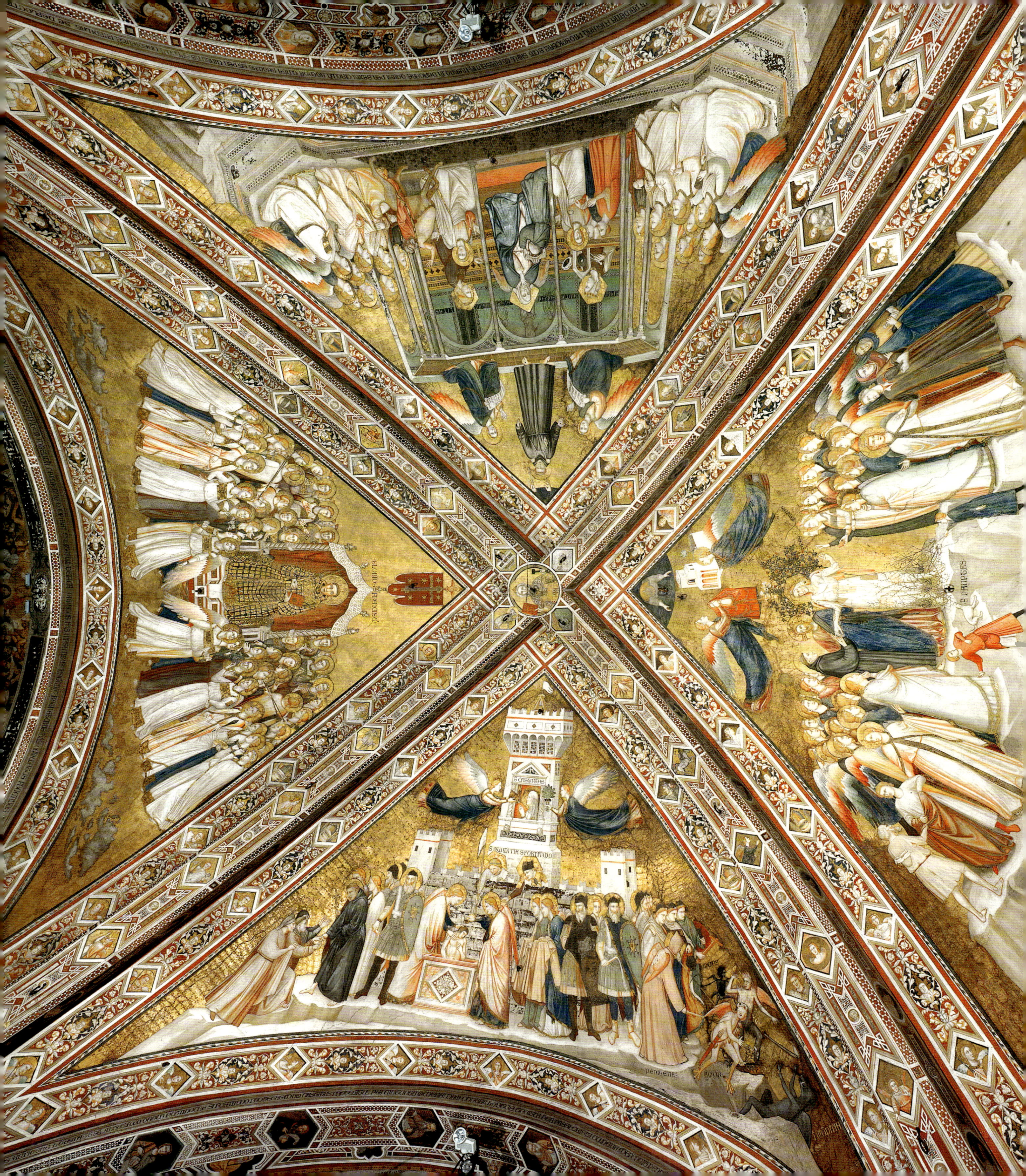

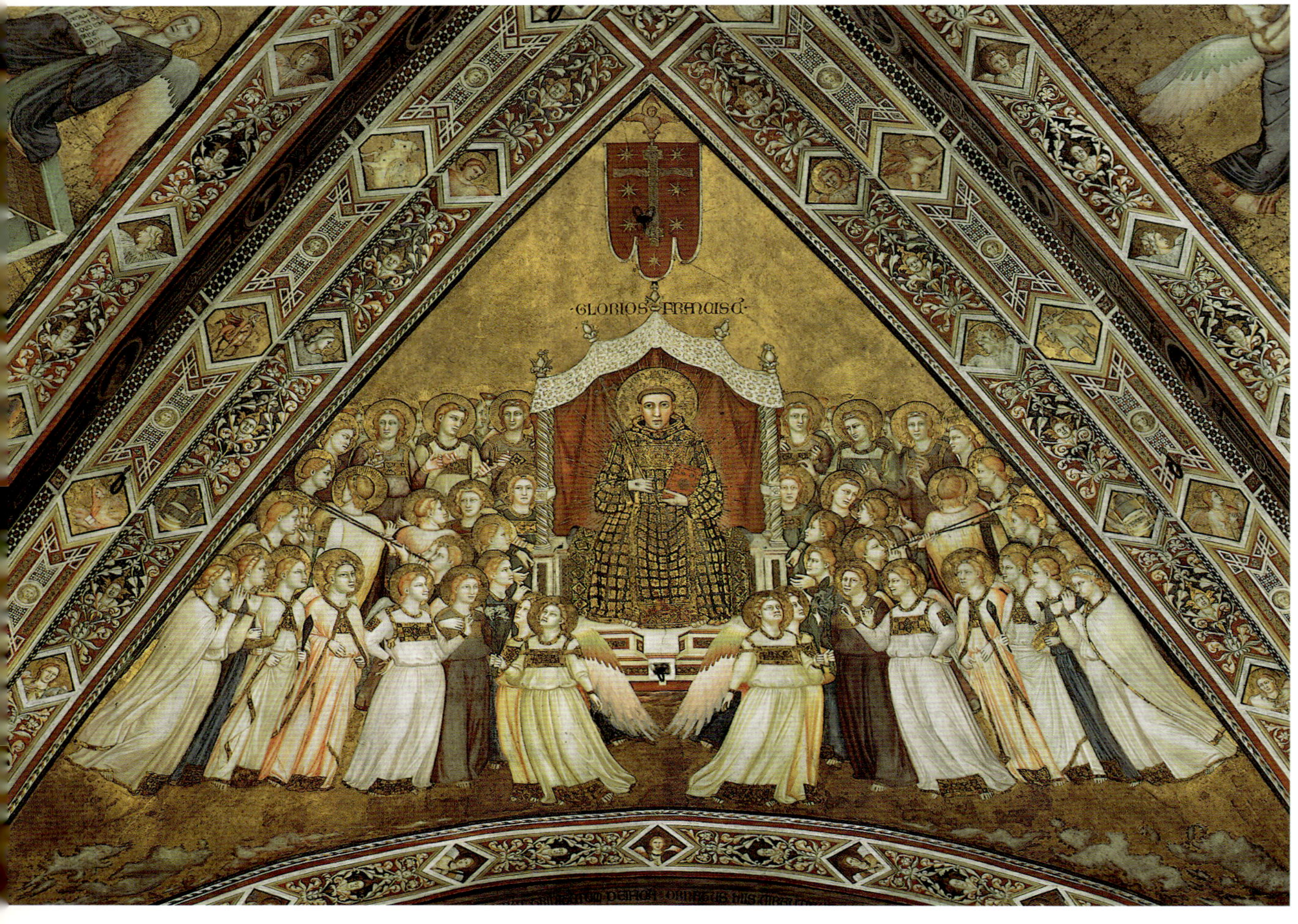

129 *St. Francis in Glory*, 1316–1319
Fresco
Basilica inferiore di San Francesco, Assisi

Worked through with gold, the triumphal procession of St. Francis comes into view. He is enthroned in the center of the triangular surface and drawn towards heaven by angels. His figure and in particular his face seem to belong to another world. The golden rays that emanate from him heighten the effect of the gold-embroidered dalmatic. The halos and the shimmering hair of the angels sustain this festive vein. The diverse figures of the angels, their music and their dancing – in which they take one another by the hand – lend the representation its liveliness.

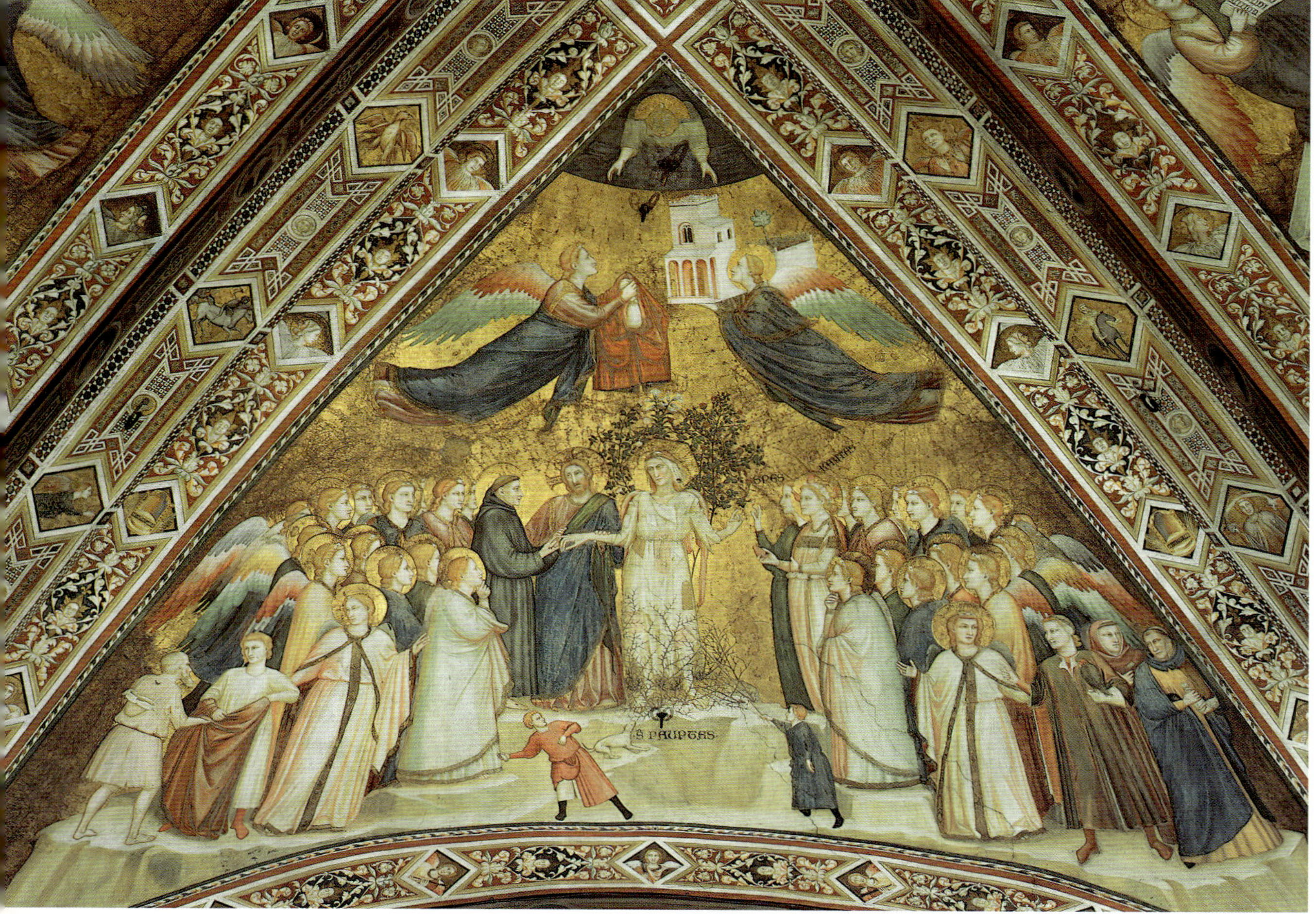

130 *Allegory of Poverty*, 1316–1319
Fresco
Basilica inferiore di San Francesco, Assisi

Poverty is a winged, gaunt woman dressed only in rags, at whom children throw stones or brandish sticks. Christ himself marries this woman to St. Francis. Numerous angels, as well as the personifications of Hope and Chastity, are present as witnesses. As offerings, two angels carry worldly goods heavenwards. The reactions of the world are depicted at either side: on the left a young man imitates Francis, and on the right the rich express ridicule.

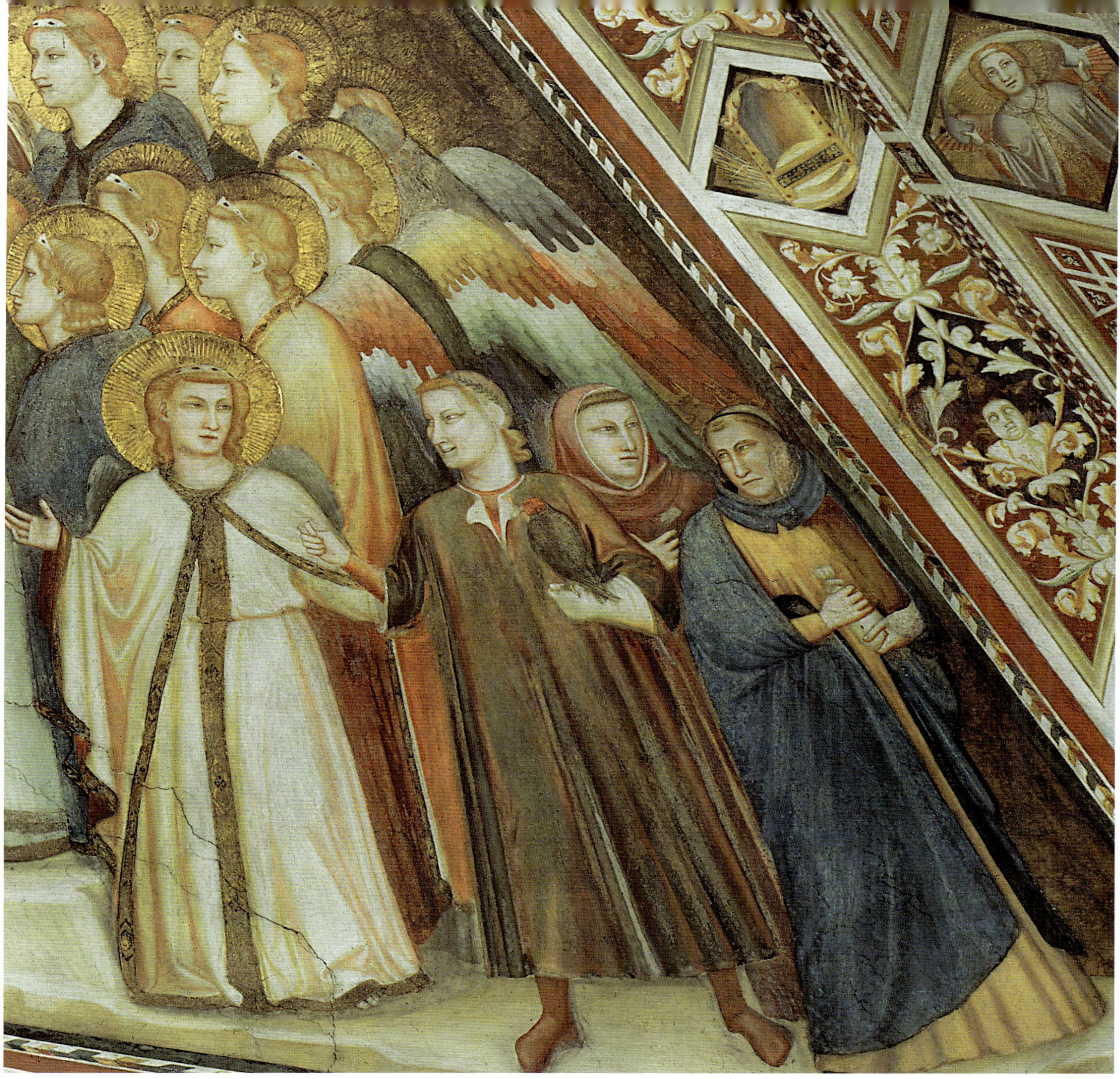

story being narrated, as can be seen in the frescoes at Padua, or through the interaction of miracle and everyday life, as is shown particularly clearly in the frescoes in the Peruzzi Chapel.

Although, in a manner of speaking, the target audience in the *Allegory of Chastity* is different, even here it is contemporary people who climb the rock in front of the well-fortified castle of Holy Chastity (ill. 134): the representatives of the three Franciscan sects – a lay brother, a Franciscan and a Clare – are greeted by Francis and an angel.

Giotto clearly connects the overall composition here

to the perspective effect of the compartment of the vault. The tower in which Chastity lives looms at its center. Proceeding from this center the walls, the phalanx of armored guards and the rows of angels are now layered towards the foreground in harmony with the curve of the dome. The impression of sound defenses and impregnability is thus reinforced without the view of the central motif of Holy Chastity being obstructed.

The scene of the action for the representation of the third Franciscan virtue is a convent environment. The view opens out onto a cloister with adjoining chapter

131 *Allegory of Poverty* (detail ill. 130), 1316–1319

The rich men do not wish to know of the angels' demands that they follow St. Francis. They cling to their sacks of money, and the elegant falconer mocks the heavenly messenger with an obscene gesture. Such narrative liveliness in art is new with respect to allegorical representations.

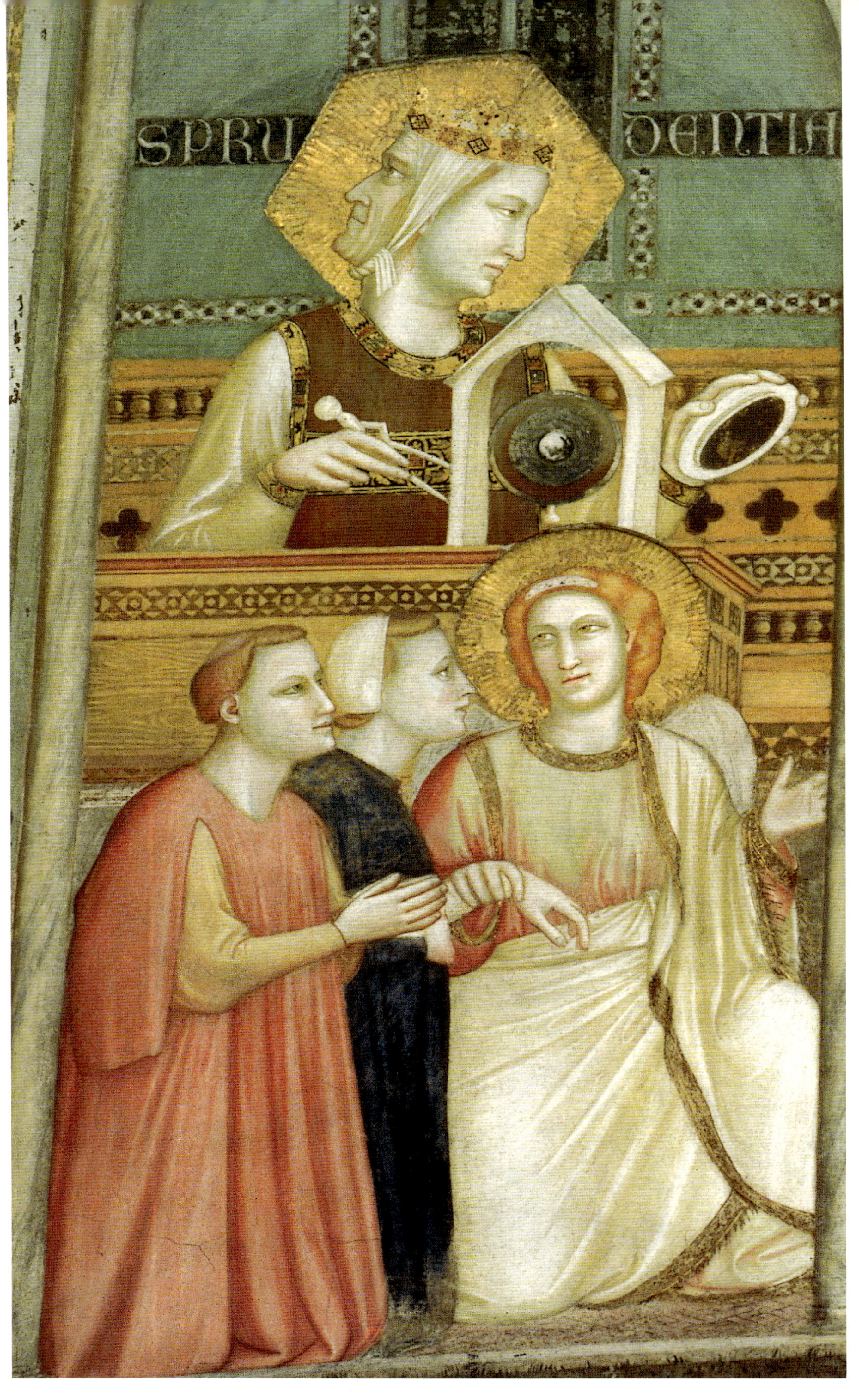

SPRU   DENTIA

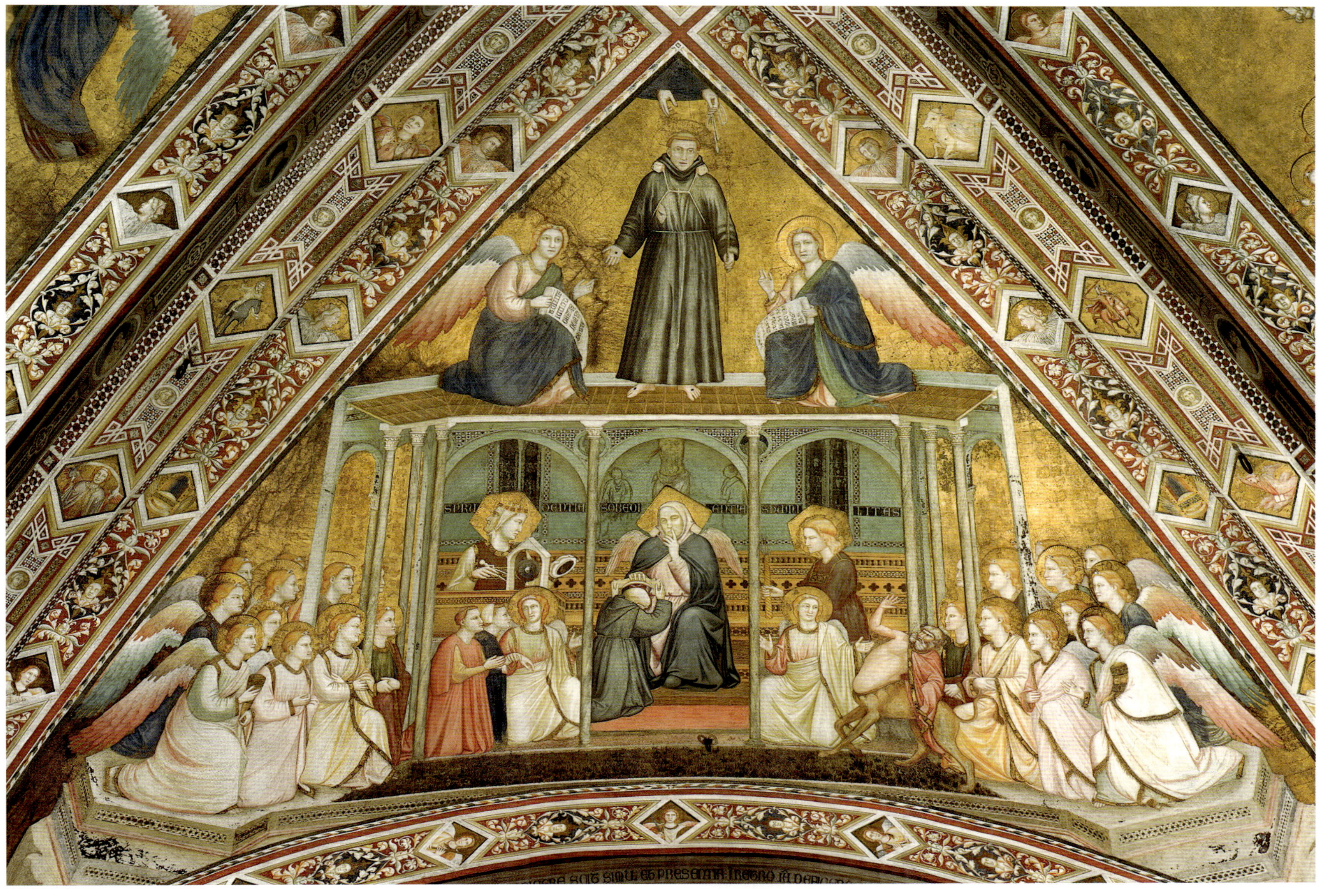

132, 133 *Allegory of Obedience* (and detail), 1316–1319
Fresco
Basilica inferiore di San Francesco, Assisi

In the chapterhouse of a cloister Obedience rules between
two observers, the dual-faced Prudence (*Prudentia*) and
the quiet Humility (*Humilitas*). Obedience commands
silence and places the yoke upon the monk who kneels
before her. Francis, who stands on the roof of the
building like an apparition between two kneeling angels,
also bears such a yoke.

The embodiment of Presumptiousness, the horned
centaur, is denied entrance. Two young men, a monk of
the order and a layman, will follow in the footsteps of the
saint. An angel has already taken one of them by the
hand. Interestingly, however, it seems to be Prudence who
presides over such a decision: with her dual face she sees
both past and future. She holds out a mirror, as a symbol
of knowledge, towards the kneeling monk, whom the
young men are following, and her astrolabe stands for the
wider context which she is able to recognize.

house. The lateral wings of the cloister absorb the curve
of the vault, while the center is set against it. The space
is restricted, no doubt to indicate the narrowness and
quietness of the cloister area. In the center of the
chapter house sits the holy Obedientia, the
personification of obedience, in a dark cloak (ill. 132).

Here, and in the other representations, the groups of
figures are organized rhythmically to emphasize the
center. On the whole, as far as color and composition
are concerned, Giotto strikes a chord in the three
allegories which harmonizes in a convincing fashion
with the radiant image of heaven in *St. Francis in Glory*.
Gold background, hosts of angels and the emphasis on
the central axis connect these representations as if they
were an opened-out fan. A most marvellous version of
the basic ideas of the Franciscans is thus created –
precious in its materials, novel in its understanding of
space and figures, and revolutionary in its conception
of the allegorical pictorial narrative. Many authors
compare this invention to Dante's "Paradiso", the third
part of the "Divine Comedy". And, indeed, the artistic
translation of abstract ideas such as obedience or

poverty into a complex visual narrative with many
levels of meaning had up till then only been attempted
in literature. Virtues were shown as personifications, as
in the *dado* level of the Arena Chapel, and the pictorial
narratives, such as those in the Upper Church of San
Francesco at Assisi, were mostly based on the legends of
the saints.

However, whether this costly arrangement
corresponds to St. Francis' demands for absolute
poverty was discussed as vehemently then as it still is
today. The *Allegory of Poverty* in the central axis of the
vault does in fact occupy a more prominent position
than *St. Francis in Glory*, and Christ also features only
in the former picture, but the saint appears without a
beard, the outward symbol of his poverty. According to
contemporary sources, Francis, like men from the lower
classes, wore a beard. He is depicted with one in the
frescoes of the Upper Church. But obviously such
emphasis on personal poverty at this late date was no
longer in keeping with the ideas of the leaders of the
order, whereas the actual rule of poverty was
emphatically stressed.

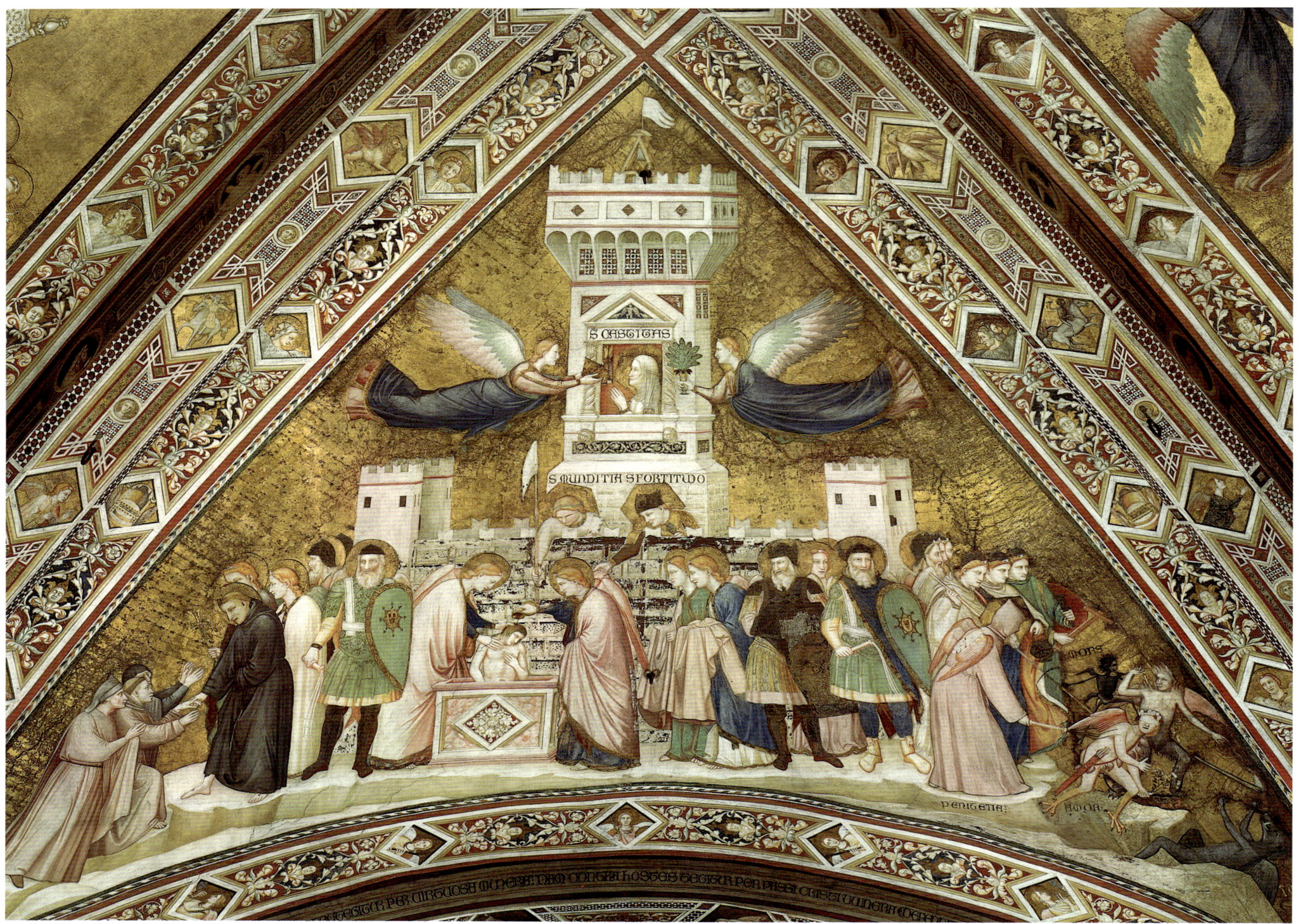

It looks as if those responsible were striving to achieve a balance between those members of the order who interpreted the rule of poverty very strictly and the more moderate forces. Following ever more bitter arguments within the order, which have gone down in history as the "dispute over poverty" the minister general of the order, Michele da Cesena, newly elected in 1316, attempted to restore unity. Initially he was supported by Pope John XXII, who was also new to the position.

When he took up office, it must surely have been a great concern of Michele da Cesena that the centenary of St. Francis' birth be celebrated in a suitable manner. The completion of the paintings in the transepts and in the crossing of the main church, the mother church of the order, presented itself as an opportunity. Since the minister general lost the support of the pope again in 1323, it is highly probable that the decoration of the crossing was executed sometime before this date. Another event narrows down the scale of time in which the frescoes in the Lower Church must have been created: in 1319 the Ghibellines, the party loyal to the emperor and opposed to the pope, invaded Assisi and removed the papal treasures from the basilica of San Francesco, where they had been stored temporarily. The reign of the Ghibellines was not broken until 1322 when an army arrived from Perugia.

Even if the normal life of a monastery could possibly have been resumed somewhat earlier, it seems very unlikely that such lavish decorative projects could have been begun or continued during this "Ghibelline" period. The fact that one wall arch and the apse remained unpainted also supports the idea of work having suddenly been interrupted.

134, 135 *Allegory of Chastity* (and detail), 1316–1319
Fresco
Basilica inferiore di San Francesco, Assisi

In a well-fortified castle, Chastity rules: only angels can enter here. In order to reach her, a long path must be followed. The representatives of the three divisions of the Franciscan order have climbed the hill. They too, as the middle scene shows, will be washed and dressed by angels. On the other side the extremely vivid and bizarre figures of demons are being cast into the abyss: They are Unchasteness (*Immunditia*) with the boar's head, Burning Desire (*Ardor*) with the flaming head, and Love (*Amor*) with the clawed feet and the hearts tied round him. The round is completed by the spider-legged, devilish Death (*Mors*).

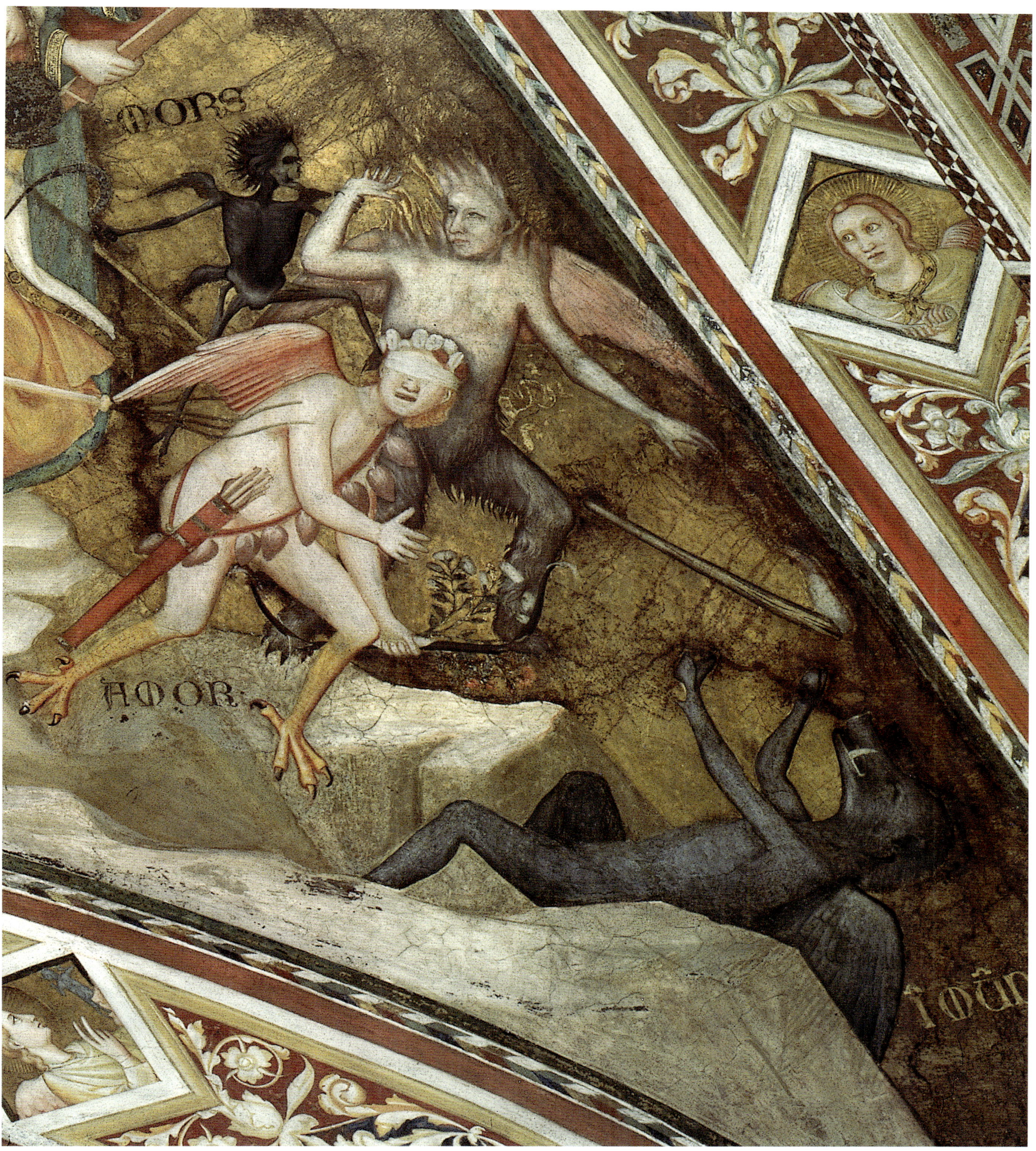
MORS
AMOR

136 *The Dream of Pope Innocent III*, 6th picture of the
Legend of St. Francis, before 1300
Fresco, 270 x 230 cm
Basilica superiore di San Francesco, Assisi

The pope lies asleep in bed, his eyes closed. The bed
curtain has been drawn back – Giotto's way of
establishing a connection with the vision: with his
shoulder, Francis supports the Lateran basilica, which is
on the point of collapse, and thus also supports the
Church as a whole.

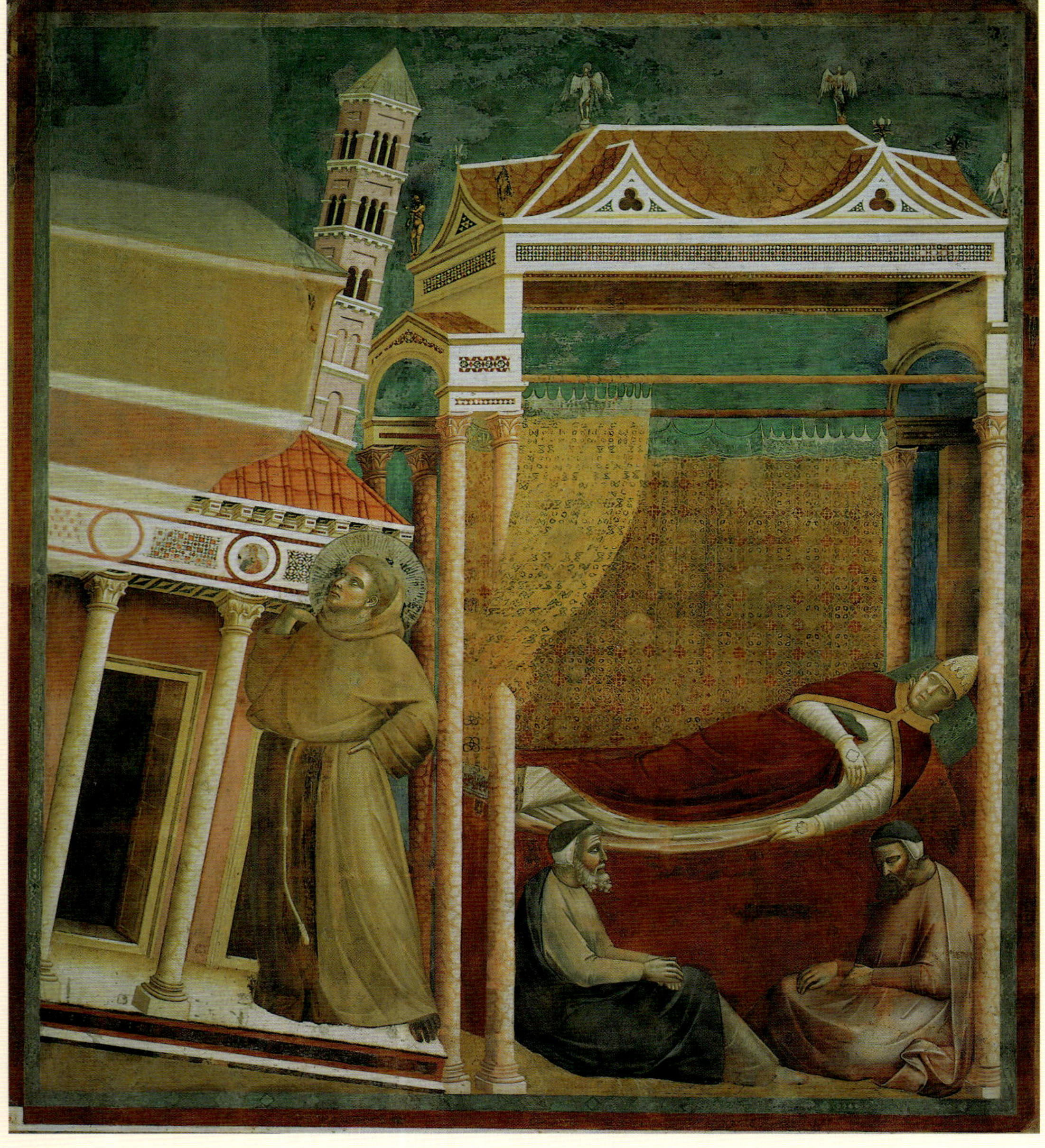

As early as the 4th century, fresh attempts at radical
poverty cropped up again and again among the followers
of Christ, sometimes as the asceticism of a single
individual, and sometimes in connection with practical
charity. Such new attempts were to be made in the
Benedictine order and, with great determination, by
Francis of Assisi. In the Franciscan order the rule of poverty
was to become a moral ideal. However, in the 13th century
a dispute began over the extent of their commitment to
poverty, which was to become a real test for the order in
the 14th century.

The development of the Franciscan order is bound up
with a more general movement towards poverty. Groups
had existed since the early 12th century which subscribed
to the ideal of preaching and to the rule of poverty. They
grew out of the displeasure with the way the Church was
being run, and took it upon themselves to live as Jesus and
his disciples had done. These groups were pursued
relentlessly up until the beginning of the 13th century and
accused of heresy, since the right to preach was only given
to ordained representatives of the Church. Church policy
changed with Innocent III (1198–1216). Attempts were
now made to bring these groups back into the Church fold,
and they were occasionally given the right to preach.

Francis and his initially small band of followers had
likewise committed themselves to living like the apostles.
However, as well as practicing as preachers, they also
combined this with services to the poor. When the rule was
first confirmed in 1209, they were also given the right to
preach (ill. 23). With the pope behind them, the new order
developed very quickly. The office of protector of the order
was created – it was always held by very influential
cardinals, and was to regulate the affairs of the order in
relation to the Church and to the outside world.

The groups settled more and more often in cities and
towns and – against the will of Francis – in monasteries
whose solid buildings, as centers of learning, became
larger and larger. The conflict between the ideal of poverty
and the necessities of a growing organization was
inevitable.

A compromise rule therefore came about under Gregory
IX (1227–1241), which distinguished between the right to
use property belonging to others, enjoyed by the order,
and ownership of that property, which was reserved for the
Curia. In this way the Franciscans could have extensive
means at their disposal without breaking the rule of
poverty. At the same time, the order was tied very closely
to the Curia and was in no way independent.

The main tasks of the friars of the order were to preach,
to hear confessions and to look after the weak and the
dying. It was precisely through these activities within the
community that the order could reunite with the Church
those people who were dissatisfied with her or who
subscribed to heretical ideas. St. Francis even appeared to
Pope Innocent III in a dream as supporter of his episcopal
church (ill. 136). It was from this that the Franciscans
derived their particular claim to renewal within the Church.
The pope in question valued and encouraged their
influence because of their power to integrate.

The rapid development of the order naturally allowed
the critics of the toned down and de facto circumvented
rule of poverty no rest. In a papal bull in 1279 Pope
Nicholas III (1277–1280) expressly affirmed the absolute
poverty of Christ and his disciples and impressed upon the
brothers of the order obedience to the rules of St. Francis.
At the same time however, he confirmed the compromise
formula regarding poverty and forbade any further
discussion.

What was meant as a settlement became the cause of a
new struggle. The group of spirituals, who claimed that

they alone represented the true teaching of St. Francis, criticized the interference of the pope and the continuing love of grandeur of individual monasteries.

Shortly before the turn of the century, and during the brief papacy of the hermit-pope Celestine V (1294), further groups began following their own path and new groups split off. These were hounded radically in the period that followed. The spirituals sought inner perfection following the example of St. Francis, the external expression of which was, for them, poverty. From this there developed a dispute on purely theological issues with the leaders of the order. But several visions, which had been condemned as heretical, and which prophesied that the end of the world was nigh, were also current among the spirituals. These people considered the successor to Celestine V, Pope Boniface VIII (1294–1303), as the personification of the Antichrist, who should be condemned along with the whole Church government. This called into question the Church's claim to power. Things became dangerous for the spirituals each time they mixed their demand for observance of the rule of poverty with these apocalyptic visions. Persecution and condemnation were the results.

However, on the whole, the conventuals, i. e. the more moderate members of the order, dominated the scene to such an extent that the dispute over poverty at first remained largely theoretical. It was only when the leader of the spirituals practically demanded a clearly more narrow interpretation of St. Francis' testament in 1311 that the opposite party attempted to intervene with the help of the pope. When the position of minister general of the order was to be filled again, Clement V (1305–1314) was willing to choose a member of the conventuals. However, the pope died in 1314 before the decision was made.

Order and Church were thus without leadership at the same point in time. In that same year Louis of Bavaria and Frederick the Beautiful were fighting in Germany over the throne and thus for the honor of being the secular head of all Christendom. Everyone was waiting for a new pope who would restore general confidence. But the cardinals did not reach agreement until 1316.

Immediately he was consecrated, John XXII (1316–1334) named Michele da Cesena the new minister general of the order. The first thing the latter did was to issue various decrees obliging the spirituals to show obedience to the monastery, and to request the pope's permission to suppress the radical spirituals. The pope replied to this request with various bulls, which ended in a complete ban on the spirituals. He thus intervened in the concerns of the order to an exceptional extent. However, worse was the fact that he gave a Dominican cardinal some papers on St. Francis' testament to consider. And so the dispute broke out anew, and this time not just within the order, but between the Dominicans and the Franciscans. More and more the pope openly withdrew his support from the Franciscans, support they had enjoyed since they were founded.

In 1322 John XXII lifted the ban on discussion of the rule of poverty, which remained the most important of the order's basic rules. Thereupon the minister general urgently requested the pope to rescind this bull. The latter responded in a relatively polemical fashion and aggravated

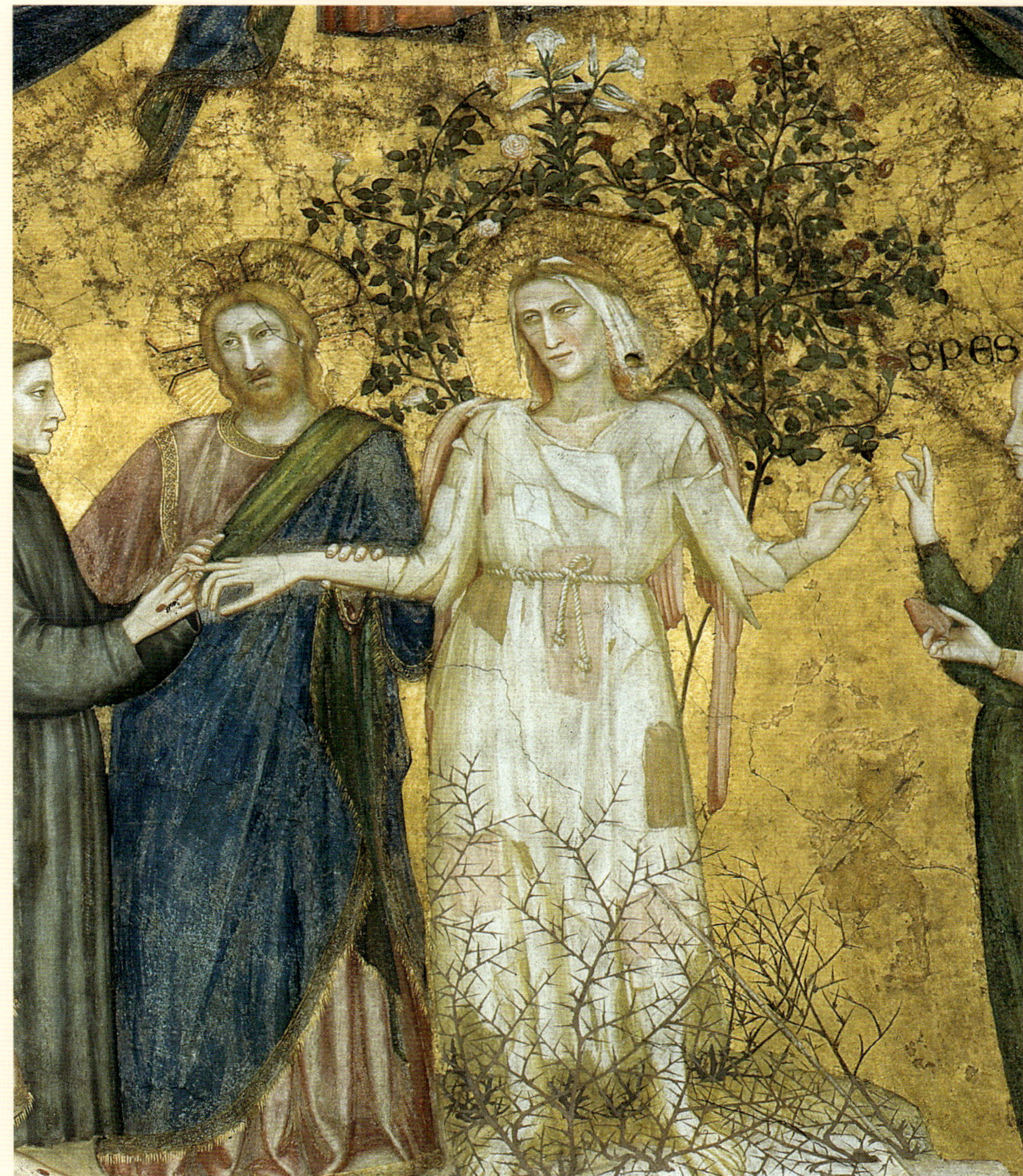

the situation by additionally annulling the regulation on property, i. e. the old compromise between use and ownership. The order more or less lost the basis of its existence.

But even worse was to come. An attempt to at least change the pope's mind about this one point resulted in a devastating blow being dealt to the whole order: in 1323 Pope John XXII declared as heresy the belief that neither Christ nor the apostles had owned any possessions. It was precisely this idea that was the most important basis for St. Francis' "Christ-likeness". To both the spirituals and the conventuals this represented the main pillar of their beliefs.

The pope's decision did away with the fundamental difference between the Franciscans and the Dominicans. As a consequence, the order never regained its original influence.

137 *Allegory of Poverty* (detail ill. 130), 1319–1328

Poverty, the bride of St. Francis, stands careworn and dressed in rags amongst withered thorns. This, however, is only how she appears in the eyes of the world, for behind her, in the heavenly regions, the most beautiful roses blossom from the undergrowth. Christ leads Poverty, who appears here beside him as his own companion, towards the saint to be wed. Before Giotto's invention, this kind of representation, which unites numerous symbolic details with a lively narrative to create an allegory, was only known in literary works.

138 Detail of ceiling vault, 1319–1328
Fresco
Chiesa di Santa Croce, Cappella Bardi, Florence

The ceiling appears to open out onto the golden heavens for a moment, and the personification of Poverty appears. As in the Lower Church at Assisi, her halo is angular and she is crowned with roses. She shrinks back from the attacking dog.

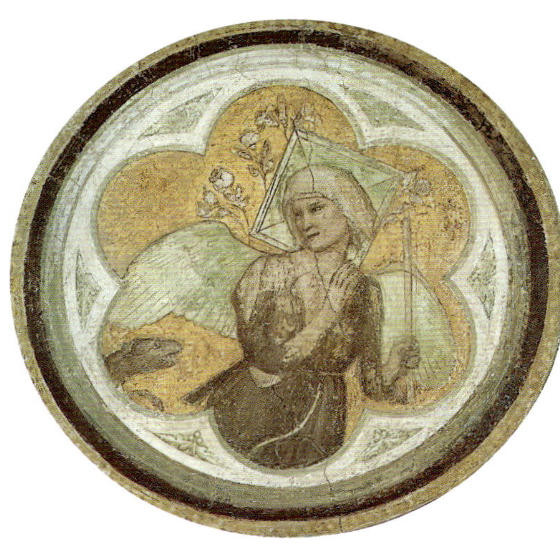

139 (opposite) *Renunciation of Wordly Goods* (detail ill. 140), 1319–1328

Crying children, curious city-dwellers and shocked clergymen observe St. Francis' decision to turn away from his earthly father for good. Compared with the work in the Peruzzi Chapel, Giotto's depiction of people in these later paintings has changed again. These figures do not seem to occupy so much space. Their movements are lithe, they have rather longer necks and their robes wider neckline — both correspond to the fashion of the time and show a certain tendency towards elegant Gothic painting.

Giotto also received the commission for the second surviving chapel in the Franciscan church of Santa Croce in Florence from a banker. The donor Ridolfo de' Bardi and his brother jointly inherited their father's banking house and commercial interests. This involved maintaining a good relationship with the powers who determined the politics of the day – with the pope, with the Neapolitan ruling house of Anjou, and with the Guelph party. He was able to go on cultivating this highly effective mixture of faith, politics and money for the next three decades until his house went bankrupt in the 1340s.

The Bardi family chapel is situated to the right of the choir, which means that it is the first chapel of the southern transept, and dedicated to St. Francis (ill. 113). As was the case with the neighboring Peruzzi Chapel, these frescoes were also painted over in the 18th century, rediscovered in the 19th century, and reworked. During their restoration in the middle of our own century, all reworked areas were removed and the ruined parts sealed with plaster. For this reason, some of the frescoes have empty spaces, although the actual painting is considerably better preserved here than in the Peruzzi Chapel, since Giotto went back to working with fresh plaster here.

As in the neighboring chapel, three frescoes framed by ornamental bands decorate each wall. But unlike in the former, these are dedicated to just the one saint, St. Francis. The *Renunciation of Worldly Goods* and the *Confirmation of the Rule* are situated in the lunettes (ills. 140, 141). In the middle register the *Apparition at Arles* and the *Trial by Fire before the Sultan* are depicted (ills. 143, 145). *The Death of St. Francis and Inspection of the Stigmata* (ill. 142) and the *Apparition at Arles* (ill. 143) can be seen at eye level. Above the entrance to the chapel the *Stigmatization* is portrayed, as it were, as a summation of the life of the saint (ill. 144). The seraphim from whom Francis receives the stigmata here appears – unlike at Assisi or in the panel in the Musée du Louvre (ills. 33, 37) – as the crucified Christ. In this way, the representation is related to the choir and to the Holy Cross, to which the church is dedicated. Moreover, the fresco has its pendant in the *Assumption of the Virgin Mary* on the other side of the triumphal

arch. Giotto, therefore, linked the decoration of the chapel with the associations of the church as a whole – an exceptional situation, which can certainly be attributed to the important position occupied in society by the donor.

On the window wall of the chapel Franciscan saints are portrayed, standing under painted arcades. One picture has been destroyed; St. Clare, St. Elizabeth of Thuringia and St. Louis of Toulouse can still be seen. The latter, along with his great-uncle St. Louis, a French king, was the most prominent saint of the Franciscan order. As the elder son of Charles II of Naples, he renounced his birthright, joined the order in 1296, and died a year later as archbishop of Toulouse. His brother, Robert of Anjou, was King of Hungary, King of Naples and, as leader of the Guelphs, who were also the party of supremacy in Florence, a supporter of the pope and a bitter enemy of the emperor.

This representation of St. Louis of Toulouse documents the power structure within which the Bardi moved, and with which the Franciscan order was also bound up, in an exemplary fashion. At the same time, the painting provides a clue to when the frescoes were executed, for Louis of Toulouse was not canonized until 1317. Furthermore, documents exist which establish Giotto's presence in Florence in the early 1320s, before he was called to the royal court in Naples in 1328. The date of execution can therefore be narrowed down to the period between 1317 and 1328. In addition, the paintings themselves allow us to place them within a chronological ordering of Giotto's works: even if the ceiling paintings are no longer complete, it is nevertheless clear that the inventions at Assisi must have preceded these. For instance, here is Poverty surrounded by roses and barked at by a dog (ill. 138). These are attributes which are only made intelligible by the scenic representation of the Franciscan virtues in the Lower Church at Assisi (ill. 130).

While the St. Francis in the paintings in the Upper Church at Assisi wears a beard, Giotto depicts him without one here, as in the vault frescoes in the Lower Church. This manifestation of the saint, favored by the order since 1316, must have been particularly agreeable

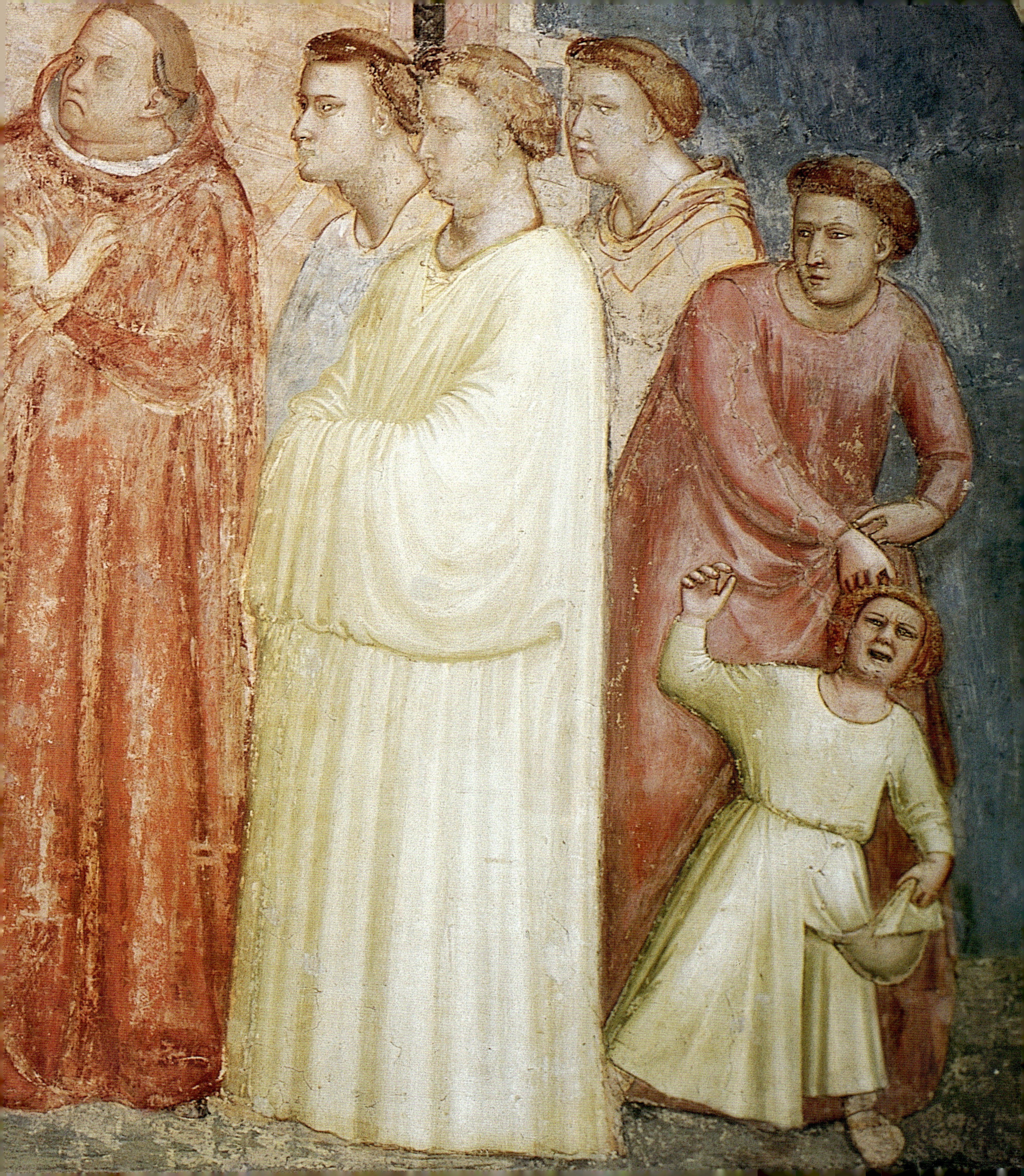

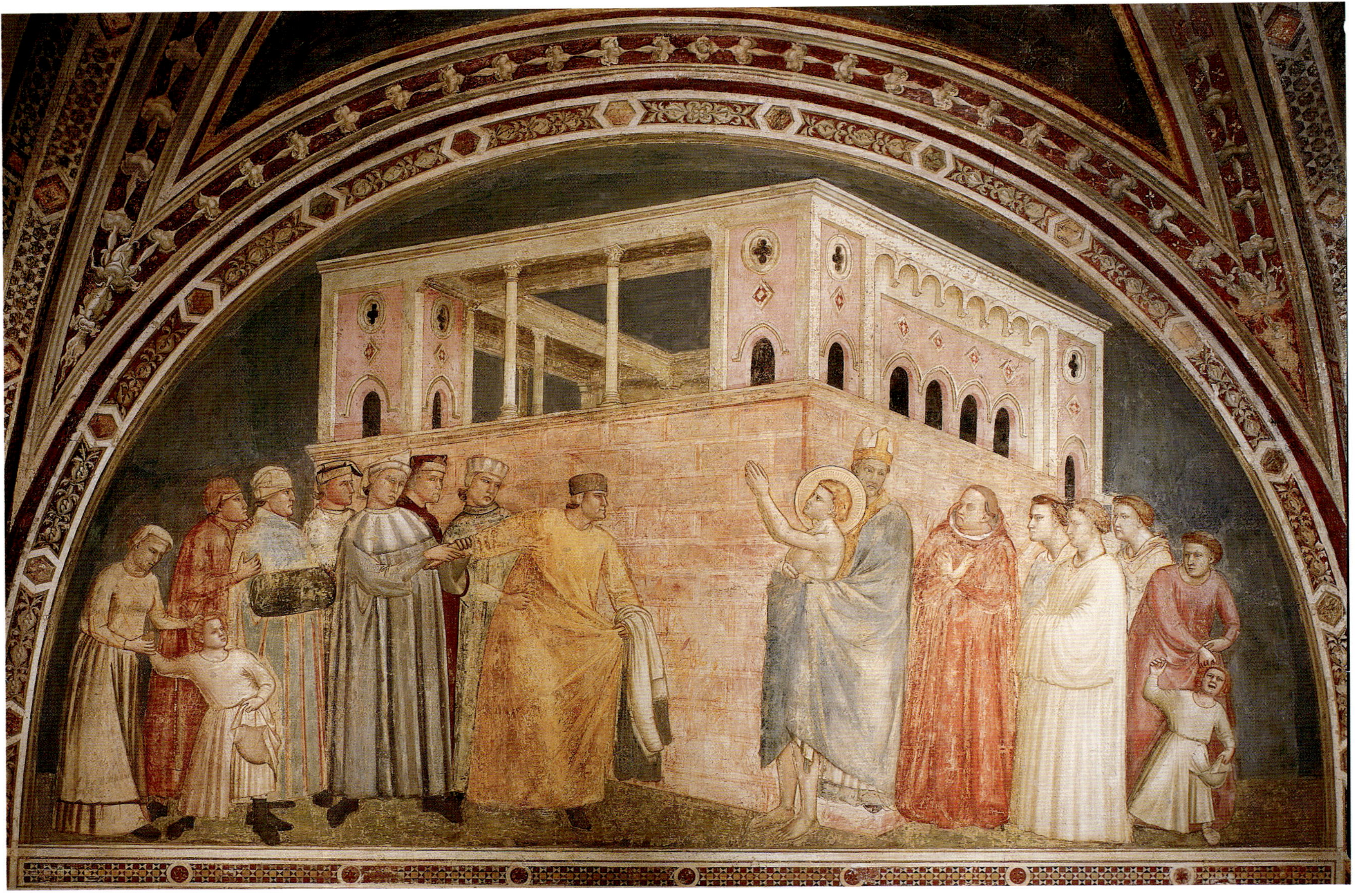

140 *Renunciation of Worldly Goods,* 1319–1328
Fresco
Chiesa di Santa Croce, Cappella Bardi, Florence

The clearly articulated palace building is set obliquely within the field of the lunette. This creates great tension, appropriate to the confrontation between St. Francis and his infuriated father. Giotto also uses the reactions of the individual figures to demonstrate the outrageousness of the saint's public decision to renounce all his worldly goods.

to a banker, since it no longer expressed the original significance of personal poverty.

Unlike the Peruzzi Chapel, the construction of the architecture portrayed in the frescoes is here based on a viewpoint within the chapel. The perspective of the architectural structures in the paintings changes with great logical consistency – the higher the register, the greater the foreshortening from below. This only increases the impression of fluidity between real and painted space.

The pieces of architecture in the paintings do not open out obliquely, as was often the case in the Upper Church at Assisi (ill. 136), at Padua (ill. 86) or even in the Peruzzi Chapel (ill. 118), but are constructed strictly parallel to the picture plane, as in the *Confirmation of the Rule* (ill. 141), or in the *Apparition at Arles* (ill. 143). Since Giotto employed Gothic decorative elements only sparingly, the frescoes in the Bardi Chapel appear almost to share the calmer, simplified qualities of classical art (ills. 143, 145). To achieve this, he again returned to his own inventions and developed them further. Thus the hall from the *Mocking of Christ* in the Paduan cycle reappears in a modified form as the location for the *Trial by Fire before*

the Sultan (ills. 90, 145), and the cloister in the *Apparition at Arles* corresponds to the convent seat of the *Allegory of Obedience* on the crossing vault in the Lower Church at Assisi (ills. 133, 143). To an even greater extent than at Assisi, space here becomes concentrated using perspective. The rows of monks are staggered continuously towards the back in a way that the eye senses to be right.

In the painting opposite, where two religions come into conflict, the situation is more dramatic than with the quiet monks, several of whom have not yet noticed the apparition of St. Francis (ill. 145). What was still being expressed in the fresco *St. Francis before the Sultan* at Assisi (ill. 26) through the two different pieces of architecture is here assembled in the contradictory gestural language of the sultan seated at the center. He points with his right hand to the fire at the side, and at the same time turns his gaze towards the priests who are withdrawing on the other side. Ashamed and at the same time rebellious, they leave the room in an impressive row. They do not want to undergo the trial by fire, which Francis on the other side is prepared to do.

The choice of this Egyptian episode from the life story of the saint offered the Bardi family the chance to

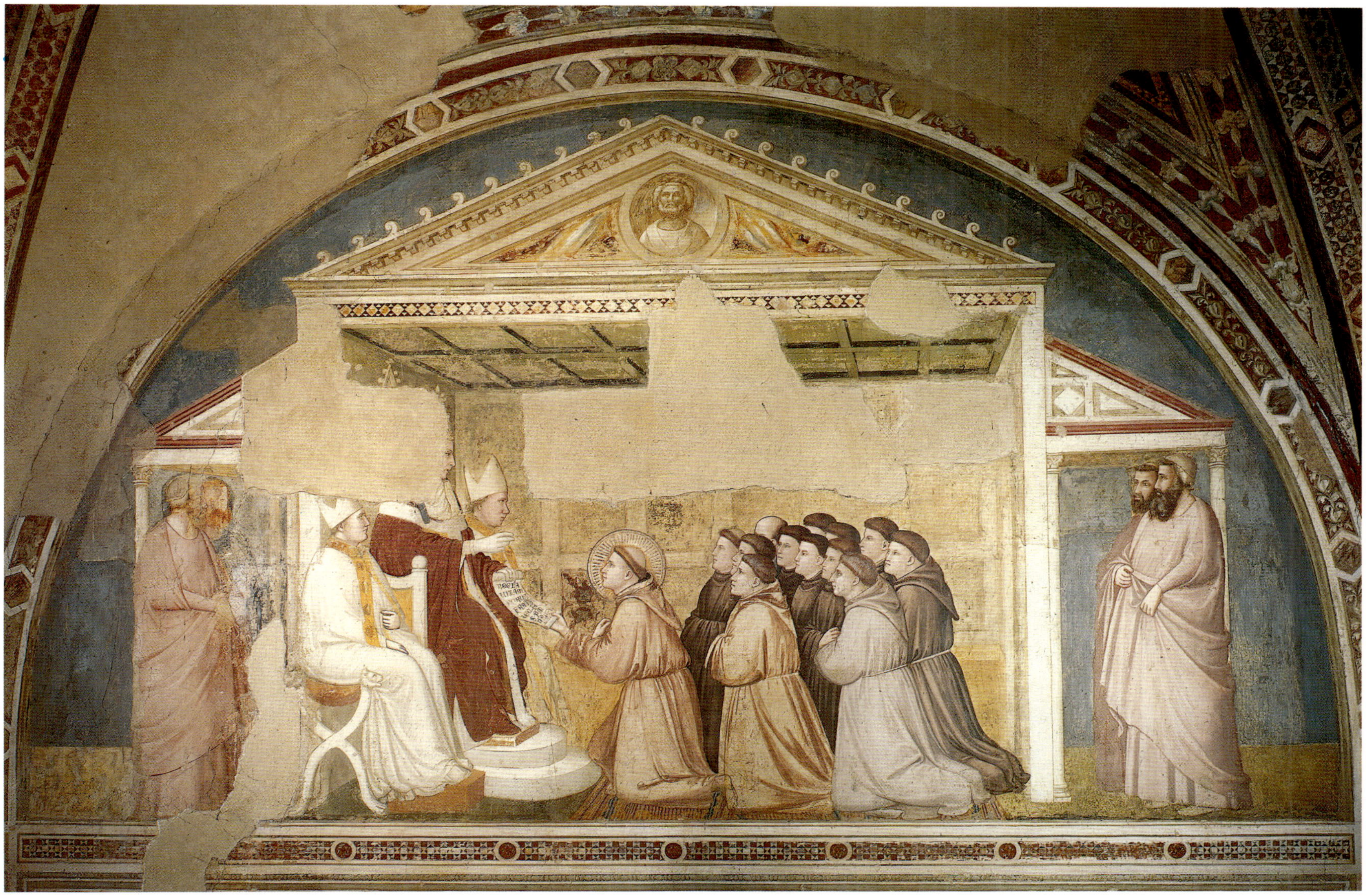

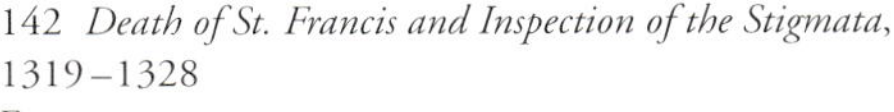

141 *Confirmation of the Rule*, 1319–1328
Fresco
Chiesa di Santa Croce, Cappella Bardi, Florence

In this representation the simple architecture is placed
parallel to the picture plane of the lunette. This creates a
strong and clearly articulated composition. Francis
kneels with his companions before Pope Honorius III,
who approves the first rule.

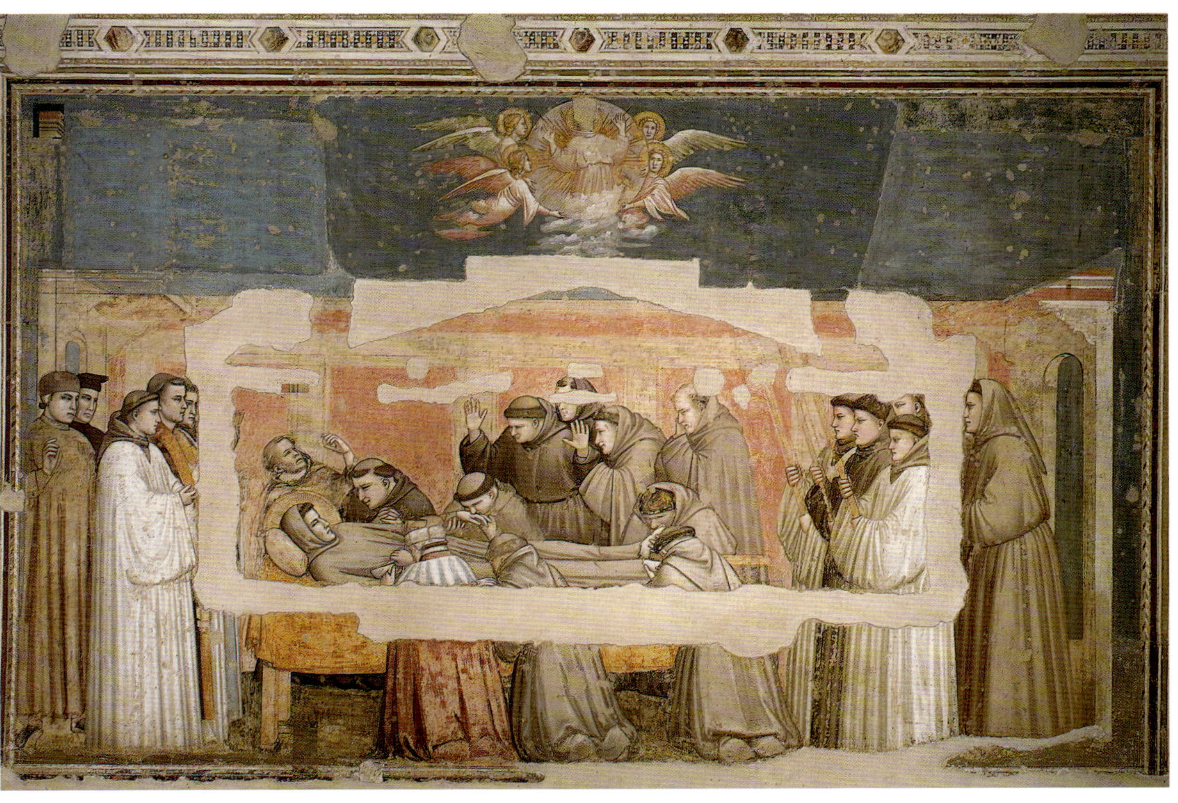

142 *Death of St. Francis and Inspection of the Stigmata*,
1319–1328
Fresco
Chiesa di Santa Croce, Cappella Bardi, Florence

In an extremely compressed space, St. Francis' disciples
have gathered for his funeral. One of them notices that
the saint's soul is being carried heavenward by angels.
While one monk kisses the stigmata, a disbelieving
nobleman examines the wound in St. Francis' side.

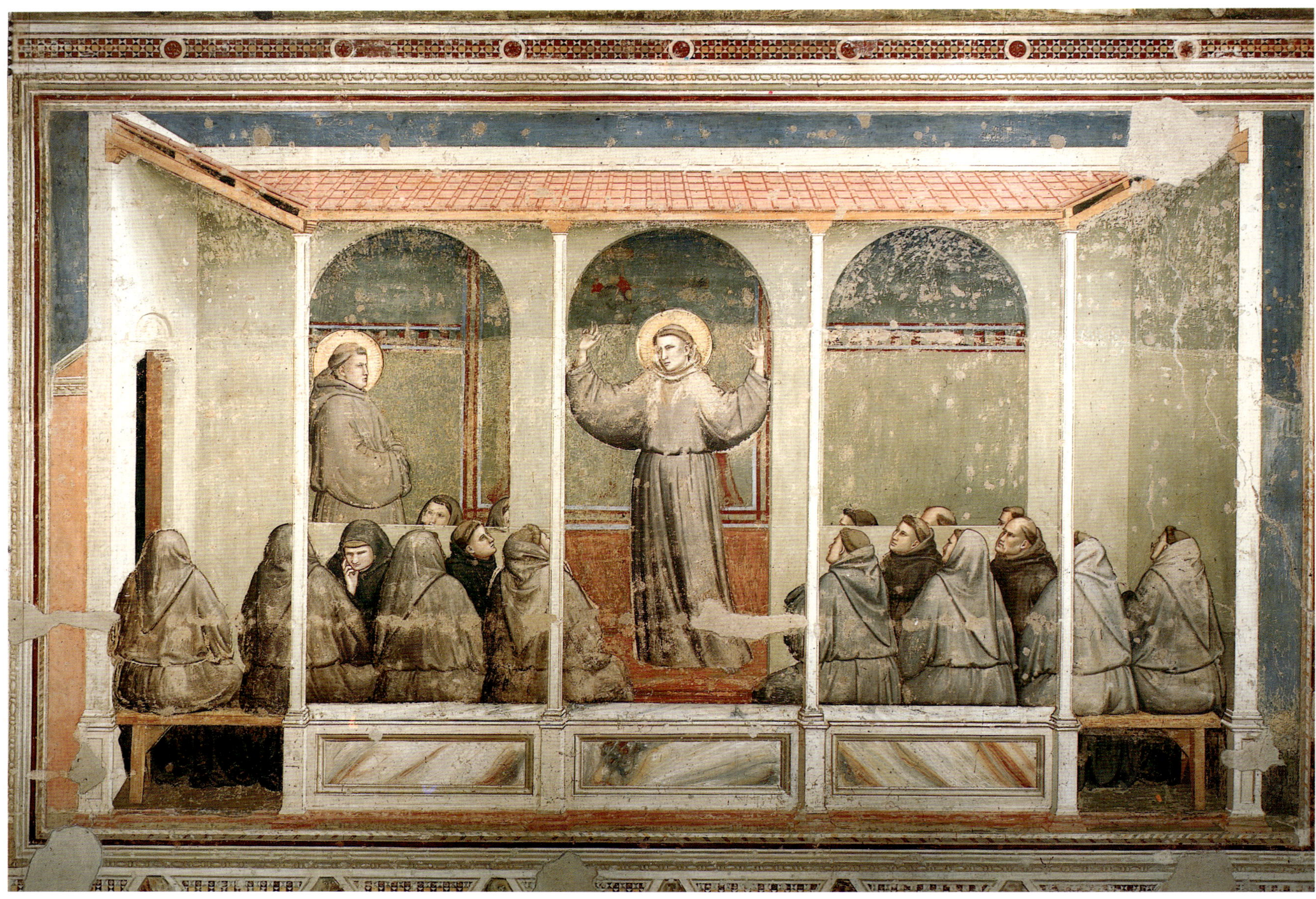

allude to their business dealings in the Near East, and at the same time to justify these as a Christian duty. In a similar fashion, the view of the city of Ephesus referred to the widespread trade relations of the Peruzzi family (ill. 120).

The cubic building in the *Renunciation of Worldly Goods* fresco brings to mind the clarity of the architecture of Ephesus (ill. 140). When conceiving the lunette paintings in the neighboring chapel, Giotto was already dealing with the arched form in an exciting and masterly fashion (ill. 114). Here, the cubic block of the father's palace, positioned at right angles, pushes its way into the foreground from the depths of the picture.

Thus the same aggressive tension that characterizes events is created between the arch of the frame and the sharp edge of the building. Just as in the trial by fire, the contrast between the two worlds is not embodied by two different buildings as at Assisi (ill. 19), but is sharpened into one element in a highly concentrated form – into the sharp edge of the corner of the building,

before which the naked Francis stands. Calm and unimpressed by all the animosity shown him, the latter turns towards heaven. The extreme nature of his decision is mirrored by the reactions of those present. And again Giotto gives those who are looking at the picture the opportunity to see themselves – in the children who throw stones, in the excited mothers who hold them back, in the angry father or in the noble city-dwellers.

Following his experiences decorating the vault in the Lower Church at Assisi, the reduction and concentration of the methods of representation are driven even further forward here. The voluminous figures of the Bardi frescoes reveal their sparing movements with a natural ease. Unlike the later art of the Renaissance, the actions of each figure are united in a rhythmically constructed, self-contained whole. Giotto never lost sight of this way of depicting things from the days of the Isaac frescoes in the clerestory of San Francesco at Assisi, and he continued to develop it in all his works.

143 *Apparition at Arles*, 1319–1328
Fresco
Chiesa di Santa Croce, Cappella Bardi, Florence

During a sermon delivered by the Franciscan brother Augustine, St. Francis appeared in support of his words. He blesses the monks and so strengthens them in their faith. The architecture is completely free of Gothic decoration, making the vividness of the faces is all the more striking.

144 (opposite) *Stigmatization*, 1319–1328
Fresco
Chiesa di Santa Croce, Cappella Bardi, Florence

Being marked with the stigmata is the high point in the saint's life. They mark him out for all to see as one of Christ's successors. Christ appears to him enveloped in angels' wings, and is here nailed to the cross – deviating from the usual portrayal. Fine golden rays emanating from Christ's wounds lead to St. Francis. In this representation the saint almost appears startled. He is in this way turned both towards the faithful and towards Christ.

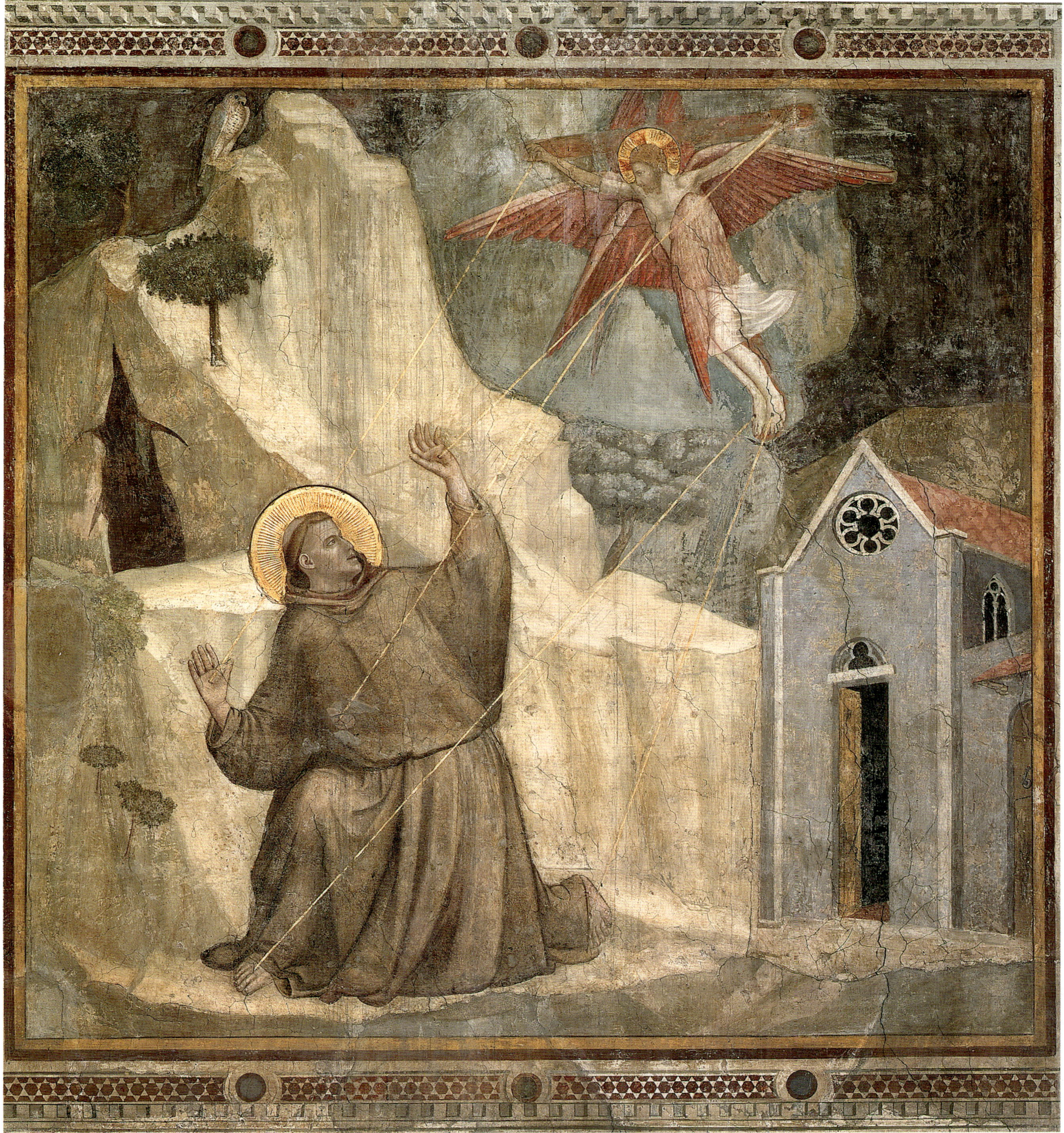

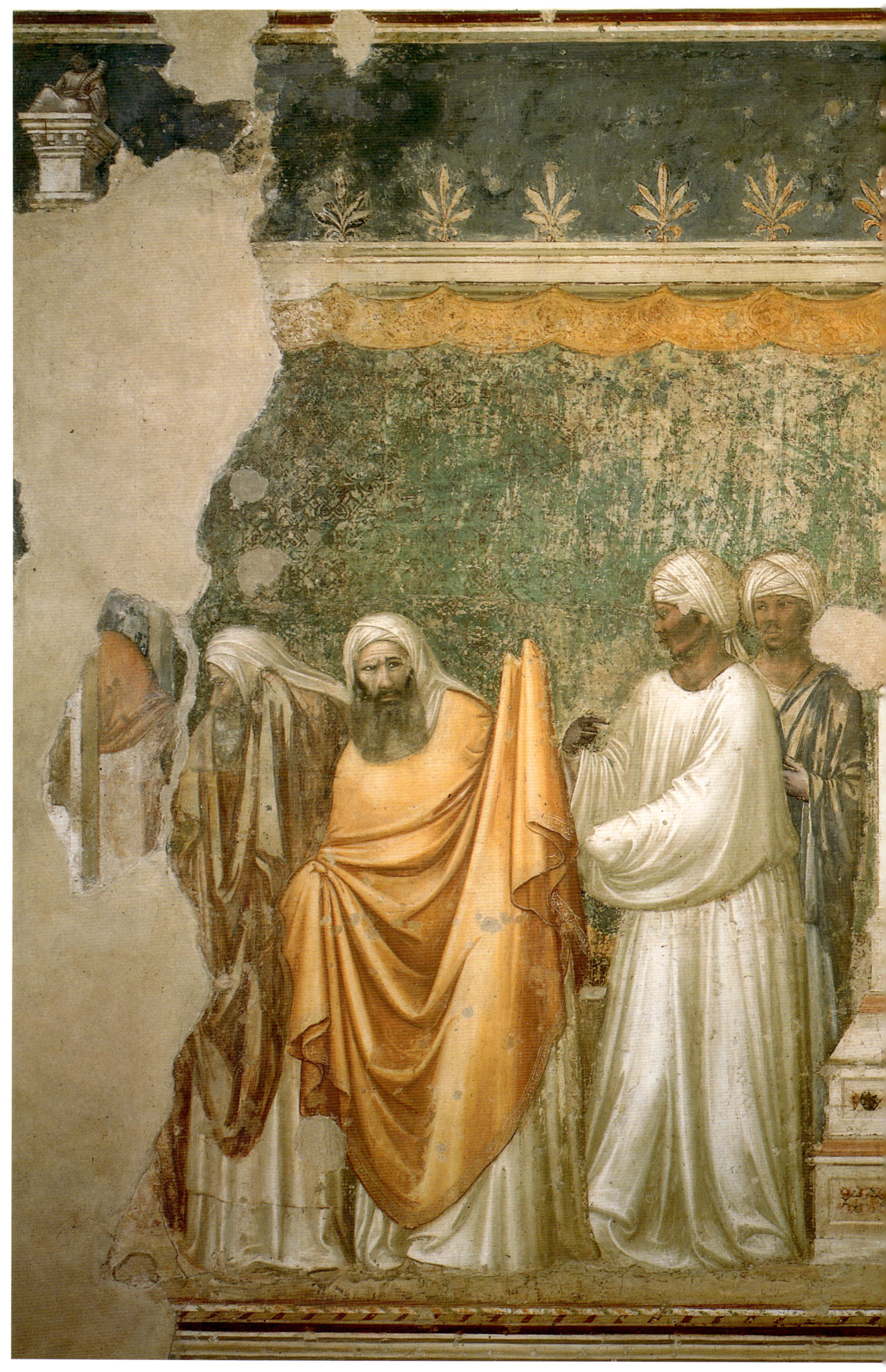

145 *Trial by Fire before the Sultan*, 1319–1328
Fresco
Chiesa di Santa Croce, Cappella Bardi, Florence

The sultan is enthroned in the center of the picture
and is referring his priests to the fire. Unlike Francis,
the latter do not wish to undergo the trial by fire, and
they steal away. In this fresco the faces of the
foreigners are painted particularly vividly. The colored
faces lead us to conclude that Nubians or Ethiopians
were present in Florence.

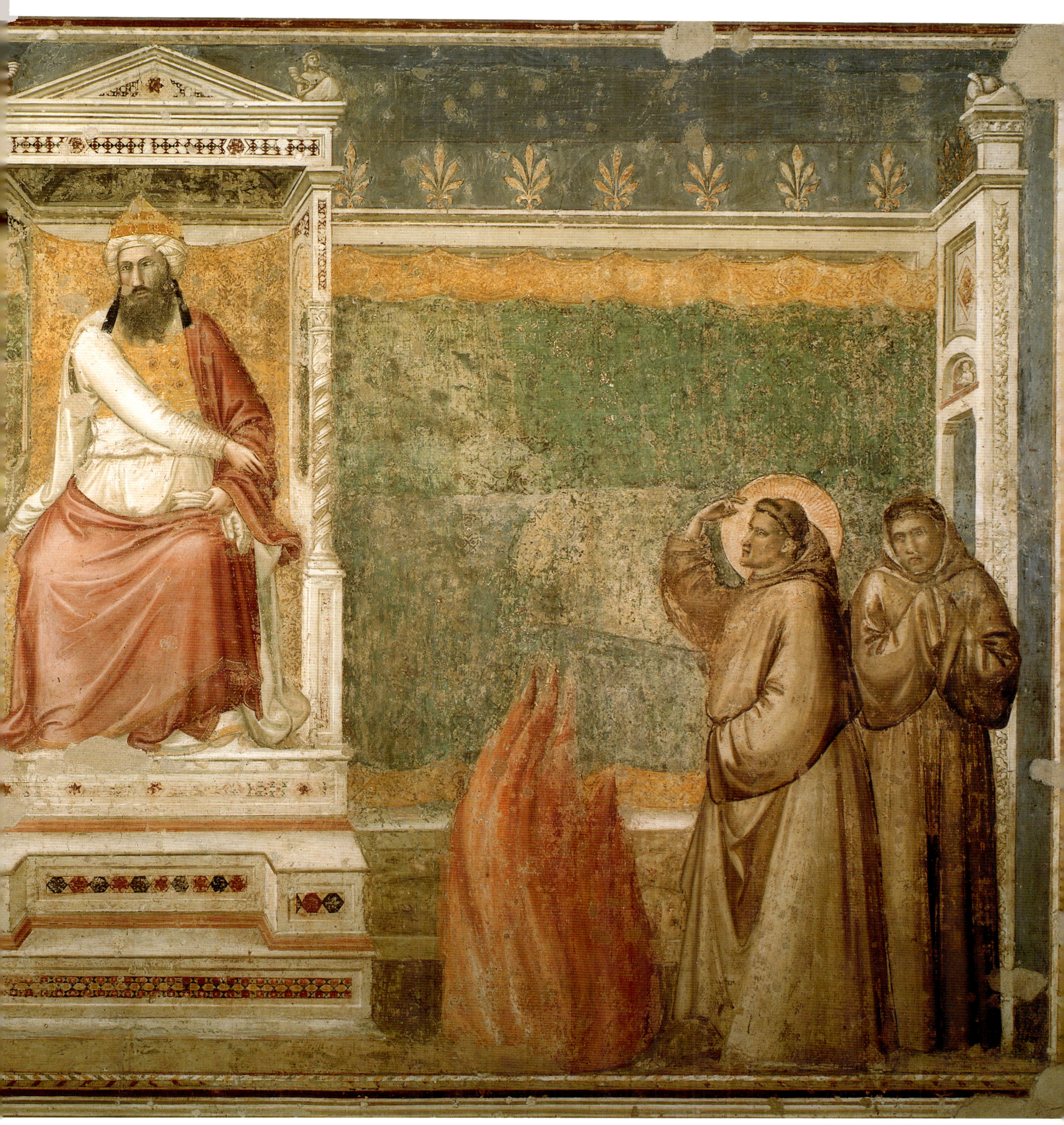

At the Height of Fame – Giotto's Last Works

146 (opposite) *Coronation of the Virgin* (detail ill. 147), after 1334

Mary and Christ sit on a broad throne. Mary bows her head reverently in order to receive the celestial crown from the hands of her Son. Mother and Son form a whole through their gestures, but mainly through their garments: both are clothed in radiant bright white and pink worked through with gold. The elegance of their clothing, in particular the trumpet-shaped sleeves on Christ's robe, indicates a great affinity with the style of courtly Gothic, a tendency which can also be observed in the frescoes in the Bardi Chapel.

147 (following double page) *Baroncelli Polyptych*, after 1334
Tempera on wood, 185 x 323 cm
Chiesa di Santa Croce, Cappella della famiglia Baroncelli, Florence

The original frame of this five-part altarpiece no longer survives. Beneath the central panel the altar is described as OPUS MAGISTRI JOCTI (Work of the Master Giotto). Many angels and saints have come together in a radiant assembly. They all want to be part of the coronation of the Mother of God by her son. In the rows at the front kneeling angels make music, in those at the back the looks and gestures of those present are oriented towards the central event.

Sources report that Giotto is said to have decorated other chapels in Santa Croce – nothing of these remains. He also received numerous commissions for altarpieces that he executed with his workshop, which obviously functioned well as a commercial enterprise. Both works by his atelier and by pupils, and those executed by his own hand, testify to its activities. However, the majority of panel paintings can no longer be seen in their original context. They were for the most part taken to pieces, and the few individual pieces that remain are scattered around the museums of the world.

The five-part altarpiece in the Pinacoteca at Bologna is one exception (ill. 150). Parts of the frame may have been lost, but the panels themselves can still be admired as a whole. The work was executed for the church of Santa Maria degli Angeli in Bologna, where building work commenced in 1328. The donor, Gera Pepoli, most likely commissioned both church and painting. At the foot of the central panel there is an inscription: OPUS MAGISTRI JOCTI DE FLORENTIA – "Work of Master Giotto from Florence". This is presumably a kind of "trademark" which Giotto's workshop applied to a work when finally completed. The somewhat wooden appearance of the saints on the side panels here strongly suggests that the assistants made a sizeable contribution. But we can assume that the overall design and the execution of the middle panel lay in Giotto's hands.

The second altarpiece of this period, the *Baroncelli Polyptych*, is also labeled with such an inscription (ill. 147). This altarpiece certainly represents the peak of Giotto's late period panel paintings, and is the only work to still be found in its original place. The name derives from the Baroncelli family, who commissioned the altarpiece in 1327 for the chapel donated by them, and dedicated to the Madonna of the Annunciation in the Franciscan church of Santa Croce in Florence. The chapel was decorated between 1328 and 1335 by Taddeo Gaddi, a pupil of Giotto's. The altarpiece – somewhat mutilated and with a 15th century frame – still adorns this chapel today. When the frame was redesigned, parts of the old frame were used to strengthen its rear side. A reconstruction has shown that the five panels were originally divided by broad,

silver-plated pilasters, that predella and altar panels therefore fitted together exactly.

The five panels are composed as one continuous pictorial space. We are looking at a heaven whose perspective is not distinct and whose width is opened out by a choir of heavenly figures on the side panels that seem to go on forever. The rows of figures throng together to form a radiant, brightly-colored assembly, observing the solemn occasion of the Virgin being crowned Queen of Heaven by her son and providing musical accompaniment. The central panel, where the main figures are portrayed on a slightly larger scale, succeeds in developing space a little more clearly.

The raiment of Mary and Christ, reminiscent of the courtly fashions of the time, and the strong colors, which remind us of the rich tones of the altarpiece at Bologna, support our dating the polyptych to the 1330s. In addition, the cutting back of space, the strict planimetric ordering, and the setting out of the figures make it appear a stylistic progression from the Bardi frescoes. The architectonic design of the frame and predella includes elements that are to be found on the campanile in Florence, which Giotto was to design as his last great work following his visit to Naples.

In 1328 the King of Naples called Giotto to his court. The house of Anjou enjoyed close contact with the Franciscans in Florence, and the Bardi family operated a branch of their bank in Naples. It is possible that Giotto was appointed on the basis of these connections. However, it is perfectly possible that Robert of Anjou, an art enthusiast, had seen Giotto's works himself in Rome and Assisi.

This appointment fundamentally changed Giotto's situation. Where he had previously been commissioned by different clients to execute works in places open to the public, and was the "independent" leader of a workshop, he now found himself an artist of the court. For the services rendered to him, Robert of Anjou awarded him the title of *familiaris* in January 1330: thus, the artist now belonged to the more intimate circles of the royal household.

Giotto received a regular salary and additional moneys for materials, assistants and apprentices. He was in charge of several "building sites" and was

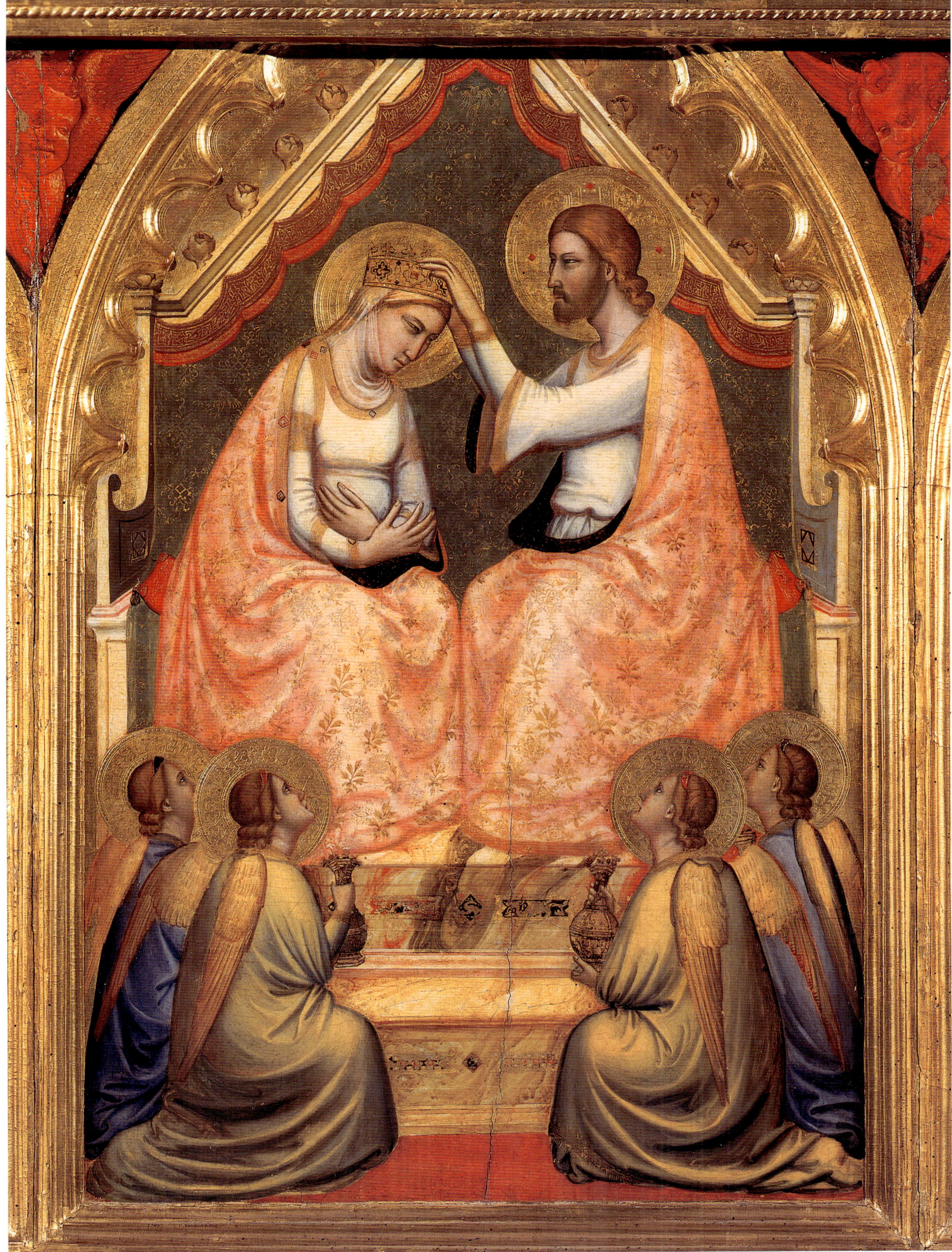

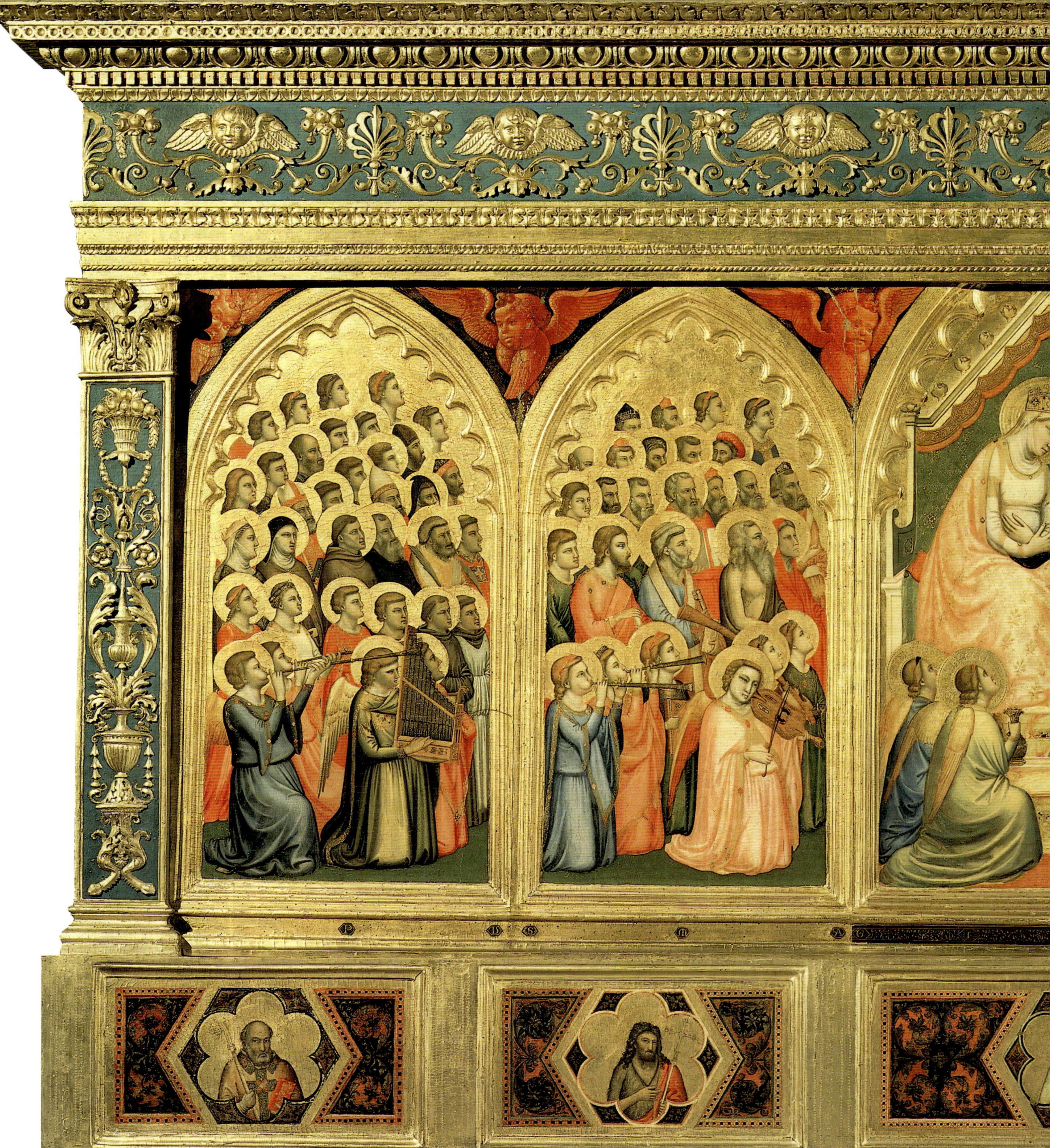

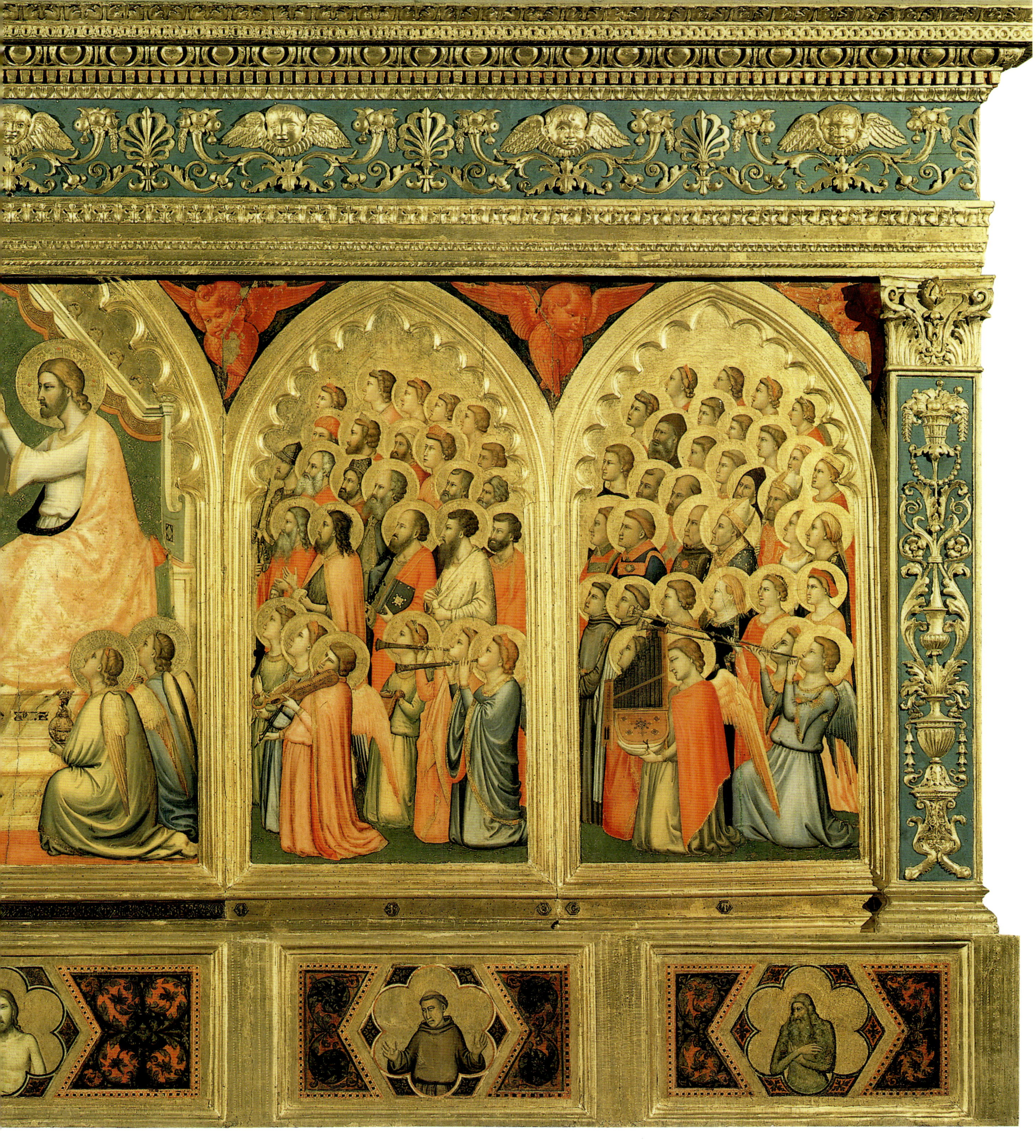

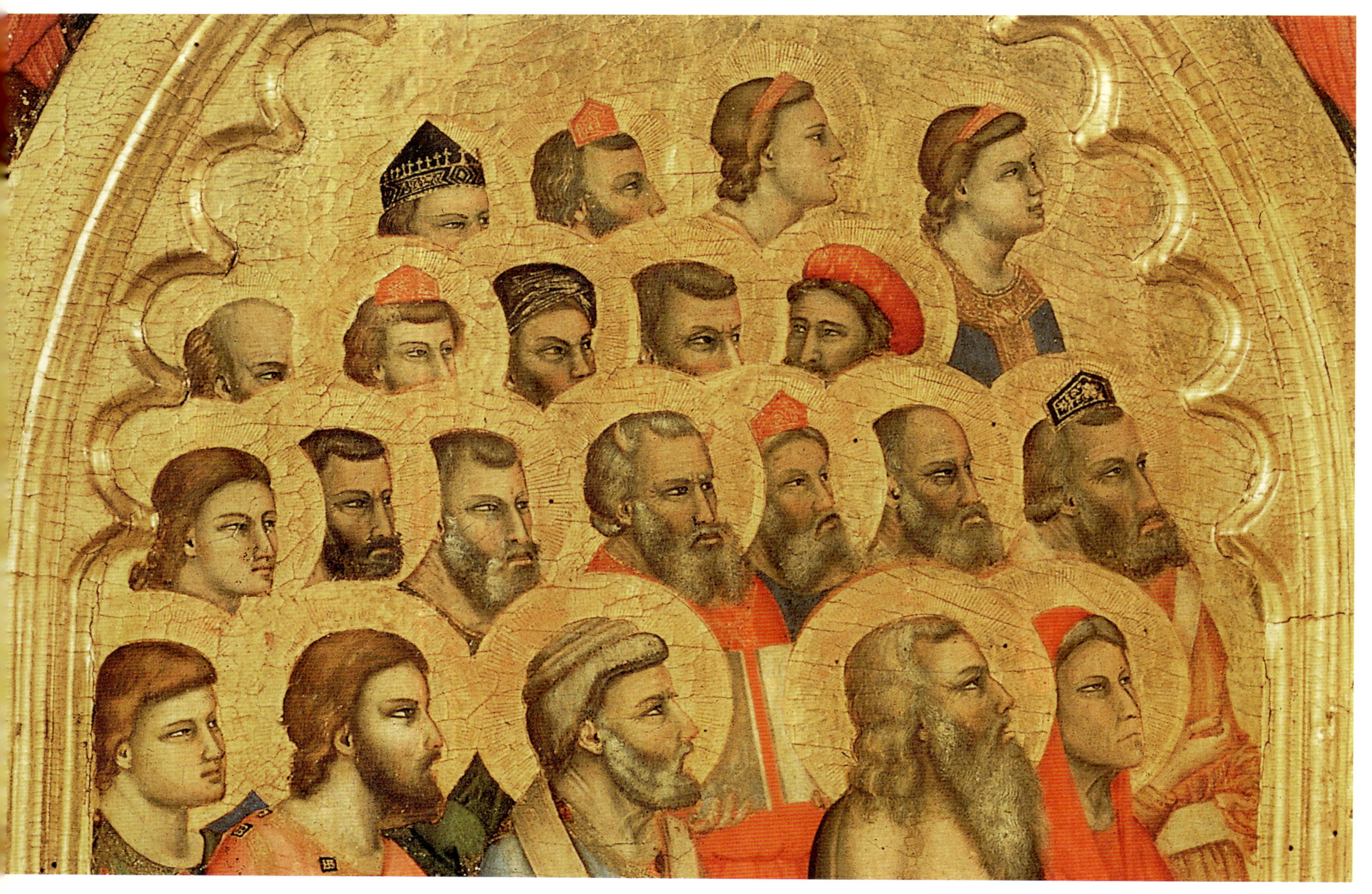

148, 149 *Saints* (details ill. 147), after 1334

As with the elegance of the clothing, Giotto also
approaches the style of international Gothic through the
condensation of space. Here on the two inner side panels
the individual figures appear almost bodiless, ranged in
lines one behind the other with no gaps in-between. The
effect of depth of the groupings that can be seen in the
Arena or Peruzzi Chapels has been abandoned here in
favor of a celebratory, radiant golden heaven without
perspectival arrangement. In spite of their supposed
uniformity, the faces of these celestial spectators are
actually fashioned in very different and varied ways.

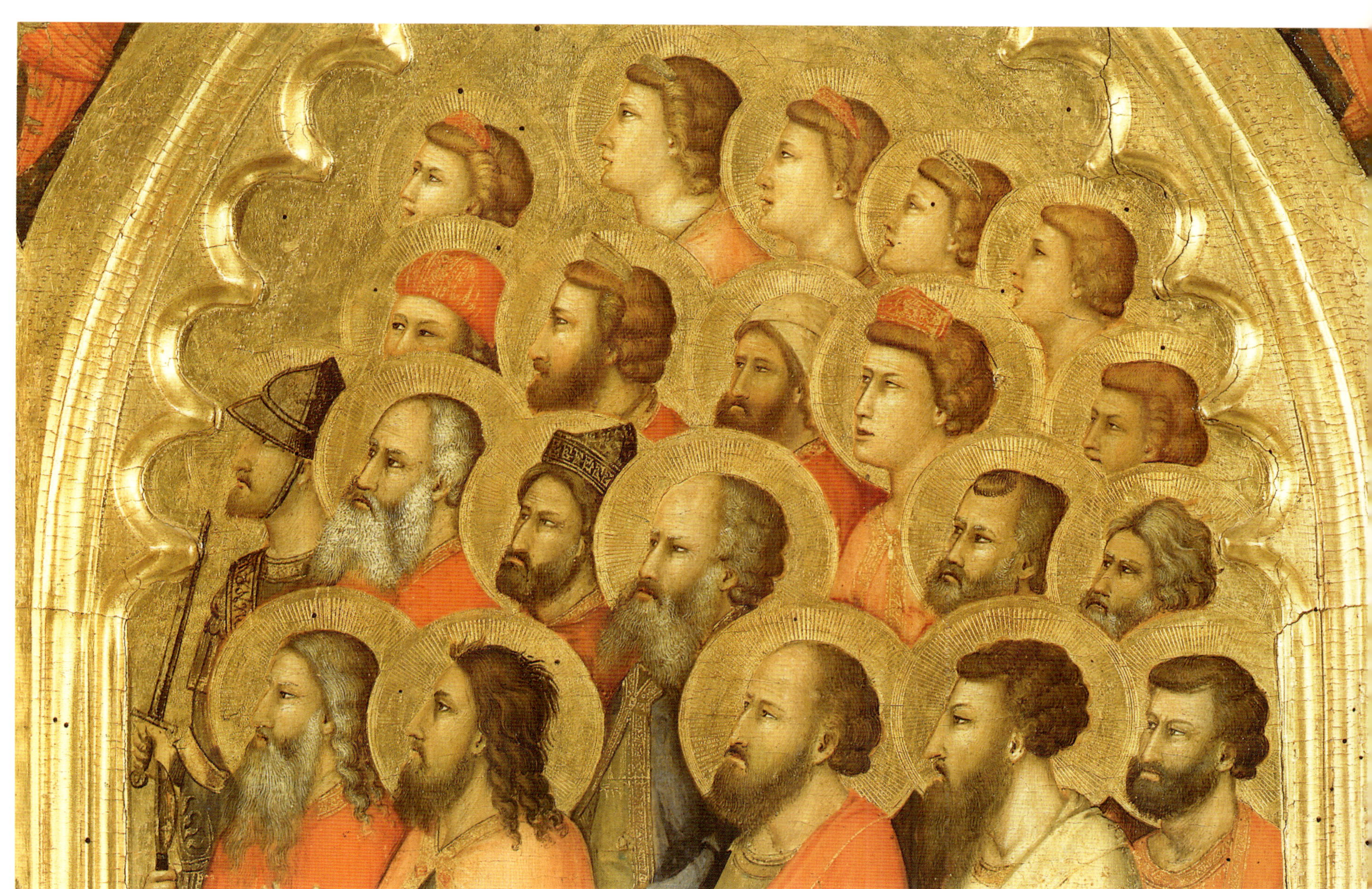

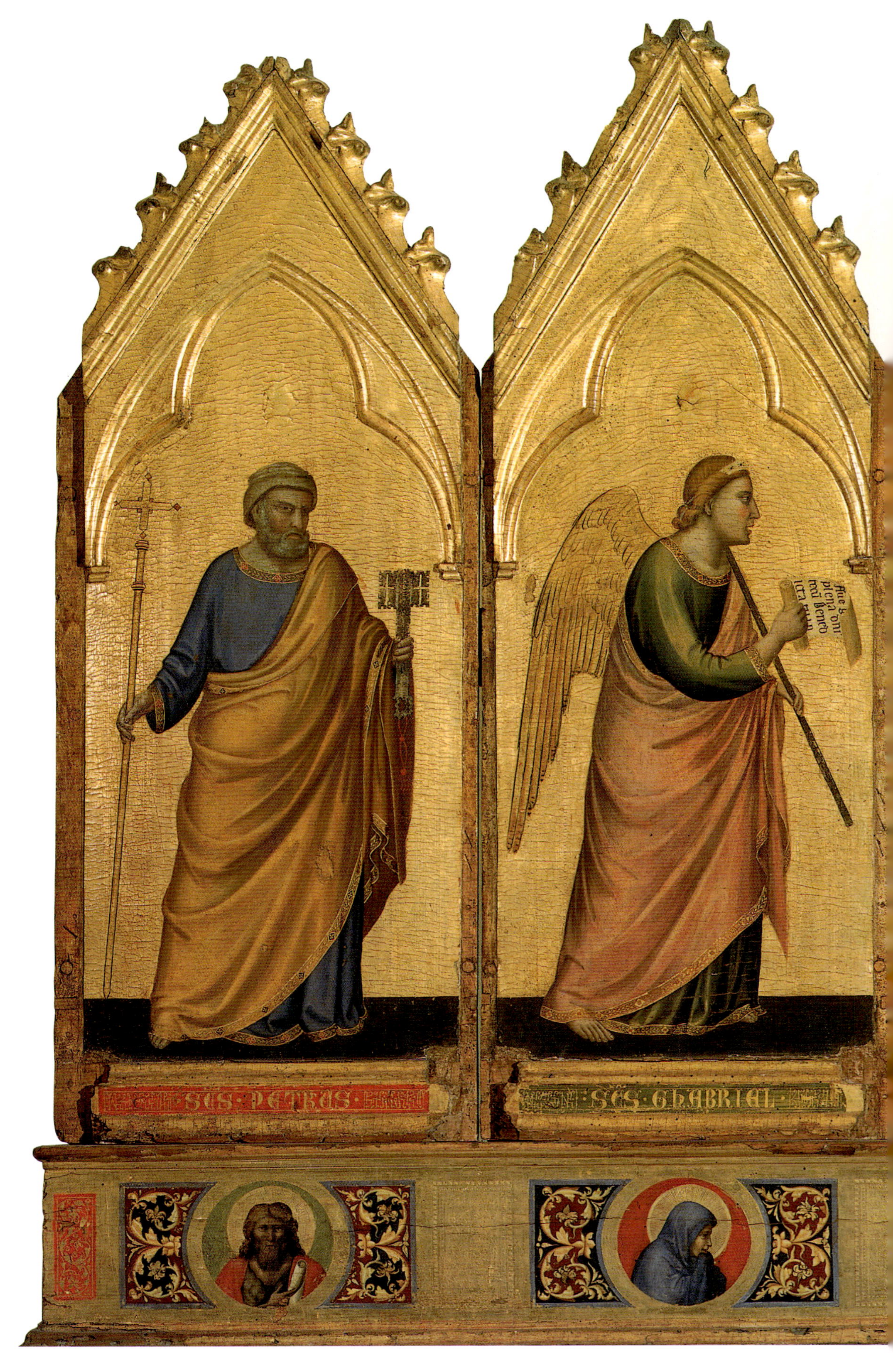

150 *Panel showing the Madonna*, after 1328
Tempera on wood, 91 x 340 cm
Pinacoteca Nazionale, Bologna

The polyptych bears the inscription OPUS MAGISTRI
JOCTI DE FLORENTIA (Work of the Master Giotto
from Florence) beneath the central panel. The Virgin
Mary is enthroned on a simple seat of marble in a radiant
blue robe. The Christ Child behaves in a very lively
manner and not at all solemnly. The Madonna is flanked
by the archangels Gabriel on the left and Michael on the
right. The two apostle-princes Peter and Paul stand on
the outside.

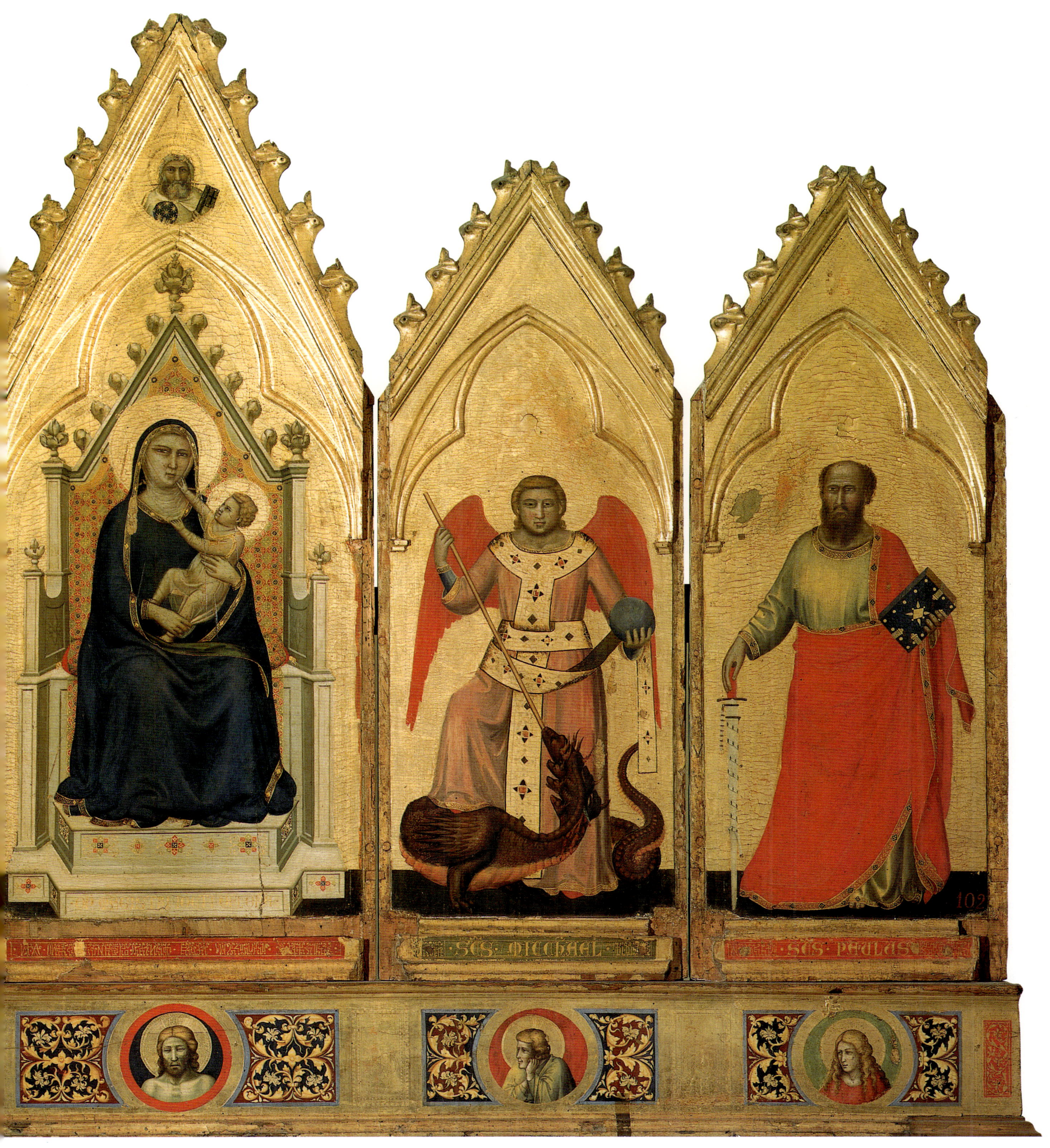
· SCS · MICCHAEL ·
· SCS · PAVLVS ·
102

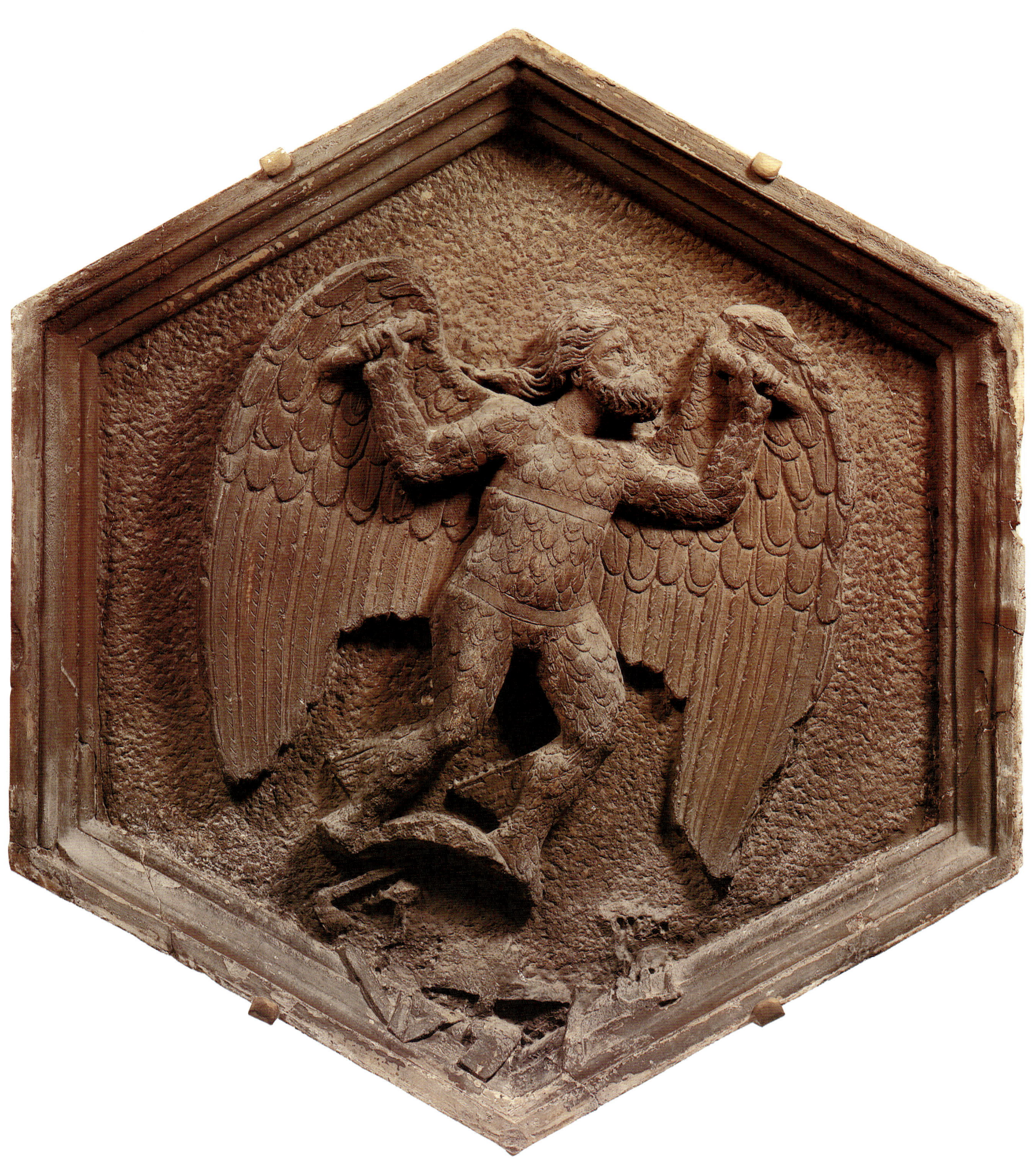

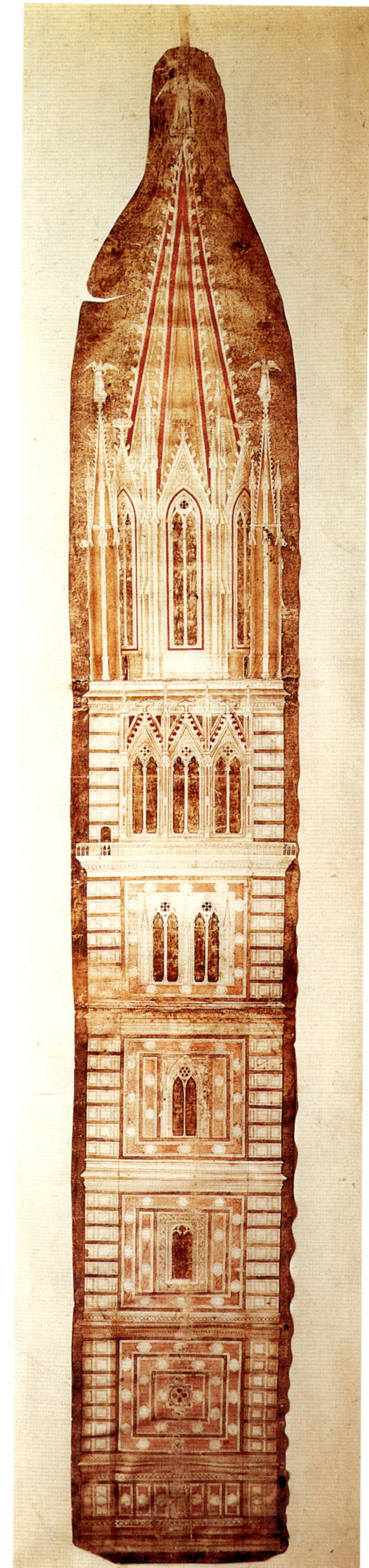

151 (opposite) *Daedalus*, after 1334
Marble
Mueso dell'Opera del Duomo, Florence

The design of this relief, though not its execution,
derives from Giotto. It shows Daedalus in a striding
posture on top of a cupola that acts as a launching pad.
All of his energy seems directed towards lifting his heavy,
feather-covered body into the air. This concentration of
energy corresponds to the energy of Giotto's painted
figures.

152 Design sketch for the Campanile, 1334
Parchment
Museo dell'Opera Metropolitana, Siena

This plan shows the design for the bell tower of the
Florentine cathedral. It most probably stems from
Giotto, who was made *capomaestro* in the year the
foundation stone was laid. Only the lowest storey was
built according to this plan.

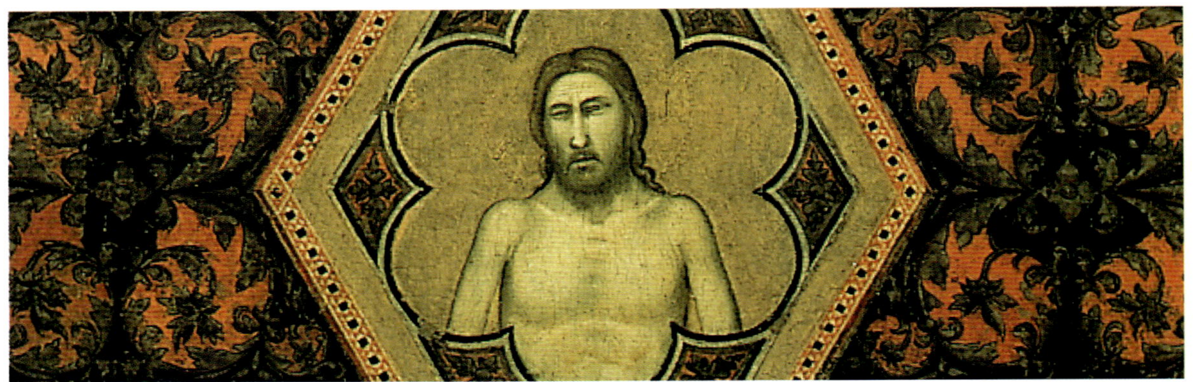

153 *Image of Christ* (detail ill. 147), after 1334

The *Coronation of the Virgin* has its theological
foundation, so to speak, in the central panel of the
predella with this iconographic depiction of Christ and
its allusion to the passion. Originally this picture of
Christ corresponded with a portrayal of God the Father
in the crowning panel at the central axis.

154 *Music-making Angels* (detail ill. 147), after 1334

These angels on the right-hand outer wing of the
Baroncelli Polyptych are making music in a lively fashion.
The strong, vivid range of colors is striking; together
with the contrasting shade of gold it spreads rich color
tones throughout the whole altarpiece. Like the
garments of the central figures, those of the angels also
conform stylistically to courtly fashion. They here form a
harmonic whole with the elegant sweeping gestures,
especially that of the wind player dressed in blue.

allocated a variety of tasks. These ranged from the
decoration of public churches via the painting of rooms
in the palace and in the private chapel of the ruling
family to the execution of altarpieces. Of all these
works, only a few fragments survive. Thus we cannot
relate this high point in his biography to a high point in
his art.

After five years in Naples, Giotto returned to
Florence. On 14 April 1334 the city appointed him
Master of Municipal Construction Works and of the
Cathedral Masons' Guild. Giotto performed this office
for three years, possibly interrupted by a visit to the
court at Milan, until his death. His attempts at
architectural clarity and his interest in spatial
conditions, such as the introduction of a unified
viewpoint or the taking into consideration of different
types of vaulting, could be found in every piece of
painting by Giotto that we have discussed so far. Even
the decorative frameworks, which separated and linked
the pictures, attest to his great feeling for architecture.
So it is not really that remarkable that we find the artist
at the end of his life as an architect.

In July 1334 the foundation stone of the campanile
of the cathedral was laid – we can assume that the newly
appointed *capomaestro* would have been given overall
control of the building work. A sketch attributed to
Giotto exists (ill. 152) which allows us to see how close
the design is to the painted architectural constructions
and the frames of the altarpieces.

Only the lower story of the bell tower was realized
from this design. There, set in the pink-colored fields of
marble, are figural reliefs, whose order and number were
changed by later alterations. The design of the original
21 reliefs very probably came from Giotto. They were
executed by Andrea Pisano (1290–1348), Giotto's
successor as *capomaestro*. A most original program is
realized in these reliefs. They are divided into three
groups of seven and dedicated to the theme of the
creative.

The Creation of Adam and Eve are the first two
representations, but they are followed not, as is usual, by
the Fall and Expulsion, but by the couple's first labors.

Even then the narrative does not continue with the usual
story of Genesis. The ancients, the inventors from the
first book of the Bible – the first shepherd, musician,
smith and wine-grower – continue the sequence.

The second group of seven shows the mechanical arts.
Since they were subordinated out of practical necessity
to the so-called "liberal arts" in the medieval system of
the sciences, their representations were normally
banished to peripheral areas. They are to be found on
capitals or on the jambs of doors.

The third group begins with the Greek hero
Hercules, who featured on the Florentine seal. He
liberated the land from a monster and made it
cultivable. The astronomer shown in the second relief
recognizes the order of the universe and its influence on
earthly fortunes. He is followed by the lawmaker, who
turns the region into a state. In a community
constructed thus, the human spirit can develop and
become creative: Architecture, Sculpture and Painting
conclude the sequence. Even the way they are portrayed
is distinctly unusual prior to this period. As artisans'
activities, they were normally subordinated to the
construction industry and did not appear in their own
right.

Daedalus appears between the basic structures of
community and the arts (ill. 151). In Greek mythology
he stands as a creative worker at the beginning of all art:
Daedalus, the inventor of the labyrinth and of flying, is
supposed to have been the first successfully to create a
sculpture with arms akimbo and parted legs. Since he is
thus supposed to have given life to figures for the first
time, he is considered as the very first artist.

With one exception, this is the only portrayal of
Daedalus to exist between the era of ancient Rome and
the age of the Renaissance. The fact that Giotto places
it at the beginning of the arts which he himself
practiced – architecture, sculpture and painting –
demonstrates that he held a particularly high opinion of
his own creations. It seems as if, in the figure of
Daedalus, the mythological son of Fame and Wisdom,
Giotto wanted in his final work to give a confident reply
to Dante's talk of the fleeting nature of earthly fame.

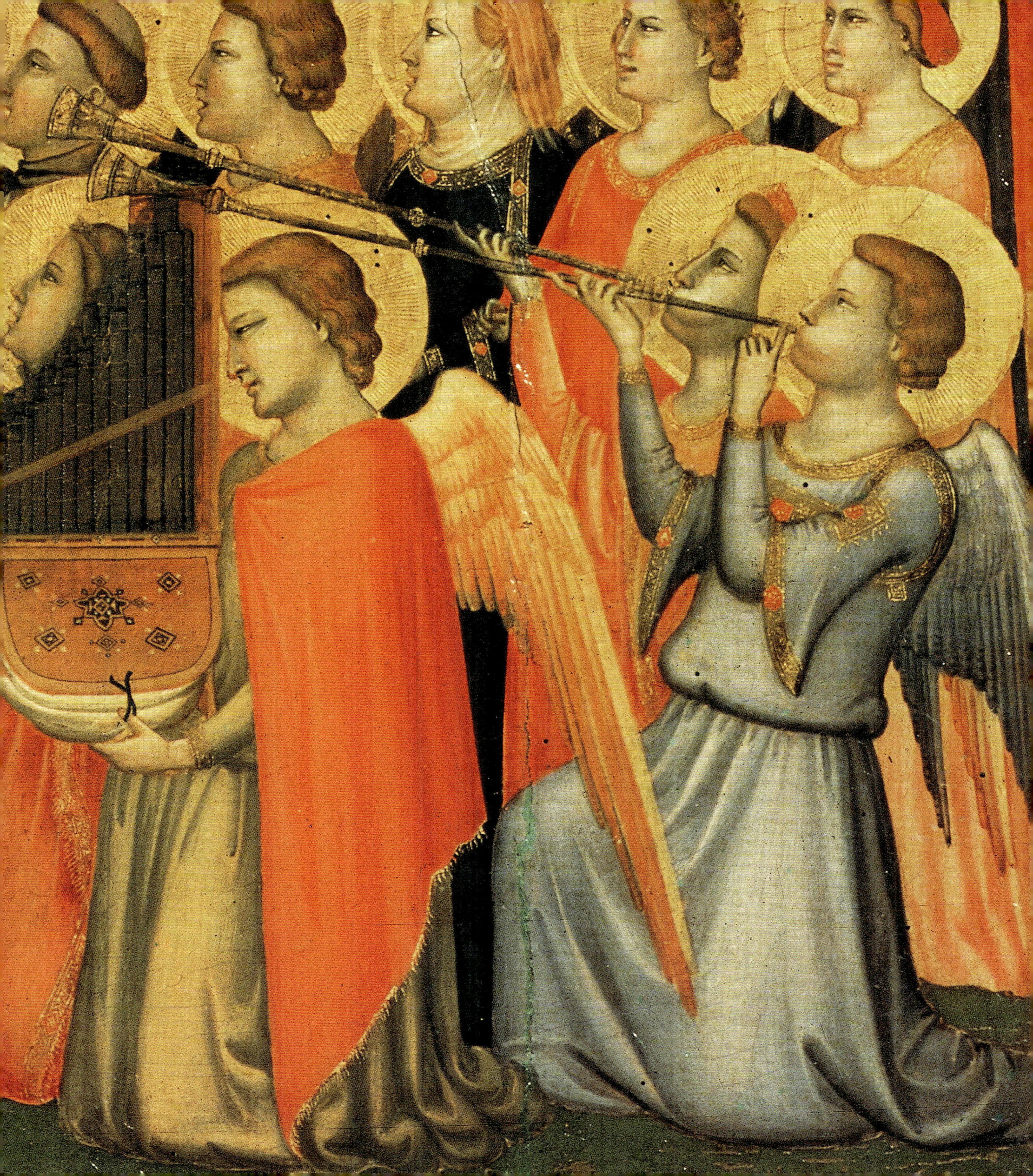

CHRONOLOGY

ca. 1267 Giotto is born in the hills of the Mugello, north of Florence.

ca. 1280 He presumably begins his apprenticeship with Cimabue, which he concludes with a trip to Rome in around 1285. After this, he probably follows his master Cimabue to Assisi.

1290–95 Giotto works independently in the Upper Church at Assisi. Sometime before 1300, he begins his first great narrative cycle of paintings, The Legend of St. Francis, in this church.

1299 He may have been in Rome, working for Pope Boniface VIII. Afterwards, the artist is in Florence. Several panel paintings are executed during this period.

1301/02 Giotto is probably in Rimini to realize several pieces of work for the Franciscan church there.

1302–1305 He paints in the Arena Chapel at Padua. During his stay here, he could have met the poet Dante, who had been banished from Florence.

1309/10 Giotto works in Rome on a great mosaic for St. Peter's. Afterwards he returns to Florence.

1313 At the end of this year, Giotto demands the return of his household property from his landlady in Rome. This means he had previously spent a considerable length of time in Rome. This is presumably the period during which the Roman altarpiece is created.

1314/15 Giotto is in Florence, as documented by various legal matters. During this time he is occupied with the paintings in the Peruzzi Chapel in Santa Croce.

1316–1320 Giotto is working in the Lower Church of San Francesco at Assisi.

1320 He is back in Florence. More works are executed in Santa Croce. He remains in the city on the Arno until 1328.

1328 The King of Naples, Robert of Anjou, appoints him to his court.

1334 Giotto does not return to Florence until this year. He becomes *capomaestro* and is in charge of all building in the city of Florence.

1336 Giotto is possibly working for the ruling house of Visconti in Milan.

1337 On 8 January Giotto dies in Florence and is buried with great honor "at the expense of the city" in the Florentine cathedral of Santa Reparata.

GLOSSARY

allegory (Gk. *allegorein*, "say differently"), a work of art which represents some abstract quality or idea, either by means of a single figure (personification) or by grouping objects and figures together. Renaissance allegories make frequent allusions both to both Greek and Roman legends and literature, and also to the wealth of Christian **allegorical** stories and symbols developed during the Middle Ages.

altar panel, a painting that stands on or behind an altar. Early altar panels were made to stand alone; gradually they came to form the central work of elaborate altarpieces that combined several panels within a carved framework.

altarpiece, a picture or sculpture that stands on or is set up behind an altar. Many altarpieces were very simple (a single panel painting), though some were huge and complex works, a few combining both painting and sculpture within a carved framework. From the 14th to 16th century, the altarpiece was one of the most important commissions in European art; it was through the altarpiece that some of the most decisive developments in painting and sculpture came about.

amphitheater, in classical architecture, a round or oval structure consisting of a central open space or arena surrounded by tiers of seats rising gradually outwards. In Roman times they were frequently used for gladiatorial contests.

Antichrist, according to Christian teaching, the final great enemy of Christ who will appear in the final days before the end of the world.

apse (Lat. *absis*, "arch, vault"), a semicircular projection, roofed with a half-dome, at the east end of a church behind the altar. Smaller subsidiary apses may be found around the choir or transepts.

arcade (Lat. *arcus,* "arch"), a series of arches supported by columns, piers or pillars. In a **blind arcade** the arches are built into a wall.

atelier (Fr.), an artists workshop or studio.

atrium, open central courtyard, especially of a Roman house; a court in front of a church, usually one lined by a colonnade.

attribute (Lat. *attributum*, "added"), a symbolic object which is conventionally used to identify a particular person, usually a saint. In the case of martyrs, it is usually the nature of their martyrdom.

aureole (Lat. [*corona*] *aureola*, "golden [crown]"), a circle of light shown surrounding a holy person, a halo.

basilica (Gk. *basilike stoa*, "king's hall"), in Roman architecture a long colonnaded hall used as a court, a market or as a place for assemblies. The early Christians adopted this form of building for their churches, the first Christian basilicas being long halls with a nave flanked by colonnaded side aisles, and with an apse at the eastern end. With the addition of other features, in particular the transept, the basilica became the traditional Christian church.

Byzantine art, the art of the Byzantine Empire, which had its capital in Constantinople (Byzantium), from the 5th century to the fall of Constantinople to the Turks in 1453. Based largely on Roman and Greek art, Byzantine art also absorbed a wide variety of influences, notably from Syria and Egypt. Byzantine art was essentially a spiritual and religious art, its forms highly stylized, hieratic and unchanging (central images were thought to derive from original portraits). It also served to glorify the emperor. Among its most distinctive products were icons, mosaics, manuscript illuminations, and work in precious metals. The strong influence of the Byzantine style on medieval Italian painting can be seen in the works of Cimabue, Duccio, and Giotto.

campanile (It. "bell tower"), a church bell tower, often standing detached from the body of the church. Well-known examples are the Campanile of St. Mark's Cathedral in Venice, and the "Leaning Tower" of Pisa.

capital (Lat. *capitellum*, "little head"), the head or crowning feature of a column or pillar. Structurally, capitals broaden the area of a column so that it can more easily bear the weight of the arch or entablature it supports. They also provide an opportunity for decoration: medieval capitals, for example, were often richly decorated with sculptures of plants, animals, demons, faces or figures.

cartoon (It. *cartone*, "pasteboard"), a full-scale preparatory drawing for a painting, tapestry, or fresco. In fresco painting, the design was transferred to the wall by making small holes along the contour lines and then powdering them with charcoal in order to leave an outline on the surface to be painted.

choir (Gk. *khoros*, "area for dancing; chorus"), in a Christian church, the areas set aside for singers and the clergy, generally the area between the crossing and the high altar.

classical, relating to the culture of ancient Greece and Rome (**classical Antiquity**). The classical world played a profoundly important role in the Renaissance, with Italian scholars, writers, and artists seeing their own period as the rebirth (the "renaissance") of classical values after the Middle Ages. The classical world was considered the golden age for the arts, literature, philosophy, and politics. Concepts of the classical, however, changed greatly from one period to the next. Roman literature provided the starting point in the 14th century, scholars patiently finding, editing and translating a wide range of texts. In the 15th century

Greek literature, philosophy and art – together with the close study of the remains of Roman buildings and sculptures – expanded the concept of the classical and ensured it remained a vital source of ideas and inspiration.

clerestory (or **clearstory**), in church architecture, the upper part of a nave, containing a row of windows.

codex (Lat. "wooden writing board"), a manuscript or book, especially of the Scriptures, a holy work or one of the classics.

coffering, an ornamental system of deep panels recessed into a vault, arch or ceiling. Coffered ceilings, occasionally made of wood, were frequently used in Renaissance palaces.

colonnade, a row of columns supporting a series of arches or an entablature.

cornice, in architecture, a projecting moulding that runs around the top of a building or the wall of a room.

Cosmati work, a colorful form of decorative work on marble altars, pulpits, thrones etc. consisting of inlays of stone and glass, and sometimes mosaic work and gilding. Flourishing mainly in Rome during the 12th and 13th centuries, it is characterized by ornate geometrical patterns that are often separated by strips of white marble. The name is derived from the Cosmati family, who specialized in this form of decoration.

crossing, in church architecture, the square space created by the intersection of the nave and the transepts. A crossing is usually covered by a tower or a dome.

crypt (Gk. *kryptos*, "hidden"), an underground chamber housing tombs or relics, usually under the choir of a church.

dado (It. "cube"), in architecture, the section between the base and the crown of a pedestal; the lower section of the wall of a room, decorated with panels.

dalmatic *(Lat. dalmatica [vestis],* "Dalmatian [garment]", made from a white wool from Dalmatia), in the Roman Catholic Church, a long wide sleeved vestment worn over an alb by deacons and bishops.

episcopal (Gk. *episkopos,* "overseer"), relating to a bishop or bishops.

Franciscans, a Roman Catholic order of mendicant friars founded by St. Francis of Assisi (given papal approval in 1223). Committed to charitable and missionary work, they stressed the veneration of the Holy Virgin, a fact that was highly significant in the development of images of the Madonna in Italian art. In time the absolute poverty of the early Franciscans gave way to a far more relaxed view of property and wealth, and the Franciscans became some of the most important patrons of art in the early Renaissance.

fresco (It. "fresh"), wall painting technique in which pigments are applied to wet (fresh) plaster (*intonaco*). Painting in this way is known as painting *al fresco.* The pigments bind with the drying plaster to form a very durable image. Only a small area can be painted in a day, and these areas (known as *giornata*), drying to a slightly different tint, can in time be seen. Small amounts of retouching and detail work could be carried out on the dry plaster, a technique known as *al secco* fresco.

Gothic (Ital. gotico, "barbaric, not classical"), the style of European art and architecture during the Middle Ages, following Romanesque and preceding the Renaissance. Originating in northern France about 1150, the Gothic style gradually spread to England, Spain, Germany and Italy. In Italy Gothic art came to an end as early as 1400, whilst elsewhere it continued until the 16th century. The cathedral is the crowning achievement of Gothic architecture, its hallmarks being the pointed arch (as opposed to the Romanesque round arch), the ribbed vault, large windows, and exterior flying buttresses. The development of Gothic sculpture was made possible by Gothic architecture, most sculptures being an integral part of church architecture. Its slender, stylized figures express a deeply spiritual approach to the world, though its details are often closely observed features of this world. Gothic painting included illuminated manuscripts, panel pictures, and stained glass windows. In painting and sculpture, the elegant style known as **International Gothic** – combining realism and courtly refinement – flourished from the 1370s to the 1420s.

grisaille (Fr. *gris,* "gray"), a painting done entirely in one color, usually gray. Grisaille paintings were often intended to imitate sculptures.

Guelphs and **Ghibellines,** in medieval German and Italy, the two rival factions in the struggle for power in the Holy Roman Empire. The conflict began in Germany in the 12th century with a dispute between two ruling families: the Welfs (known in Italian as Guelfs) and the Hohenstaufen (known in Italian as the Ghibellines). The conflict spread to Italy, where the Guelfs supported the pope's claim to power, and the Ghibellines supported the Holy Roman Emperor's claim to sovereignty (northern Italy being part of the Holy Roman Empire). Long and bitter, the struggle became an integral part of Italian life in the late Middle Ages, each city being dominated by one group or the other. The conflict was over by the end of the 14th century.

Horsemen of the Apocalypse, according to the Book of Revelations, the four horsemen who symbolize plague, war, famine and death who will appear at the end of the world.

humanism, an intellectual movement that began in Italy in the 14th century. Based on the rediscovery of the classical world, it replaced the medieval view of humanity as fundamentally sinful and weak with a new and confident emphasis on humanity's innate moral dignity and intellectual and creative potential. A new attitude to the world rather than a set of specific ideas, humanism was reflected in literature and the arts, in scholarship and philosophy, and in the birth of modern science.

iconography (Gk. "description of images"), the systematic study and identification of the subject-matter and symbolism of art works, as opposed to their style; the set of symbolic forms on which a given work is based. Originally, the study and identification of classical portraits. Renaissance art drew heavily on two **iconographical** traditions: Christianity, and ancient Greek and Roman art, thought and literature.

Imitatio Christi (Lat.) the imitation of Christ, the Christian ideal of a life lived in complete accordance with Christ's own life and teachings.

jamb, in architecture, the vertical elements of a doorway, archway, or window.

journeyman, a person who has served an apprenticeship in a trade or craft and is now fully qualified to work for others.

keystone, in architecture, the central, wedge-shaped stone of an arch or vault.

Legenda Aurea (Lat. "golden legend"), a collection of saints' legends, published in Latin in the 13th century by the Dominican Jacobus da Voragine, Archbishop of Genoa. These were particularly important as a source for Christian art from the Middle Ages onwards.

lectern, a reading stand or desk, especially one at which the Bible is read.

liberal arts, in medieval education, the seven main subjects studied: grammar, rhetoric, logic, astronomy, geometry, music and arithmetic. These intellectual disciplines were thought the proper subjects for a "free man" (Latin *liber*) and were clearly distinguished from the mechanical or practical arts (such as painting and sculpture), which were thought to be of a lower status.

lunette (Fr. "little moon"), in architecture, a semicircular space, such as that over a door or window or in a vaulted roof, that may contain a window, painting or sculptural decoration.

Maestà (It. "majesty"), a depiction of the Madonna and Child enthroned in Heaven and surrounded by saints and angels. They were particularly popular in Italy during the 13th and 14th centuries.

mandorla (It. "almond"), an almond-shaped radiance surrounding a holy person, often seen in images of the Resurrection of Christ or the Assumption of the Virgin.

maniera greca (It. "the Greek style"), the Byzantine style of painting in Italy. See: Byzantine art.

mosaic (Gk. *mouseios*, "belonging to the Muses"), an art form in which picture or designs are built up by setting small pieces of colored stone or tile in mortar. Extensively used in ancient Rome, it later became popular for wall and vault decorations in medieval Byzantine and Italian churches. During the early Renaissance it was largely replaced by fresco.

nave (Lat, *navis*, "ship"), the central part of a church stretching from the main doorway to the chancel and usually flanked by aisles.

panel painting, a portable painting on a rigid support (usually wooden boards) rather than canvas. It was not until the 15th century that canvas began to replace wooden panels.

parchment (Lat. *Parthica* [*pellis*], Parthian [leather]), the skin of an animal, usually sheep or goat, prepared so that it can be used for writing or painting on; a document made of this material.

perspective (Lat. *perspicere*, "to see through, see clearly"), the method of representing three-dimensional objects on a flat surface. Perspective gives a picture a sense of depth. The most important form of perspective in the Renaissance was **linear perspective** (first formulated by the architect Brunelleschi in the early 15th century), in which the real or suggested lines of objects converge on a vanishing point on the horizon, often in the middle of the composition (**centralized perspective**). The first artist to make a systematic use of linear perspective was Masaccio, and its principles were set out by the architect Alberti in a book published in 1436. The use of linear perspective had a profound effect on the development of Western art and remained unchallenged until the 20th century.

pilaster (Lat. *pilastrum*, "pillar"), a rectangular column set into a wall, usually as a decorative feature.

podium (Gk. *pous*, "foot"), an elevated platform.

poverello (It.), the "little poor one," a reference to St. Francis of Assisi, who swore a vow of poverty.

predella (It. "altar step"), a painting or carving placed beneath the main scenes or panels of an altarpiece, forming a kind of plinth. Long and narrow, painted predellas usually depicted several scenes from a narrative.

rood-screen, in church architecture, a high screen between the nave and the choir. Usually in wood, they were often richly carved and decorated, and were surmounted by a crucifix (rood = cross).

sacristy (Lat. *sacer,* "sacred"), a storeroom attached to a church, generally used for housing vestments and sacred vessels.

seraph pl. **seraphim** (Hebrew "angel"), an angel. In the Medieval hierarchy of celestial beings, they are the first in importance. They are usually depicted with three pairs of wings.

stigmata, sing. **stigma** (Gk. "mark, brand, tattoo"), the five Crucifixion wounds of Christ (pierced feet, hands and side) which appear miraculously on the body of a saint. One of the most familiar examples in Renaissance art is the **stigmatization** of St. Francis of Assisi.

symbolic perspective, in medieval art, a way of clearly indicating a person's importance by means of size. A saint, for example, would usually be larger than a donor but smaller than the Virgin Mary.

tempera (Lat. *temperare*, "to mix in due proportion"), a method of painting in which the pigments are mixed with an emulsion of water and egg yolks or whole eggs (sometimes glue or milk). Tempera was widely used in Italian art in the 14th and 15th centuries, both for panel painting and fresco, then being replaced by oil paint. Tempera colors are bright and translucent, though because the paint dried very quickly there is little time to blend them, graduated tones being created by adding lighter or darker dots or lines of color to an area of dried paint.

tracery, in architecture, decorative work consisting of interlaced or branching lines, usually found in the upper parts of windows, but also on screens, doors and vaults. Elaborate tracery was a characteristic feature of Gothic architecture.

transept, in church architecture, the two lateral arms that project from the nave to form the shape of a cross.

Trecento (It. "three hundred"), the 14th century in Italian art. This period is often considered the "proto-Renaissance", when writers and artists laid the foundation for the development of the early Renaissance in the next century (the **Quattrocento**). Outstanding figures of the Trecento include Giotto, Duccio, Simone Martini, the Lorenzetti brothers, and the Pisano family of sculptors.

triptych (Gk. *triptukhos*, "threefold"), a painting in three sections, usually an altarpiece, consisting of a central panel and two outer panels, or wings. In many medieval triptychs the two outer wings were hinged so that they could be closed over the center panel. Early triptychs were often portable.

triumphal arch, in the architecture of ancient Rome, a large and usually free-standing ceremonial arch ways built to celebrate a military victory. Often decorated with architectural features and relief sculptures, they usually consisted of a large archway flanked by two smaller ones. The triumphal archway was revived during the Renaissance, though usually as a feature of a building rather than as an independent structure. In Renaissance painting they appear as allusion to classical antiquity.

vault, a roof or ceiling whose structure is based on the arch. There are a wide range of forms, including: the **barrel** (or **tunnel**) vault, formed by a continuous semi-circular arch; the **groin** vault, formed when two barrel vaults intersect; and the **rib** vault, consisting of a framework of diagonal ribs supporting interlocking arches. The development of the various forms was of great structural and aesthetic importance in the development of church architecture during the Middle Ages

Vices and Virtues, the. In the medieval and Renaissance Christianity there were seven principal virtues and seven principal vices, a classification that brought together ideals of both Christianity and classical Antiquity. Personifications of both appear in medieval and Renaissance art. The seven Vices (also known as the seven Deadly Sins) were: Pride, Covetousness, Lust, Anger, Envy, Gluttony, and Sloth. The seven Virtues were: Faith, Hope, Charity, Fortitude, Temperance, Prudence, and Justice.

SELECTED BIBLIOGRAPHY

Arcais, Francesca Flores d': Giotto, Milan 1995

Bellosi, Luciano: Giotto, Florence 1981

Bandera Bistoletti, Sandrina: Giotto. Catalogo completo dei dipiniti, Florence 1989

Belting, Hans: Malerei und Stadtkultur in der Dantezeit, Munich 1989

Blume, Dieter: Wandmalerei als Ordenspropaganda. Bildprogramme im Chorbereich Franziskanischer Konvente Italiens bis zur Mitte des 14. Jahrhunderts, Worms 1983

Cämmerer, Monika: "Giottos Polyptychon in der Baroncelli-Kapelle von Santa Croce: Nachtrage und neue Beobachtungen" in: *Mitteilungen des Kunsthistorischen Institutes in Florenz*, vol. XXXIX, 1995, pp. 374–392

Gioseffi, Ducio: Giotto architetto, Milan 1963

Gosebruch, Martin: Giotto und die Entwicklung des neuzeitlichen Kunstbewußtseins, Cologne 1962

Gosebruch, Martin: "Giottos Stefaneschi-Altarwerk aus St. Peter in Rom" in: Miscellanea Bibliotheca Hertzianae zu Ehren von Leo Bruhns u. a … Munich 1961, pp. 109–330

Hetzer, Theodor: Giotto, seine Stellung in der europäischen Kunst, Frankfurt 1941

Kempers, Bram and Sible de Blauw: "Jacopo Stefaneschi, Patron and Liturgist. A new hypothesis regarding the date, ikonography, authorship and function of his altarpiece for Old Saint Peter's" in: *Medelingen van het Nederlands Instituut te Rome*, vol. XLVII, n.12, 1987, pp. 83–286

Lisner, Magrit: "Die Gewandfarben der Apostel in Giottos Arenafresken. Farbgebung und Ikonographie" in: *Zeitschrift für Kunstgeschichte*, 1990, pp. 309–375

McWilliam, G. H.: Boccacio's Decameron, London 1972, pp. 456–459

Previtali, Giorgio: Giotto e la sua bottega. 3rd edition, A.Conti (ed), Milan 1993

Poeschke, Joachim: Die Kirche San Francesco in Assisi und ihre Wandmalereien, Munich 1985

Ruf, P. Gerhard: Franziskus und Bonaventura, Assisi 1974

Sinclair, John D. (ed.): The Divine Comedy of Dante Alighieri. Purgatorio, London 1971, pp. 146–147

Zanardi, Bruno: Il cantiere di Giotto: le storie di San Francesco ad Assisi. Note storico-iconografiche di Chiara Frugoni, Milan 1996

PHOTOGRAPHIC CREDITS

The publishers would like to thank the museums, collectors, archives and photographers for permission to reproduce the works in this book. Particular thanks go to the Scala photographic archives for their productive cooperation.

© Archivi Alinari/Archivio Seat – Photo: R. Sigismondi (91); © Archivio Fabbrica di San Pietro in Vaticano, Vaticano, Roma (92); Archivio Fotografico del Sacro Convento di Assisi, Assisi (13, 15 top); The Metropolitan Museum of Art, New York, New York: Hewitt Fund 1917 (93); © RMN, Paris – Photo: Daniel Arnaudet (6); Scala, Istituto Fotografico Editoriale, Antella/Firenze (8, 9, 10, 11, 12, 15 bottom, 16, 18, 21, 23, 24, 25, 26, 27, 28, 30, 31, 32, 33, 34, 35, 36, 38, 39, 40, 44, 46/47, 48, 49, 50, 51, 52, 53, 54, 55, 56, 57, 58, 59, 60, 62, 63, 64, 66, 67, 68, 70, 71, 73, 74, 75, 77, 80, 81, 95, 96, 99, 100, 102, 105, 107, 108, 111, 112, 114, 116, 118, 119, 120, 121, 122/123, 125, 126/127, 130/131, 132, 133).